SACRED SPEAKERS

SACRED SPEAKERS

Language and Culture
among the Haredim in Israel

Simeon D. Baumel

Berghahn Books
New York • Oxford

First published in 2006 by

Berghahn Books
www.berghahnbooks.com

©2006 Simeon D. Baumel

Library of Congress Cataloging-in-Publication Data
Baumel, Simeon D.
 Sacred speakers : language and culture among the Haredim in Israel / Simeon D.
  Baumel.
   p. cm.
 Includes bibliographical references and index.
 ISBN 1-84545-062-0 (alk. paper)
  1. Ultra-Orthodox Jews—Israel—Language. 2. Ultra-Orthodox Jews—Israel—
Intellectual life. 3. Language and languages—Religious aspects—Judaism. 4. Hebrew
language—Social aspects—Israel. 5. Hebrew language, Talmudic—Social aspects—
Israel. 6. Aramaic language—Social aspects—Israel. 7. Yiddish language—Social
aspects—Israel. I. Title.
BM390.B37 2005
296.8'32095694—dc22

                                                                    2005053085

British Library Cataloguing in Publication Data
A catalogue record for this book is available from the British Library

Printed in the United States on acid-free paper

ISBN 1-84545-062-0 hardback

To my parents, Yona and Miriam Baumel, with love

CONTENTS

ACKNOWLEDGEMENTS

It is my great pleasure to thank a number of groups and individuals who assisted me throughout the research and writing of this book. First and foremost, to Prof. Bernard Spolsky and Prof. Joel Walters of the English department at Bar-Ilan University, who acted as beacons in my path of linguistic study and guided the dissertation upon which this book is based. To the staff and editors of Berghahn Books, and especially to its publisher, Dr. Marion Berghahn, go my thanks for believing in this book and enabling its publication. Sections of this book have appeared as part of an articles in *Jewish History* 16 (2000): 161–186, *Language Policy* 2:1 (2003): 47–68 (with the kind permission of Kluwer Academic Publishers) and *European Judaism* and my thanks to the editors and publishers for allowing the material to be reprinted here.

A number of scholars, colleagues and friends assisted me during the researching and writing of this book. I wish to give special thanks to Yitzhak Alfasi, Muhammad Amara, Gershon Bacon, Sarah Benor, Zippi Berman, Deborah Dienstag, Bayla Eisenberg, Menachem Friedman, Lewis Glinert, François Grin, Brenda Idstein, David Kranzler, Jean-Paul Lellouche, Leah Makovetsky, Gita Malka, Ephraim Shakh, Tali Tadmor-Shimoni, Kenneth Stow, Eli Tzur and Hanna Yablonka. I also thank friends, family members, Haredi educators, Haredi pupils, and especially members of the four Haredi families (A, B, C, and D) who graciously tolerated my intrusion into their daily lives and included me in experiences that the average researcher does not merit.

I wish to give special thanks to friends and family who encouraged me throughout my research and writing. To my friends and colleagues at Achva College, and particularly Hila Hadas and Yosef Tzelgov go my heartfelt thanks for providing me with a warm academic home in which I completed the manuscript for this book. Special thanks also to my friends and colleagues at Bar-Ilan University, Sapir and Lipschitz Colleges and particularly to my Haredi students who taught me much about language and culture in the Israeli Haredi world.

To my parents Yona and Miriam Baumel, my aunt Sadie Pitkowsky, my sister and brother-in-law Osna and Daniel Haberman and their family, my mother-in-law Shirley K. Tydor, and last but not least, to my wife Judy and daughters Rivka and Rina my thanks and love for bearing with me throughout it all.

Simeon D. Baumel, Ramat Gan, April 2005

1

Introduction: Who are the Haredim?

A story is told about an American Jewish senior citizen who embarks upon a long-awaited heritage trip to Israel. Returning home, he regales his friends with stories from his tour, emotionally describing the scenery and sites he visited and the people he met. Concluding his tale, he remarks that only one thing marred his visit: "How can it be called the Jewish State if almost no one there speaks Yiddish?"

The connection between language and culture is an ancient one, formed when the first languages began taking shape in the world. Once a multitude of languages and dialects began to be spoken, tribes and other ethnic groups became separate entities from each other as a result. Whether one accepts the Biblical narrative placing the linguistic watershed event at the time of the Tower of Babel, or prefers a more scientific theory of linguistic evolution, the use of language as a contemporary ethnic variable is hardly in doubt. The link between language and culture, two of the basic variables influencing the daily existence of the ethnic groups that populate the world, is an intrinsic one.

This book focuses upon the language and culture of a particular ethnic minority that has retained its uniqueness in spite of its urban character—the ultra-Orthodox Jews in Israel known as *Haredim*. The term *Haredi* literally means "fearful," with the reference being to fear of the Almighty. Initially utilized by speakers of Hebrew to denote any Jew who was punctilious about his religious practice, the term gradually came to designate those Jews whose style of life, worldview, ethos, and beliefs went beyond what many people seemed to understand by "Orthodox."

The emergence of such a Jewish minority was originally dictated by the historical Jewish tradition of separatism throughout the ages, whether by pressure of outside forces or by internal religious or social choice. The decision to concentrate upon Haredim (plural of Haredi) in the present study stemmed from the fact that after the eighteenth and nineteenth centuries, when Western and Central European Jewry underwent the dual processes of emancipation and assimilation, Haredim were the only major Jewish groups that continued to adhere to a separatist tradition. The ways of Israeli Haredim were a factor in various research lacunae, as few scholarly studies exist about Israeli Haredim in general or about their language policies in particular. Stereotypically, the connection between Yiddish and the Haredi world, popularly considered to be the bearers of authentic old-world European Jewish culture, is almost a foregone conclusion, as reflected in the expectations of the American Jewish tourist at the beginning of this chapter. Yet there are growing numbers of Haredim in Israel who do not use Yiddish as their language of daily communication or who do not speak Yiddish at all. This book concentrates upon four such groups found in contemporary Israel and the relationship between their language and culture.

Although Haredi enclaves may be found throughout the world, I decided to focus on Israeli Haredim for several reasons. The first is demographic density: Israel contains the largest number of Haredim found in any one country. The second is population variation: in Israel one finds Haredim belonging to all ultra-Orthodox sectors, something that is difficult to find in Haredi enclaves outside of Israel. The third is political: as the only country in which Haredi political parties function, Israel acts as a research arena in which the political factor plays a significant role in Haredi life. This combination of factors makes Israel the ultimate field for study of various aspects of Haredi life, linguistic aspects notwithstanding.

As my research progressed I realized the difficulties in distinguishing between Haredim as a religious minority and as an ethnic minority. A religious minority can be defined as a group consisting of people who share a common religious basis and beliefs, whereas an ethnic minority is considered a group of people who share a unique social and cultural heritage that is passed on from generation to generation. As I will show further on, in the case of Haredim these definitions often overlap; I will therefore view Haredim as a hybrid group embodying qualities of both ethnic and religious minorities. To further narrow my scope of research I decided to concentrate upon four Haredi groups found in Israel today that best express this hybrid nature while simultaneously representing a large proportion of what is known as contemporary Israeli Haredi society. These are the Habad (Lubavitch) Hassidim, the Gerrer Hassidim, the Mitnagdim, and the Sefaradi Haredim.

Origins of the Haredi Community

According to sociologist M. Friedman (1991), who has long studied the Haredi population, Haredim throughout the world are composed of four main sectors. The *Mitnagdim* (opponents) who originated in Lithuania (and are thus often referred to as the Lithuanians), represent the lifestyle formulated in the large *Yeshivot* (pl. of *Yeshiva*, religious Jewish school for boys and men) in Poland and Lithuania at the end of the nineteenth century. The Polish Hassidim represent the Hassidic tradition of that country as developed from the third generation of the Hassidic movement onward. The Hassidic and/or Orthodox traditions of Hungarian Jewry which were formulated under the inspiration of Rabbi Moshe Sofer, known as the *Hatam Sofer.* The Jerusalemites represent a hybrid tradition that was elaborated in the Old (Ashkenazi) *Yishuv* (Jewish settlement) in Jerusalem (Friedman 1991; Heilman 1982).

In the wake of the Second World War many people now separate Haredim into two catchall categories: the Hassidim and the Mitnagdim. The Hassidim are divided into many different dynastic groups known as "courts," each headed by its own *rebbe* (Hassidic rabbi) and follows its own particular customs. Many of these courts are related to each other through family or marriage and thus may have similar, though generally not identical, customs. As for their views on the outside world (including the state of Israel), these different groups range from the extremist-rejectionist Satmar and Neturei Karta to the more accepting Habad, which engages in Jewish outreach throughout the world, coming into contact not only with non-religious Jews, but with Gentiles as well.

The Mitnagdim (also known as *Litvaks*—Lithuanians) traditionally differed from the Hassidim in several ways. Most visibly, they adopted Western-style attire. A second difference was socioeconomic: unlike Hassidim, who joined the workforce soon after marriage, Mitnagdim often continued learning in Yeshivot and *kollelim* (religious study frameworks for married Haredi males) for many years. Another difference was in the realm of study and prayer. The Hassidic Torah study program was less rigorous than that used in the Lithuanian style Yeshivot. Even today, the Hassidim pray according to *nusach Sefarad* (Sefardic liturgy, used by the sixteenth century kabbalist R. Isaac Luria of Safed), while the Mitnagdim pray according to the Northwestern European *nusach Ashkenaz* (Ashkenazic liturgy). Traditionally, Hassidim were known for their enthusiasm and *shuhkelin* (swaying) during prayer; Mitnagdim prayed in a more reserved manner. Finally, there was the attitude toward the *rebbe*, considered a *Zaddik* (Holy man), and his court. Although Mitnagdim always venerated their Yeshiva directors and Rabbinical sages, they did not customarily turn to them for guidance in household or mundane matters, as became the custom in Hassidic circles. Indeed, up until recent times, the centrality of the *rebbe*, or the *zaddik,* in Hassidic life, and the existence and impact of his court upon the lives of the Hassidim, had little counterpart in the Mitnagdic communities (Heilman 1992). Many of these differences underwent change during the last decades of the twentieth century; and I will discuss the impact of this fact upon Haredi language and culture in a later chapter.

In the past two decades a third group has joined the ranks of the Haredim: those of Sefaradi (Oriental) origin. Almost totally lacking their own educational establishments in Israel, the United States, and most European countries until the 1980s, the devout Sefaradi population often sent their children to be educated in Ashkenazi (European-style) Haredi schools and Yeshivot. But the ethnophobic nature of Ashkenazi Haredim rarely permitted graduates of these institutions to marry into Ashkenazi Haredi families; nor were they accepted into the Ashkenazi Haredi social milieu. Lacking a strong political establishment in Israel until recent years, even the most capable activists were barred from absorption into the Ashkenazi Haredi political world and never reached any position of power.

Since the early 1980s the state of Israel has seen the rise of Sefaradi political parties such as the shortlived "Tami" (Tenuat Masoret Yisrael, Traditional Israel Movement) and later the growing "Shas" movement (Sefaradim Shomrei Torah, Sefaradi Torah Guardians). One consequence was the formation of a powerful Sefaradi political and educational establishment, which encouraged and enabled large groups of Sefaradim in Israel (and subsequently throughout the world), to form a Sefaradi Haredi subculture of their own. Usually characterized by Ashkenazi Haredi dress but Sefaradi educational, religious, and cultural norms, this group has gained adherents among both the *hozrim betshuva* (newly religious) and *mesorati* (traditional) Sefaradim, who are mobilized by slogans of ethnic pride and simultaneously provided with assistance, for example subsidized long school days and free lunches, in the fields of education and social welfare (Willis 1993; Peled 1998).

Demographic Data on the Haredim

How many Haredim exist in the world in general, and in Israel in particular? Heilman (1992) claims that of some 12 million Jews worldwide, about one and a half million are Orthodox. Of these around 550,000 are Haredi, with about half living in Israel. Funke (1998), citing official counts, states that of Great Britain's 300,000 Jews, some 27,000 are Hassidim, but admits that all the official numbers may be questionable. Abraham-Glinert (1997) counts 3–4 percent of British Jews (9–12,000) as Hassidim, while of the Jewish school population of 15,300 students of all ages, 36 percent were at strictly Orthodox schools, and most of these were Hassidim. Glinert (1999b) cites Shilhav (in a personal communication) as stating that there are 250,000 Ashkenazi Haredim in Israel (of whom 100,000 are in Jerusalem), with an additional 15,000 in Great Britain (based on 1983 figures). Kranzler (1995b) notes 35,000 Satmar pupils worldwide, implying a total Satmar population of 100,000. Glinert (1999a) cites the American Jewish Yearbook of 1990 as stating that there are 250,000 Orthodox Jews in the United States (6 percent of all Jews there), with only a small proportion of that being Haredi. However, Kranzler (1988) claims that there are at least 40–57,000 Haredi Jews in the Brooklyn, New York neighborhood of Williamsburg alone. This is in addition to the estimated 5–6,000 Satmar Hassidim in Kiriyas Yoel, Monsey, New Square and Tash in upstate New York. In contrast to the American Jewish Yearbook, Mintz (1992) claims that 8–10 percent of Jews in the United States are Orthodox, with 5 percent being Haredi. He claims a Hassidic population of 35,000 in Williamsburg (for 1974), a Jewish (mostly Haredi) population of over 70,000 in Boro Park in 1983, and a Hassidic (Satmar) population of over 8,000 in Kiriyas Yoel in 1990.

Glinert (1999a) also notes that there are some 25,000 Haredim (mostly Sefaradim) in France—5 percent of the country's Jewish population. Both Mintz and Kranzler note that the natural growth rate among the American Haredim is much higher than that of all the surrounding ethnic groups, including non-Haredi Jews. There are no precise statistics regarding the number of Sefaradi Haredim throughout the world, and it is only by examining election data that one can approximate the numbers of Sefaradi Haredim in Israel. Based on the seventeen Knesset seats that the Shas political party gained in the 1999 Israeli elections (each seat representing approximately 20,000 adult voters), five of which seems to have come from its Haredi hard core, there appear to be over 250,000 Sefaradi Haredim living in the state of Israel alone. In short, the Haredim represent a significant and growing fraction of the Jewish people, particularly in the state of Israel.

The Four Groups Chosen for this Study

Numerous studies have dealt with various aspects of the Haredi world (a full list may be found in the bibliography); however none address my basic research topic, the means by which social, economic, religious and political constraints influence Israeli Haredi language policy and through it, Haredi culture. In order to analyze this issue, I will examine four groups of Israeli Haredim, each of which represents a major trend in Israeli ultra-Orthodoxy. Again, these are the Habad (Lubavitch) Hassidim, the Gerrer Hassidim, the Mitnagdim, and finally, rating their own separate chapter, the Sefaradi Haredim and particularly those in the Shas movement. The ensuing chapters will show that each of these four movements is connected to the others in an almost Gordian knot formed by religious-political machinations of the Haredi world in the state of Israel during the last decades of the twentieth century.

The outreach policy of the Habad Hassidim has traditionally lent them a reputation for a greater openness to outside influences; however, they maintain a full Hassidic lifestyle. For a period of over forty years the movement was under the leadership of one man—Rabbi Menachem Mendel Schneerson, the seventh Lubavitcher *rebbe*—who left his unique mark upon both his Hassidim and the entire Hassidic world. The particular style of Habad, based on the philosophical tradition of each *rebbe* building on the traditions of his predecessor, provides us with a fascinating chain of linguistic and cultural tradition within a particular Haredi sect.

Gerrer Hassidim, considered by historians to be the largest group of Hassidim up to the Second World War, have traditionally set the standards for mainstream Hassidic groups that tend toward separatism but, unlike the Satmar or Neturei Karta sects, have not adopted a totally separatist lifestyle. During the 1920s the Gerrer *rebbe* in Poland, Rabbi Avraham Mordechai Alter, was one of the first Hassidic leaders to give his blessing to the ultra-Orthodox Beis Ya'akov girls' school system, incorporating secular and religious studies under one roof. His followers were among the first ultra-Orthodox adherents to send their daughters to this school system, which functions today in various locations throughout the world and was the model for similar girls' schools later established by other Haredi groups (such as Beis Rivka of Habad and Beis Rochel of Satmar). Rabbi Alter was also one of the few Hassidic leaders who encouraged those of his followers who desired to move to Palestine to do so, and he was instrumental in purchasing land and supporting institutions in the Holy Land. Thanks to these prewar Palestinian real estate investments, the postwar Gerrer *rebbes* were among the few Hassidic leaders in Israel and the Diaspora who were independently wealthy, a fact that shaped the form and nature of this particular Hassidic group. Too, the Gerrer faction's succession of five leaders each with his own policies, within almost as many decades, each with his own policies, makes this a fascinating Hassidic movement to examine in terms of changing leadership and its influence upon Haredi language and culture.

The Mitnagdim, chosen as an example of non-Hassidic Ashkenazi Haredim, maintain an ultra-Orthodox lifestyle that differs somewhat from that of Hassidim. Unlike the Hassidic groups, the Mitnagdim have no declared leader. The result is a certain amount of variation within the Mitnagdic world, ranging from the extremely separatist Hungarian Mitnagdim in Jerusalem to the more Zionist ones found elsewhere. In the last decades of the twentieth century their acknowledged public leader was the late Rabbi Eliezer Menachem Man Shakh, head of the Ponevezh Yeshiva in Bnai Brak; their *halachic* (Jewish law) authorities were Rabbi Yosef Shalom Eliashiv, and the late Rabbi Shlomo Zalman Auerbach. Shakh was not the supreme religious leader in terms of his theological standing; however, his practical influence over tens of thousands of Mitnagdim, combined with his political machinations (such as founding the political party Degel Hatorah), made him a major player in the Haredi world.

Many Sefaradi Haredim in Israel are part of the Shas Sefaradim Shomeri Torah, Sefaradi Torah Guardians movement. Although the appellation was originally the voting letters assigned to the party (*Shin, Samech*), it later caught on due to its religious association with the original acronym of that term, *Shisha Sidrei Mishna* (The six books of Oral Law). This relatively new phenomenon is the only large politically organized group of Sefaradi Haredim. In addition to being a political party, it is a social, educational, and religious movement, and I will refer to it primarily as such, rather than as a political entity. Headed by former Israeli Chief Rabbi Ovadia Yosef, the movement was nurtured during its formative period by the Lithuanian Rabbi Shakh, who conceived of it as an important player in his internecine Haredi struggles. Having broken away from Shakh's influence and dictates during the early 1990s, Yosef and his associates succeeded in turning the movement into a powerful political and social force in the state of Israel. Like Habad, the movement places great importance on the concept of outreach, if only among Sefaradi Jews, locating it in the forefront of the *Teshuva* (repentance) movement. It is therefore interesting to juxtapose it with Habad, the largest Ashkenazi-Haredi outreach movement in the Jewish world (Feldman 2001).

There are several other Israeli Haredi sects that could have provided a vivid contrast to the aforementioned movements, such as the more separatist groups of Satmar and Neturei Karta, or those that are almost solely Yiddish-speaking. However, early overtures toward these and other Hassidic groups such as Vizhnitz and Karlin, revealed their members and leaders to be unwilling to participate in the type of academic survey in question. It is hoped that the linguistic variation among the four groups that ultimately were chosen (Habad, Gur and the Mitnagdim include both Hebrew and Yiddish speaking groups) will compensate for my inability to research the more separatist groups.

Questions of Language Policy and Its Relationship to Culture

Three of the most important methodological steps in my study were delineating the dimensions of the term "language policy," defining the languages in question, and determining the extent of the terrain covered by the term "culture." Language policy is a relatively new term, initially appearing in book titles at the end of the Second World War (Cebollero 1945). Sometimes known as language planning (Kaplan and Baldauf 1997), the field developed in parallel with sociolinguistics, a specialty that also included practical matters of language policy and development (Paulston and Tucker 1997). By determining the language policy of a particular group, policy makers can allow its members access to information and cultural knowledge (Kahane 1986), enable them to adapt to marketplace phenomena (Coulmas 1992), or strengthen their religious and/or national identity (Fishman 1969).

Spolsky and Shohamy (2000) have proposed that language policy be seen as involving three intertwining elements: language ideology, language management, and language practice. Language ideology—the consensus on what varieties are appropriate for what purpose—is determined by a number of factors, including language status and the preferences of the active leadership of various groups in power. Language management—the attempts by someone in authority to modify or influence someone else's practice or ideology—leads us once again to these active leaderships. Although they do not always have complete authority over their groups, they nevertheless act as controlling agents by selecting the language of instruction and making other determinations ranging from language acquisition or education policy to orthography planning, lexical elaboration, and ensuring language purity. Language, therefore, becomes a determinant of power, with language management being either an expression of existing power or of the attempt to use language as a vehicle for obtaining such power. Language practice—the ethnography of communication (Hymes 1974)—is the form of language used in a particular speech community (Hymes 1967), with the term "speech" taken as a surrogate for all forms of language, including writing. Together these three variables create the linguistic policy, and consequently the linguistic culture (Schiffman 1996), of a particular group wishing to implement language rights for socio/cultural, economic, religious, or political reasons.

The next methodological step was to define the languages being examined. Some of the languages that I will deal with in this study are in fact progressions and expansions of a single language that is commonly, though not always precisely, referred to as "Hebrew." In some cases, the various forms of the language overlap so much that treating them as separate languages may be construed as artificial and misleading. A number of Hebrew versions are considered sacred languages. Though they vary slightly in lexis and grammatical structure, their primarily differences lie in their era of origin and social milieu of use. One such language is Ancient Biblical Hebrew, the original language of the Bible (Netzer 1999; Tourgeman 1999). A second is Talmudic Hebrew, with or without a high proportion of Aramaic (Sharvit 1996), with Aramaic itself being considered a separate sacred Jewish language (Kaddari 1990; Hurvitz 1996). For my purposes, a low proportion of Aramaic is defined as the appearance of the occasional Aramaic word within the Hebrew text, and a high proportion of Aramaic is the use of full Aramaic sentences within the Hebrew text with at least ten percent of the entire text being in Aramaic. Medieval Hebrew, used primarily for sacred purposes, was the sacred language in which prayers and responsa were written (Kaddari 1993). Of the sacred categories of Hebrew, this study will deal primarily with Talmudic Hebrew with various proportions of Aramaic. To refer to this form of Hebrew, I will follow various studies of language (such as Kutscher 1982; Bogoch 1999; Isaacs 1998a, 1999) in using the term *Loshon Kodesh* (the Holy Tongue).

Non sacred registers of Hebrew are chronologically among the more modern versions of the language. Here I will refer primarily to the modern Israeli Hebrew with Sefaradi pronunciation that was used initially among the pioneers in Eretz Yisrael to distinguish themselves from the Old Yishuv and later became the language of modern Israel (Schwarzwald 2001). I will refer to this language as *Ivrit* and will also refer to the colloquial or slang Ivrit that is commonly spoken in Israel today (Nir 1978). Following the accepted definition of the Webster's dictionary (Webster's 1958), I have defined colloquialisms as words, phrases, and idioms characteristic of informal language, although not indicative of substandard or illiterate usage. Slang is defined as a kind of jargon marked by its rejection of formal rules (Spolsky 1998). In generic references—that is, those not dealing with any of the specific variations—the Hebrew language will also be termed "Hebrew."

Aramaic raises a separate dilemma. It is true that Aramaic is no longer spoken today as an independent language, and it is possible to argue that its main use among Haredim is as part of Loshon Kodesh. Nevertheless, there is a gendered aspect to the use of Loshon Kodesh that should not be overlooked. The Loshon Kodesh used by Haredi women in their studies includes very little, if any, Aramaic apart from those phrases that have become well known in Haredi society, for women do not study Talmud, the major source today for Haredi knowledge of Aramaic. In addition, more Aramaic is used in Sefaradi Haredi Loshon Kodesh than in Ashkenazi Haredi Loshon Kodesh because certain Sefaradi populations were descended from groups whose Jewish language was heavily based on Aramaic. When referring to Loshon Kodesh I will occasionally mention the proportion of Aramaic used in order differentiate between the various types of Loshon Kodesh used commonly by men and women, or by Haredim from different ethnic backgrounds.

Bearing in mind the wider repercussions of a linguistic study and the fact that all four of the groups I am examining are Hebrew-speaking and based in

Israel, I decided to focus on two broad categories, which I have termed inclusion and omission. Under the first category I explore the verbal and written expressions used in the Haredi groups that are being examined. Of particular note are the distinction between Loshon Kodesh and Ivrit, something particularly important in view of the fact that all four Haredi groups studies here are primarily speakers of Ivrit; the attitude towards and use of a quasi sacred tongue (Aramaic), either alone or within Loshon Kodesh; the role of non-sacred Jewish languages and especially Yiddish in the Haredi community, particularly on the verbal level; and the use of the non-Jewish vernacular. I will also examine the use of gendered speech, particular dialects, generational factors, the attitude toward prestige languages (those given higher regard in a particular society), and language loss and maintenance. The category of omission uncovers the linguistic lacunae that exists in the Haredi sects and attempts to explain them. Here I ask what words, speech patterns, dialects, and even languages are missing from the Haredi vocabulary and propose a linguistic and cultural hypothesis that explains my findings.

This leads me to the issue of "culture," defined as the concepts, habits, skills, arts, instruments and institutions of a given people in a given period. The interaction between language and culture, particularly among ethnic minorities, can be pictured as a three-stage process. Its first stage, is that of reaction: how ethnic minorities' language and culture are molded under the influence of various external factors. The second stage, to which I will allude both throughout my analysis and in my conclusions, can be termed definition: how the linguistic, and thus cultural, policies that an ethnic minority adopts help to define its essence not only vis-à-vis itself, but also in comparison with similar or related ethnic groups, and finally, as opposed to its general surroundings. The third stage, which is discussed primarily in my concluding chapter, can be termed expression: the statement that the ethnic minority's language policy attempts to make in relation to the surrounding majority. But the process does not necessarily conclude here. As in the famous Escher sketch of two hands, each drawing the other, an unexpected type of mutuality arises when this statement begins to influence the very factors that molded the ethnic minority's linguistic and cultural policy—and thus it itself—in the first place. And as in the case of the drawing, the onlooker is left unsure which created which.

This process becomes evident when we remember that language ultimately determines the interaction between a minority ethnic group interaction and what it considers to be the outside world. Because it delineates the degree of familiarity that the majority framework—which often serves as the minority group's economic cushion—has with the ethnic minority, language often has wide-ranging repercussions. Haredi language policies not only delineate internal Haredi cultural parameters; they also determine the extent of Haredi cross-cultural interaction with the larger Israeli society. Those outside Haredi groups—particularly Israeli government functionaries—often view Haredi language policy as an indicator of the degree of Haredi willingness to ultimately assimilate economically (although not socially or culturally) into Israeli society rather than remaining economically separate and dependent primarily upon government welfare allocations. Consequently, Israeli government policy makers' perceptions of Haredi language (and through it, their culture) have already been known to affect the scope of government educational allocations for adult-Haredi vocational training. This is but one example of how a group's attitude to language may ultimately hold great significance for their continued economic existence.

Does culture include a geographical component? Within a particular sect one finds linguistic, and at times, cultural variations in different parts of the country. For example, while Habad Hassidim in the veteran Habad communities of Kfar Habad and Kiriyat Malachi use Yiddish at home as much as or more often than they use Ivrit, this is not necessarily true of Habad elsewhere in Israel. The same holds true for Gerrer Hassidim found in Bnai Brak and Jerusalem as opposed to those found in peripheral communities such as Arad or Ashdod. Does this linguistic differentiation mean that Haredim living in these communities are culturally less separated from their outside environment than those in the major centers? In order to answer these and other questions I will examine at least two geographical centers of each group, one central to each movement and one more peripheral.

Another component of linguistic and cultural importance, that I have already noted is gender. Gender studies have underscored how women's society, speech patterns, and literature are often different from those of men (Coates 1993). I will therefore discuss these issues with regard to Haredi women in the four groups featured in this study. My examination will include observations of women and girls in the domestic and educational spheres, and will also refer to Haredi women's periodicals and those parts of the Haredi press geared towards women ("family pages," etc.).

If culture is both public and personal, it also becomes political. This alludes to the fact that all of the sects studied here are either pro-Zionist (Habad and Shas) or neutral towards Zionism (Mitnagdim and Gur). This is an important factor when discussing their attitude towards Ivrit, the linguistic representation of contemporary Israeli, and thus Zionist, culture.

For purposed of this study I have chosen to view the Haredi world as being composed of three spheres: the public domain, the domestic realm, and educational frameworks. Whereas each of these spheres is influenced by the others, there is a definite hierarchy of influence among them. The largest of the spheres, and the one that encompasses all Haredi action, is that of the public domain. This sphere is characterized by its theological component, one that is often considered theoretical: that of *da'at Torah*, religious beliefs as formulated or interpreted by the movement's leaders (Bacon 1986). This may be analyzed as a form of language management, as it is this sphere that determines what the *de jure* language policy will be in each Haredi group, thus making it the most influential of the spheres. Drawing heavily upon the particular movement's traditional attitude to languages, this sphere has also been influenced by the contemporary interpretations of da'at Torah as it reinterprets the past, thus setting the new traditional and halachic boundaries for the future. An example of how such a da'at Torah influenced Haredi language policy in the past is the Jerusalem *herem* (ban) of the late nineteenth century on the teaching of foreign languages (in that case, Arabic), intended at the time to allow members of the community to obtain local employment. One of the ways that various groups circumvented this ban was by teaching foreign languages not in large classes but groups of two and three students instead (Spolsky 1993). Apart from theological writings, written proclamations and verbal expressions from which one can glean information relating to the da'at Torah, language, and culture of a particular group, an additional source—under direct Rabbinical supervision and expressing the *de jure* linguistic policies of a given movement—is its newspaper.

The second sphere, which is also under the jurisdiction of the movement's leader and includes everyone in Haredi society, is the domestic realm of the home and family, in which daily language policy is carried out. To represent the transition between public domain and family, I use Bourhis' typology (Bourhis 1984a) to place the concept of Haredi space (landscape, linguistic and otherwise) within the second sphere and examine it as an element thereof. In doing so I include what is colloquially known as the Haredi "street," the neighborhood or community, in which one can note general trends in contemporary Haredi life.

The third, smallest, sphere is the educational realm, divided into the pre-elementary and elementary levels, the high school level, and the post–high school level of higher Yeshiva or vocational training. In this section I examine how educational settings act as a vehicle for promoting Haredi policies on language and culture.

Prior to focusing on the Haredi public domain, domestic realm, and educational frameworks, I will discuss the Jewish attitude towards languages and present a short history of each of the four Haredi groups under examination. This will lay the basis for understanding their traditional da'at Torah with regard to language and culture as stipulated by the movement's leaders and followed in the past. This is a particularly important consideration in a discussion of Haredi groups, which claim to venerate the past and look to past leadership as a guideline for contemporary behavior and future policies. As I will show, the challenges of modernity have often made it necessary to reinterpret the past in every generation in order to ensure a future for the movement in question. Although all Haredi groups adhere to an avowed policy of continuity, one can often detect the seeds of change, which are portrayed as slightly different interpretations of past policy or behavior. These are usually grounded in statements or writings stemming from the movement's formative leadership or founders, enabling the new interpretation to be portrayed as yet another means of continuing the past traditions.

Following the discussion of the three spheres in which Haredi language policy is formulated and executed, I devote a special chapter to the comparatively recent phenomenon of Sefaradi Haredim. In another chapter I compare Israeli Haredi language and culture to that of the same sects of Haredim living abroad, locating the subjects of this study within a larger framework and providing the reader with a more panoramic view of the topics covered. I conclude my study with a typology of Haredim as a linguistic and cultural minority group and summarize the various factors influencing their attitude toward language and culture.

Conclusion

In traditional Jewish imagery the world is often depicted as being surrounded by the Leviathan, an enormous fish whose mouth closes upon the end of its own tail. The meaning of this juxtapositioning of symbols is uncertain: some consider it a divine warning; others see it as saying that all beginnings come an end and all ends are connected to a new beginning. A third group views it as referring to the relationship between framework and content, with man acting as the molding, guiding force between the two. It is this third interpretation that brings me to the end of this opening chapter, after which I shall begin my exploration of Israeli Haredi language and culture as expressed during the last decades of the twentieth and the beginning of the twenty first century.

Before concluding this introduction, I wish to mention two aspects of framework and content that may initially appear obvious and even superfluous, but have ultimately proven instrumental in determining the dimensions and nature of this entire study: the disciplinary framework and the nature of the researcher. At its outset, this project appeared to be grounded in the field commonly known as sociolinguistics, defined as "the study of language in its social context," which usually means the study of linguistic variation (Coates 1993, 4). But as my research progressed I realized that it actually belonged to a slightly different and possibly broader discipline, that of cultural linguistics. As Halliday states in a study of language as a social semiotic (1978, 23), "language is culture," and culture shapes our behavior patterns in almost all fields of life. In addition to the usual sociolinguistic explorations, I often found myself drawn to broader research parameters similar to those of sociologists and anthropologists. Although my study is heavily grounded in sociolinguistics, certain sections include observations that may be considered more the domain of cultural anthropologists than that of students of language. Aware of the need for occasional forays into other fields in order to better understand my own, I have retained some of these observations in deference to the theory that claims that artificially constructed disciplinary limitations often prevent one from viewing the broader picture and can thus lead to misinterpretation of research results. It is my sincere hope that the extradisciplinary details help me turn what can often wind up as a binary exploration of a very limited discipline into a three-dimensional study of language and culture.

The second instrumental aspect is the nature of the researcher. Students of language and social scientists have long debated the preferred qualities of sociological, anthropological, and linguistic researchers (Fishman 1989). Obviously the first prerequisite is a basic knowledge of the languages involved in the study. Having overcome this technical requirement, one faces the issue of ingroups and outgroups. Should the researcher belong to the group being examined, or at least have some type of personal connection to the group? Or is it better if the group is examined by a complete outsider who is cognizant of its characteristics but does not share them? As Poll (1965) has shown in his study of Hungarian Haredim in Williamsburg, his education in a Hungarian Yeshiva did not provide him with an advantage; rather, he was considered an outsider even by those who had known knew him in Europe because he did not follow the dictates of Haredi life. As El-Or (1994) states in her study of literacy among Gerrer Hassidic women, her status as being a completely nonreligious outsider enabled many of the women to be more open to her than they would have been to someone who was religious but not Haredi; such a person would have been perceived as a possible threat to their lifestyle.

Helmreich once explained this paradox with the following story: a six-year-old American Haredi child on vacation was asked by two slightly older, modern religious boys what he wanted to be when he grew up. "A baseball player," replied the little boy. "But you are a Hassid; you have *peot* [sidelocks] and *tzitzit* [ritual fringes]," they said incredulously. "You can't become a baseball player, only *goyim* [Gentiles] can become baseball players." "OK," he said, "so first I'll become a *Goy*, and then I'll become a baseball player." For the six year old Haredi child in America, saying that he would become a Gentile was the equivalent of saying that he would become a professional ball player or even a Martian, something that was beyond the realm of possibility, and thus, not threatening. On the other hand, concluded Helmreich, this story could not taking place in Israel, where no six-year-old Israeli Hassidic child would state that first he would become a nonreligious Jew—perceived as a blatant and serious threat to Israeli Haredi life—and then a soccer player.

The same often holds true for interviewers. A questioner who is viewed as a nonthreatening creature "from outer space" can often gain better access to groups than one who is perceived as a mutant of that group—in other words, a modern religious researcher attempting to garner information about the Haredi world. Yet, a student who lacks familiarity with the inner Haredi codes, both behavioral and linguistic, is often unable to correctly interpret what is observed. In other words, the ideal interviewer would be a total outsider with a complete working knowledge of insider codes. In view of the rapidly growing insularity and radical separatism of Israeli Haredim, particularly the Mitnagdim and many of the Hassidic groups, there is little chance for a nonreligious researcher today to touch upon anything but the most superficial level of Haredi life. It is certainly impossible to conceive of such a person entering the inner sanctums of learning and family and truly understanding their codes. On the other hand, my being a modern religious Jew with family connections to the Haredi world and a cognizance of many Haredi codes made it possible for me to penetrate into the levels of Haredi life that would enable me to perform my research. In the words of Garlick (1999), all ceremonies are indeed performances, with participants and spectators each playing their part. At times I acted as spectator to the scenes being performed by the various Haredi groups I was investigating; at other times, particularly during religious ceremonies, I was a full participant, notwithstanding my colorful knitted *kipah* (skullcap), as opposed to the black cloth or velvet kipah of the Haredim. Positioned, in the eyes of many of my Haredi subjects, somewhere between a Martian and a practicing religious Jew who could ultimately be converted to Haredi life, I entered this study with the perspective of a sociolinguist and ended it in the hope that there are few gaps—linguistic and other—that are truly unbridgeable.

2

JEWS AND LANGUAGE
THROUGHOUT THE AGES

As a young boy growing up in Brooklyn, I was certain that everyone could speak at least two languages. My schoolmates and I spoke to each other in English, although many of our subjects were taught in Hebrew. Those of my friends with European-born parents often spoke Yiddish at home. In my house, Hungarian—my father's mother tongue, in spite of the fact that he was born in America—would have been considered a third language, while my mother's Lithuanian relatives spoke Yiddish when they didn't want the children to understand. This multilingual society was not limited to Jews. The school janitor spoke Greek in addition to English, while the conversation among the workers in my father's knitting factory buzzed in Italian, a language that Dad ultimately picked up as his fourth or fifth language. In short, although heavily based in English, in retrospect my boyhood was a mixture of efforts to maintain various languages within an ethnic melting pot of immigrants.

At first glance, the atmosphere that I have just described appears very different from the traditional nativist *Ivri—daber Ivrit!* (Hebrew Jew—speak Ivrit!) exhortation that reigned in Israel for over a half a century, from the period of the second Aliya (wave of immigration), 1904 to 1914, until the mid 1960s or early 1970s. Which situation was an anomaly among Jews: the efforts to turn Israel into a monolingual society or my polyglot Jewish childhood? I will begin my answer to this question by examining the attitude towards languages traditionally held by Jews as a minority group.

Traditional Jewish Attitudes to Languages

There does not appear to be a single "Jewish" attitude toward the teaching of foreign languages. In Biblical times Jews were conversant in the various Middle Eastern languages, which enabled them to communicate with their neighbors.

Having developed Hebrew as their own Jewish tongue, they maintained a separate language not only in their own land but even after in exile following the destruction of the First Temple and the Babylonian dispersion in 586 B.C.E. (Esther 8, 9).

Only during the Hellenistic period (from the second century B.C.E. onward), by which time another sacred Jewish language, Aramaic, had become a Jewish vernacular, did Jewish linguistic separatism become an issue. This was primarily because language and culture were considered parts of the same package. In spite of a pragmatic Jewish attitude towards the use of Greek, other foreign influences remained suspect. The basis for this policy was cultural, language being considered the great divide that could prevent assimilation into local culture. Foreign languages were categorized with "foreign wine," "foreign bread," and other non-Jewish phenomena, all of which were forbidden as barrier breakers between Jews and their surroundings. Aramaic enjoyed special status, as the Jewish mother tongue (*Babylonian Talmud*, Tractate Bava Kama 92b), while Hebrew maintained its status as the holy language.

Following the dispersion and exile of Palestinian Jews after the destruction of the Second Temple (70 C.E.) and the Bar Kochba revolt (135 C.E.), almost all Jews found themselves living in a foreign country and having to learn its language while attempting to maintain their own tongue. Over the ensuing centuries the Jews in almost all diasporas—in Europe, North Africa, and the Orient—were traditionally triglossic, speaking the local vernacular with the natives, their own language among themselves (often affected by the co-territorial vernacular), and Loshon Kodesh for religious purposes (Rabin 2000).

Our focus now moves to the European venue, the cultural framework within which a large part of the Haredi population would ultimately develop. Jewish settlement in Europe began in the Mediterranean basin, and by the early Middle Ages Jewish communities were established in central and northern Europe, in areas later known as Ashkenaz, that were parts of the Holy Roman Empire. Apart from having at least a working knowledge of Loshon Kodesh, Jews in these areas spoke the local tongue. Some were even conversant in Latin, the legal language of the period. Jewish settlement in Eastern Europe began during the Crusader period, when large numbers of Jews fleeing from the Rhineland sought refuge from marauders in the newly opened eastern territories. Bringing with them their German-Jewish culture and religious customs, these Jews maintained a form of Middle High German that would metamorphose into Yiddish (Weinreich 1973), a language that over time acquired a quasi sacred status. After the Holocaust, in which the bulk of Yiddish-speaking secular and religious Jews were annihilated, Yiddish would continue to act as a linguistic and cultural barrier, this time from other Jews, keeping many Haredi Jews separate from the less religious elements of the Jewish people (Glinert and Shilhav 1991).

During the period of the Emancipation (the late eighteenth and nineteenth centuries), Jews throughout Europe were forced to teach official languages in their schools so that they would be assimilated into the local culture and society—to ensure their *verbesserung* (betterment), in the words of the local enlightened despots. Rabbinical opposition ensued, and the modern cultural battle for and against the teaching of languages began. This was true particularly in Western and parts of Central Europe, where local languages were ultimately successfully introduced to Jewish schools in countries such as France under Napoleon, and in some Germanic states even before the unification of Germany under Bismarck. The Reform movement, in particular, was instrumental in influencing acquisition and maintenance of the German language among Jews in Western Europe (Meyer 1986). Jewish schools in Eastern Europe did not teach the local vernacular; it was learned on a "need to know" basis (Weinryb 1972). Only in Jerusalem in the late nineteenth century did several Ashkenazi Haredi authorities actually prohibit the teaching of foreign languages, and even this ban (herem) was rejected by major rabbis in Egypt and Europe. A century later, this herem is still considered by some to be in effect. It is obeyed in a number of the schools I investigated, including one where English is taught.[1]

Until the end of the nineteenth century, despite laws mandating the introduction of the official state language in all school frameworks, in practice various Jewish communities throughout Central and Eastern Europe were granted a great deal of educational autonomy in terms of both school administration and curriculum (Weinryb 1972). As a result, boys could receive a full Torah education without learning about the country in which they lived, or becoming proficient in its language. After the First World War, when many central and eastern European countries became independent, state governments in such countries as Poland, Russia, Hungary, and Czechoslovakia took firm control over school curricula and demanded that certain secular subjects be taught, including the local language. By necessity boys were taught these subjects, but most Haredi schools managed to schedule the secular subjects at the worst possible hours in terms of the pupils' lowest attentiveness (i.e. late afternoon), while the best hours were reserved for Jewish subjects (Sourasky 1967). A similar policy is implemented today in many Haredi schools throughout the United States (Kamen 1985; Kranzler 1995a; Rubin 1997).

As Haredi schools were always segregated by sex, Haredi girls were usually sent to study in Gentile local schools, a factor that proved detrimental to the maintenance of their religious standards and subsequently acted as a deterrent to their finding a religious Jewish matrimonial partner. In 1917 a Cracow seamstress, Sarah Schenierer, established the first Haredi girls' school, known as Beis Ya'akov (The House of Jacob), which later metamorphosed into an entire school network that included elementary and high schools along with a teachers-training seminary (Weissman 1976). The establishment of an Orthodox Jewish girls' educational network was considered a radical innovation as it provided Orthodox and ultra-Orthodox girls and young women with both serious religious and comprehensive secular education. One of the main reasons that Schenierer managed to obtain rabbinical approval was the leeway traditionally given to girls in terms of secular education (Baumel and Schacter 1992).

Following the Second World War, the Haredi attitude toward language teaching became geographically focused on three loci. One was the United States, with its growing Haredi population. A second was certain Western European communities such as Antwerp, Paris, and London, where remnants of the once flourishing Haredi Eastern European communities—particularly those of Hassidic origin—had taken root. The third was Israel, home to members of both the former Old Yishuv, composed of the descendents of early nineteenth-century Ashkenazi Haredim, and those who had made Israel their home after the Holocaust. Attempting to rebuild the world that had been lost in Europe, certain Haredi leaders heightened their opposition to all factors that they saw as a threat to their ethnic and cultural separatism, among them the use of the local vernacular (including Ivrit), and the study of non-Jewish languages. Despite this common attitude in practice, different language policies developed in Israel and abroad among various Haredi groups.

The attitude to languages among the Oriental Jewish populations differed somewhat from that of European Jews. Until the nineteenth century, Jews in Eastern lands also developed a form of triglossia, speaking a Jewish variation of the local vernacular (Ladino, Judeo-Arabic, etc.) at home, understanding enough of the local vernacular for trade and commerce, and knowing enough Loshon Kodesh for prayer and Torah study (Laskier 1991). When colonialism, and with it the Enlightenment, reached these countries in the mid-nineteenth and early twentieth centuries, the issue of teaching a fourth language—the colonial language (instead of the local vernacular)—arose (Schwarzfuchs 1992). In spite of the fact that French (in Morocco, Tunis, Algeria, Iraq, Lebanon, Syria), Italian (Libya), and English (Egypt) were considered vehicles of the Enlightenment, Jewish separatists put up surprisingly little opposition to teaching these languages (Stillman 2000). This was possibly due to the traditional broadmindedness of Sefaradi Jewry toward external influences, may also stem from a lack of tradition of radicalism or extreme Jewish separatism, other than that which was forced upon them by Moslem leaders. Upon moving to Israel in the mid-twentieth century, large numbers of Sepharadic Jews were triglossic, or even tetraglossic, speaking a Jewish vernacular, the local vernacular of their country—usually Arabic—and a colonial language (usually French), and having some knowledge of Hebrew.

Conclusions: Where do the Haredim fit in?

In a classic Mel Brooks movie there is a scene where a Jew, traveling west, spies two Amish men on a porch, bearded and dressed in black. Delighted to see what he thinks are his coreligionists, the weary traveler comes running up to them, eyes twinkling, arms outstretched, shouting *"Yidden!"* (Jews!). He stops short, as the bewildered facial expressions of all three men make clear that he has mistaken their identity. Although the unspoken punchline "Amish, Jewish, what's the difference" hangs in the air, the one Yiddish word uttered in the entire scene points to the chasm ranging between linguistic minorities, regardless of what appear to be their other—in this case, visible—similarities.

Where does Haredi language policy fit into these differences and similarities? Obviously, it is impossible to answer this question without first discussing various Haredi attitudes towards language and culture, the topic to which this study is devoted. But even before such an exploration is commenced, the above discussion has shed light on several of the salient issues that must be addressed in any study of a minority group. These include the interaction between majority and minority groups in terms of language use, the influence that the relative prestige of different languages has upon minority language maintenance, the impact of immigrant assimilation on maintaining ethnic languages, and the impact of minority group economic status on language shift. In addition, one must also take into account any impact that cultural affinity or antagonism between majority and minority groups may have upon language maintenance and shift.

Can the study of Haredim be treated as an examination of an ethnic immigrant community? Although in many countries we are dealing with language policies of native-born Haredim, this group may often be considered an immigrant group as the Haredi communities in question were usually founded only some fifty years ago. There are those who consider Israel to be an exception to this rule; however, we must remember that the existing prewar Haredi communities in that country received their vital demographic push only after the Holocaust, with the immigration of Orthodox and Haredi Holocaust survivors. In 1948 there were 4,910 children enrolled in the Haredi Agudat Yisrael elementary schools throughout Israel. By 1956 their number had risen to 18,536, and by 1964 there were 27,407 children registered in such schools, and in 1998 there were 68,900 pupils in the Agudat Yisrael and Shas Haredi school systems.[2]

If one speaks of Haredim as an ethnoreligious minority, we must note that, in contrast to separatist groups such as the Molokans and Doukhobors (Poll 1962), who have chosen physical separation in rural as opposed to urban areas, Haredim have shown themselves capable of maintaining their separatist way of life in an urban setting. Although there have been attempts to create rural Haredi communities abroad (particularly in Monroe, New York, or Tash in Canada) and Haredi agricultural settlements in Israel (such as the agricultural collective kibbutz and moshav settlements of Poalei Agudat Israel), most Haredim throughout the world reside in urban communities.

There is no doubt that Haredim are a religious minority, but are they a religious-fundamentalist group? In their study of religious fundamentalism and religious Jews, Heilman and Friedman (1991) find it difficult to definitively locate Haredi Jews within a fundamentalist category and even more so, to define them as an ethnic-separatist fundamentalist group. Unlike the Amish (Hostetler 1968; Redekop 1989), the Haredim do not reject the products of science and technology, but rather use them to support their way of life. The means by which the Haredim maintain their partial separation from the society at large is first and foremost by the use of religious prohibitions. To this one must add visible and audible factors that are used in maintaining ethnic separatism by Haredi but not by Orthodox Jews of the more modern persuasion. The first such factor is the use of language (Yiddish) among certain—though as we will see further, not all—Ashkenazi Haredim; the second is the adoption of different Haredi dress (Poll 1962; Rubin 1997).

While the adoption of Haredi dress may act as a physical barrier between Haredim and the surrounding majority, for a long time it appeared to be the linguistic factor that limited the assimilation of Ashkenazi Haredim into the majority culture. This was often the first impression received by sociologists, anthropologists, and students of linguistics who approached Ashkenazi Haredi society throughout Israel and almost all Haredi places of residence in the Diaspora as well (Berger-Sofer 1978; Kamen 1985; Epstein 1999). Such conclusions often appeared to be buttressed by what was known about Ashkenazi Haredi linguistic policy as early as the late nineteenth century, particularly in Palestine. Although Haredim living in the Holy Land were somewhat conversant in Loshon Kodesh, it was considered the sacred tongue and thus was not to be used for mundane matters. At the end of the nineteenth century, when Zionists began using Ivrit as their language of communication, Ashkenazi Haredim in Palestine insisted on maintaining Yiddish as their vernacular. This was done not only because Hebrew was sacred, but also in order to erect a linguistic barrier between themselves and what was becoming a secular Zionist majority. Those few members of the Old Yishuv who used a form of Hebrew adopted Old Yishuv Ashkenazi Hebrew with borrowings from Yiddish (Friedman 1991). The Haredi attitude to other languages also appeared to be negative at that time. While the school teaching of Arabic—the language of the local population—was limited by the Jerusalem herem in order to prevent Haredim from mingling with the native populace (although Palestinian Yiddish was marked by its borrowings from Arabic), European languages such as English, French, and German were rejected because they were used for assimilationist purposes (Sourasky 1967).

In the Diaspora, the Ashkenazi Haredi use of language as a separatist factor became apparent only after the Second World War, when the annihilation of the world's largest Yiddish-speaking population in the Holocaust almost caused the demise of Yiddish. However, soon after the war, much of the Haredi society in Western Europe and the United States that maintained Yiddish as a living language sanctified that language, not only as a linguistic memorial for millions of Jewish martyrs but as a means of maintaining their uniqueness—and thus separation—from their surroundings (Seidman 1997). This rule held for their Jewish as well as their Gentile milieu. Being a double religious minority—a minority within the Jewish world and part of a Jewish minority within the Gentile world—it was doubly important for them to erect linguistic barriers between themselves and others. Being Orthodox Jews, it was politic to imbue their chosen language policies with the theological significance that would grant them special stature in the eyes of Haredi Jewry. What was in fact a means of maintaining ethnic separatism was given the aura of a fundamentalist prohibition that, with the exception of the Jerusalem herem, had little basis in reality.

The aforementioned conclusions, which are sometimes cited in sociological and anthropological literature dealing with Haredi society throughout the world (Poll 1962; Kranzler 1995b; Rabinowicz 1997), do not take into account the great variations existing today within Haredi society. Although in certain cases Haredim more strongly resemble ethnic separatist groups rather than religious fundamentalist groups (S. Baumel 2000), the multifaceted nature of Haredi society—both Ashkenazi and Sefaradi—consistently thwarts pigeon-holding. Unlike the case of some ethnic separatist and nonseparatist minorities who consider the local vernacular a prestige language and therefore a desired acquisition, the religious prohibitions that certain Ashkenazi Haredim added on to separatist linguistic policy turned the question of prestige and non-prestige languages into a non-issue. Although there are still sizeable numbers of Ashkenazi Haredim who maintain what appears to be linguistic and cultural separatism, particularly in the state of Israel, an equal number of Haredim now use the local vernacular in everyday life and have been influenced to varying degrees by the surrounding majority culture.

The term that animates the nucleus of this study is "communication," the means by which individuals and groups make their wishes known to their surroundings, project themselves before others, or have contact with other human beings. Communication involves a certain amount of interface between individuals or groups. In the following chapters I will examine the various expressions of ingroup and outgroup Haredi communication and their impact upon the life and culture of the members of the four sects featured in this study.

Notes

1. Interview with Mrs. Pinter, Bnai Brak, 15 Feb. 1999.
2. Figures are taken from *Statistical Abstract of Israel,* Jerusalem 1949–1999.

3

HISTORICAL OVERVIEW

For an outsider, telling the various Haredi sects apart is no mean feat. Any Hassidic child can immediately differentiate between Gerrer and Habad Hassidim, but to non-Haredim who are unaware of each sect's subtle dress and behavioral codes, the Haredi world looks like a monolith of white shirts and black hats. Trying to explain the external differences between Haredi sects to a friend, I was reminded of the two Israeli old-timers in the early 1980s who were attempting to understand the changeover in currency from *lira* to *shekel*. After a few minutes of explanation to his bewildered companion, the older of the two solved the problem with one short Yiddish sentence. "*Kik*" ("look" in Galician dialect], he said, "*dus is an alter piaster, und dus is a neier piaster*" (this is an older *piaster*—the Eastern European equivalent of a penny—and this is a newer *piaster*'. In other words, it really makes no difference; all are variations on a similar theme.

How similar is the recurring theme among all Haredi sects today? To what extent does their historical background affect their modern manifestations? In order to answer these questions I will review the history of the three Ashkenazi Haredi sects spotlighted in this study in an attempt to deconstruct the Gordian knot that binds all of these contemporary groups. By doing so I will lay the foundation for understanding contemporary Haredi language and culture, providing insights into the reasons behind the development of Haredi linguistic dynamics.

What makes a Haredi?

The term Haredi first appears in the biblical phrase "Hear the word of the Lord, you who tremble [*haredim*] at his word" (Isaiah 66:5). Although there are those who claim that legitimacy, identity, and territory are the major distinguishing factors of Haredi groups (Shnall 1989), in practice, Haredim can often differ from other Orthodox Jews in appearance, the central religious authority that they accept, lifestyle, and philosophy of Judaism among other variables. Each of these distinctions factors heavily into daily life and often acts as a visible or invisible barrier between the Haredim and their surroundings.

I have chosen to present the history of the three sects by depicting the historical emergence of each, beginning with the history of the Hassidic sects of Habad and Gur. The Mitnagdic circles arose in opposition to Hassidism; consequently, I will deal with them as a third Haredi group, bearing in mind that chronologically they preceded the formation of the Gerrer (the adj. of Gur) court. Only in another chapter will I turn my sights to Sefaradi Haredim and particularly Shas, examining it as an ultra-Orthodox Oriental religious and social movement rather than merely a political party.

What makes a Hassid?

Based upon the teachings of Israel Ben Eliezer, known as the Ba'al Shem Tov (Master of the Good Name, 1700–1760), the Hassidic movement began in the mid-eighteenth century among the Jews of the Ukraine and later spread to White Russia, Poland, and Galicia. Sprung up in the wake of the physical devastation of the Chemielnicki pogroms (1648–9) and the moral debacle surrounding the false messiah Shabbetai Zvi (1666), the movement drew a great following among the impoverished Jews of Eastern Europe. Emphasizing the mystical connection between man and God, an important part of the movement's philosophy was grounded in *devekut*—cleaving to God through prayer, Torah study, and ultimately every aspect of life—and *kavannah,* proper intention in carrying out one's good deeds. Drawing heavily on the Kabbalistic teachings of "the Ari," R. Isaac Luria of Safed in the land of Israel, members of the Hassidic movement prayed according to a variation of the Sefaradi prayer liturgy known as *nusach Ha'Ari* (liturgical form of the Ari) or *nusach Eretz Yisrael* (liturgical form of Israel)(Loewenthal 1994a).

Although the Ba'al Shem Tov, a folk healer and scholar, had originally placed primary emphasis on intellectual study of Judaism alongside its emotional component, he soon found himself leading a movement with mass appeal, necessitating a shift in emphasis and a change in structure. Mysticism slowly took the place of intellectual pursuits in the dynamically expanding social movement, changing the lives of thousands of ordinary Jews (Loewenthal 1990).

Following the death of the Ba'al Shem Tov, the second and third generations of the Hassidic movement (under R. Dov Ber, known as the *Maggid*—preacher—of Mezritch, and R. Elimelech of Lizansk) instituted two innovations that would become central to the movement. The first was the doctrine or concept of the zaddik or rebbe surrounded by his followers, the Hassidim (Dresner 1960; Robinson 1995). Within a short time each Hassid came to be known not generically but as belonging to a specific rebbe, i.e. a Gerrer Hassid, a Lubavitcher Hassid etc. (Poll 1995; Etkes 1996).

The second innovation was the Hassidic court, the bureaucratic institution that would locate a Hassidic movement in a particular geographical location and facilitate its demographic development. Ultimately becoming the economic basis for most Hassidic movements, the creation of the court and its financial reserves enabled Hassidism to merge the politics of identity with the politics of distribution, assuring its place as a mass movement within Judaism (Dan 1989; Wilson and Frederiksen 1995; Loewenthal 1994b).

One of the main weekly events of most Hassidic courts was the *tish* (table). On Friday night, or during the third meal at the close of the Sabbath, the rebbe would hold court at his table, blessing the food, taking a small bite, and distributing the rest to his Hassidim, who would vie for the honor of receiving the rebbe's leftovers. The *tish* was an opportunity for the rebbe to deliver sermons to his eager Hassidim, and be honored by them in turn. A pivotal event in the life cycle of the Hassidic court, the *tish* was often one of the major public events that reinforced the connection between the Hassid and his rebbe.

The Beginnings of Habad

The Habad (Lubavitch) movement, an offshoot of the Hassidic movement, was founded in Russia during the late eighteenth century. Today the term Habad evokes images of bearded young men at various public locations—airports, train stations, outside department stores—energetically trying to convince Jewish males to put on *tefilin* (phylacteries). Another image that surfaces is that of young men in Habad "*mitzvah* [good deeds] tanks" distributing sugar-dusted jelly doughnuts to outlying Israeli army outposts on Hanukkah. A third, more contemporary image, displayed worldwide on the huge billboards erected by the Habad movement, is the portrait of the late Lubavitcher Rebbe atop a phrase welcoming the coming of the Messiah. But each of these images gives us insight into various characteristics of the Habad movement, none of them captures its philosophy or historical development.

During the third generation of Hassidism, while the when Galician leader R. Elimelech developed the concepts of the zaddik and the Hassidic court, his Russian counterpart, R. Shneur Zalman of Liady (1745–1812) founded the Habad school of Hassidism. Introducing his philosophy in 1772 after the passing of the maggid, R. Shneur Zalman was credited with a following of thousands of Hassidim throughout Russia (Mindel 1969; Dalfin 1998). Calling his movement Habad, an acronym of the three *sefirot* (kabbalistic circles) of *Hochma Bina* and *Da'at* (wisdom, understanding, and knowledge), he developed a philosophical system that was basically a synthesis between mystical Kabbalah and Halacha (Jewish law). In 1796 he published what would become the central philosophical text of Habad—the *Tanya*—which had been circulated in manuscript form for several years (Loewenthal 1990; Koskoff 1995, 90).

By the nineteenth century Habad—also known as Lubavitch, the name of the town where the second to sixth rebbe resided over a total of 112 years— became recognized as a rationalist form of Hassidism that could appeal to the educated (Mindel 1969). Each generation of Habad rebbe built its own philosophical teachings on the basis laid by R. Shneur Zalman while adding its scholarly and practical innovations to the movement. The generations were those of Shneur Zalman's son and successor, R. Dov Ber (1773–1827), and the third *Rebbe*, R. Menachem Mendel (1789–1866), known as the Tzemach Tzedek (from the title of his book) who was the first to assume the Habad surname Schneerson (referring to the descendents of Shneur Zalman). In the face of the challenge and threat of secular enlightenment in Russia, he was the first Habad *Rebbe* to confront the issue of secular learning, including The study of foreign, non-Jewish languages. Although the movement's founder had had a range of secular knowledge, the Tzemach Tzedek considered total separation from secular influence to be the only way to preserve Habad. Consequently, he fought vehemently against the urging of the *maskilim* (enlightened Jews) to open the Jewish community to secular learning.

The fourth rebbe, R. Shmuel (1834–1882), headed the movement during a wave of antisemitic pogroms against Russian Jewry. His son, Shalom Dovber (1860–1920), grappled with the political and ideological influences that were making inroads into Jewish life in Eastern Europe during the years prior to the First World War. Recognizing that Habad had to create an education stronghold for the movement in order to hold its own intellectually against Zionism and communism, in 1897 Shalom Dovber established the first Habad Yeshiva, Tomchei Temimim, instituting Hassidic thought as a major part of the curriculum (Loewenthal 1990; Dalfin 1998; Littlewood 1995; Dein 1992).

The Concept of "Communication" in Habad

Throughout its entire history, an important characteristic of the Habad movement was its attitude to the written and spoken word. Known for its bibliomania, as the Habad fixation on publishing was called by at least one scholar (Landau 1993), the seven rebbes published dozens of books, pamphlets, and lectures, making Habad the most prolific Hassidic movement in terms of number and scope of publications and the only one to record its own history (Dalfin 1998; Gries 1987; Faierstein 1991). This is but one facet of what Naftali Loewenthal calls "the Habad communication ethos," a central factor affecting the movement's attitude towards language (Loewenthal 1993; 1994a).

Many scholars agree that the Hassidic experience is characterized by efforts to make the highest level of the Jewish mystical experience accessible to the Jewish people at large. In Habad it was the zaddik who presented a mystical theosophy for the elite and a simplified version for the average man (Loewenthal 1994b). From the time of R. Shneur Zalman onward, Habad placed primary emphasis on the goal of communication, distinguishing itself from other groups of Hassidim. When this communication ethos merged with the dual Habad activity of outreach and messianism in the mid-twentieth century, it would change the face of the movement and of Jewish society at large.

Messianism and Outreach as Central Habad Tenets

In contrast to the rationalist nature of traditional Habad, one of the characteristics distinguishing the movement's twentieth century version from other Hassidic groups was its gradual focus on radical messianism. In her study of Lubavitch messianic resurgence Rachel Elior states that Habad had no messianic character at its inception (Elior 1998). This philosophy was transformed during the leadership of the sixth rebbe, R. Josef Isaac (1880–1950) who propagated a more apocalyptic perception of the world as oriented toward a transcendental messianic turning point (Greenberg 1992). The rebbe escaped the Holocaust and settled in the United States, and Habad took on a twofold role in dealing with the cataclysm's aftermath: professing a testament and carrying out a mission. To further carry out this resurgence of religious devotion and repentance, R. Josef Isaac, along with his son-in-law and successor, R. Menachem Mendel, started an all-encompassing educational program and developed a philosophy of outreach to all Jews. Unlike other Haredi communities that were trying to rejuvenate themselves after the Holocaust, Habad turned outward sending emissaries to Jews throughout the world. At this point, Habad policy muffled its outspoken messianism and subordinated it to the aim of outreach.

During the reign of the seventh rebbe, Menachem Mendel (1902–1994), messianic hope eventually led to practical activity (Redman 1992). Born in Nikolaiev in southern Ukraine, Menachem Mendel was a sixth-generation direct descendent of his namesake, the Tzemach Tzedek, and strengthened the Schneerson familial ties by marrying R. Joseph Isaac's daughter. Following a stay in Berlin and Paris, where Menachem Mendel completed his studies at the Sorbonne, he reached the United States in 1941. There he utilized his secular studies and knowledge of close to a dozen languages, acting as a translator for his father-in-law and preparing materials in English, Yiddish, and Loshon Kodesh that would be used in Habad's new outreach program. Reluctantly assuming the mantle of Habad leadership in 1950, the new rebbe developed the outreach program further and began printing material about Hassidism in various languages. An early example was the weekly periodical, *Talks and Tales,* which featured both Torah and Talmud stories as well as a column about nature from a Torah perspective (Dalfin 1998).

The seventh Lubavitcher rebbe stood out from all of his predecessors. Truly a "people's Rebbe," this visible leader was courted by Jewish and Gentile politicians from all over the world. Receiving and greeting followers and supplicants once a week at his Brooklyn residence, in place of collecting the customary Hassidic *pidyon* (a sum of money given to a rebbe as redemption for one's soul), the rebbe would instead distribute dollar bills and blessings. Thus he used this forum as a stage in the outreach program that he considered a cornerstone of postwar Habad Hassidism.

The fervor of the Habad community's embrace of the outreach program was expressed in both word and deed. Adopting a quasimilitary terminology, enthusiasts bestowed on Habad outreach vehicles the nickname "mitzvah tanks."

Similarly, the groups that were sent on outreach missions were called "Habad commandos," outreach youth groups were known as the "Army of Light," and the children's organizations were dubbed the *Tzevaot Hashem* "Army of the Lord" (Ben-Rafael 1998). Habad was now an "army," and all its members were devoted "soldiers" doing the Lord's work by proselytizing other Jews. At a recent Habad wedding in Israel, I observed a group of young men asking each other where they were "serving," terminology that is usually reserved for army service in that country.

From the 1950s to the 1990s, the last rebbe of Habad, who died childless without naming a successor, became more vocal in promoting the messianic issue side by side with the growing Habad outreach movement (Shaffir 1993). Various circles in Habad ultimately personified the general Jewish idea of redemption as the person of the rebbe himself, orchestrating a future gathering at which the rebbe was to be proclaimed the Messiah. During these years the traditional communication ethos merged with outreach and messianism, giving rise to numerous Habad publications in Hebrew, English, French, Yiddish, Spanish, Portuguese, Russian, Italian, and German and spurring printings of the *Tanya* printed in thousands of locations throughout the world. Habad efforts in both the Israeli *Teshuva* movement and the worldwide Jewish outreach program replenished the movement's ranks with thousands of *hozrim betshuva* who were unfamiliar with Yiddish and, indeed outside of Israel, with any form of Hebrew. This necessitated that Habad emissaries be fluent in foreign languages and that Habad publications be available in the local vernacular (Loeb 1995; *Challenge* 1973; Salinger 1991).

In the late 1980s messianic expectations flamed, and the messianic majority in Habad, whose hopes crystallized around the figure of the rebbe, began to fight the rationalist minority. In the early 1990s, the rebbe suffered a stroke that affected his mobility and left him unable to speak. The issue of messianic doctrinal interpretation was now left open to the leaders of various Habad factions. Following the rebbe's death in 1994, the movement splintered when one group refused to acknowledge the Rebbe's demise, claiming that the coffin in which his remains were ostensibly buried was, in fact, empty. At present there are two trends in Habad to which more than one Habad Hassid refers as the *Rebbe z"l* (the rebbe of blessed memory), as opposed to the *Rebbe Shlita* (the rebbe, may he be blessed with a long life). Both groups have representatives worldwide and each publishes its own material, reflecting its philosophies.

Habad in Israel

Traditionally, Habad has always had a special connection with the land of Israel in that the movement's founder, R. Shneur Zalman, intended to follow Hassidic leader R. Menachem Mendel of Vitebsk to the Holy Land in 1776, although in practice he did not do so. The attraction to the Holy Land continued with his son and successor, R. Dov Ber, who in turn encouraged his son-in-law to settle in Hebron and start a Kollel in the city. As the Hebron colony grew steadily, additional Habad colonies were established in Jerusalem and Jaffa (Rabinowicz 1982).

With the rise of Zionism, the Habad rebbes were forced to distinguish between their antagonism to the new political movement and the age-old Jewish tradition of settling the Holy Land. R. Joseph Isaac was the first rebbe to visit Palestine, meeting with religious and secular leaders throughout the country in the summer of 1929. (*Challenge* 1973). Following the establishment of the state of Israel he urged his followers to establish a rural community that could serve as the movement's national center. The result was Kfar Habad, founded in the Lod Valley in 1949. Surrounded by settlements peopled with new immigrants, the original seventy four families were joined by another fifteen from Morocco and later by numerous Russian immigrants. Placing education at the forefront of their activities, the founders of Kfar Habad established a Talmud Torah, a Kollel for married students, a yeshiva combining Torah study and vocational training, and in 1959, a girls' school (Beit Rivka). Habad was the only Hassidic group active among Yemenite and Moroccan immigrants, an important step in establishing itself as an outreach movement in the state of Israel (Loeb 1995). Expanding its geographical settlements throughout Israel, Habad launched communities in Kiryat Malachi, Jerusalem, Lod, and in the ancient holy city of Safed.

From the late 1950s onward the Habad motto of outreach became its calling card in Israeli society. Habad adopted a program of caring for Israeli war orphans, periodically gathering groups of orphaned boys together at Kfar Habad in order to celebrate their Bar Mitzvah. From the 1970s onward, Habad mitzvah tanks traveled to army bases on Hanukkah, distributing delicacies to soldiers even in the most remote outposts. Additional outreach activities—activists encouraging Jewish men to put on *tefilin,* the erection of public Habad *succot* (tabernacles), the kindling of public Hanukkah lights (Redman 1992)—earned Habad a reputation as the most approachable Hassidic sect, both in Israel and in the rest of the world.

Habad has made its mark on the Israeli political scene. In his last years the rebbe expressed support for a more extreme religious position (for instance, in the case of the legislative debate over "who is a Jew") and a right-wing territorial position, while simultaneously involving his movement in Israeli Haredi political machinations (Landau 1993). During the 1996 elections a last-minute Habad-sponsored campaign helped to propel the right-wing Likud political candidate Binyamin Netanyahu ("Netanyahu is good for the Jews") into the prime minister's seat. With this bold movement Habad exchanged its identity as an outreach organization for that of a vocal player on the political map and was consequently ostracized by left-wing groups that once had welcomed what they considered the movement's benign cultural and religious activities. Habad mitzvah tanks have been barred from army bases and the movement is now publicly affiliated with a right-wing territorialist camp.

Contemporary Habad

Since the Habad center moved to the United States after the Holocaust, the major centers of the movement have found homes in New York, London, Israel,

Canada, and Belgium. It was generously estimated that by the 1980s there were perhaps 250,000 Habad adherents and close sympathizers worldwide, and that approximately 10,000 Habad-affiliated families now live in Israel, concentrated in Kfar Habad, Jerusalem, Safed, and various other locations (Sharot 1991).

What makes a Habad Hassid different from any other Hassid? Four distinguishing characteristics are ideology of Judaism, appearance, lifestyle and central religious authority. Habad ideology developed throughout the reign of the seven rebbes, linking the Hassidic elements of *devekut, kavannah,* and mystical thought. Until the past half-century Habad was considered one of the more, if not the most, rational of the Hassidic movements.

Walking down the street, a member of Habad can at times be indistinguishable from fellow pedestrians. As members of an outreach movement, Habad Hassidim can be found dressed in anything from jeans and a t-shirt (for the newly religious) to the traditional men's garb of a wide-brimmed pinched hat, plain dark pants, a short suit jacket, and a light-colored shirt, preferably white. Wearing their *tzitzit* (ritual fringes on a four cornered garment) out of their shirttails is often all that distinguishes them from a Western businessman. While many Habad men grow *peot* (sidelocks), they often do not let them grow very long, as do other Hassidim, and many tuck them behind their ears. Habad women dress modestly, with unrevealing necklines, sleeves covering their elbows, skirts below their knees, stockings, and for married women, a wig covering their own hair. In other Hassidic sects the dictates of female modesty can be instrumental in keeping women out of the public eye, but in Habad physical modesty does not mean remaining exclusively within the realm of the family. Habad women act as emissaries along with their husbands, appearing at public gatherings and taking to the podiums to spread the word of God, primarily to other Jewish women (Belcove-Shalin 1989). Indeed, to be a woman who is a Hassidic follower in her own right was traditionally encouraged in Habad, particularly by the sixth rebbe who encouraged practical activism by Habad women in Poland during the 1930s (Loewenthal 2000). This lead was followed by his son-in-law, who encouraged women's empowerment in Habad, declaring it acceptable for Jewish women to study not only the laws that pertained to them but mystical thought as well.

Although some consider Habad to be a rejection of modern society (Davidman 1990), this is true with regard to only one of the three attributes that sociologists claim characterize Haredi rejectionist philosophies: chastity (Friedman 1975). As for the other two attributes—rejection of Western dress and education—Habad is more lenient than other Hassidic sects, as long as the concept of *tzniut* (modesty) is followed. Habad Hassidim can be found in all professions, from Rabbis to ritual slaughterers, stockbrokers to lawyers, doctors to college professors, computer technicians to refrigerator repairmen. A large number of white-collar Habad professionals, both male and female, are former secular Jews. Like many groups within the Haredi world, Habad Hassidim often provide services to their own communities. As an outreach sect, it dispatches a great proportion of its adherents to remote outposts throughout the world, making it necessary for emissary parents to send their children away at a young age to a major Habad center such as London or New York for education at a yeshiva or girls' boarding school.

Since the death of the seventh rebbe in 1994, the issue of the movement's central religious authority has been a thorny one. Hassidim continue to consult the rebbe for posthumous advice by randomly inserting questions written on slips of paper into a book of his responsa; the answer to the question is then found on that page. In daily matters there are several leaders who deal with formulating and implementing Habad policy (Shaffir 1993). Among them are the primary movers in the two Habad factions mentioned earlier, the less messianic one that considers the rebbe to be dead, and the hard-core messianic group that still refers to him as if he were alive.

A final issue worthy of note is Habad's use of language. It is too simplistic to say that Habad Hassidim in Israel speak Ivrit, although almost all of the veteran Habad members are fluent in that language. As we will see in a future chapter, some veteran Habad Hassidim speak Yiddish among themselves, while other Habad Hassidim born abroad speak to each other in their native tongue, be it English, Russian, or any other language. As for the Yiddish used in Habad, the correct pronunciation of Yiddish is held to be the Russian-Lithuanian pronunciation of the last rebbe used. Yet in spite of its Russian-Lithuanian origin, Habad Yiddish, both in Israel and abroad, incorporated a great deal of Loshon Kodesh in its vocabulary.

Habad Hassidim are probably the most well known Haredim in the world. Coming into contact with Jews and non-Jews in the most far-flung regions throughout the world, they are a familiar sight to many people who have never seen another Jew. In the following chapters I will explore how the unique nature of Habad influences its language and culture, marking it as a Hassidic group which can be compared to no other.

What is Gur?

In the late 1970s the Israeli Hassidic world appeared to undergo a socio-economic revolution as the Haredi population explosion began to make itself keenly felt. Aware that Hassidim, blessed by large families and unable to resist social pressures, were taking out exorbitant loans to marry off their children, the Gerrer Rebbe of that time, R. Simcha Bunim Alter, issued a series of sumptuary laws intended to save his Hassidim from bankruptcy. Apart from the most immediate family, no more than two hundred guests could be invited to a wedding. Apartments for young couples could cost no more than fifty thousand dollars, making it necessary for many to leave the confines of the traditional Hassidic territories of Jerusalem and Bnai Brak and create Gerrer communities elsewhere. These stipulations applied to all Gerrer Hassidim, regardless of their economic status. When a wealthy Gerrer Hassid remonstrated that he could easily afford to invite a thousand people to his daughter's wedding, the rebbe replied tersely: "Invite as many people as you desire, but if you desire more than two hundred guests, you will not find your rebbe among them!"[1]

It is interesting to note that this growing economic distress was first addressed by a scion of one of the wealthiest Hassidic dynasties at the time. Unlike the various Hassidic courts that subsisted on the *pidyon* system, where followers would present the rebbe with a sum of money before asking his advice or blessing, the Gerrer rebbes had been made independently wealthy by the family's successful real estate purchases throughout the twentieth century. Yet of all Hassidic leaders of the time, it was the former businessman R. Simcha Bunim who realized the acuteness of the situation and took steps toward ameliorating his Hassidim's lot (Gerlitz 1995b).

Many outsiders identify Gerrer Hassidim through their appearance: the men wear their trousers tucked into their socks. Others think of them as the "strict Hassidim" due to their stringent sexual norms and complete separation of the sexes, enforced even between husband and wife in public. In one of the better known Gerrer jokes, a Hassid's friend remarks on having seen him walking in the street near a woman. "It wasn't my wife!" the first Hassid responds with alacrity. Yet the Gerrer court is also known for its political and economic power, not only in the Hassidic world but in contemporary politics as well. No prime ministerial candidate in Israel can afford to campaign without making overtures to the reigning Gerrer rebbe; for many years the chairman of the Knesset Finance Committee was a Gerrer Hassid, a close associate of the *Rebbe* and an extremely powerful former businessman. To many, Gerrer Hassidim are an enigma, expressing a dichotomy of extremes in the Hassidic world.

The Beginnings of Gur

The Gur dynasty began in the mid-nineteenth century under the leadership of R. Isaac Meir Rothenberg of Gur (Gora Kalwaria) in Poland (1789–1866), whose father had been a disciple of the Hassidic master R. Levi Isaac of Berdichev. Orphaned at a tender age, R. Isaac Meir was raised under the tutelage of his grandfather and later sent to study with the famous Hassidic rebbe R. Simcha Bunim of Przysucha. In that small town he became inseparable from another student who would be instrumental in his life—Menachem Mendel of Tomashov, the future rebbe of Kotzk, Poland. Having fled the unsuccessful Polish uprising against the Russians in 1830–31, the two found refuge in eastern Poland, changing their names so as to go unrecognized by the authorities. From that time on "Rothenberg" was replaced by "Alter," the name by which the Gur dynasty would be known. An unreserved supporter of Menachem Mendel throughout the stormy controversy that divided the Kotzker Hassidim during their leader's twenty-year period of voluntary isolation, Isaac Meir accepted the mantle of Hassidic leadership only after his old friend's death in 1859 (Alfasi 1993).

Known by the acronym of his name and the title of his major work, the *Rim* (R. Isaac Meir) displayed an awareness of his Hassidim's public needs and the difficulties besetting Polish Jewry of his time. As opponent of the *maskilim,* who wished to make innovations in the fields of education, profession, and dress, he was incarcerated by local authorities for refusing to make concessions to educational modernization. In contrast to the isolationist, and "iron fist" system of spiritual guidance of Kotzk, the Gerrer system involved a great deal of contact with the masses, with the rebbe taking personal interest in their daily problems. As in the case of the Kotzker Hassidim, the Gerrer teachings placed Torah study at the center of spiritual life, attempted to develop followers' enthusiasm for Torah study, and constantly searched for truth and inner perfection. Every subsequent *Rebbe* would add his own personal mark to the movement, emphasizing concepts of belief and behavior or creating new customs that would bind his Hassidim (Alfasi 1993).

Upon R. Isaac Meir's death the mantle of the Gur dynasty passed to R. Isaac Meir's grandson, Judah Aryeh Leib Alter (1847–1905). Orphaned as a child, R. Judah Aryeh Leib had been raised by his grandfather, who instilled in him the special teachings of Gerrer Hassidism, including dialectic truth, belief, and *devekut* (Ya'akovson, 1986; Piekarz 1986). R. Judah Aryeh Leib established the group's spiritual and political leadership in Congress Poland under Russian domination, winning the confidence of rabbis throughout the area. Like his grandfather, he played a significant role in public affairs and concerned himself with contemporary Polish Jewish problems. It was through his influence that Hassidism in Poland disassociated itself from Zionism, and under his guidance that the Gerrer Hassidic movement began to make inroads among Jewish youth (Alfasi 1993).

In the early years of the twentieth century he was succeeded by his eldest son, Abraham Mordechai Alter (1866–1948), under his leadership the movement reached the height of its religious, social, and political influence among Polish and world Jewry. A lover of order and precision, he provided his Hassidim with an organized framework for life, restoring the recitation of morning prayers from a later time to their regular time and providing a break during the Sabbath service for public study (Levin 1977). R. Abraham Mordechai was a prominent figure in European Orthodox Jewry and a founder of the Agudat Yisrael (Agudath Israel) political movement (Rabinowicz 1982). Particularly sympathetic to young people and their needs, he established a Gerrer yeshiva, which functioned as both a showplace for the movement and a vehicle for bringing more young men to the Gerrer way of life (Stampfer 1988). In addition, he was one of the major supporters of the Beis Ya'akov girls' educational movement, founded by the Cracow seamstress Sarah Schenierer in 1917, which ultimately revolutionized Orthodox female education throughout the world (Weissman 1976, 1995).

Gur in Israel

Despite his opposition to organized Zionism, R. Abraham Mordechai promoted the idea of Jewish settlement of the Holy Land, visiting it five times while still based in his native Poland. Accompanied by several of his children, he escaped to Palestine at the outbreak of the Second World War and later reconstructed his movement from the ashes of the Holocaust. At the time of his arrival, there were between 1,500 and 2,000 men belonging to the Gerrer sect in Palestine with eleven Gerrer *shteiblach* (small Hassidic prayer houses) in Tel Aviv, five in Bnai Brak, one in Haifa, and one in Kiriyat Ata.[2] In 1948 he succumbed to illness, passing away during the War of Independence (Alfasi 1993). The next rebbe, his son R. Israel Alter (1892–1977) known as the *Beit Yisrael* (house of Israel), was a noted scholar of great personal charm, whose influence extanded far beyond the immediate circle of his followers. Having lost a wife and children in Europe, he remarried before assuming the mantle of leadership (Gerlitz 1995a). In his youth, he was already known for his asceticism and precision in matters of Jewish law, something that later expressed itself in his stringent interpretation of sexual mores between husband and wife (Levin 1977; Helman 1994). Following the tradition begun by his father, R. Israel Alter was active in developing and leading the Moetzet Gedolei Hatorah (Council of Torah Sages) of Agudat Yisrael, which was the guiding force and deciding board behind the decisions of the Haredi Agudat Yisrael political party in Israel. He was also the primary force behind Agudat Israel's political separatism. Leaving no children, in 1977 he was succeeded by his younger brother, R. Simcha Bunim (1898–1992).

A down-to-earth businessman, R. Simcha Bunim was familiar with the day-to-day problems of both the country and his Hassidim in a way that his older brother never had been. A fourth son who had never thought that he would lead the Gur dynasty, the *Lev Simcha* (heart of joy), "a true gentleman" who tempered his older brother's asceticism and attempted to solve his Hassidim's financial tensions, brought a collective sigh of relief to the Gerrer community.[3] More relaxed than his older brother, the *Lev Simcha* made his mark on the world of Gur primarily through the sumptuary laws mentioned earlier. Consequently, he expended a great deal of effort trying to promote the concept of rental housing for young couples and was instrumental in establishing Gerrer communities in areas with inexpensive housing such as Arad, Ashdod, and Hatzor Haglilit. Having fallen ill in the mid 1980s, R. Simcha Bunim in his final years of leadership was leader in name only; the daily running of his court was left to others (Gerlitz 1995a).

Although he left a son, R. Ya'akov Arieh, R. Simcha Bunim was succeeded by his half-brother, Pinchas Menachem (1926–1996). Unlike his brothers, whose Hebrew was peppered with Yiddish (or rather, whose Yiddish was often peppered with Hebrew), the *Pnai Menachem*, who had come to Israel as a young teenager, was more comfortable in Ivrit than in Yiddish, and it was common to hear him use very modern expressions. Known for his sharp tongue and wit, he was capable of using slang phrases such as *eizeh fashla* (what a blooper), something unheard of from other Rebbes of his time.[4] Primarily self-taught, the *Pnai Menachem* had the broadest secular education of the three brothers owing to the influence of his mother, who had been an educated woman. Apart from his fluency in Ivrit and Yiddish, he was the only one of the three brothers to have a working knowledge of Polish or to keep a modern secular reference—the Hebrew Encyclopedia—in his drawing room. An astute politician versed in both intra-Haredi machinations and contemporary Israeli politics, R. Pinchas

Menachem used his clout to offer, or refraining from offering, support to various coalitions, even before being chosen as rebbe (Helman 1997).

In 1996 the *Pnai Menachem* was succeeded by his nephew, R. Ya'akov Arieh Alter (1939–), the first contemporary Gerrer rebbe to be groomed for the task since birth. Unlike his father, who was known as a "people's *Rebbe*," he is extremely introverted and eschews almost all outward signs of his rank. He has no secular knowledge and knows only Yiddish and Ivrit. It is difficult to determine his particular style of leadership and the impact which he will ultimately have upon the Gur dynasty, but his desire for religious and social separatism is well known. Unlike his father, uncles, and grandfather, R. Ya'akov Arieh refuses an audience to secular Jews, individuals and politicians alike (Katzover 1999). His separatist philosophy is also expressed in statements rejecting religious compromise, and in the ultimate desire of the sect of Gur—which never initiated an outreach policy similar to that of Habad—to make inroads into secular Israel (Cohen and Susser 2000).

Contemporary Gur

There are no precise statistics regarding the number of Hassidim belonging to the Gerrer sect. Statistics from the early 1980s mention 4,000 families belonging to Gur (Rabinowicz 1982), while more recent estimates name over 7,000 Gerrer families, almost all of whom live in Israel.[5] Many are descendents of the original 1,500–2,000 Gerrer Hassidim mentioned earlier, or of the thousands of Hassidic Holocaust survivors who reached Israel in the late 1940s and early 1950s.[6] In addition, several hundreds of Hassidim from other sects have married into Gur. One of these families will be discussed in a future chapter. The leadership is headquartered in Jerusalem, and Gerrer communities are thriving in Bnai Brak, Tel Aviv, and outlying areas such as Ashdod, Arad, and Hatzor Haglilit (Shilhav 1993). Outside of Israel there are small Gerrer communities in Antwerp, London, and Brooklyn numbering several hundred families in all.

As evidenced by their preference for the singular "Gur" as a self-referent, Gerrer Hassidim never count themselves as individuals, or even families; instead they show their growing numbers by counting their Yeshivot and *shteiblach* throughout the world. In 1992 there were eleven Gerrer Yeshivot in Israel and eight *shteiblach* in Brooklyn alone (Landau 1993). A newspaper article on Gur's political power in Israel quoted the rebbe's right-hand man, Knesset member Ya'akov Litzman, who often enumerates the movement's schools and synagogues to show its power: "Seventy boys' schools throughout the country, thirty-one synagogues in Bnai Brak, twenty in Ashdod, etcetera."[7]

What makes a Gerrer Hassid different from any other Hassid? In addition to the usual Hassidic beliefs of *kavannah* and *devekut*, Gur believes in separatism, stringent Torah study, and personal striving for truth and inner perfection. As each of the Gerrer rebbes has left his stamp on the movement, to this one must add sexual asceticism (the *Beit Yisrael*), sumptuary regulations (the *Lev Simcha*), sharpness in language (the *Pnai Menachem*), and biting wit. Despite their separatism and asceticism, Gerrer Hassidim are famed for the secular jokes, that they tell about subjects that other Hassidim would consider risqué. For example, the following was heard at the Gerrer *Beis Medrash* (study hall) during a break between prayers: "What did Eve do when Adam would come home late? She would count his ribs." In an aside, the listener—an expert on Hassidic life—stated that such a joke would never be heard in any other Hassidic *Beis Medrash*.[8]

A male member of the Gur sect is instantly recognizable on the street by his three quarter–length black coat, flat wide-brimmed hat (or *spodik* [high fur hat] on the Sabbath and holidays), and trousers tucked into socks. The latter tradition stems from a mid nineteenth century government decree in Congress Poland forcing Jews to choose between Western dress and that of Russian peasants. Eschewing any Western influence that might bring his Hassidim closer to the dreaded ideas of the enlightenment, the first Gerrer rebbe chose to emulate Russian garb, including the tucking of pant legs into high boots. When such boots were no longer worn, Gerrer men continued to tuck their pants into their socks, creating a visible separation between themselves and other Hassidim. Also, the hats of Gerrer Hassidic men have more rounded tops and broader brims than those of other Haredi groups. Like almost all Hassidim (with the exception of the more modern groups within Habad), Gerrer Hassidim never wear ties, and they wear their *tzitzit* out of their trousers. Gerrer Hassidim grow *peot* and often gather them up under their skullcap or hat. Gerrer women dress modestly, covering their hair with wigs.

Gur has been a prime player in modern Israeli politics, with the rebbe and his inner court being extremely familiar with current events in Israeli society, belying the separatist doctrine of ignorance of non-Haredi lifestyles. On the individual level the situation is different. Although most Gur families speak Ivrit among themselves, the Gerrer lifestyle is one of separatism, not only from Israeli culture, but often from other Haredi groups as well. This may be seen by the recent creation of a Gerrer Beit Ya'akov in Bnai Brak in order to offer a different educational and social atmosphere to girls being raised in the Gur tradition. Although Hassidim customarily worked after marriage and did not devote themselves to full-time Torah study, the Israeli army deferment for Torah students has motivated Hassidic society to embrace this custom. Older Hassidim in the Gerrer community work in business, services, and in the diamond industry.

The central religious authority in Gur is always the current rebbe. A pivotal member of the Moetzet Gedolai Hatorah, the decisions of that group are law for Gerrer Hassidim in most matters. In terms of culinary specifications, Gerrer Hassidim only eat food that has received the seal of approval of the Badatz, the High Court of the Eda Haredit. Gerrer Hassidim subscribe to the Haredi newspaper *HaModia*, a prominent mouthpiece for that group.

A final issue is language. Forbearing to subscribe to the Habad communication ethic that expresses itself in copious writings, the Gerrer rebbes best express themselves in oral discourse, often during the *tish*. Although these discourses are occasionally written down after the Sabbath, the rebbes are not known for their prolific authorship. In oral communication, Gerrer Hassidim tend to speak more Ivrit than other Hassidic groups, reflecting their attitude toward contemporary Israel. Gur has always been a political Hassidic movement, a behind-the-scenes mover first in Jewish interwar politics in Poland and later in modern-day Israeli political manipulations. This tends to foster an intimate knowledge of the local vernacular and facilitate its use among members of the sect. The separatist tendencies, and the influences of Hungarian Hassidim, have also manifested themselves in contemporary Gur life, leading toward a linguistic separation and a desire to expand the use of Yiddish in everyday life. The extent of this phenomenon, and the tensions between the Ivrit and Yiddish speakers within the Gur community, will be examined in later chapters.

Who are the Mitnagdim?

For over fifty years, every spring a flag ceremony has been held in Bnai Brak from one of the highestt points overlooking the city. On Israeli Independence Day the national flag is raised over a bastion of the Mitnagdic sect, the Ponevezh Yeshiva, founded during the Second World War. This custom, introduced by the Yeshiva's founder, R. Joseph Kahaneman (1888–1969), whose educational establishment boasted a pre-state military underground, symbolizes his multifaceted relationship with the Zionist entity. The custom continued under the leadership of his successor, R. Eliezer Menachem Man Shakh. When elderly R. Shakh became incapacitated during the 1990s, anti-Zionist militancy among the students caused the custom to be questioned, though it was not abolished. These days the flag is removed by the students within hours of its being hoisted, thus giving lip service to both the founders' quasi-Zionist *weltanschauung* and their own anti-Zionist sympathies.

The Beginnings of the Mitnagdim

The Mitnagdim (opponents), as they are called in the Haredi world, were known as such because their major characteristic as a group was their opposition to Hassidism. Under the leadership of a major historical opponent to the Hassidic movement, R. Elijah B. Solomon Zalman, the Gaon of Vilna (1720–1797), their way of life became characteristic of much of Lithuanian Jewry.

The Vilna Gaon's opposition to Hassidism did not stem from direct contact with the movement; rather, he was influenced by his contemporaries and disciples who recounted stories about the practices of followers of the Ba'al Shem Tov. On the theological level the Gaon opposed what he considered neglect of Torah study and disrespect toward Torah scholars in a movement that failed to emphasize unceasing Torah study and stringent interpretation of Judaic law. Simultaneously, he suspected certain aspects of the Hassidic movement of being influenced by Sabbateanism, a belief focused on the bizarre practices that Hassidic Jews were rumored to have introduced into everyday life, including dancing during prayer and other unheard-of innovations (Morgenstern 1998). Even relatively staid customs such as praying by a liturgy other than that used in the rest of the community widened the gap between Hassidim and their surroundings.

On the communal level, Hassidism was seen as a suprageographical factor that would weaken the status of the local rabbinate. Hassidim's refusal to eat from the ritual slaughtering of non-Hassidim created a separation in the community that had repercussions in many fields (Wilensky 1991). Although the Gaon did not mention such economic factors as loss of revenue to local functionaries, those, too, played a role in his disciples' support for his public opposition to the new religious movement, which they felt would protect their own position and the status quo. Another important reason for the Mitnagdic opposition to Hassidism was timing. This was the period when Jewish autonomy in Poland was threatened by to the dissolution of the Council of Four Lands (1764) and the first partition of Poland (1772). Consequently, the attitude toward Jewish communal institutions and their powers became a central public issue, and the alternative leadership set up by the Hassidic movement indirectly contributed to a decline in the centrality of the existing Jewish communal leadership (Hasdai 1988).

From the outset, the Mitnagdim were shaped by the iron will and intellectual perseverance of the Vilna Gaon; however, along with the opposition to Hassidism, they developed institutions, tendencies, and a way of life that formed a specific culture. One of these expressions was a pronounced skepticism, a reaction to the mysticism attached to the Hassidic movement in general. Another was a criticism of authoritarianism, a response to the charismatic leadership of the Hassidic rebbes (Etkes 1989).

Following the death of the Vilna Gaon, opposition to Hassidism reached new heights, but by the mid nineteenth century the hostility began to abate as both movements faced a common enemy: the *Haskala* (Jewish Enlightenment) (Etkes 1989). As time passed the gap between the Hassidim and Mitnagdim closed, though the basic differences remain apparent in dress, prayer liturgy, ritual slaughtering, and the existence of a Hassidic court. Various institutions of Mitnagdic Jewry took form, including a Yeshiva movement that would ultimately become the basis for all Haredi society (Friedman 1992).

The first modern Lithuanian Yeshiva was founded in 1802 by R. Haim of Volozhyn. Unlike other learning environments, which were usually centered around a particular rabbi and required students to fend for themselves outside of the very unofficial hours of study, Volozhyn offered fixed lessons for single young men, a stipend, and an alternative community detached from a secular environment (M. Friedman 1991; Stampfer 1995). Ultimately, Yeshivot based on the Volozhyn model provided an all-embracing residential framework, which cut students off from their families and separated them from their community of origin (M. Friedman 1991). Some, such as the Slobodka Yeshiva, combined Torah learning with a desire to further the ethical standards of the learner. An offshoot of the *Mussar* movement founded by R. Israel Salanter (1810–1883), this response to the Hassidic innovations which put great emphasis on intention and spiritualism instead of concentrating solely on the letter of the law (Helmreich 1982). Another, almost hybrid Mitnagdic group was the Hungarian school of thought founded by R. Moshe Sofer in Pressburg during the early nineteenth century. Combining stringent application of the law with depth in

Torah studies, his school created a new form of non-Lithuanian opposition to Hassidic custom (Silber 1992).

The question of including secular studies in the Volozhyn Yeshiva's curriculum was a major issue during the institution's later years. As part of their policy of modernization and Russification, during the late nineteenth century the authorities insisted upon introducing secular studies—and particularly lessons in the Russian language—into the Yeshiva. Although initially willing to permit Russian to be taught alongside Talmudic study for two hours a day, the head of the Yeshiva, R. Naftali Zvi Yehuda Berlin, known as the *Natziv*, balked at having to formally introduce secular language studies into the official curriculum. The *Natziv's* opposition to secular studies was not a blanket condemnation, and he himself often read secular newspapers (Schacter 1990). However, he did not find such studies fitting as an integral part of a Yeshiva curriculum and preferred to close the Yeshiva in 1892, rather than acquiesce to the authorities' demands. Three years later the Yeshiva reopened and continued to function until the First World War; meanwhile he had managed to articulate his position against including secular language studies in a Yeshiva (Katz 1998).

During the nineteenth and early twentieth centuries the Mitnagdic movement grew in strength, but it was far surpassed numerically by the growing Hassidic movements. Unlike the dynastic Hassidic leadership, Mitnagdic Rabbis were not always characterized by a family succession. Consequently, the movement often had a number of spiritual leaders at one time, each with his own Yeshiva or following and his own system of learning.

The Lithuanians in Israel

By the 1930s, several major Lithuanian Yeshivot, such as Slobodka, Novardok, and Lomza, were transplanted to Palestine. Unlike the ultra-Orthodox Hungarian groups that attached themselves to the Old Yishuv and lived off donations brought in from abroad, the students in these Yeshivot affiliated themselves with the New Yishuv of modern Zionists, which they hoped would eventually economically absorb them after they left their studies (M. Friedman 1991).

A great Mitnagdic luminary of that period was R. Abraham Yeshayahu Karlitz, known as the *Hazon Ish* (1878–1953), who settled in Bnai Brak in 1933. Although he never held a formal public position, he became one of the major figures to mold Mitnagdic Jewry. In 1942 he established a Kollel in Bnai Brak, that provided a framework for married men who chose a life of Torah study. The establishment of such an institution within the New Yishuv society—an extended moratorium from work for married Haredi men—was an innovation which would leave its mark on the entire Jewish world, a symbol of the transition from the religious-traditional Eastern European Jewish world to a Western and Israeli Haredi society. Following the establishment of the state and the army exemption granted to men who claim Torah study as their full-time profession, the Kollel would become the accepted framework for Haredi men of army age. This Mitnagdic innovation made inroads into Hassidic society as well, which now organized Yeshivot and Kollelim in order to become "a society of scholars" rather than exclusively a society of piety (M. Friedman 1986; Heilman and Friedman 1991).

Another figure of stature was R. Joseph Kahaneman, who founded the Ponevezh Yeshiva in December 1943. Initially numbering seven students, by the mid 1950s it had become a major Yeshiva in the Jewish world owing to Kahaneman's acceptance of both religious and secular financial support, taking advantage of the postwar romanticism and nostalgia that Eastern European Jews often displayed for a world that had been destroyed. In contrast to other Haredi leaders of the time, he also turned to government sources to further his aims. He was therefore meticulous in making sure that the Israeli flag would be raised above the Yeshiva each Independence Day, a symbol of the *modus vivendi* he had reached with the Israeli government (M. Friedman 1991).

A third educational figure who made his mark on both the Mitnagdic and Hassidic worlds was R. Abraham Joseph Wolff, founder of the Beit Ya'akov teaching seminary in Bnai Brak. Although a Tel Aviv seminary had existed since the mid-1930s, it was Wolff's seminary that taught girls that a Haredi wife's purpose is to financially support her Torah-learning husband, and thus to share his portion of the world to come. In spite of initial parental opposition, by the late 1950s this pattern had become the norm in the Haredi world, making it another step in institutionalizing Haredi separatism through the creation of a society of scholars (M. Friedman 1991).

Another strong imprint was left on the Mitnagdic world by R. Eliezer Menahem Man Shakh (1898?–2001), who succeeded R. Kahaneman at the helm of the Ponevezh Yeshiva. Although not considered the most prominent Torah personality in Mitnagdic circles (a position held then by the late R. Shlomo Zalman Auerbach and presently by R. Yosef Shalom Eliashiv), for almost three decades Shakh was one of the primary movers in the Mitnagdic world, often appearing to be the Israeli Mitnagdic politician *par excellence*. The convoluted mergers and dissolutions of alliances that he maneuvered during this period usually had a theological justification. From a historical perspective, however, they were just another phase of Haredi power plays. One example was his changing the balance of power within the Moetzet Gedolai Hatorah, in response to Habad's foray into the Israeli political elections of 1988. In defense of his political territory, Shakh came out strongly against the Lubavitcher Rebbe, scornfully calling Habad "the outside sect closest to Judaism." Thus, contemporary Israeli politics acted as the catalyst for a new era in the Hassidic-Mitnagdic rivalry that had lain dormant for over a century (Landau 1993).

Contemporary Lithuanians

It is impossible to estimate how many Mitnagdim exist today. At a rough estimate based on voting patterns, at least 15,000 families belong to Mitnagdic groups in Israel (Arian and Shamir 1995). Most are located in Bnai Brak and Jerusalem, although one can find small Mitnagdic communities in outlying areas such as Ashdod (Shilhav 1993). Outside of Israel there are small Mitnagdic communities in major Jewish centers, in the U.S., Canada, England, and South Africa.

How does one distinguish between a Mitnaged and other Haredim? Originally, the Lithuanians were the only sect to put a major emphasis on Torah study as opposed to emphasizing the mystical or emotional aspects of Judaism. Until this rigor was tempered by the *Mussar* movement, they appeared to be almost single-mindedly focused upon deep immersion in the legalistic aspects of the Talmud as the only way to attain spiritual elevation. With the amelioration of Mitnagdic stringency and the creation of Hassidic Yeshivot, the two movements moved closer to each other in this respect.

Mitnagdic garb differs from that of Hassidim in several aspects. Aside from Rabbis, who wear frock coats, Mitnagdic men dress in dark Western suits, often with ties. *Tzitzit* are worn out of trousers, sometimes in pockets or around belt loops to be less visible. Hats are dark and slightly broad-brimmed. While almost all Hassidic men grow beards and *peot*, Mitnagdic *peot* are short and many men are clean-shaven. Mitnagdic women dress modestly but fashionable; married women cover their hair with wigs.

Attempting to create a society of scholars in Israel, Mitnagdic lifestyle deepened its separatism, particularly regarding secular education for men. Since the late 1950s young men devote themselves to full-time Torah study while women support the family. Older Mitnagdic men can be found in various trades and industries. While the custom of learning full-time has made inroads abroad, outside of Israel it is possible to find Yeshivot that allow their students to simultaneously pursue high school and college studies during the late evening hours (Gurock 1988).

Unlike the dynastic succession of Hassidic courts, which usually allowed for one central rabbinical authority per sect at any given time, the Mitnagdic world often had several *Gedolim* (Great Torah Scholars) to turn to in one generation. From the 1970s until the late 1990s R. Shakh was the major rabbinical authority in terms of daily issues, and his political machinations were instrumental in creating a new form of Mitnagdic separatism. Having broken away from the heavily Hassidic Moetzet Gedolei Hatorah in the late 1980s, Shakh founded a new Haredi political party (Degel Hatorah), started a new Haredi newspaper, *Yated Ne'eman,* and created the She'erit Yisrael kashrut authority. From the late 1990s until his death in November 2001, the aged, bedridden leader no longer communicated with his followers. As of yet, he has no successor, and although R. Eliashiv of Jerusalem acts as supreme Mitnagdic Halachic authority, the lack of a central temporal authority has been keenly felt in the Mitnagdic community.

A final word on the Mitnagdic use of language. In terms of communication forms, the Mitnagdic world appears to fall somewhere between that of Habad and that of Gur. Although Mitnagdic spiritual leaders have authored weighty Talmudic tomes, these are not their main vehicle of communication with followers. Mass communication takes place orally or via *Yated Ne'eman.* As for spoken communication, most Mitnagdim in Israel are fluent in Ivrit and communicate in that language. However, Yiddish is heard in the Mitnagdic community, where it is used in various settings. As for foreign languages, the attitude towards their study and use will be examined in a future chapter. In a discussion about language in the Mitnagdic world, R. Shakh's son, a high-ranking official in Israel's Ministry of Education, mentioned to me that although the elderly Mitnagdic leader had never received any formal secular education, he was fluent in Ivrit, Yiddish, and Polish (thanks to his wife), with a working knowledge of Russian. And in spite of what appeared for many years to be insularity from secular society, he was fully aware of the importance of foreign languages in the modern world. Describing R. Shakh's reaction to his decision to leave Israel for South Africa to study abroad for the first time, Ephraim Shakh recalled his father's major question: how was he preparing himself linguistically for the move? "He was quite aware of the language problem if it were necessary for someone to leave Israel to live abroad," his son recounted. "He had no doubt that one needed languages to survive in the Diaspora if you weren't going there to be a *Rosh Yeshiva* [Yeshiva Director]."[9]

Conclusions

Shortly after the 1988 Israeli elections, a specialist in Jewish Hassidism and mysticism wrote an article, wryly entitled "The Dance of Rabbi Elimelech," in which he showed that contemporary Haredi life was slowly becoming a variation on a common theme (Dan 1989). Acknowledging the traditional opposition between Hassidim and Mitnagdim, the essay showed how both ultimately adopted the two main innovations of R. Elimelech of Lizansk: the centrality of the Zaddik and the bureaucratic institution of the court. Like Hassidic Rebbes, Mitnagdic rabbinical leaders have been semideified by their followers, who turn to them for intercessions, blessings, and advice in mundane matters. In order to maintain the various institutions surrounding their leaders, the Lithuanians have developed a court, replete with the very bureaucratic apparatus typical of Hassidic courts—*pidyon*, assistants, kashrut supervisors, financial arrangements—against which Mitnagdim had long railed.

"Hassidim are no longer Hassidim and Mitnagdim are no longer Mitnagdim," echoed Hassidic expert R. Dr. Yitzhak Alfasi over a decade later. "They all have the Zaddik, Rebbe, Rav and the court. They all *shokel* [sway] when they *daven* [pray]. With the exception of the *streimel,* the *spodik,* and the *gartel* [Hassidic prayer belt], they dress alike, and the only differences are in the *nusach* they use in *davening,* and the *tish.* As for the Sefaradi Haredim, they are a mixture of everything."[10]

Yet when it comes to language policy and practice, things become more complex. Tradition and history begin to play an important role, and in Israel, all of the sects that I have targeted use Ivrit as their basic language, but they vary in their attitude to that language, and even in the forms of Ivrit which they use. As for other languages—sacred, quasisacred, Jewish vernacular, and foreign— each sect adheres to a different policy influenced by its historical background and contemporary praxis as presented here in brief. Even in issues of gendered language—the languages, or even the type of Ivrit used among Haredi women, or by Haredi men when speaking to Haredi women—there is variation among the groups. All of this will become apparent upon exploration of the three spheres that comprise Haredi life—the public domain, the educational frameworks, and the domestic realm—in the following chapters.

Notes

1. Author's telephone interview with Rabbi Dr. Yitzhak Alfasi, 14 Feb. 2001.
2. Author's telephone interview with Rabbi Dr. Yitzhak Alfasi, 30 Aug. 2001.
3. Author's telephone interview with Rabbi Dr. Yitzhak Alfasi, 14 Feb. 2001.
4. Author's telephone interview with Rabbi Dr. Yitzhak Alfasi, 14 Feb. 2001.
5. *Ma'ariv*, 27 April 2001, Shabbat Supplement, p. 14.
6. Author's telephone interview with Rabbi Dr. Yitzhak Alfasi, 30 Aug. 2001.
7. *Ma'ariv*, 27 April 2001, Shabbat Supplement, p. 14.
8. Author's telephone with Rabbi Dr. Yitzhak Alfasi, 14 Feb. 2001.
9. Author's telephone interview with Dr. Ephraim Shakh, 14 Feb. 2001.
10. Author's telephone interview with Rabbi Dr. Yitzhak Alfasi, 14 Feb. 2001.

4

DA'AT TORAH AND THE PUBLIC DOMAIN

"I can understand the problem with women, but tell me, what in the world do they have against rabbits?" Thus remarked a left-wing kibbutz member upon reading Sefaradi Haredi leader R. Ovadia Yosef and R. Eliezer Shakh's comments on the peccadilloes of secular Israeli Jews, which they saw as sinful. Referring to R. Yosef's denigration of Israeli Supreme Court judges as "sexual defilers of impure women" and R. Shakh's tirade against "rabbit-eating kibbutz members," my friend bewilderment notwithstanding was an example of how Haredi turns of speech, once an entirely internal Haredi matter, are now exposed to a broader cross-section of the Israeli population. One explanation is the growing secular interest in Haredi life, often explained by scholars and journalists as a combination of ethnic voyeurism and the desire to know where their taxes are going (Dan 1998; Anaki 1999; Golan 2000). A second is the growing use of electronic media among a number of Haredi groups, which makes their leaders' talks accessible to all listeners, secular and religious alike.

Unlike the Gerrer rebbe whose pronouncements have often been handed down during the course of a Sabbath *tish*, during the 1990s the Lithuanian R. Shakh delivered politically laden Torah speeches at mass gatherings held in places such as the Yad Eliyahu Stadium. While the *Tishes* are never covered by newspaper reporters and rarely attended by secular Jews, the latter conventions were widely reported upon by both the print and the electronic media. Outdoing his competitors, each Saturday night Shas leader R. Ovadia Yosef delivers a satellite-carried *derasha* (speech) from the podium of the Yazdim Synagogue in Jerusalem, combining political diatribes with a discussion of the weekly Torah portion. Broadcast by pirate Shas radio stations throughout the country, R. Yosef's *derasha*, which becomes instantly available to reporters from the major dailies, has given a new Haredi meaning to the phrase "Saturday night live." Less than twelve hours after eliciting the requisite responses from his followers, R. Yosef's more vehement linguistic gems, particularly the soundbites dealing with political matters, leave the Haredi public domain to become widely quoted among the general Israeli population.

One of the make-or-break issues in the lifespan of almost every political and ideological movement or organization is communication: the conduits through which leadership makes its wishes known to the rank and file; the means by which information is disseminated, either officially or unofficially; the forms via which particular dictates or decisions are brought to the attention of both membership and the public at large (Castells 1989). These issues lie at the root of this chapter, which concentrates upon several aspects of Haredi language policy creation, expression, and communication in the public domain.

In the first section of this chapter I examine the language used in rabbinical theological writings, written proclamations, and speeches given by the leaders of the three Ashkenazi Haredi movements featured here, highlighting the way that their choice of language affects the linguistic policy of each movement. Turning from rabbinical sources to those under the Rabbi's direct supervision, the second section of this chapter scours the newspapers of these movements to glean information relating to the language and culture of a particular group. The chapter's final section looks at publicaions issued under more general rabbinical supervision: family and women's magazines read by the Haredi community, including members of all four movements in my study. By examining both official and unofficial forms of communication, I will chart the course of the linguistic aspects of what is known in the Haredi world as *da'at Torah*—the accepted theoretical-theological religious beliefs regarding specific issues—as expressed within each of the Haredi movements.

Movements, Language, and Culture

Two of the salient terms found at the root of this linguistic study are "literacy" and "culture." Literacy and the use of the written word are key factors in a group's maintenance of its cultural identity. Culture exists as a product of social interaction and organization. Cultural identity is the mutual influence of the individual and his social environment. On the group level, this entails a shared sense of cultural features that identify the group. On the individual level, there is an assumed uniformity within the group, although any one individual's perception of what this uniformity is may differ from that of another (Ferdman 1991). The use of the written word enables the group to maintain and spread its cultural values regardless of the passage of time, and despite geographical diffusion. Changes in a group's values can be charted by following changes in the group's writings over a period of time, while noting internal and external influences that may have brought about the changes.

Culture and literacy are constructs that are also expressed in language choices. Particularly on the group level, language choice is valuable not only functionally but also symbolically. In racial groups, for instance, the use of a particular word is a cultural indicator. As Shirley Brice Heath (1983) shows in her study of two Appalachian communities, even a word's pronunciation or inflection, as taught to groups at home and school, can serve as an indicator of a particular racial experience. In ethnic groups, the identification with a particular language often represents their difference from the majority culture. Even if individuals in that group are not literate in their minority language, their desire to preserve even some degree of speaking ability may be a veiled attempt to remain distinct from the surrounding society. For many Puerto Ricans in the United States, Spanish is not only a means of communication but also a marker of their identification as Latinos who are separate from the majority culture (Ball, Giles, and Hewstone 1984). Similarly, the fragmented Yiddish spoken among certain groups of late middle-age American Jews who are not really literate in that language, may be indicative of their desire to preserve at least a vestige of their childhood ethnic identity.

Breaking down the broader category of language choice into its individual variables, it appears that even the decision to use a particular word or expression can be an indicator of cultural identity. The interspersion of minority-language code words within a majority-language conversation or text may be a cultural symbol indicative of the desire for separatism. On the other hand, the reverse phenomenon—the introduction of majority language expressions into the minority-language text—is not necessarily indicative of a desire for assimilation but may be the result of the subliminal influence of majority culture on a minority group (Hakuta, Ferdman, and Diaz 1987).

The cultural identity of the various Haredi groups is symbolically represented in their use of language. This representation relates to the politics of social identity: the group's place in society and the individual's sense of his or her integration into the cultural group (Erickson 1984). Under the assumption that a person's cultural identity can change, and in turn be changed, by the process of literacy (Ferdman 1991), language becomes a charged subject in Haredi society, based as it is on the transmission of cultural identity and its long-term preservation.

The direct and indirect linguistic messages handed down to followers by the leaders of Haredi sects are important forms of language management influencing Haredi language practice. In this chapter I will examine some of these leaders' directives, and the derivatives of these directives, as seen in their own speeches and writings, expressed in the newspapers of the various Haredi sects, and in Haredi family and women's magazines. This use of language may be divided broadly into matters of inclusion, such as the use of Loshon Kodesh, Ivrit, Yiddish, foreign languages and orthography, translation, and transliteration; and issues of omission, such as the absence of various topics and expressions, and the exclusion or inclusion of gendered language. My exploration of these topics will reveal the development of the Haredi leaders' *de jure* da'at Torah in the linguistic sphere, which ultimately makes its impact on *de facto* Haredi language practice.

What did the rabbi say?

In Haredi movements the rabbinical leader holds a unique position. Not only is he the supreme figure whose actions express the contemporary *de jure* policy of his movement in every sphere, but in addition, his policy automatically becomes the official da'at Torah, the accepted theoretical-theological religious belief of the movement which is binding upon all of its members (Bacon 1986). As scholars have shown, contemporary da'at Torah is often a process of reinterpreting the past to suit the present, thus setting new traditional and halachic boundaries for the future. Here I will show how such reinterpretation takes place in the linguistic sphere, gradually altering Haredi groups' language policy and practice in other spheres, such as the domestic realm and the educational frameworks that are covered in later chapters.

During the last decades of the twentieth century each of the Haredi movements featured here adapted to a different form and style of leadership. Until 1994 Habad remained under the leadership of a single one Lubavitcher rebbe, Menachem Mendel Schneerson, while the Gur dynasty has experienced a succession of four different rebbes as contemporary leaders. Lacking a Hassidic-style dynastic leader, for over three decades the Lithuanian Haredim accepted R. Shakh as their chief spokesman in public matters until his incapacitation in the late 1990s and his death in 2001. While not ignoring the religious centrality of other leaders such as the late R. Shlomo Zalman Auerbach or R. Yosef Shalom Eliashav, here I will only examine the writings and recorded speeches of the figures who took public center stage within their movements.

Habad

Habad is one of the most prolific of the Haredi sects in terms of literature, with the seventh Lubavitcher rebbe being especially well known for the large number of books, primarily compilations of his speeches, that were published under his name in various languages during his lifetime. The movement's pivotal text, the *Tanya*, also known as *Likutei Amarim*, regards speech as being one of the garments of the divine soul through which a person can immerse himself in the study of Torah. In order to reach the soul, the speech of the Lord, comprehended as Torah, has undergone a process of being lowered from loftier realms, a descent which that enables the parallel process of transforming the lower, the profane, into the higher, the sacred. In Habad belief, this tenet applies to spoken and written language, laying the theoretical (and theological) basis for the use of all languages in the pursuit of Torah (Shneur Zalman of Liadi 1987).

Writings of the first Habad rebbe were geared to a learned readership familiar with Talmudic Hebrew and rabbinical linguistic shortcuts and abbreviations (Shneur Zalman of Liadi 1982, 1987; *Maamorei* 1991; Schneerson 1977). From Hassidic stories we know that the various Habad rebbes were often known for their turn of phrase, even using foreign expressions in their writings, such as referring to Rosh Hashana as *Karanatzia Nacht* (Coronation Night) (A. Friedman 1997).

The seventh Lubavitcher rebbe delivered his advanced religious lectures in Loshon Kodesh and Aramaic. But similar to his Eastern European predecessors, who gave their *Reydn* (talks) in Yiddish so that women and uneducated persons would understand, he delivered his more general *Sichot* (chats) and *Ma'amarim* (speeches) in Yiddish in order to make direct contact with the masses of American Jews, many of whom were themselves immigrants fluent in Yiddish. For the same reason, his *Likutei Sichot* (Collected Talks) were initially printed in Yiddish, which despite not being an official sacred language was transcribed in Hebrew orthography and therefore considered by Habad to be a quasisacred tongue (Dalfin 1998). During the 1960s and 1970s, when the younger generation of Habad was no longer fluent in Yiddish, the rebbe encouraged a group of his Hassidim to translate his *Sichot* and *Ma'amarim* into various languages, including Hebrew, English, and Russian (Schneerson 1992, 1994b; Schneerson 1994c). These efforts provided his outreach program with written material to be used when dealing with a larger Jewish public (Salinger 1991). In addition, he personally examined the Yiddish translation of the *Tanya* that Habad published in 1958, and transcripts of *Tanya* lessons in English broadcast over the radio in New York from the 1970s onward (Shneur Zalman of Liadi 1987). This was possible because of his unique facility in languages, which also allowed him to vet translations of the *Tanya* into French and other European languages (Lobenstein 1998). Similarly, although he used Loshon Kodesh in his religious Hebrew compositions, he could speak fluent Ivrit, and used it in greeting Israeli visitors and dignitaries (*Challenge* 1973).

The fact that he could delegate the translation project to select groups of his Hassidim was also an indication of Habad's unique ideology and composition, as a Haredi group that did not consider language a cultural barrier and an outreach movement boasting large numbers of members who were fluent in foreign languages and familiar with non-Jewish culture.

An examination of those *Sichot* whose official translation into Ivrit was approved by the rebbe provides us with a number of examples of his language policy in action. Yiddish expressions were retained in the text, particularly when quoting previous rebbes. Yiddish and Hebrew were often interspersed in the footnotes of the translated *Sichot* (Schneerson 1964). Aramaic terms appear without translation, hinting to the fact that the readership was supposed to be fluent in these terms. Because they were delivered to an American audience, the original *Sichot* occasionally included words in English when the rebbe wished to make a point. In a talk delivered to women on Shavuot 1956 he spoke of being "'all right' with the Lord," with the two English words appearing in the written *Sichot* in transliteration (Schneerson 1965, 225). As this particular *Sicha* was addressed to women, the use of English words in this context may be considered a form of gendered speech. Aware of a lack of Hebrew literacy among Habad women and girls, he was careful to approach these groups in languages with which they would feel familiar (Schneerson 1994a). This also follows the accepted Haredi pattern of allowing more secular leeway to women than to men, a tradition evident in Europe during the nineteenth century, judging from the fact that women were not required to spend their days studying Torah (Parush 2001).

In addition to governing the language choices for his talks and books, the rebbe also referred directly to the issue of language in several of his *Sichot*. In a 1986 *Sicha* he spoke of the need to adhere to his father-in-law's policy of disseminating the teachings of Hassidism throughout the world "in seventy languages," like the Septuagint (*Sicha, Parshat Vayera, Cheshvan* 1986, individual *Sichot* pamphlets). In other *Sichot* he discussed the importance of knowing the meaning of names and words, including those in foreign languages, which often have deep philosophical significance. All in all, Habad's outreach ideology is a major force in the positive attitude towards non-Jewish languages. The theological justification for this comes from the founder of Habad, R. Shneur Zalman, who claimed that letters are like stones used in building. But just as the ordinary can become sacred according to Hassidic thought, all language is potentially Hebrew. According to this belief, the sacred tongue, Hebrew, is the source of all language, and all languages can be elevated to the sacred tongue. Consequently, although Habad rabbinical tradition posits a hierarchy of language (from Loshon Kodesh with Aramaic to Yiddish as a quasisacred tongue, other Jewish languages and non-Jewish languages), all language is imbued with potential sacredness and is therefore permitted for use.

Gur

Whereas the Habad bibliophilic tradition was expressed in a broad publication campaign, Gerrer Hassidism was not known for prolific publications but rather for a specific compilation of the teachings of each rebbe. In some cases these compilations of Torah exegesis appeared during a rebbe's lifetime (A. M. Alter 1925, 1937; P. M. Alter 1990, 1995). In other cases they were published after his death by his successors (Y. Alter 1978; S. B. Alter 1992, 1993, 1994; P. M. Alter 1997). There are also memorial volumes composed of excerpts from *shmussen* (informal talks) delivered by various rebbes, and collections of a rebbe's letters on various topics (A.M. Alter 1925; A.M. Alter 1937; P.M. Alter 1995; P.M. Alter 1998). As opposed to the Lubavitcher rebbe who addressed some of his *sichot* and writings to women, the Gerrer rebbes addressed all their talks, letters, and other writings to men. These publications thus pertain to the issue of gendered speech by virtue of their being directed at a male audience.

Each Gerrer rebbe had his own style of leadership and method of holding the Sabbath *Tish*, which also found expression in his use of language. Fluent in Yiddish and archaic Hebrew, with some knowledge of Polish, the *Imre Emet* (R. Abraham Mordechai Alter) spoke Yiddish with his followers and wrote his Torah exegesis in Loshon Kodesh and Aramaic (Amirot 1994). His letters on political and religious matters, meanwhile, were written in Loshon Kodesh, but used Yiddish words for emphasis (A. M. Alter 1925, 1937), probably because most of his life was spent in Poland within a Yiddish-speaking milieu.

Although their mother tongue was Yiddish, each of his three sons, who in turn became rebbes in Israel, exhibited a slightly different use of language based on their background, education, personality, and individual inclinations. The *Beit Yisrael* (R. Yisrael Alter) was fluent in Ivrit but, having spent over half of his life in Poland, preferred Yiddish for daily speech (Y. Alter 1978). The *Lev*

Simcha (R. Simcha Bunim), who was less formal than his older brother, spoke in a combination of Yiddish, Loshon Kodesh, and Ivrit. When his *drashot* (speeches) were published posthumously in the early 1990s, Yiddish phrases were followed by their Hebrew translation in parentheses, acknowledging the fact that younger Gerrer Hassidim in Israel spoke Ivrit among themselves and were not as fluent in Yiddish as their European-born parents (S. B. Alter 1992). The third of the brothers, the *Pnai Menachem* (R. Pinchas Menachem), had reached Israel in his early teens and was the only one of the three to have a working knowledge of Polish yet be completely comfortable in Ivrit—including slang—which he utilized in everyday speech. (P. M. Alter 1990, 1997). The present Gerrer rebbe, R. Ya'akov Arieh, is fluent in his mother tongue, Ivrit, and in Yiddish but speaks no foreign languages.

Gerrer Rabbinical language policy is characterized by several trends. The first is the growing use of Ivrit among the rebbes as the language of oral communication, interspersed less and less with Yiddish as the reigning rebbe became more removed chronologically from a European background. This linguistic tendency characterizes the Israeli Gerrer community in general, with the rebbes having set the tone. The second tendency is the tempering of Loshon Kodesh used in Gerrer religious talks with a growing amount of contemporary Ivrit expressions. Traditional Gerrer ideology of religious separatism but political activism necessitated fluency of contemporary speech, as may be seen by the last two rebbes complete fluency in Ivrit, including slang expressions that were unheard of in other Hassidic courts. The third trend is a loss of knowledge of foreign languages in the present generation, far removed from the European background that once provided the necessary input.

Mitnagdim

As opposed to the leaders of the two Hassidic groups discussed so far whose leaders continuously address their followers during communal rituals such as the *tish*, Mitnagdic leaders usually address their followers in the setting of a more formal gathering. Such contact often takes place during mass lectures delivered to their students. Like Hassidic rebbes, many Mitnagdic rabbis have authored volumes of Torah exegesis, and compilations of their letters have been published. In addition, one can find Mitnagdic tracts on various subjects as well as responsa to questions of Jewish law.

As head of the Ponivezh yeshiva in Bnai Brak, Mitnagdic leader R. El'azar Menachem Man Shakh authored numerous volumes of Talmudic commentary (Shakh 1948–93), addressed students on various occasions (Shakh 1992, 1998b, 1998c), and delivered opening lectures at mass study sessions (Shakh 1983, 1986). Many of his addresses and lectures were transcribed by students and later published in pamphlet form (Shakh 1970, 1971). In addition, he wrote exhortations to his followers (Shakh 1978, 1998a), published numerous letters and responsa (Shakh 1988, 1993), and penned eulogies for public figures that also appeared in various compilations (Sefer 2000). All of his written addresses, responsa, and Torah commentaries have been published in Hebrew, with the exception of one volume of his collected responsa published in English by his son-in-law (Shakh 1999).

R. Shakh's mother tongue was Yiddish, and he had a working knowledge of Ivrit and some degree of fluency in Polish and Russian. Many of his addresses to students were delivered in Yiddish, but were transcribed into an archaic form of Hebrew. In his later years, when speaking in Ivrit to large crowds at Torah-related gatherings, R. Shakh would often lapse into Yiddish when agitated, particularly when referring to contemporary political issues. At a gathering at the Yad Eliyahu Stadium during the early days of Shas, R. Shakh slipped into Yiddish during a speech, disconcerting R. Yosef, with whom he shared the podium and for whom a rapidly whispered translation had to be provided. Here, too, as is common procedure, the written versions of these speeches, which later appeared in collected volumes, include only a Hebrew text (Sefer 2000). This may stem from the editors' desire for linguistic continuity in the volume, but is also an acknowledgement of the fact that often, the younger generation of Mitnagdim was no longer fluent in Yiddish in comparison to the older, primarily European-born generation.

Several of R. Shakh's letters and responsa deal with the issue of secular studies, including language study both in Israel and abroad (Shakh 1995). Writing about yeshivot in Israel, he exhorted his followers not to allow students to prepare for matriculation exams, including those in subjects such as English, because reading the necessary books at such a young age ruins the soul (Shakh 1995, 126–129). For the same reason he deemed it impermissible to introduce secular studies into the boys' *metivta* (high school). Emphasizing this point in a letter to educators in Israel, he stated that the most important accomplishment in the realm of education is "the founding of more religious schools … that are free of all foreign influences. When secular studies are introduced into the curriculum, the outlook of the school inevitably changes and the Torah perspective that has been handed down from generation to generation becomes adulterated" (Shakh 1999, letter of 6 May 1976, 110–111). Foreign languages were considered to be the ultimate conduit of foreign influences.

R. Shakh was not adamantly opposed to teaching secular studies and languages in girls' schools, as he acknowledged Mitnagdic women's need to ultimately support their husbands (Shakh 1999, letter of 13 June 1980, 112–113). Nevertheless, he joined other Mitnagdic luminaries such as R. Ya'akov Kaminetzky and R. Moshe Feinstein in their call to forbid girls to study at Touro College in New York, which combined secular and religious studies under one roof (Shakh 1988, 130–131).

As for introducing secular studies, including language study, in yeshivot abroad, he wrote that although there was a desire and a demand to do so in order to attract more pupils, stringent Torah followers should not bow to these demands as they endanger the Jewish people. Acknowledging that Jewish sages and medieval commentators had studied secular studies and were fluent in foreign languages, he emphasized that they had had a need to do so, whereas Haredi young men today would be spending their lives learning Torah and had no such need (Shakh 1993, 61–62). When asked by educators abroad what language *Humash* (Pentateuch) should be taught in, he replied that the boys should be taught in Yiddish because *shiurim* (lessons) in the yeshiva are taught in Yiddish, and even if they speak English among themselves, they should learn to be comfortable in Yiddish. Girls studying in the diaspora should be taught in Loshon Kodesh, and if they do not understand Loshon Kodesh they should be taught in English, if that is the language they are used to speaking. His ultimate exhortation was to familiarize both boys and girls with Yiddish, the language, he claimed, that is spoken by all Jews. He also referred children to schools that teach completely in Yiddish, including continuous translation of Torah and Talmud into Yiddish. Reminding the questioner that although learning Yiddish would further the children's Haredi education, he stressed that it should not be to the exclusion of Loshon Kodesh, for they should be able to understand *Humash* and other religious teachings in the original (Shakh 1988, letter 313, 29).

These last letters appear to deliver a very direct linguistic message, while simultaneously presenting a contradiction. On the one hand, R. Shakh refers to Yiddish as the ultimate Jewish language, granting it a status both sociological (the language of the Jewish people) and theological (the language of the yeshiva). Indeed, for many years Talmud study in Israeli Mitnagdic yeshivot took place in a combination of Loshon Kodesh and Yiddish, a situation that still holds true in certain Mitnagdic yeshivot today. But in the next sentence he warns educators abroad against letting their students get used to studying everything in Yiddish translation, lest they lose the ability to understand Loshon Kodesh on its own. In Israel, R. Shakh usually spoke to his students, and to the Haredi public at large, in Yiddish and sometimes in archaic Hebrew, often changing the nature of the language to suit his listeners, the topic being covered, or his own emotional state at the time. Similar to the earlier European-born Gerrer rebbes who spoke a combination of Yiddish and Ivrit, he tended to intersperse the two languages in public addresses.

Linguistic typology

It is difficult to speak of a unified religious opinion regarding linguistic matters among the three groups of rabbinical leaders I survey to this point, or even an unchanging ruling in the case of the Gerrer court, which has been led by five different rebbes over a fifty-year period. Nevertheless, it is already possible to chart the beginning of a linguistic typology with cultural overtones.

The outreach ideology of Habad expresses itself in the language used by the leaders of these groups: a willingness to use foreign languages, to translate publications, to include non-Hebrew orthography, to address spoken and written material to women in a form that they will readily understand. In most cases the material is directed to a male audience, but in the case of Habad women are addressed as well at times, with an according shift in the nature of the language.

How does the da'at Torah of the various movements' leaders express itself in compositions written under their direct supervision but not by them? For this I turn to the official organs of the various movements, the newspapers and magazines that express the accepted language policy of each movement's leader.

Newspapers and Communal Magazines of the Four Movements

In early August 1990 the Mitnagdic Haredi world appeared to be up in arms. Numerous irate phone callers to the offices of the Mitnagdic daily *Yated Ne'eman* threatened to cancel subscriptions. Mothers, embarrassed by their children's questions, swore that the paper would not cross their doorstep; dozens of rabbis called to ask how something like this could have happened. This deluge of complaints was triggered by a syndicated article that had appeared in the paper, detailing an attack on a female soldier at an army base near Hadera. A suspect was now in custody, the article stated, held on charges of both attack and rape. How did such a word—rape—which should never pass the lips of a Haredi person, get by the paper's censors, everyone asked? Explaining that the censor had been exhausted by the *Tisha Be'av* (Ninth of Av) fast of the previous day, the publishers apologized for the mishap that had caused him to overlook one small, but extremely loaded, word. Acknowledging the necessity of a Haredi paper of their own, the Mitnagdic community accepted the explanation, with the understanding that neither feast nor fast would prevent the censor from carrying out his sacred task in the future (Michelson 1990).

This anecdote exemplifies several of the differences between a secular and a Haredi newspaper: the language permitted, the topics recognized, even the knowledge that one is working with a captive audience. Each of the Haredi newspapers and magazines in Israel is published under the aegis of either a particular movement or a general Haredi umbrella. Most of them directly or indirectly supervised by a rabbinical leader, and their editorial policy reflects his dictates.

Each of the Haredi movements has its own tabloid newspaper or magazine. Since 1981 the Habad movement in Israel has published a glossy weekly magazine in Ivrit entitled *Kfar Habad*. Not a newspaper devoted principally to recounting current events, its contents include articles and commentary on issues of the day, memoirs by religious figures, tales of Habad sages, editorials with religious content, and a large number of advertisements, which keep the journal financially solvent. In 2001, each edition of *Kfar Habad* appeared in 20,000 copies. Of these, 5,000 were sold abroad, primarily in the United States, England, France, and Australia.[1]

Each edition is vetted by a spiritual board composed of three members. Articles dealing with Habad in various countries are in addition read by a board member specializing in that country. Apart from the spiritual board, there is also an administrative board that reviews the text of each issue prior to publication to ensure that it contains nothing unsuited to Habad standards.

Oversight by a spiritual board is a common phenomenon for ultra-Orthodox publications, one that applies to Haredi newspapers, including dailies, as well as weekly or monthly magazines. The board is always composed of men, usually rabbis, and they are chosen only from among the sect that stands behind the particular publication. One will not find a Hassidic rabbi on the spiritual board of a Mitnagdic publication, nor will one find a Satmar Rabbi on the spiritual board of a Belz publication even though both groups are Hassidic. The composition of a board can change from time to time, but it is rare for a change in personnel to bring about a change in publication policy. Policy is actually set by the head of a particular movement—the rebbe guiding a particular Hassidic movement, the rabbis heading the Mitnagdic world. In practice, the existence of a spiritual board ensures that a publications' content will always reflect the party line of the movement publishing the paper or journal, which is handed down from above by the movement's rabbinical leader.

The spiritual board bases its decisions on a number of factors. Material published must adhere to the rules of modesty accepted in the Haredi world as interpreted by the spiritual guidance behind the publication. Freedom of thought may exist in the Haredi world, but freedom of the press has its constraints: content must also conform to the respective movement's political leanings and be free of slander. Nevertheless, interpretation of this last issue depends upon one's definition of what constitutes slander. In the daily Haredi press it is common to find satirical diatribes against enemies of the Haredi group issuing the publication in question.

HaModia (The Announcer), the daily journal of the Gur Hassidim, has appeared in Ivrit since 1950, making it the oldest of the Haredi papers. A weekly English version services a foreign Haredi audience. The paper claims to be the official newspaper of the entire Agudat Yisrael political movement. From the onset, the paper's contents were vetted by representatives of the Gerrer rebbe, and today all sections of the publication, from columns to advertisements, are scrutinized by a board of spiritual censors. In mid 2001, HaModia has a circulation in Ivrit of 28,000 copies, 3,000 of which were subscriptions. Several thousand copies were published in English for sale both in Israel and abroad.[2] As there are only an estimated 7,000 Gerrer families in Israel, it is obvious that the newspaper's readership comes primarily from other Haredi groups. Nevertheless, it is the Gerrer rebbe who sets the tone for HaModia, and nothing appears in the paper without his approval.

Much of HaModia's format and some of its content, too, is reminiscent of Israeli daily political organs like Davar (Mapai-Labor), Al Hamishmar (Mapam), Herut (Herut-Revisionist), and Hatzofe (Mizrachi-Hapoel Hamizrachi), which were published in Israel during its first decades as a state. HaModia was indeed conceived as a Haredi equivalent of these newspapers, and today, after all but Hatzofe have closed, HaModia stands almost alone as a truly mobilized publication. The paper's weekday version is six pages long though, several are devoted primarily to advertisements. The Friday paper has several sections, and the current events portion, at twelve pages, is double the size of the weekday version. It also features a children's supplement called HaModia Hatzair (Young HaModia), a religious supplement, and a weekend magazine. While the paper routinely runs advertisements for women's clothing emporia and wig-sellers, there are no gossip or fashion columns. Nor are there astrological forecasts, or articles that deal with music, entertainment, sports, or criminal activity. The only way for a *HaModia* reader to keep abreast of the cultural aspects of general Israeli news, such as a local sports team winning an international tournament, is to read the editorial columns, which kill two birds with one stone. Leading with a mention of, for example, an Israeli success in sport, music, or the like, an editorial will immediately continue by condemning the event as typifying a non-Haredi way of life. It is in this world of verbally denoted "right" and "wrong," of a simultaneous "absence" and "existence," that one begins to detect acculturational patterns. Readers report that they turn to the editorial columns first, and this is true of both *HaModia* and its rival, *Yated Ne'eman*.

The Mitnagdic daily newspaper *Yated Ne'eman* (literally "The Faithful Peg," although *Yated* is actually a skewed acronym of the expression *Yomon Da'at Torah* The Torah Opinion Daily) was an offspring of the internecine Haredi wars that began when R. Shakh left the Moetzet Gedolei Hatorah in 1982. From that time onward *HaModia* no longer covered his activities, and though it refrained from attacking him directly, its editorials were extremely critical of his rabbinical associates. In late 1985, a number of R. Shakh's followers decided that it was time for the Mitnagdim to have a daily newspaper of their own, which should rival *HaModia* and serve as a mouthpiece for their movement. With the elderly rabbi's blessing, they went about raising funds and attracting reporters (Michelson 1990).

R. Shakh decided, again indicative acculturationally, that the format would be similar to that of the eight-page left-wing Mapam daily *Al Hamishmar;* it would even be printed by the same publisher. Initially intervening in everything from the type of lettering used to advertising format, he finally approved the new paper, which he then placed under the supervision of a seven-member board of censors committed to him: yeshiva heads, rabbinical judges, and halachic experts. These censors themselves do not frequent the paper's offices, but their representatives do, and they read every word before it goes into print. The paper contains the same disclaimer as does *HaModia:* that it is not responsible for the contents, kashrut, or quality of products advertised. Yet censors have been known to eliminate offending words from ad copy, or even an entire advertisement that does not suit the policies, politics, ideology, or lifestyle of the movement's leadership. R. Shakh's opposition to settlement in Judea and Samaria resulted in a refusal to advertise the Haredi city of Emmanuel—which also happened to be a project sponsored by the rival Gerrer Hassidim.

Yated Ne'eman advertises itself—justifiably—as the largest Haredi daily in Israel. The paper's Hebrew edition circulates in over 100,000 copies of which between 70,000 and 80,000 go to subscribers. Over 4,000 people subscribe to the English edition in Israel alone. But there are only about 15,000 Mitnagdic families in Israel. The other subscribers and readers belong to the *Hardal* (an acronym for Haredi *Leumi,* Nationalist Haredi, which differs from the Haredim in its pro-Zionist, more modern orientation, and from the modern religious in its tendency to adopt certain Haredi trappings and its more punctilious attitude towards observing the commandments) public, the modern Orthodox, and even Sefaradi Haredim.[3]

The daily paper's format is similar to that of *HaModia*. Several pages of each issue are devoted to local and world news, collected mainly from wire services. The rest of the paper is taken up by advertisements and communal announcements, a brief classified section, an editorial column, letters to the editor, and news from the Jewish world. The Friday edition is double the size of the weekday one and includes many more announcements and advertisements. It also has two supplements, *Shabbat Kodesh* (the Holy Sabbath), which deals with current events from a religious viewpoint, topics of religious interest, stories of rabbis and other leaders, and a digest of contemporary news, op-ed columns, articles about nature and technology, and stories with moral value. In addition, the paper publishes a Thursday family supplement called *Bayit Ne'eman* (the Faithful Home). Directed primarily at women, it includes articles about the dilemmas of balancing work and family, health matters, children, education, recipes, and other domestic items. There is also a Tuesday children's supplement entitled *Yated Shelanu* (Our Yated) targeted at preadolescent boys and girls.

The importance of these newspapers in the Haredi community is enormous. The Gur Hassidim and the Mitnagdic community read only *HaModia* and *Yated Ne'eman*, much as hardline partisans read only their party-centered papers in the early years of the state. The Gerrer will not even casually read the paper of the Mitnagdim, and vice versa. Furthermore, the probability of either group reading a secular newspaper is very small. The two papers thus have great political clout in their respective communities. Politicians of all stripes, religious and secular, go to great lengths to be promoted in these papers, for this publicity is the surest way to bring their activities to the attention of the rebbes or rabbis, who will ultimately decree how devotees should vote. Rabbinic leaders generally do not waste their time perusing a daily newspaper, but their assistants do, purposefully to keep the leadership informed (Katzover 1999). Too, newspaper as a public message board is the fastest way to make a decision public. Rabbinic decisions regarding the kashrut of various products and other such proclamations can rate front-page coverage, sometimes before they have appeared elsewhere; these decisions have an immediate impact, for instance the boycotts that occurred when the Shemen company was accused of producing cooking oil on the Sabbath.

Language and Its Settings

Haredi newpapers exercise a virtual monopoly over the Haredi ability to stay informed, and thus over Haredi public opinion.[4] They exercise this monopoly most effectively by paying careful attention to detail, especially linguistic detail, exerting a microinfluence through nuances of style and language particular to the Haredi press. Most striking is the technique of internal linguistic codes, such as those found in expressions used to preface and distinguish between persons being discussed. The hierarchical position of an *Admor* or a person of highly respected rabbinical rank will be recalled by the appellation *Harav Hagaon* (Brilliant Rabbi). A "plain" rabbi will be called just Rabbi. A respected Jew without rabbinical standing receives the honorary title *Reb*. Women, who receive many fewer titles than men, are referred to as either Mrs. or *Rebbetzin* (Rabbi's wife) (Munchik and Kantor 2000). On the other hand, a modern Zionist rabbi with whom the Haredi world is at loggerheads might have his name mentioned, but without a title, most notably in the case of former Ashkenazi chief rabbi of Israel, Rabbi Shlomo Goren, whom *HaModia* treated this way for years.

Other linguistic codes are found in words that have unique meanings for Haredim. These include *zman* (time), the Haredi equivalent of semester (as in *bein hazemanim*, the Haredi expression for the intersession between periods of yeshiva study), or *marbitzim* (hitting), used for serious Torah study (Zilberschlag 1998). Regardless of fluency in Ivrit, an uninitiated reader confronted with such terms may be bewildered, much like a beginning student of a foreign language: the words are intelligible, but the sense of the sentence or the article is not. A similar issue is the exaggeration common in personal announcements like those regarding engagements, weddings, and funerals. Haredi groups vie for status in the Haredi hierarchy by trying to outdo each other in the number of superlatives attached to the subject of the message. Congratulatory announcements in *HaModia* (15 June 2001) sponsored by two different yeshivot upon the engagement of the son of a yeshiva director, each attempted to raise the father of the groom to higher rank by referring to him as, respectively, "our honorable scholarly leader, great in Torah knowledge" and "the world-reknowned scholar, of the highest Torah rank." The Haredi world is one of extremes: good becomes wonderful, or unparalleled; bad is the worst, the lowest on earth.

A final overt difference from the secular press is the use of quotation marks to generate irony or sarcasm, whereby "wonderful boys" or "brilliant young men" of a particular secular (or even rival Haredi) group are actually called hopeless fools, or the like. This technique, known in Aramaic as *lashon sagi-nahor* (blind-light language, with its inherent contradiction), is well known to Haredi readers. Here, Haredi papers come into their true element, following the pattern, begun in the late eighteenth and early nineteenth century, of polemics between Mitnagdim and Hassidim, or between Enlightened Jews and the Orthodox and ultra-Orthodox world. Haredi columnists often appear to be competing with each other to include the most ironic statements in a single article, for example, the political diatribe that appeared in *HaModia* on 14 February 2001, which boasts a record eighteen such expressions in a thirty-line column.

But if the linguistic usages just noted are unique to Haredi newspapers in general, Haredi papers differ from each other by subtle differences in these same usages: the choice or exclusion of words, style, inclusion and omission of topics, the use of specific abbreviations and acronyms, the tone and content of advertisements, and the inclusion or omission of illustrations when discussing women and women's concerns. Linguistic variants thus enable distinctions to be drawn between specific Haredi groups, revealing both degrees and modes of Haredi acculturation. They also show how these same groups wrestle with the overall Israeli outside.

Language and Linguistic Consciousness

Language is an issue to which the editorial board of the weekly *Kfar Habad* devotes much thought. The bulk of its subscribers live in Israel, and its primary language is Ivrit. The editors clearly prefer "proper Ivrit," but slang such as "bleeding-heart liberals" (*Kfar Habad* 946, 29 March 2001) or "a ticking bomb" (*Kfar Habad* 941, 22 Feb. 2001) also appear, primarily in editorials.

What most dictates the choice of language is the nature of a column or the topic being discussed. The largest amount of Loshon Kodesh and archaic Hebrew grammar is found in rabbi's columns and memoirs by religious figures. A small number of Aramaic quotations also appear, primarily in quotations from the rebbe's writings. Although these terms usually appear in the original text of a *sichot* without translation, the editors of *Kfar Habad* almost always follow Aramaic words with a Hebrew translation to aid the uninitiated, newly religious, women, and even the general public. Yiddish phrases appear in texts, usually as parts of quotations from the various writings of the rebbes. Complaints from readers who did not understand Yiddish, however, provoked an editorial decision always to provide a Hebrew translation following a phrase in the Yiddish original. Even among Habad in Israel, it appears, Yiddish is disappearing. The rule of translation is suspended when *Kfar Habad* reprints facsimiles of Habad publications from the late nineteenth century and early twentieth century—all, of course, in Yiddish (*Kfar Habad* 946, 29 March 2001).

Because a quarter of subscriptions are sold abroad, and because Habad's outreach ideology makes the use of non-Jewish vernacular permissible, no policy mandates that all texts be solely in Ivrit or Jewish vernaculars. Consequently, one can occasionally find English words interposed with Ivrit, often as a direct quotation being cited and occasionally even in non-Hebrew orthography. This is a common practice in secular Israeli newspapers, often verging on the use of slang (Rabi 1974; Kantor 1992). English words in English orthography also appear in facsimiles of Habad documents, such as the recently published passport of the sixth rebbe (*Kfar Habad* 959, 5 July 2001). In addition, several articles deal in my research with the issue of languages or mention the knowledge of non-Jewish languages in a positive context. One example is the story of a Hassid who was told by the sixth rebbe to study German upon moving to Germany, and to use it fluently for his personal safety (*Kfar Habad* 946, 29 March 2001).

Language is equally important to the editors of *HaModia*, who accord it great cultural significance. The newspaper's language is Ivrit; however, the Friday religious supplement is rich in Loshon Kodesh and sometimes Aramaic. The choice of linguistic style is determined by the nature of the column; in a direct excerpt from a religious work. Aramaic can appear wholly untranslated. In the magazine section, Aramaic expressions are interspersed in the text, but these expressions are normally familiar to the Haredi public. Op-ed articles contain interesting combinations of colloquial Ivrit and Aramaic terms.

Yiddish makes its way into several sections of *HaModia*. Although it is rare to see Yiddish expressions in the news columns, many of which are syndicated from wire services, Yiddish is frequently found in the magazine sections, both the religious supplement and the more general one. For example, in an article about travel to Israel during the intifada, the author interjected the expression "*Mashiach zoll shoin kumen*" ("the Messiah should come already!") with no translation (*HaModia*, 15 June 2001). Yiddish is also mentioned in letters to the editor. Commenting on the frequently bad handwriting of many Haredi boys, one reader suggests this is a result of the fact that less than two hours a day are devoted to secular studies in the Talmud Torah, leaving little time to practice handwriting (*HaModia*, 21 Feb. 2001). Several letters in *HaModia* recount the difficulties that the lack of secular studies has created for the Haredi world and offer corrective suggestions (see also *HaModia*, 11 Feb. 2001 and 14 Feb. 2001).

Consciousness of language and linguistic choice is detectable in *HaModia's* news and magazine sections. An army poster showing dirty hands that exhorts soldiers to keep "*Klalei Nikayon*" (cleanliness rules) to prevent intestinal disorders is accorded the terse comment: "Jews call it *netilat yadayim* (ritual washing of hands), the army calls it *Klalei Nikayon*" (cleanliness rules) (*HaModia*, 15 June 2001), a not-so-subtle claim to (Haredi) moral and cultural superiority—and to its practical rewards. Such claims, common in Haredi newspapers, are the mirror image of secularized formerly religious terms (Kantor 1989).

Consciousness of language is found even in the letters to the editor of the children's supplement. In response to a young reader who had written about the names chosen for books, the editor mentions that names have both a national and a religious significance, and that the same is true of the names of people. "Even in our internal community, there are several levels and you can see the difference in names," the editor concludes (*HaModia Hatzair* 779, 213, 15 June 2001), referring to the choice of names given to children as a linguistic expression of their family's religious observance, their standing in the Haredi community, and even the particular Haredi sect to which they belong.

A special linguistic problem is the integration of English (and other foreign words) and Yiddish with the Ivrit that is all of the papers' basic language. English has even been integrated into *HaModia*, particularly in the Friday general supplement. While English orthography does not appear in the news columns, it may make its way into advertisements. As in *HaModia*, the basic language of *Yated Ne'eman* is Ivrit and its columns and editorials are written in what one of its editors refers to as a combination of "proper language" and more up-to-date expressions, although never slang.[5] The general tone is that of a modern newspaper, with a larger amount of colloquial Ivrit than in *HaModia*. This choice of language is similar to that of the intellectual secular press in Israel during the 1970s in such dailies as *Ha'aretz* (Rabi 1974). In fact, *Yated Ne'eman* presents itself as a daily newspaper that attempts to walk the fine line between religious dictates on the one hand and on the other, a spirited journalism seeking to offer readers a more modern style of writing, range of topics, and presentation of advertisements than the veteran *HaModia*.

Both columns and editorials in *Yated Ne'eman* liberally use Aramaic expressions without translation, and, as in *HaModia*, editorials occasionally that use colloquial Ivrit expressions and Aramaic in the same sentence. In line with other Haredi newspapers, the topic and nature of the column determines the language used. The largest proportion of Loshon Kodesh, religious abbreviations, and Aramaic (without translation) is found in columns of a rabbinical or Torah nature. Columns on religious topics sometimes include Rashi Hebrew script (in which the biblical commentary by Rashi—R. Shlomo Yitzhaki—is printed), usually in their headlines.

Yiddish is rarely used in *Yated Ne'eman*. Its infrequent appearances are usually in short quotations from rabbinical figures (*Yated Ne'eman*, 16 Feb. 2001), emphasizing that the Israeli Mitnagdic world primarily speaks Ivrit. English words that have become part of Ivrit often appear as such, for example, "credit," repeated eight times in the Friday edition of 6 August 2001. Uncommon English words are usually transliterated or explained, to wit, "*bulimic—milashon bulmus, ra'av hazak*" (bulimic, from the term bulmus, a strong hunger) (*Yated Ne'eman*, 15 June 2001). Much like the Israeli secular press, *Yated* Ne'eman seldom allows English orthography to appear, except in mentioning the name of a non-Israeli organization, listing medical or technical terms, or advertising and positioning a product.

Absence and Inclusion of Expressions

In the matter of absence versus inclusion, the differences between the two Haredi dailies are most evident, especially with respect to religiously oriented terms, where *Yated Ne'eman* is more punctilious than *HaModia*. It refers to the Knesset, for example, as a "building" (*binyan haKnesset*) rather than by the usual *mishkan haKnesset*, a word reserved solely for the tabernacle. Neither paper, however, will write that the Israeli Supreme Court *pasak* (ruled); rather, it *hichlit* (decided), for only religious authorities make "rulings."

Haredi papers often employ key words understood fully only to members of that sect. Habad's key word, found often in *Kfar Habad*, is *Mamash*, literally "actually" or "truly," which appears at the end of sentences or paragraphs for emphasis, to strengthen hopes for the immediate future: *techef umiyad mamash* (immediately, actually). In fact, some of Habad's Messianic faction interpret the word as an acronym of the seventh rebbe's name, Menachem Mendel Schneerson.

Abbreviations and Acronyms

The abbreviations and acronyms used in the Haredi press are characteristically those of Haredim rather than the general public. The Habad weekly appears to be aimed at a general Habad readership, not only a learned one. Hence its many rabbinical abbreviations are generally confined to those that are well known, including the abbreviated names of Habad organizations. Widespread use of religious abbreviations and acronyms appear in all sections of *HaModia; Yated Ne'eman*, too, uses abbreviations and acronyms. All abbreviations, however, except in religious or reflective articles found in the religious supplement, are familiar to the general Haredi public, both male and female. Elementary abbreviations appear in articles directed at young people.

Advertisements

The language of advertisements in *Kfar Habad* is fruitful ground for insights into the particularized Habad ethos. Like the entire weekly, advertisements are basically composed in Ivrit. However, English orthography, rarely found in articles, appears often in the advertisements, most noticeably in full-page ads that are almost entirely in English. Some advertise educational establishments in Israel and abroad intended for Habad students from all over the world, for example, the summer yeshivot held in Israel for young Habad emissaries (*Kfar Habad* 944, 15 March 2001). Others are for holiday symposia and similar religious gatherings held in the diaspora, such as the Passover symposium or Hassidic *fabrengen* (gatherings) held at the Habad synagogue in midtown Manhattan (*Kfar Habad* 941, 22 Feb. 2001). There are even advertisements for stores outside of Israel, like the full-page list of prices at a Brooklyn electronics store (*Kfar Habad* 946, 29 March 2001).

Yet here English tends to have acquired special tics that say a great deal about the interface between Habad and general culture, as when the wholly English advertisement for the Brooklyn store highlights a "*kosher* Walkman," a cassette player without the radio portion some religious leaders deem improper (unkosher). The inclusion of a sentence in *Ivrit* in the advertisement reveals that it targets two distinct Habad components, the Israeli Habad traveling abroad and the Habad Hassidim living in the diaspora who subscribe to the Israeli publication (Kantor 1997).

English orthography is used in naming products and their producers, for instance, Isomil from Abbott Laboratories, or a logo like Coca-Cola. Active ingredients such as "LA-Pufa" in Materna baby formula also are spelled out in English. This follows the usage of the secular press, which, similarly guided by marketing surveys, believes that using English creates a scientific impression (Rabi 1974; Kantor 1992). In this respect, Haredim are no different from the rest of the Israeli public.

Advertisements in *HaModia* and *Yated Ne'eman* also say much about Haredi speech, particularly that which overrides sectarian divisions, certainly in the Ivrit-speaking Haredi world. This is most visible in topics dealing with physical modesty, sexuality, or crimes of passion, whose mention is a linguistic taboo. For years, these topics were not even euphemistically referred to publicly and to this day they cannot appear in any Haredi news column. But they do appear in advertisements, suggesting an admission, even among Haredim, that there are limits to avoidance. Both newspapers advertise a "urological clinic" called Habayit Hashalem (The Complete Home), the Haredi equivalent of the well-known Israeli medical chain Klinika On (Virility Clinic). Like ads for the secular chain, the Haredi advertising copy promises medical secrecy and private treatment rooms. The only real difference is that the Haredi urological euphemism is even more discreet than the claim of the secular chain that "one will improve" after treatment, the improvement, of course, being in male sexual function. Still, in a combination of Ivrit and Aramaic affirming that the clinic is under the supervision of *morei hahora'a, shlita* (the rabbinical teachers, may they have long lives), the Haredi advertisement states openly, and in large typeface, that "Besiata Dishmaya [Aramaic], Anachnu matzlichim liftor 98% mihaba'ayot! [Heb.]" (With the Assistance of Heaven we succeed in solving ninety-eight percent of the problems). The advertisement's wording raises no questions in the field of modesty. Yet it is difficult to imagine it appearing several years earlier, even if it is only with the final phrase that the acculturational cycle is completed, namely that the importation of non-Haredi culture is "Haredized," accorded a Haredi religious affect by the reference to rabbinic guidance.

The story extends even further. Such an advertisement would not appear in the publications of the more isolationist Haredi sects, nor would it be found in a community magazine like *Kfar Habad*. Yet it has appeared in the three Haredi dailies, *HaModia*, *Yated Ne'eman*, and the Shas *Yom Leyom*, which will be featured in a later chapter. However, it did not appear in all three at once. Rather, knowing *Yated Ne'eman*'s openness to innovation—and perhaps aware that the Mitnagdim are sometimes more in touch with their secular surroundings than other Haredim—the clinic's marketers turned there first. The paper's censors made a halachic inquiry, whose results indicated the advertisement's acceptability, whereupon it appeared in a weekend edition. Once it had run for several weeks, the marketers approached *HaModia*, also seeking a slot in the weekend edition. In their desire to present *HaModia* as being more rigorous in its standards than its Mitnagdic rival, the editors initially rejected the advertisement as immodest. But eventually they relented, wishing to show that the Gerrer were every bit as aware as the Mitnagdim of the need for such an institution in the Haredi world.

Finally, the marketers felt bold enough to turn to *Yom Leyom* of Shas. Initially, the editors of this Sefaradi paper had difficulties. Should they advertise such a delicate issue? They agreed they should. Yet for some time, the advertisement appeared on alternate weeks because the decision whether to include it had been left in the hands of differently opinionated religious censors who were rotated weekly. Ultimately, however, the precedent of the Ashkenazi Haredi dailies, and the knowledge of the economic loss that would otherwise occur, produced a decision to publish the advertisement regularly.[6] Whether to include the accompanying picture of a male doctor or to make the advertisement's language even more euphemistic than in the other papers was debated to the last. Yet in the end, the advertisement in *Yom Layom* turned out to be identical to that in the other Haredi papers. It even added a direct plea rejected for its immodesty by the Ashkenazi papers: "Do not defer your treatment, the solution to your problem will remain between us" (*Yom Leyom,* 14 June 2001).[7]

Practical factors overcame any hesitancy to follow the Ashkenazi lead, a choice many Sefaradi Haredim consider regrettable, recalling that precisely this reluctance was de rigueur, back when they had no choice but to study in Ashkenazi yeshivot. Acculturational impetuses are varied indeed.

Women and Their Concerns

During certain periods in its published history, *Kfar Habad* has included a women and children's supplement. The language considered by the editors to be appropriate to these publics, included no Aramaic or Yiddish; abbreviations were kept to a minimum. Today, the entire periodical addresses both a male and female readership, with few discernible instances of gendered language. As in most Haredi publications (*Yated Ne'eman* excepted, as will soon be seen), pictures or even drawings of women and girls do not appear, although the organization of Habad women publishes full-page advertisements on special occasions (*Kfar Habad* 944, 15 March 2001; 946, 29 March 2001). Announcements of engagements, weddings, and births, however, include full names of women: daughters, wives, mothers, and brides. This is rare in Haredi circles, which usually do not mention women's names but instead refer to women as "and wife," mentioning a woman's full name only when she becomes a bride. The free mention of women's names in *Kfar Habad* is an expression of Habad's attitude toward women as shaped by the seventh rebbe, although it may also reflect Habad's outreach ideology and, no less, the fact that before becoming observant, many Habad women hold important public posts or are leaders in the business sector, positions they do not relinquish when they join Habad. Indeed, in distinction from other Haredi groups, Habad women often take public stances or act as emissaries in their own right.

In *HaModia*, divisions are more evident. In the weekly news and magazine sections of the Friday edition, the language is ungendered, as is also true of the *Yom Leyom*'s family section which is directed at both male and female readers. But the religious supplement, reminiscent of rabbinical writings, appears to be linguistically directed—according to Haredi dictates—primarily at a male audience, at least in the sense of intellectual expectations derived from the presumption of (the exclusively male) study in the yeshiva. Loshon Kodesh lexis and grammar are used freely, as are Aramaic, without translation, and the large number of abbreviations familiar to those initiated in religious texts. The same applies *Yom Leyom*, as well as to the Shabbat Kodesh religious supplement of *Yated Ne'eman*. By contrast, in the *Bayit Ne'eman* section of this paper, which is clearly directed at women, the language has no learned baggage. In this sense, the language in these two supplements is gendered, adapted to "men's society" and "women's society" as Haredim interpret these terms (Coates 1993). Implied gendering also extends to the children's supplement, certainly in *HaModia*. Ostensibly addressed to both boys and girls, in language that appears free of gendering, the articles seem to be authored predominantly by women—who sign their pieces with names like Yehudit or Yochi, but without a surname (*HaModia*,

15 June 2001)—but nonetheless, the topics covered relate particularly to the experiences of young boys, a gender preference that appears to be built in.

Yated Ne'eman seems less stringent than *HaModia* on issues of visual modesty, the concept dictating that women's photographs never appear in a printed medium. Modesty also requires that women's full names appear only to announce their marriage, death, or events dedicated to their memory. *Yated Ne'eman*, however, alone among the Haredi papers, allows drawings of girls and young women in the youth magazine *Yated Shelanu*. The practice initially angered rabbinical authorities, who wished the pictures removed. But the women who headed the editorial board of the magazine stood firm claiming creatively, that the drawings were only that, not photographs, and that the figures depicted not women but young girls of pre-Bat mitzvah age. Furthermore, unlike *HaModia*, where female authors are listed by initials or first name only, at *Yated Shelanu* the (female) editors insisted that the author might specify whether her full name appeared, and that of the artist, too. Surprised at this vehemence, the rabbinical censorship board ultimately backed down, and on both issues.[8] This journalistic innovation is a sure sign of changing attitudes among Haredi women, certainly in the Mitnagdic world, whether on the cultural, professional, or domestic level. It does not, per se, explain the changes, but it does signify a need for cultural linguists to hunt these changes down in order to chart a transition in Haredi society.

English-Language Editions

Unlike *Kfar Habad*, which appears solely in Ivrit, *HaModia* publishes a weekly edition in English for readers outside Israel that is sold primarily in Haredi enclaves in the United States, Great Britain, and Belgium, and is also found in yeshivot. The paper is written in modern English, interspersed with Hebrew orthography, sometimes in headlines, at other times as part of text. The spelling of the Hebrew is according to Ashkenazic pronunciation. Like the Hebrew edition, the English edition addresses both men and women, and it follows the same rules about modesty, illustrations, and women's names. Family and childrens' pages—there is no separate supplement as in the Hebrew—are indistinguishable in linguistic style and usage from articles on religious subjects, unlike the Hebrew version, where the language is gendered. However, in the English edition Yiddish is rarely translated, and there are references to Yiddish being the preferred Jewish home language. One example is the conclusion of a story appearing in the family pages: "In our home, Yiddish is spoken and traditions of the *shtetl* are being kept alive. I hope and pray we make her proud." (*HaModia* English edition, 16 Feb. 2001). Here, comment on acculturational resistance here, as well as on the greater permissibility of Haredi acculturation in the Israeli setting, whatever dangers the Haredi world considers inherent in that country's secular Judaism or even modern Orthodox format, would be superfluous.

The occasional uniqueness of the Ivrit in *Yated Ne'eman* is also seen in its weekly English edition, which is sold in the United States, Great Britain, South

Africa, and Australia. Containing primarily Israeli and Jewish news from communities throughout the world, the paper also offers opinion columns, family
and children's pages, announcements, and classified advertisements. Transliterated, italicized Hebrew words are used throughout the paper. Other words
are written in Hebrew orthography, such as the names of books or the titles of
columns, like that on the weekly Torah portion. Full-length announcements,
primarily death notices, often appear in Hebrew alone. Aramaic is seldom used.
Yiddish too is rare, apart from the colloquialisms that are part of everyday
Ashkenazi-Haredi parlance, such as *davening* (praying) or *benching* (reciting
grace after meals), terms that, needless to add, are not translated (*Yated Ne'eman*
English edition, 1 June 2001). When an uncommon word is used, such as the
Arabic term *shahidim* (martyrs—people killed during the Intifada), the term is
translated (*Yated Ne'eman* English edition, 15 June 2001). Finally, and distinc-
tively, following the practice of the Hebrew edition, *Yated Ne'eman*'s English
edition reproduces, in translation, stories from the Hebrew children's supplement that include drawings of girls and young women.

Discussion

Haredi newspapers in Israel have much in common. In all of them, language
and its use express the cultural uniformities that clearly distinguish Haredim
from the rest of Israeli society, secular and observant. However, within the uniformity, there is difference. *Kfar Habad* differs by including material from non-
Jewish vernaculars, both in the texts and in a large portion of the advertisements.
HaModia is distinguished by its claim to be the official newspaper of the Agudat Yisrael (political movement) and the Gerrer, who see themselves as the
guiding light of the Hassidic, if not the entire Ashkenazi Haredi, world, and
whose geographical range is reflected in the circulation of *HaModia*'s English
edition. The paper is read in the same homes that subscribe to other Agudat
Yisrael–sponsored English and Yiddish monthlies, including the New York–
based *Jewish Observer* and *Dos Yiddishe Vort*. At the same time, the Hebrew edition is distinguished by the growing use of Ivrit, even with a large number of
colloquialisms. This, in turn, reflects the increased use of Ivrit, along with the
colloquialisms and slang, too, that marked the speech of the late Gerrer rebbe,
Pinchas Menachem Alter and, even more, the present, Israeli-born rebbe Ya'akov
Aryeh Alter. A similar pattern of increasing familiarity with popular spoken
and written Ivrit (and hence with Israeli culture as a whole) may be observed
in the columns of *Yated Ne'eman*. This linguistic turn is rooted in the accepted
Mitnagdic ideology that acknowledges, but does not promote, the interface between the Mitnagdic world and contemporary Israeli society.
   However, *Yated Ne'eman*'s constant linguistic evolution suggests that practice
may be outpacing theory. Some might explain this gap, manifest in a certain
linguistic and visual modernism in the journal—certainly as compared to *Ha-
Modia* at any rate, by noting that since the early 1990s, and the incapacitation
of R. Shakh, the spiritual board censoring *Yated Ne'eman* has not been respon-

sible to a central and universally recognized rabbinical figure. R. Yosef Shalom Eliashiv may have taken the place of R. Shakh as the Mitnagdic halachic authority, but in the temporal sphere R. Shakh's successor has yet to be found. This vacuum seems connected to the concerns of reporters and columnists with *Yated Ne'eman*, who, when queried, spoke of constant tension between religious dictates and the desire to produce an interesting, competitive journalistic product combining quality, interest, and something to pique readers' curiosity.[9]

Haredi newspapers, in short, may look alike, but borders there are. Borders represent the distinguishing qualities of the movements behind each of these papers, and it is these borders that the language of each of the different Haredi newspapers seeks to preserve, apparently with success. Indeed, studying the languages of the various Haredi papers reveals the Haredi continuum, the shadings and dialectics of Haredi opinion and life: for instance, the outreach of Habad, as opposed to the turning inward, to the extent it is still possible, by the Gerrer. But the same time, a certain linguistic slippage betokens the slow erosion of borders between secular and Haredi societies, in Israel at least— even to the point of feminism, as evidenced by the use of women's names in *Yated Ne'eman*. The degree of this erosion, however, should not be overestimated. All Haredi papers distinguish sharply between sacred and profane, Haredi and non-Haredi; the question of advertisements and their propriety makes this point perfectly clear. Openings to broader Israeli society there may be, but traditional Haredi stances, couched in appropriate Haredi language, plaster these openings over, seeking to keep the small cracks in the wall from becoming real fissures.

Women's and Family Magazines

In addition to buying the newspapers belonging to each of the Haredi movements, many of their members subscribe to women's and family magazines. The journals that will represent the genre here are the weekly *Marveh Latzame; Olam Hahasidut* a family magazine geared to men, with a family supplement aimed at women and children the weekly magazine *Mishpacha*, which also publishes an accompanying news magazine by the same name, and the monthly *Mishpacha Tova* (Anaki 1999). Some are sold only by subscription; others are also found in stores and on newsstands. Some are only available in Israel; others are also available abroad. Unlike the newspapers and communal journals that belong to a specific group, most of the women's and family magazines are not affiliated with a particular sect but are read by the general Haredi public. Yet although they all promote themselves as being Haredi, these journals differ in language and content, level of religious supervision, and orientation, thus tacitly expressing the cultural inclinations and *weltanschauung* of a particular Haredi group or set of sects. As a result, many of the women who subscribe to one magazine will not read another, a factor that reinforces the nature and design of these magazines, whose editors are well aware of the variations within their Haredi market and the subtle cultural shifts within the contemporary

Haredi world. The lines of demarcation may be religious (Hassidic versus Mitnagdic), ethnic (Ashkenazi versus Sefaradi), chronological (younger women versus older women), or demographic (Haredim worldwide versus solely Israeli Haredim).[10]

Marveh Latzame (The Thirst Quencher) has been published weekly since 1976 by the Organization of Daughters of Israel and Haredi Youth in Israel. The magazine's cover identifies it as "a weekly education and doctrine magazine for the head of the family, the housewife, teenagers and youth." Edited by a Sanzer Hassid, R. Yisrael Pollak, it to attract a general Haredi readership and even has a number of subscribers among the more modern Orthodox in Israel. The magazine is not distributed abroad and is available by subscription only.

In mid 2001 the magazine's publishers stated that it had approximately 10,000 subscribers from all over Israel. The publication's authors are of both sexes. Several of the articles examined for this study were written by men, among them rabbis, who are connected with the Sanzer court. Especially popular among Hassidic women, this magazine is eagerly read by female members of the Gerrer community in particular. It does not express the ideology of any single movement, nor is it printed under the stamp of approval of a particular leader; it can therefore boast a general Haredi readership.

The magazine is printed on cheap paper reminiscent of Israeli women's magazines of the 1960s and 70s. It includes a discussion of the weekly Torah portion, letters to the editor, stories for yeshiva students, children's pages, mothers' pages, nature stories, a crossword puzzle, serialized stories, and a serialized story in cartoon form. According to the magazine's secretariat, there are no advertisements in *Marveh Latzame* so as not to "slide into irrelevant [immodest] issues," or draw the reader's eye away from the important moral message of the stories.[11] As the publication lacks an archive, I could not check whether this attitude developed out of a desire to attract readers from strict Hassidic sects such as Gur, or whether it was an outgrowth of the fact that women from such families began reading the magazine and voiced their demands of modesty.

This policy of modesty (*tzniut*) in all female matters is expressed even in bylines. All authors identified by full name are male. Other authors are either unidentified, or have only a first initial and a last name. In certain cases this is a pseudonym and in others, a signifier that the author is a woman whose modesty has been preserved. Unlike other women's publications in the Haredi world, *Marveh Latzame* includes no pictures or drawings at all of girls or women, even those under the age of three, which are permissible by Jewish law. This, too, is an expression of the dictates of extreme modesty adopted by which the editorial board of this publication, either as a response to its readership or *a priori* in order to attract a particular readership.

Olam Hahasidut—The Hassidic World—published monthly since 1994, was created after a number of Kollel directors, and particularly those from the Vizhnitz and Sanz courts, noted the lack of quality reading that could take the place of the secular newspapers that had made their way even into the yeshivot.[12] The result was a glossy Hassidic monthly magazine, sold in stores, at newsstands, and by subscription. In mid 2001 the publishers stated that the magazine was printed in close to 13,000 copies a month of which almost 7,000 were sent to subscribers in Israel, and 2,500 to subscribers abroad in the United States, Mexico, England, France, Belgium, the Netherlands, Russia, and Australia. Although most readers, among them Gerrer and Habad Hassidim, belong to one of the various Hassidic courts, subscribers in Israel are found not only in Hassidic enclaves, but also among the more modern religious public in many of the settlements in the West Bank of Judea and Samaria and Gush Katif in the Gaza Strip.[13] According to the magazine's publishers, because the journal finds its way not only into the home but also into the Kollels, special care is taken regarding the language of texts and advertisements appearing in each issue. A spiritual board vets each advertisement, and the entire magazine board meets at least once a month to review the text and advertisements prior to publication.[14]

Olam Hahasidut is composed of two sections. The main section, whose cover boasts the slogan "Clean of gossip and politics," contains articles about various rebbes past and present and religious customs, letters to the editor, short stories on religious topics, moral parables, a focus on a Jewish community in the world, and a consumer column. The use of an abbreviation for gossip and the Yiddish term *politik* (instead of the Ivrit term *politika*) in the slogan are symptomatic of the magazine's dual focus: the desire to produce a "clean" publication that does not even write out the full word for gossip but instead substitutes an acronym; and the intention of presenting readers with a publication that combines the old and the new, juxtaposing traditional Haredi values and stories, often from the Yiddish-speaking European pre–World War II world, with newer topics such as technology, package tours, and consumerism. Many of the columns in this section of *Olam Hahasidut*, particularly those about the comings and goings of the various rebbes, replete with photographs, are in fact the Haredi equivalent of the gossip and celebrity columns of the secular press. Eschewing the forbidden gossip-style language of these types of columns, the Haredi version provides readers with visual stimuli along with a modern form of hagiography reaching the proportions of secular hero-worship. An example is the lead article in the magazine's *Lag Ba'omer* issue (*Olam Hahasidut* 80, Iyar 5761, April–May 2001). Well illustrated with pictures of past and present rebbes holding bows and arrows in various positions, the issue provides readers young and old with the Hassidic parallel to secular articles lauding sports stars, right down to the pictures of them at various athletic events.

The smaller supplement is called *Habayit Hahasidi* (The Hassidic Home), with a subtitle in Yiddish and Ivrit: *A Hasidische Shtub Livnei Habayit Vehaneurim* (A Hassidic Home [Yiddish] for the family and youth [Hebrew]). The words *Livnei Habayit* are a euphemism for girls and women, a verbal expression of the modesty guiding the lives and expressions of the Hassidic world. This section contains stories for and about children, a nature column, a consumer column listing new products for the younger members of the family, and a riddle and crossword puzzle page. *Olam Hahasidut* does not express a particular ideology; its authors are primarily Hassidic writers from various courts.[15] Acknowledging the Haredi community's need for a form of popular literature

with religious content, *Olam Hahasidut* presents its readers with visual and textual hero worship, religious-historical serials, and educational/moral parables,
in a reader-friendly form. Part of the reader-friendly format is the language,
which is old-fashioned enough to be considered "proper" but not so archaic as
to be unreadable or—even worse in the case of a journal of this type—boring.

The existence of such a journal is an expression of changes taking place
within the Israeli Hassidic world as modernization combines with a form of
consumerism. Although the Hassidic world is popularly held to be closed to outside influences, this is far from being true in practice. This magazine's framework is ostensibly a Hassidic one, with its socialized rules of modesty, slander,
and linguistic style, whereas the format—a glossy magazine replete with photo
opportunities and even a modern consumer column—are evidence of the encroachment of the outside world into the Israeli Hassidic one.

The desire to present the Haredi community with a family-style magazine
that was neither boring nor archaic was also the impetus behind the publication of *Mishpacha* (Family), a weekly geared to the "Haredi public," as it states
on its front cover. Consisting of two sections within one cover, the glossy magazine, published since 1991, and its children's supplement *Betoch Hamishpacha*
(Within the Family) cover topics that are not typical of Haredi women's publications. These include contemporary political issues, an economics column,
and feature articles on various subjects from consumerism to the Israeli secu-
rity services. In mid 2001 the publishers stated that the magazine was circulating in 15,000 copies (of which 500 were subscriptions) and was sold in Israel,
North and South America and Europe. Among its readers were families from
various Haredi groups: Hassidic, Mitnagdic, Sefaradi-Haredi, *Hardal*, and others.
In practice, this magazine appears to be read by more Mitnagdic and Sefaradi-
Haredi women than those of other Haredi groups.[16] This is possibly due to the
fact that its publishers do not have a Hassidic orientation, as do the two magazines previously mentioned. Neither does it present an ideology of any particular movement, which frees it of any particular linguistic focus. In addition
to the magazine, the publishers put out a weekly news supplement under the
same name (*Mishpacha: News of the Haredi Community*), which, unlike the
magazine, is geared to both sexes. Genre and topic do shape language. The magazine includes a special column entitled *Hadashot Ans* (News of Ans, the abbreviation for *Anshei Shlomeinu*, "our people") that provides the latest personal
news about rabbis, rebbes, and various Hassidic courts, again the equivalent of a
Haredi gossip column. Geared towards men, this column abounds in religious
abbreviations familiar to most Haredi male youngsters. A person familiar with
Ivrit but not with the cultural associations or linguistic abbreviations of the
Haredi world will find him or herself reading the text but not understanding
its meaning.

Articles and advertisements in the publication are approved by a spiritual
board consisting of one Hassidic and one Mitnagdic representative aiming for
parity in political matters and compromise where Hassidic and Mitnagdic circles differ in interpretation. Although the board does not interfere in the polit-

ical content of articles, it censors any mention of gossip, immodest language, or expressions that would hurt various groups or individuals. An article on the special education frameworks established in the Israeli Haredi community was barred from labeling parents who for years had hidden children with severe retardation from the community as "primitive."[17] In such a case, linguistic particulars are in reality a cultural indicator, delineating not only permitted and forbidden topics but also acceptable and unacceptable responses to various phenomena with which the Haredi community grapples today.

Mishpacha prides itself on not being under the supervision of a particular Haredi movement, stating that it can better serve its purpose as a magazine for the entire Haredi community. Although it has lost readers from among those groups who want their specific rabbinical leader's stamp of approval on the cover, more modern Hassidic and Mitnagdic families, who are not put off by the magazine's contemporary flavor, are avid subscribers.[18] Its language (Ivrit with almost no Loshon Kodesh) and topics (contemporary politics, modern feature reports) locate it in a more modern camp than *Marveh Latzame* or *Olam Hahasidut*. However, it is still a closely supervised publication in terms of both language and content. Despite its claim of Haredi pluralism, it draws the line at running a photograph of a secular event, or of secular Jews, even on the front page of its inner family section. The editorial comment about the readers was "they don't want to see secular faces staring up at them"—testimony to the internal cultural separatism that still guides much of the Haredi world. Its editors subscribe to an axiom attributed to one of the contemporary rebbes, still greater than such a journal's responsibility to let the public know is its responsibility "to make sure that the public will *not* know certain things."[19]

Published since 1999, the monthly Haredi magazine *Mishpacha Tova* (The Good Family) is a Haredi version of the secular *Lehiyot Mishpacha* (To Be a Family), targeted at expectant mothers and women with small children. Replete with color pictures in a high-gloss format, the magazine is the most visually attractive of the four Haredi women's and family publications surveyed. The chief editor and several of the writers are Haredi women who are familiar with the cultural and linguistic nuances of the various Haredi sects. They carefully revise the articles also published in the magazine's secular version, tailoring them to their female Haredi readership.[20] While the text usually remains the same, the Haredi version bears a particular Haredi cultural slant in terms of examples given, photographs used, etc. The publishers state that 30,000 copies of the magazine are printed each month, of which 15,000 are subscriptions, all in Israel. The remainder are distributed in clinics and hospitals throughout the country, primarily in religious areas.

Mishpacha Tova is not aligned with a particular Haredi sect, and its readership includes women from among the Hassidim, Mitnagdim, Sefaradi-Haredim, *Hardal,* and modern Orthodox. As half of the copies are distributed in healthcare facilities, it is difficult to know how many Haredi women apart from those on subscription lists, are exposed to the magazine, or how many read it on an irregular basis while in hospital or clinic waiting rooms.[21] The editors assume that it is read on a regular basis primarily by those young Haredi women with more modernist tendencies, and they gear the magazine's language and topics to these groups. The decision is based on economics—a financial decision of the publishers, based upon market surveys—and not ideology or theology.

Mishpacha Tova, which is considered more modern than the other publications surveyed here, prints the full names of all the women reporters and editors connected with the magazine, something that was not done in the publication's early days. However, *Mishpacha Tova* adheres to the visual limitations of its rival *Mishpacha,* and does not include photographs of girls or women, over the age of three. It does include drawings of girls and women who are always modestly attired.

Before concluding this section, let us examine the issue of circulation figures, which in themselves are an indicator of trends in the Haredi world. In the cases of all four publications surveyed, circulation figures were provided by the publishers only. It proved impossible to verify them through independent sources because general publication surveys in Israel have consistently ignored Haredi publications. However, from my observations in the Haredi communities in Israel over a period of several years (1998–2002), these figures appear to convey some truth when juxtaposed with one another. That is, although it is impossible to document whether the exact figures presented are correct, the proportional circulation of the four publications surveyed in this article, vis à vis each other, is correct. The most widely disseminated publication of the four is the more modern and consumer-oriented *Mishpacha Tova,* after which comes the glossy-format, slightly less modern *Mishpacha.* This is followed by the sectoral *Olam Hahasidut,* and, finally, *Marveh Latzame,* the least circulated and least modern publication, available by subscription only. The significance of this comparative circulation list points to two separate trends. The first is the slow encroachment of cultural modernization in the Haredi world, expressed by reading preferences. The second is capitalization by secular publishing houses on this fact, something that has led to the creation of new, modern Haredi publications that could not have existed in Israel a decade ago. A continuous dialectic is therefore created between manufacturers and Haredi consumer, in this case, the manufacturer is a disseminator of information for which the Haredi community appears to thirst.

Language as Expression of Haredi Culture in Women's and Family Magazines

Marveh Latzame is written completely in Ivrit, and its style is old-fashioned in terms of both grammar and vocabulary. The language, reminiscent of Hebrew publications from the 1920s and 30s, contains almost no colloquial Ivrit or slang. The magazine permits few of the English words that have made their way into Ivrit, and no non-Hebrew orthography. Loshon Kodesh appears only when quoted directly from sources, either in the weekly Torah portion exegesis, or in articles quoting Torah sages. The same holds true for Aramaic, which usually appears as part of a quotation or in the form of a colloquial expression (*Marveh Latzame,* 11 Iyar 5761, 4 May 2001), in either case without translation.

Yiddish words are rarely interspersed in *Marveh Latzame* and always appear with translation. A decision was made to include material translated from speeches given in Yiddish but not to publish the original Yiddish text, even with translation. This respects the fact that the magazine aims for a general Haredi readership, Sefaradi and Ashkenazi alike.[22] In spite of the enthusiasm of past demands for a Yiddish translation of the entire paper, the publishers have declined to publish one for fear that there are not be enough Yiddish speakers among the Haredi readership to make such a magazine economically viable. This decision was recently reinforced by research confirming that large numbers of Israeli younger Hassidic girls and women are much more fluent in Ivrit than in Yiddish.[23]

Most columns in *Olam Hahasidut* are written in an archaic form of Hebrew (not Loshon Kodesh), but some of the content, particularly the stories and the consumer column, is written in colloquial Ivrit, as are almost all the columns in the *Habayit Hahasidi* section. In these columns one can even find foreign words such as *chroni* (chronic), *masivi* (massive), or *fiziology* (physiological) that have made their way from other languages into Ivrit. Abbreviations and Aramaic words familiar to the general Haredi community appear without explanation. So do short Yiddish interjections, which appear as parts of quotations from other volumes. Longer Aramaic or Yiddish expressions are usually accompanied by a translation. When asked if this was indicative of the fact that the younger Hassidic community was no longer fluent in Yiddish, the magazine's representative replied in the negative. Instead she emphasized that the translations from Aramaic appear "primarily for women who do not understand the language and those from Yiddish for readers from the 'Mizrachi' settlements," the modern Orthodox readers from Judea, Samaria, and Gush Katif who subscribe to the magazine.[24]

Mishpacha (and even more so, its news supplement) is written in Ivrit, and many of its columns include not only foreign words that have made their way into colloquial Ivrit, such as *kolektzia* (collection), *tip* (tip), or *dekorativi* (decorative) (*Mishpacha* 499, 10 May 2001), but also contemporary slang such as *ba lo al* (he likes) (*Mishpacha* 500, 17 May 2001) or *out* (in its English slang meaning of "unfashionable") (*Mishpacha News* 499, 10 May 2001). With the exception of common expressions such as *besiata dishmaya* (with the help of Heaven), or *lav mideorayta* (a Torah prohibition) (*Mishpacha* 498, 3 May 2001), no Aramaic appears in the magazine, and the only abbreviations used are those that are commonly understood by both male and female readers. Loshon Kodesh is rarely found, usually only in short quotations. Long Yiddish quotations appear only in translation, while individual Yiddish words and expressions are usually accompanied by a translation in parentheses. Words from other languages, such as Russian, that are an integral part of a quotation or a story, are printed in Hebrew transliteration with a Hebrew translation in parentheses (*Mishpacha* 496, 19 April 2001). English orthography rarely appears in the magazine, except in the form of product logos found in the advertisements.

Mishpacha Tova is geared to a particularly modern Haredi readership and is written completely in Ivrit, with almost no Loshon Kodesh. The language is quite colloquial, admitting expressions such as *levalbel et hamoach* (to drive someone crazy, *Mishpacha Tova* 22, Tevet 5761, January 2001), and often verges on slang (e.g., *srufim*, crazy about, *Mishpacha Tova* 24, Adar 5761, March 2001). English words that have made their way into colloquial Ivrit, such as *informatzia* (information), *kognitivi* (cognitive), and even *intimiyut* (intimacy) (*Mishpacha Tova* 27, Iyar 5761, May 2001)—in other Haredi publications a taboo word for reasons of modesty—appear in every issue. Except for occasional expressions that have become part of daily Haredi speech, Aramaic does not appear in the magazine. The editor explained that "for the fun of it," she has been known to use Aramaic expressions in the titles of articles to produce a play on words. Examples are *Lechem Oni Behamisha Cochvaya* (The Five-Star Bread of Affliction), about Passover vacations, or a consumer exposé entitled *Had Gadia Bitrei Zuzei Bimkom Arba* (One Goat for two *zuzim* instead of four), a play on the Passover song entitled *Had Gadia* (*Mishpacha Tova* 26, Nissan 5761, April 2001). It is interesting to note that the slang expression *bishvil haketa* (for the fun of it) used by the editor (a Haredi woman) is rarely heard in common Haredi parlance, which may reflect the influence of the journalistic work environment on her daily speech.[25]

The use of languages in these journals appears to point to three distinct cultural groups within Ivrit-speaking Haredi society. The first, and is the most traditional in terms of cultural separation from the surrounding society, is a Haredi subculture characterized by stringency in word and deed. Adhering to rigid linguistic patterns, it yearns for a return to a Yiddish-speaking subculture, although in practice it admits the cultural/economic impossibility of bringing this desire to fruition. Encouraged by those small enclaves of Haredi society that have still managed to remain Yiddish-speaking (Satmar, Neturei Karta, Vizhnitz, and others), this group is often reactionary in terms of its consumer trends, professional aspirations (if they exist), and gender-related roles. These are the readers of *Marveh Latzame,* and to a lesser extent *Olam Hahasidut.* At the other end of the cultural spectrum is a second Haredi group that expresses more modern tendencies and, in fact, takes its cues on many issues from secular Israeli society while giving each point at issue a Haredi shading to provide it with a modicum of respectability. These are the readers of *Mishpacha Tova,* with its up-to-date expressions and contemporary Israeli slang. In between are a large body of Israeli Haredim who do not wish to be identified with the extremely modern Haredi world, verging on that of the nationalist-Haredim, yet in practice have moved away from the first, most traditional group mentioned. They are found among the readers of *Mishpacha* and *Olam Hahasidut,* both of which write in a style that can easily be identified as Haredi as opposed to general or secular in terms of vocabulary and even syntax, not to mention the topics being covered. This last group may for now be considered the mainstream Haredi world; however, as the lines of demarcation in this world are in a constant state of flux, it is impossible to know how long this delineation will apply.

Advertisements in Periodicals as Reflecting Haredi Cultural Nuances

Unlike articles, which require initiative and input from a publication's editorial board and reflect its cultural composition or that of its readership, advertisements allow more freedom than features and similar material. Their very existence or absence is indicative of cultural trends, and of the orientation of a particular journal and its readership. As mentioned earlier, for example, *Marveh Latzame* does not carry advertising, intending to refrain from distracting the reader with diversions that might dilute the sanctity of the topics being discussed. This noteworthy abstinence from a known source of profit follows the publication's linguistic and cultural lead, discussed in the previous section.

The existence of advertisements in a publication gives us a field for observation not only of the readers' consumer cultural world, but also their ethical and moral beliefs and ethnic variations. Advertisements also reveal much regarding gender-based division of labor among various Haredi sectors.

The editors of *Olam Hahasidut* imposed strict guidelines on its advertisements, as its rabbinical board was well aware of the overt and subliminal messages that ads send to their readers, and of the magazine's presence in various Hassidic institutions of study.[26] One example of how these guidelines work in practice may be seen in the way the spiritual board dealt with advertisements for the "urological clinic" Habayit Hashalem, mentioned earlier. Although the marketers of the Habayit Hashalem clinic approached the publishers several times about the possibility of running their ad in the journal, it was not accepted for publication. The publisher explained that, knowing that the magazine makes its way into sacred places such as Kollelim the spiritual board based its decision on the belief that even the euphemistic language in the advertisement was inappropriate for a hall of study. This is consistent in view of the fact that whereas the major Haredi newspapers, which all carry that very advertisement, are by definition, not supposed to enter houses of study, the Hassidic journal *Olam Hahasidut*, a vehicle for Hassidic hagiography that eschews political, cultural, or economic issues is customary reading "behind the scenes" in yeshivot and kollelim.

Bearing in mind similar nuances in the Hassidic world, the spiritual board rejected an advertisement for the *Mifal Hapayis* lottery, as the faces in the picture were not considered suitable for Haredi society. It is difficult to explain to the uninitiated how a face can be "suitable" or "unsuitable" for Haredi society; however to understand how such decisions are made one might paraphrase what was once said about pornography: you may not know precisely how to define it, but you know it when you see it.[27]

Advertisements considered acceptable by the spiritual board and publishers of *Olam Hahasidut* include those for religious products such as *kiddush* goblets and candlesticks, disposable diapers (this ad ends with a moralistic appeal to mothers: now that they no longer have to deal with the "technical side" of children's hygiene, they are exhorted to spend their time on the child's development and future education), the electric company, meat products under Hassidic rabbinical supervision, and cellular telephones. This last ad depicts a notice on a bulletin board stating that after *seder erev* (the evening learning session in yeshivot and kollelim), a certain person's cellphone will be on (*Olam Hahasidut* 80, Iyar 5761, April–May 2001). This advertisement is particularly interesting in view of the fact that large numbers of Mitnagdic rabbis and heads of yeshivot have recently forbidden yeshiva students to possess a cellular telephone.

Can we divine from this that Hassidic readers spend their time using ritual objects, diapering babies, eating, using electricity, and talking to one another on cell phones? As strange as the question may sound, the answer is a resounding "yes." Ritual is a central part of the Jewish world and becomes increasingly so along the spectrum from secular to the Orthodox and on to the ultra-Orthodox communities. One uses a ritual washing cup numerous times in a day: upon rising, before prayer, before eating, and to purify one's hands before reciting the blessing after using the restroom. Other ritual objects, such as silver *kiddush* goblets and candlesticks, are a focal point in the Haredi glass-front living room credenza; a *mezuzah* is placed on every doorframe in the house except that of the restroom. It is therefore no surprise that advertisements for ritual objects are prominently featured in a Haredi publication that is by definition for men as well as for women.

The large number of children in the average Haredi family, and the rare gender-division of labor when it comes to care of infants in these families, explains the widespread placement of advertisements for disposable diapers, changed by fathers as much as by mothers. Even the moralistic addition does not detract from the fact that these advertisements are directed at parents of both sexes. Electricity is another nongendered subject necessary for the Haredi family, while the topic of food, and particularly meat with a particular supervision, is considered a bridge between the genders (women prepare it, men eat it). Finally, the advertisements for cellular telephones are an expression of the widespread use of the device among men in the Haredi world, and particularly the Hassidic world, even in yeshivot and kollelim. One Haredi woman who does not have a radio at home related that on 11 September 2001, only minutes after the first plane crashed into the World Trade Center, her son called from his yeshiva to give her the news. He and his friends had just heard it from the older students, who had received word via cell phone from yeshiva students in the U.S.[28]

The advertisements appearing in *Mishpacha*—a publication geared more to women than *Olam Hahasidut*—are of a slightly different nature but cover many of the same topics. Because the journal is targeted at women, comparatively more advertising deals with family and childcare matters. But the most interesting aspects of the advertising language in *Mishpacha* are those that fall in the category of omission. Strictly adhering to dictates of modesty, the spiritual committee forbids many key terms such as "pregnancy," "breast-feeding," "nipple of a bottle," and so on. Instead these exemplary concepts are referred to by expressions like "a woman before giving birth" or "after giving birth," "the natural way of feeding a baby" or "the opening of a bottle." Such decisions are not even made by the lay spiritual board but by the editorial board, for it is self-understood in moderate Haredi circles that although various topics are no longer taboo, one discusses them via circumlocution instead of words that could evoke blatantly sexual thoughts.

Advertisements are scrutinized for both topic and language. Certain ads, such as those for internet service providers, have been rejected on the grounds that they are a temptation to readers in view of the recent Haredi rabbinical prohibition on using the Internet, at least from the home.[29]

The questions asked by the spiritual board of each publication are indicative of the cultural associative world of the religious elite in various sectors of Haredi society. In certain cases, this cultural world is still removed somewhat from that of the publication's readers, particularly in the case of more modern publications like *Mishpacha* and *Mishpacha Tova*. Several times, members of the spiritual board of these publications have had to ask the authors about the meaning of certain words that were unclear to them. One female writer remembers being asked by a rabbi on the board of *Mishpacha* what a *nonchalantiut* (with nonchalance) was, and whether it should be considered a forbidden item for the Haredi public.[30] On the other hand, there were times when the tables were turned, and the editors were surprised to discover the extent of rabbi's knowledge of Ivrit slang. Having decided to permit the magazine to publish advertisements for the Habayit Hashalem clinic mentioned earlier, one of the rabbis on the spiritual board questioned the language used where the ad promoted alternative treatments such as *massage veharpaya* (massage and relaxation). Despite the fact that the clinic was in fact advocating nothing more than the pure meaning of each term, the rabbi insisted that the words be removed because in the secular press they were euphemisms for sexual services.[31]

Mishpacha Tova allows itself the most leeway, both in advertising and in the more general matter of consulting its spiritual board, which is involved only in those cases that the editors deem questionable. This policy, indicative of greater modernity, facilitates the use of a larger vocabulary than in other Haredi publications and leads to what may appear to the uninitiated to be inconsistent linguistic decisions regarding categories of inclusion and omission. While the word "uterus," forbidden in magazines such as *Mishpacha* can appear in *Mishpacha Tova*, "bottle nipple" does not. Here one can find expressions such as *hituv haguf* (body shaping), in an ad for diet supplements boasting that their product has been checked and approved by the Badatz of the Eda Haredit (The Kashrut supervision of the Eda Haredit in Jerusalem) (*Mishpacha Tova* 15, Sivan 5760, June 2000). Yet a baby's backside, colloquially called a *tusik* (tush) in the secular version of an advertisement for skin cream, is called *aizor tifrachat hachitul* (the diaper rash area) (*Mishpacha Tova* 28, Sivan 5761, June 2001).

The well-choreographed linguistic dance executed by even the more modern Haredi publications around words and expressions that could evoke thoughts or associations of a sexual nature, is indicative of the centrality of this issue in contemporary Haredi society, whether in its own right or owing to the amount of attention given publicly to such topics in the secular world. In Haredi society, as in Haredi publications, one can discern several means of dealing with this issue. A traditional means of dealing with the topic of sexuality, seen as a threat to the basic fabric of Haredi, is the Victorian attitude of sublimation in which the topic is ignored culturally, textually, and verbally to avoid any mention of something that would open a libidinous Pandora's box. This attitude still prevails among large sectors of Haredi society, and is expressed more in the pages of *Marveh Latzame* and *Olam Hahasidut* than any of the other publications covered here. A second attitude, one of compromise, refers to a topic but uses linguistic circumlocution to keep it in a proper (nonsexual) setting. This is a common device in *Mishpacha*, which gears itself to a Haredi public that does not consider itself old-fashioned in the sense that it admits the existence of various topics, although it finds ways to mention them without being linguistically blatant. The third attitude, which is evident in *Mishpacha Tova*, is still more liberal than the second, using various slang expressions as indicators of its level of modernity while still not crossing the invisible linguistic line that would remove it from the framework of Haredi society. Here we see how that in Haredi society even advertisements, often considered by the uninitiated to be a demilitarized zone, accent the cultural differences between various parts of the contemporary Haredi world, which in their own words define each other as "primitive" versus "too outspoken" while seeing themselves as "traditionalist" as opposed to "progressive."

Gendered Language and Gender-Role Changes in Contemporary Haredi Society

Although the opening page of *Marveh Latzame* states that it is a "magazine for the entire family", the publication is primarily oriented to a female readership. One therefore finds omissions characteristic of gendered writing, such as the limited use of abbreviations. While none of the Haredi men I asked were willing to admit that they peruse the magazine, it seems to be a common phenomenon. In an informal survey taken after a women's *shiur* (study session) in Bnai Brak, some wives mentioned that their husbands occasionally pick up the magazine at home and leaf through it, ostensibly checking the contents in order see what type of reading material is being brought into the house. And although their older sons were often away from home studying in yeshivot, the younger boys would occasionally look at the magazine if they found it at home.[32] Bearing in mind this tacit mixed-sex readership, the editor presents *Marveh Latzame* as a magazine for the "head of the household, housewives, youth and children." Thus the magazine becomes the product of two factors existing in tandem. The first is the desire to provide Haredi women with quality reading, mixing household hints with Torah vignettes in a nondenominational Haredi spirit. The second is the realization that Haredi boys and men thirst for literature of their own that has received rabbinical approval but is not composed solely of Torah studies.

The issue of gendered language in *Olam Hahasidut* becomes apparent when the language and content of the main and supplementary sections of the magazine are compared. The magazine's main section is aimed primarily at a male readership and teems with stories of rebbes' activities, Loshon Kodesh with a large proportion of Aramaic expressions, and references from religious sources. In contrast, the Habayit Hahasidi supplement, which is written for female readers, offers stories with women protagonists who deal with domestic subjects, female interrelationships, and *shmirat halashon* (the laws of gossip and slander, considered to be female failings). The language of the stories and articles, including those geared to adult female readers, is plain compared to that appearing in the main section, with no plays on words and almost no Biblical or Talmudic metaphors. References to religious texts are few and there is very little use of Loshon Kodesh, which commonly appears in the main part of the magazine. Reading the supplement after having finished the main section, the impression is one of an attempt to simplify both language and concepts for female readers.

Although *Mishpacha* is oriented to the entire family, the publishers are aware that whereas a large proportion of the magazine's readers are female, the majority of the news supplement readers are men.[33] One reflection of this is the inclusion of an "Inside the Family" supplement to the magazine and a rabbinical news column in the news section. Except for domestic columns in "Inside the Family" that are written in the feminine, in contrast to the rest of the magazine, it is difficult to point to gendered language of any kind. Subtle differences between the main section and the "Inside the Family" supplement are manifested in terms of modesty; for instance, pictures of girls under the age of three and drawings of women and girls that accompany stories are included in the supplement but not in the main section. But overall, few language differences can be discerned between the two sections. Some female columnists use a full name in the article's byline; others are identified only by a first initial.

As a Haredi version of a secular magazine geared to young mothers, all of *Mishpacha Tova* would be expected to use gendered language and address gendered topics. And in practice, all content deals with motherhood, women's health, mother and child consumer products, and the like. Because Hebrew is by definition a gendered language, articles appearing in *Mishpacha Tova* are usually written using female verb forms. At the level of gendered Haredi codes, there is an absence of religious abbreviations, and of *Loshon Kodesh* tempered with the varying proportions of Aramaic found in magazines that are even tacitly geared to a mixed-sex readership.

On the surface, one would assume that the use of gendered language in Haredi publications is indicative of the specific gender roles allotted to members of that society. Men learn Torah; women support and raise their families. Men provide religious sustenance and exist socially in a single-sex society; women work outside the home and care for home and family while living socially in a parallel but equally segregated women's society. In practice, however, this delineation has shown itself to be no longer absolute, particularly in matters of home and family related to childcare and consumerism, in which Haredi men have begun to play an active role. I have already commented in the previous section on the advertisements for disposable diapers and meat that appeared in *Olam Hahasidut,* the most male-oriented publication surveyed in this article.

Analysis of gendered language exposes another crack in the once impenetrable wall of distinct men's and women's society—that having to do with Talmudic learning and linguistic codes. As girls' education in certain sectors of Haredi society has recently broadened to include religious topics that were omitted in previous generations, young Haredi women have become more familiar with the host of Aramaic codewords or abbreviations that were once the impenetrable fence surrounding a male domain. The inclusion of a certain amount of such terminology in the more modern family and women's Haredi journals is an expression of this educational change taking place in the more modern Haredi circles. Opposed to these groups, however, are the traditionalist Haredi educators closer to the circles of *Marveh Latzameh*, who believe in an educational system that anthropologist Tamar El-Or, referring to its approach to girls' needs, has termed "Educated and Ignorant": girls are taught that they should use the education they receive to deepen the chasm between them and cultural modernity. This education gap is also evident in a comparison of the gendered language in the various journals explored in this study.

Discussion

To the outsider, the Haredi world appears to be a monolithic society of white shirts and black hats, almost hermetically sealed from outside influences, where unfashionable dressed Jews persist in old-fashioned religious education and linguistic patterns reminiscent of the 1930s and 1940s. The reality, however, is quite different from the popular image. Haredi society is multifaceted and dynamic, influenced by both internal and external factors in the field of communication as well as that of linguistic culture (Friedman 1991). Haredi culture is also not a monolithic entity, and in the various women's and family magazines examined here the differences among subgroups are expressed in the same ways as in the various Haredi dailies and weeklies.

During the past few years the Haredi world has undergone various changes those in the spheres of gender, language, and culture, among others. The changes are often not revolutionary but evolutionary, subtly expressing themselves in various spheres of Haredi society. For example, the limited number of teaching positions available in the Haredi world has forced young women breadwinners to make their way into fields that require daily contact with nonreligious society, broadening their vocabulary and expanding their associative cultural world. The growing numbers of Haredi women who are working in Haredi communications and advertising have opened Haredi publications to gendered influences.

Even the fact that a number of Haredi groups are supporting the establishment of Haredi colleges with separate study groups for men and women has changed the linguistic and cultural climate in various parts of Haredi society. One example is the Shas Sefaradi-Haredi college for women headed by Rebbetzin Adina Bar-Shalom, daughter of the former Sefaradi chief rabbi and present spiritual leader of the Shas movement, Rabbi Ovadia Yosef. Another segregated school for both genders is the Academic College in Kiriyat Ono, which offers degrees in law for Haredi men and women; a third is the separate B.A. programs launched for Haredi men and women at Touro College's Jerusalem branch, the Lander Institute, which will be discussed in a later chapter. Thus the various subgroups now being created in Haredi society are not always characterized by the traditional lines of demarcation between Ashkenazi and Sefaradi, Hassidic and Lithuanian, and so on. In the same way, the different form of differentiation that is emerging within the Haredi world—one based on the coordinates of gender and culture—has created a basis for publishing modern Haredi women's and family magazines, several of which have been discussed here.

Conclusions

In his study of the spatial separatism of Israeli Haredim, Yitzhak Shnall (1989) states that legitimacy, identity, and territory are the three main defining parameters of Haredi life, and that Haredi publications are a central tool in analysis of these values. Here we have seen the degree to which a publication's language praxis reflects a particular movement's cultural and spiritual outlook as set down in the da'at Torah of the movement's leader.

The official publication of a movement obtains its legitimacy by receiving the stamp of approval from the movement's chief rabbinical authority. When the source of that authority is blurred (such as in the case of the Lubavitcher rebbe's death or R. Shakh's incapacitation) the existing language policies usually continue to be carried out, as originally set down by the movement's leader. In time they may themselves begin to blur or slowly metamorphose as a result of pressure from below, in other words, in acknowledgement of the linguistic dynamics manifested among its readership. As the chain of command in certain areas—such as deciding upon a movement's published political directives—becomes problematic, not only will language policy change, but even a publication's orientation can undergo a metamorphosis. When a movement's leadership changes, such as in the case of the Gerrer faction, the language appearing in the movement's publications may also undergo change, taking its cue from the new leader's policy and linguistic style.

In the case of all of the movements, subscribing to a particular publication is an expression of a member's identity. In one case (Habad), such a subscription is not all-inclusive, nor does it necessarily preclude the reading of other, nonmovement newspapers. Where the sectoral nature of Haredi family and women's magazines is blurred, the lines of demarcation reflect sex, age, ethnic background, and personal tendencies, not adherence to a particular movement. Schisms that have developed within movements—as in Habad after the rebbe's death or, within today's Gerrer court; if slowly—are only now beginning to have no repercussions for subscriptions to the movement's official publications.

As for the territorial component, Haredi newspapers and periodicals, disseminated over a broad geographical range, create a social and cultural definition of space or territory, delineated not so much by geographical boundaries as by linguistic, social, cultural, and theological inclusions or absences. What may appear to the secular public as a monolithic group of "black-hat" publications are actually magazines and newspapers between which run a number of fine lines that for certain groups act as the borders between the permitted and the forbidden. Moving from internal Haredi demarcation lines to those separating the Haredi and secular public, the language, acronyms, and style of publications, even those written in Ivrit, can act as an effective barrier to the uninitiated, who may grasp the form of what they are reading, but rarely its deeper meaning.

The official publications of a movement—newspapers and journals—will obviously express its leader's da'at Torah in terms of language more than will the general Haredi family and women's magazines that I have surveyed in this chapter. What happens when the language policy and practice of the various movements moves directly into the Haredi domestic realm? My next chapter will answer this question by focusing on language praxis within Haredi communities—the home and family, store, street, and neighborhood.

Notes

1. Author's telephone interview with *Kfar Habad* administrator Shmuel Steinmetz, 16 July 2001.
2. Author's telephone interview with H. R., *HaModia* subscription department, 23 July 2001.
3. Author's telephone interview with Z. R, *Yated Ne'eman* subscription department, 23 July 2001.
4. In order to explore the linguistic expression of Haredi acculturation and changes in the Haredi world, I have examined five months of the journals and weekly newspapers (20 issues from mid February to mid July 2001) and six weeks of the daily newspapers (40 issues from mid February to early March; early June to mid June 2001; early July to mid July 2001) mentioned above.
5. Author's telephone interview with N. M. *Yated Ne'eman* editorial staff, 23 July 2001.
6. Author's telephone interview with Haya, *Yom Leyom* subscription department, 23 July 2001.
7. Ibid.
8. Author's telephone interview with Pnina, *Yated Ne'eman* staff, 23 July 2001.
9. Author's telephone interview with *Yated Ne'eman* representatives who requested anonymity, 23 July 2001.
10. For purposes of my survey I examined 20 issues (five months) of each of the three weekly magazines (February–June 2001) and 13 issues of the monthly magazine (May 2000–May 2001).
11. Author's telephone interview with unnamed secretary of *Marveh Latzame,* 23 July 2001.
12. Author's telephone interview with Rachel, secretary of *Olam Hahasidut,* 25 July 2001.
13. According to a telephone interview with B.S. the director of the subscription department of *Olam Hahasidut,* 25 July 2001.
14. Interview with Rachel, 25 July 2001.
15. Ibid.
16. Author's telephone interview with Ya'akov Pali, Assistant general manager of *Mishpacha,* 26 July 2001.
17. Ibid.
18. Author's informal survey among the participants of a women's *shiur* in Bnai Brak, 27 July, 2001.
19. Author's telephone interview with Ya'akov Pali, Assistant general manager of *Mishpacha,* 26 July 2001.
20. Author's telephone interview with Esti Rider-Reichmann, editor of *Mishpacha Tova,* 26 July 2001.
21. Author's interview with Rabbanit Gita Malka, Tel-Aviv, 8 August 2001, who mentioned how she and her friends read the magazine when they are at the local children's health clinic, *Tipat Halav.*

22. Interview with unnamed secretary of *Marveh Latzame*, 23 July 2001.
23. Ibid..
24. Interview with Rachel, secretary of *Olam Hahasidut* 25 July 2001.
25. Author's telephone interview with Esti Rider-Reichmann, editor of *Mishpacha Tova*, 26 July 2001.
26. Author's telephone interview with Dvora, advertising section of *Olam Hahasidut*, 25 July 2001.
27. Interview with Rachel, 25 July 2001.
28. Author's interview with Rebbetzin Z. Berman, Bnai Brak, 23 Sept. 2001.
29. Author's telephone interview with Malka, advertising section of *Mishpacha*, 26 July, 2001.
30. Author's telephone interview with E. Dar, who writes for *Mishpacha* under a pseudonym, 26 July 2001.
31. Interview with Ya'akov Pali, Assistant general manager of *Mishpacha*, 26 July 2001.
32. Author's informal survey of fifteen Haredi women at a women's *shiur* in Bnai Brak, 21 July 2001.
33. Interview with Ya'akov Pali, 26 July 2001.

5

THE DOMESTIC SPHERE: LANGUAGE IN HAREDI "SPACE"

The Jewish month of Elul, coming in early autumn, is a time of personal reflection and repentance as the religious world prepares itself for the divine judgement that is pronounced on the High Holidays. Expressed in both group and individual activities, the special atmosphere of this period is evident on the spiritual plane as well as the temporal. Late at night or in the early hours of the morning weary, bleary-eyed Jewish men make their way to synagogues to re-cite *slichot* (prayers of repentance). On the individual level men and women make special efforts to refrain from gossip or slander. The month of Elul is also one of the more lucrative months for revivalist preachers, religious figures delivering public *mussar* (ethics) exhortations, and even wives of prominent rabbis, who appear in the evenings before groups of Haredi women to spiritually prepare them for the holy days of judgement. These gatherings, which are a major part of Haredi life, provide women with a permissible social framework for meeting friends and act as a religious version of popular thought-provoking entertainment. In the Mitnagdic circles there are even women's groups that are addressed by prominent rabbinical speakers, a breach of modesty rarely found in the Hassidic sector.

At the conclusion of one such gathering in Bnai Brak, a group of young Mit-nagdic women walked home together through the darkened streets, discussing the charismatic rabbi whom they had just heard lecture. "Something was different this year," said one of the participants to the group. "What was this talk about *hesed* [charitable deeds] all of a sudden?" "Didn't you see the crowd in the back?"replied a second woman. "They weren't all 'ours' this year, they must have seen posters about him in Pardes Katz [a nearby neighborhood with a large Sefaradi population]." "Ah, that explains everything", said another, "it was for them. All they talk about is *hesed, hesed, hesed,* almost like the Hassidim who at least have finally learned to say 'Torah' as well. That's the most they can strive for. With us it's different; we talk about our sons and husbands reaching heights of *limud* (Torah study), *bekiut* (well-versed in Talmud), and *harifut* (sharpness of study)." "That's how you can tell their speakers right off," remarked one of her companions as she turned towards her corner, "You wouldn't catch one of ours talking about *hesed* as if it's the most to be expected of us. But with them." She left her sentence unfinished.

This brief conversation provides us with one example of the cultural and linguistic differences existing between the various Haredi "spaces": the terminology by which one can identify a particular sect. The linguistic aspect is obvious to the listeners—the ubiquitous use of the term *hesed* as an identifying marker for Sefaradi Haredim, as opposed to Ashkenazi ones, primarily the Mitnagdim. However, the importance of the linguistic difference is actually its deeper, cultural significance. The fact that in Mitnagdic speech that term, used on its own and not as part of the expression *gemilut hasadim* ("charitable deeds"), indicates what some consider to be the absolute religious inferiority of Sefaradim, and the relative religious inferiority of Hassidim. Language therefore becomes a marker of culture, expressed in social and religious hierarchy and delineating the framework in which all of Haredi society functions.

This chapter, dealing with language and culture in the Haredi domestic sphere and space, analyzes the juxtaposition of two of the most common Haredi separatist factors, "territory" and "tongue". As Glinert and Shilhav (1991) succinctly state in the introduction to their study of language and ultra-Orthodox Jewish ideology, these are the basic components for creating a community separate from its surroundings and united by ongoing, active ideological ties.

The idea of a community is one of the basic elements of a social system, providing content with meaning and connecting individuals to the various institutions that they utilize (Suttles 1972). Although there are examples of international, suprageographical communities that have existed for long periods of time, the space within which a segregated community forms usually requires a territorial component. Religion, as an intentional and operative functional system, can also be a basic factor in forming these communities (Poplin 1979). But because society is an entity that constitutes itself through the continuous and recursive production of a connected series of communications based on meaning, it is the communication factor (and not the people) that lies at the heart of a social system.

How are Haredi language, and thereby, culture, translated into expression in the domestic realm as part of the communication factor in the community, within what can be considered Haredi space? Is there a connection between *de jure* policy and *de facto* praxis, or are the dynamics of modern life stronger than even the decrees of a rabbi, rebbe, or *Admor*? How does daily speech differ among the sects focused upon here? What differences become evident when examining what Bourhis defines as space, something that includes street signs, notices in store windows, wall posters, and even graffiti (Bourhis 1984a; 1984b; 1992; Bourhis and Sachdev 1989; Landry and Bourhis 1997)? In answer to these questions this chapter will focus on Haredi language and culture as expressed within three realms of the Haredi domestic and public space. The first is the Haredi family domain, where interchanges occur between husband and wife, parents and children, siblings, and members of the extended family. One of the ways that researchers in sociolinguistics or cultural linguistics study deal with their subject is to live immersed within a community, basing the research on carefully recorded field notes. This I did by observing and questioning three large Haredi families in their usual surroundings for six months during the spring and summer of 2001. Each of the families belongs to one of the sects upon which this study focuses. During this period I took copious notes and asked questions about the various language habits and choices I observed. It must be added that I had been familiar with three of the nuclear families for many years, although not as a researcher.

The second realm to be explored is the language used in Haredi public space. I examined the store window signs, public advertisements, and wall posters in areas containing enclaves of Haredim from each of the sects explored herein. In addition, I recorded and analyzed graffiti and notes found at Haredi sacred spaces, particularly on the walls surrounding the graves of Zaddikim that are frequented by various groups of Haredim. The third Haredi realm I examined here is the language used among friends, at work, in places of religious ritual, and at public gatherings such as the lecture described above. For this research I returned to my Haredi families, using their extended families, places of work, study, and religious practice as a source of data.

In the course of my fieldwork I became acutely aware of certain difficulties involved in carrying out such a study. The first is the complexity of nuances. A word used by one Haredi sect can sometimes have a completely different connotation in another. Noting the use of a particular word is therefore only one stage of observation and must be followed by an extensive exploration of its meaning in a particular context and within each group. The second difficulty is assessing the degree of intruder influence—in other words, how much my subjects' awareness of my presence influenced their choice of words or the language used around me.

A third challenge was posed by the issue of sexual segregation in the Haredi world. As journalist Amnon Levy (1989) notes in his study of Haredi life in Israel, it is almost impossible for a strange man to carry on a long conversation with a Haredi woman, let alone converse with her in private. Consequently, the families I chose for observation in this chapter were by necessity those with whom my extended family had close personal connections. This was what enabled me to participate in mixed-sex family gatherings, and to observe and discuss matters of language with the females of the family in a public setting. As for totally segregated activities, I could (and did) readily participate in communal religious activities along with the males of each family, but I was, naturally, barred from doing so with the women. I therefore enlisted the assistance and observation of a female member of my own family, trained in research practice, who supplied me with data on all-female activities among these sects. She recorded both spoken language and language used in the signs and wall posters hanging in places of ritual practice such as the sites of women's *shiurim*, and even noted the graffiti found in the women's sections of Zaddikim's graves. These observations were confirmed in my conversations with women from each of the sects.

Although much of my data on the domestic realm was gathered through observation, my research methodology in this and the next chapter (on educational frameworks) was also based in part on the responses from of oral interviews. Such survey research, traditionally divided into three stages (constructing variables based on research goals; approaching subjects; interpreting answers and relating them to content theory and research goals), is premised on a common understanding between questioner and respondent regarding the broader meaning of terms used and questions posed (Belson 1981). In asking the same questions of different sects, I often found it necessary to use different expressions in keeping with what I saw as the group's *lingua franca*. One must meanwhile bear in mind that the response elicited by a particular term can depend on the context in which it is used. Even simple responses such as "yes" and "no" have different meanings in various situations. For example, a Haredi man who is asked if he "loves all Jews" may answer "yes"; however, this does not preclude his also answering "no" to the question of whether he loves secular Jews. This linguistic problem is particularly evident in the forbid/allow asymmetry, where answering "no" to forbid is not the same as answering "yes" to allow (Holleman 2000). Agreeing to forbid implies a real act of opposition, but to disagree with allowing means merely to abstain from support (Clark and Schober 1992). For example, if a Haredi father says that he would forbid his children to study at a secular school, this may be taken as a real act of opposition. On the other hand, if he states that he disagrees with the educational methods of a particular school belonging to his own Haredi sect, he can be understood as merely abstaining from supporting that school.

A final consideration if the intensity of underlying attitude that a particular question measures and the degree to which a question's wording influences the response (Foddy 1993). Recognizing that respondents tend to modify extreme positions, I attempted to phrase questions in a neutral fashion, so that they might express their opinions on various subjects to the fullest, instead of trying to fit themselves into a set pattern determined by my form of question.

The Domestic Realm: Language Used within the Family

The initial unit for language development is usually the family, which forms the social and cultural context that creates the input factors for individuals and groups. As Heath (1983) shows, in certain societies, roles that children will eventually play in larger society are often predestined in the conceptual structures they have learned at home, and which are reinforced in school and numerous other associations. In her study of language in two Appalachian communities, she charts how, long before reaching school, children have made the transition from home to the larger societal institutions that share the values, skills, knowledge bases, and language patterns of the school. Using a technique grounded in observation and comparative analysis of the two communities, Heath ultimately reinforces the conclusion that it is their language and culture at home that structures for them the meanings that will give shape to their experiences in classrooms and beyond (Bernstein 1975).

The development of language in a community is densely intertwined with the way it structures the families that comprise the community, defines the roles that community members can assume, and plays out these community members' concepts of childhood, which guide child socialization. In communities throughout the world, these and other features of the cultural milieu in which the family exists and functions affect the ways in which children learn to use language and continue to use it as adults (Brown 1973).

The place of language in the cultural life of each social group is linked with the habits and behavioral values held in common by members of that group. The different social legacies and even the ways of behaving in face-to-face interactions are pivotal in shaping the different patterns of language use (Heath 1983). Only after determining factors like the different gender roles, the expected standard of living, or the generational or gendered hierarchy of authority within a group is it possible to gain a fuller understanding of the subtle language choices that evidence themselves in a particular group. Even what is ostensibly a study of language must at times become an ethnographic exploration, probing the cultural framework within which language is an inseparable factor. My analysis of Haredi language and culture in the family setting therefore looks at the families' lifestyle, constructions of gender, and internal hierarchy, all of which serve as a crucial background for their linguistic choices and language patterns.

It is the interdependence of culture and language that was decisive in my selection of families to be observed for this chapter. At first glance, it may seem to the reader that instead of choosing mainstream Haredi families—in which both parents are longtime members of the sect and the home is a Haredi ghetto inhabited almost solely by members of that sect—I have chosen "lames" (Labov 1973), a term used by sociolinguists to designate peripheral members of a community. In truth, I chose these particular families because they represent the reality of pluralism within the Haredi community. In my mind, the families I picked were more typical of Haredi families of each group as it exists today, as opposed to the popular image or stereotype that the general public holds of Haredi families of each group.

Each of the three Haredi families featured in this study lives in a Haredi neighborhood, though not necessarily one inhabited only by Haredim of their own sect. In modern Israel, a mix of sects in a complex web of neighborhoods (Isaacs 1998a; 1999) is a common result of Haredi demographic growth. For example, the Habad family featured in this study does not live in Kfar Habad—like the majority of Habad families in Israel, who live neither in Kfar Habad nor even in large Habad communities. Still, along with many a Habad family who lives in a general Haredi area, they are part of a Habad "community within a community" and are far from being the only Habad family in their neighborhood in Bnai Brak. In all four cases, one member of the couple was a longtime member of the Haredi sect in question while the spouse joined the sect only after marriage. For example, in the Gerrer family, the wife came from a veteran Gerrer family, whereas the husband, who had belonged to a different Hassidic sect, became a Gerrer only as an adult. Ties between their sects were strengthened by their marriage. Although as recently as half a century ago Haredim tried to marry only within their sect, intermarriage is commonplace today as a result of the demographic changes that have taken place in the Haredi world. This is particularly true among Hassidic groups, many of which were decimated during the Holocaust. It is less common to find marriages between Hassidim and Mitnagdim, and rarer still to find an Ashkenazi Haredi married to a Sefaradi Haredi.

Another characteristic that mirrors contemporary Haredi reality (but not public image or stereotype) concerns place of birth. In each of the families I observed, one parent had been born in Israel or brought there as an infant, while the other parent had moved to Israel as a teenager or even later. For example, although the Mitnagdic family observed belongs today to the Mitnagdic mainstream in terms of lifestyle, neighborhood, education, and occupation, the father was born abroad and spent his early years in a diaspora-Mitnagdic environment with a great deal of linguistic interface with the local non-Jewish community. While such a man, today a prominent rabbi in Israel, may not fit the secular public image of the Mitnagdic Haredi background, it is much closer to the reality than they can imagine (Levy 1989). The non-Israeli background of one member of each family is an expression of the suprageographical nature of Haredi life, common to Hassidim, Mitnagdim, and as we will see in a later chapter, the Sefaradi Haredi elite. In Israel it is common to see engagement announcements listing pairs of cities—Bnai Brak and Antwerp, Jerusalem and Brooklyn, London and Melbourne, Paris and Marseilles—as the places of origin of the young couple who intend to make their home in Israel.

Because the two parents in each family have different birthplaces, they also have different mother tongues. This is interesting in view of the fact that two of the three sects represented do not object to adopting the local vernacular as part of their commonly spoken language, which is in fact what happened in these families.

Habad

The Habad family that I observed and interviewed (I will refer to them as the A family) lives in Bnai Brak. Although connected by family ties to Kfar Habad, the movement's center in Israel, like many Habad families, the A couple chose to live in a mixed Haredi area inhabited by enough Habad members to form "a community within a community," where they are now raising their seven children aged nine to twenty-one. Both parents are in their early fifties. The father, an engineer, is one of seven children born in the Soviet Union to a veteran Habad family that moved to Israel in the early 1970s. Having been brought up speaking Yiddish at home and Russian outside the home, Mr. A's mother tongue was Yiddish, and the language of his education and daily speech in his youth was Russian. In addition to Ivrit, in which he became fluent after moving to Israel, he has some command of English and German. The mother, an Israeli-born lecturer and researcher whose mother tongue is Ivrit, grew up as is one of three children in a *Hardal* family and joined Habad only after her marriage. Both parents hold graduate degrees from Israeli universities.

Despite the fact that Mr. and Mrs. A come from different linguistic backgrounds, there was never any debate regarding what language they would speak at home, both to each other and to their children. Although Mrs. A can read several languages including English, French, and German, she has no knowledge of Russian and only a limited command of Yiddish, the language that Mr. A continued to speak with his parents after immigrating to Israel. Before marrying, the couple decided that they would speak Ivrit at home, as it was the only language in which both were fluent. Mr. A noted that this was a common practice in Habad families where one parent came from the USSR and the other was a *sabra* (Israeli-born). Even when both spouses were Soviet Habad immigrants who initially spoke Yiddish or Russian to each other, couples tended to switch into Ivrit after their children were born. This shift appears to be influenced by the fact that Habad, being an outreach movement, conducts its linguistic life in Israel primarily in Ivrit. Mr. and Mrs. A both noted that there are Russian Habad families in Kfar Habad and Kiriyat Malachi who still speak Yiddish at home. In many cases the younger generations in these families now communicate among themselves primarily or even entirely in Ivrit, just as Mr. A now speaks Ivrit to his siblings although he continued to speak Yiddish with his parents until their death.

None of the seven children of A family has been educated in official Habad educational establishments before the stage of seminary for girls or higher yeshiva studies for boys. This appears to be common practice among Habad families with professional backgrounds, among whom are formerly secular families and Habad families from other countries, including both the United States and the former Soviet Union. These families wish their children to receive professional education but also eventually to study at Habad institutions. Preferably, the children are formally educated at Habad institutions only at a later stage in their studies because the parents have a low opinion of the level of secular education at many of the Habad elementary and high schools in Israel. Like many educated Habad families, the adults in the A family decided to enroll both their sons and daughters in more modern Haredi educational programs up to the end of high school. This enables them to continue their professional studies if they chose to do so in the future. The children were not sent to other Hassidic educational establishments, as many of these are opposed to the ideology of Habad.

All of the children study in a combination of Loshon Kodesh and Ivrit and in their Talmud studies the boys use Loshon Kodesh with a large proportion of Aramaic. All of the children study English at school, although they speak neither Yiddish nor Russian. One daughter has studied French as well as English. When asked how they feel about studying non-Jewish languages, all of the children—both boys and girls—responded that knowing foreign languages is a necessity and they know that they will need languages for their work in the future, particularly if they become Habad emissaries. In the next chapter, where I discuss the educational frameworks at Kfar Habad, we will see how this differs little from the language practice in the Kfar Habad elementary and high schools, with the exception of the talmud torah and yeshiva, in which English is not taught to the boys.

Following the tendency of the more modern Habad families to prefer educational excellence over studies in Habad institutions that instead emphasize ideological indoctrination, the girls in the A family are encouraged by their parents to continue their post–high school education outside the Habad framework. This is primarily because the mother believes that the Habad girls' seminary, Beit Rivka, is not as good in terms of either secular studies or vocational preparation. The older children have studied the teachings of Habad either on their own, with their father, or in study frameworks outside their elementary or high schools. Whereas the daughters in the A family are not pressed to study in Habad institutions at any age, a formal Habad education at some point is considered a necessity for the sons. After their oldest son (age 16) completes high school, the parents have said, that they would like him to study at a Habad yeshiva, preferably the Habad world center in Brooklyn.

In her study of Yiddish vitality and language choice, Isaacs (1999) notes how Haredi language study and use are shaped by separate linguistic and social environments in the Haredi school-world that are expected to continue into adulthood. This expectation appears to be true to a lesser degree within Habad, the Haredi group that probably has the highest rate of both male and female professionals and consequently, more intermingling between the sexes and exposure of both men and women to the local vernacular. Despite that fact that Mr. A was raised in a triglossic Haredi linguistic pattern, as professionals, he and his wife are immersed in Ivrit all day at work. In addition, the sect's outreach orientation and its leaders' positive attitude toward the use of the local vernacular in general and towards Ivrit in particular, has made it less important for Habad families in Israel to maintain a minority language as a means of creating separation. In spite of its being his mother tongue and the typical Haredi minority separatist language, Mr. A does not intersperse Yiddish into conversations with his wife and children. This is strengthened by the language patterns observed among his Russian-born siblings, all of whom now speak Ivrit with each other. According to Mr. A., the absence of a separatist minority language in the family (in this case Yiddish) is a language pattern evidenced among the majority of Habad families in Israel. The only Habad-style speech that evidences itself in the A family is Mr. A's occasional punctuation of his sentences with the characteristic ending *mamash* for emphasis, something I have noted in chapter four as a Habad expression that may have messianic overtones. This term is used neither by Mrs. A nor by the children in the family. It may also be an echo of Mr. A's Habad-style education and upbringing, as opposed to the more modern Mitnagdic or even *Hardal*-style education that his children are receiving in non-Habad educational establishments.

Habad's positive attitude towards Ivrit is reinforced in the A family by the fact that both parents and children have incorporated Ivrit slang in their daily speech. Among the slang terms that both parents and children in the A family use are words such as *balagan* (a mess), or *lachtof* (to grab), as in "do you want to grab something to eat?" When they talk to their parents, the children's Ivrit is more restrained; it becomes more colloquial among themselves even though they refrain from using the derogatory terms that may be heard among secular children. The harshest expressions the children use toward each other are along the lines of *metumtam* (stupid) or *idiot*. Seldom do they use an expression such as *psichi* (crazy), and after doing so they are harshly rebuked by their parents. In the course of my observations I noted no differences between the way the parents speak to the boys in the family as opposed to the girls, nor were there any expressions used only by the sons as opposed to the daughters, or vice versa. I noted that some language patterns in talk between children and adults were the same as those observed during the time I spent in families and schools in Kfar Habad, and among Habad members in Arad.

Apart from using Ivrit at work or school, the A family is exposed to colloquial language through their written and broadcast media. Like most Haredim, the family does not own a television set. However, all family members listen to the radio, particularly to news programs and talk shows. Mrs. A and several of the children are interested in music and listen to musical programs. Except for the father, who limits his reading to professional journals and religious volumes, all other family members, including the boys, are exposed to daily newspapers—and not necessarily only those of the Haredi variety—along with the weekly magazine *Kfar Habad*. The mother and girls do not read family magazines, but they do read non-Haredi books, voluntarily limiting themselves to what they call "classical literature," which excludes books that raise topics of a questionable moral nature for what the mother called a "proper family." In the A family there is little attempt at home to control the texts that the children read; rather, they are allowed free access to both religious and secular subjects.

How different is the A family from those Habad families found in Kfar Habad or in other Habad communities such as those in Safed, Jerusalem, Kiriyat Malachi, or even Arad? According to Mr. and Mrs. A, the A family's lifestyle and linguistic patterns are typical of a professional Habad family, such as those in the Safed community who immigrated from the United States in the late 1970s, or the Russian professional Habad families in Kfar Habad. Mrs. A also added that in a certain sense, they are also typical of some of the formerly secular Habad members, a large number of whom reached Habad after a career in the professional world, or left this world after joining Habad.

It appears that the A family's exposure to and use of Ivrit and slang may be a result of the interface that certain Habad families have with conduits of secular cultural. Mr. A noted several times that in what he called the "hardcore" Habad communities of Kfar Habad, Kiriyat Malachi and Jerusalem, there are families, primarily from the USSR, who still speak Yiddish at home. However, he also noted that they are few and cannot be considered representative of the Israeli Habad community in general.

Since they are not being schooled in Habad educational establishments, the A family boys and girls are not exposed to Yiddish in their studies. If the boys opt to study in Habad yeshivot either in Kfar Habad or in the United States, they will probably study a certain amount of Yiddish in the future. Group identity and cultural continuity is not a factor of minority language use among Habad in Israel. To whatever degree, Yiddish appears to play a larger role in Haredi communication in the diaspora, making it more significant outside Israel as a vehicle, along with territory or space, for ethnic minority identification.

Gur

The Gur family that I observed and interviewed (I will refer to them as the B family) lives in Jerusalem in a mixed Haredi area populated by a large number of Gerrer Hassidim. This is a not an uncommon practice among the various Hassidic groups, whose members prefer living near members of their own community. In major Israeli cities with large Haredi populations such as Jerusalem or Bnai Brak, they form a "community within a community." In peripheral areas like Arad, Ashdod, and Hatzor Haglilit, they form their own community to provide their own services, separating themselves both from the other Haredim in the area and from their secular surroundings.

The B family, the youngest of the four families I observed (both parents are in their late twenties), has four children age two to seven. The father is one of six children born in Antwerp to a family of diamond dealers who are connected not to Gur but to a large Galician Hassidic sect; Gur, however, was known as the largest and most powerful Hassidic group in central and northeastern Poland at the time. Owing to his upbringing in the multilingual Jewish community of Antwerp, Mr. B knew French as his mother tongue and he was exposed to Flemish (spoken and written) in his secular studies and Yiddish (spoken only) at home and in his Jewish studies. Studying in an Israeli Yeshiva in his late teens, he began to speak Ivrit with his friends but continued to speak French and Yiddish with his family, a large number of whom moved to Israel during the 1970s. Mr. B had been was drawn to the Gerrer community in Jerusalem soon after coming to study in Israel. Ultimately, after a year of participating in Gerrer activities, he was offered a bride from that Hassidic group and is now a full-time Kollel student. Mr. B's family subsists on his Kollel stipend along with his wife's earnings. Mrs. B is Israeli-born, the oldest of five children from a veteran Gerrer family that came to Israel from Poland after the Second World War. She was a secretary before her marriage and now works part-time as a typist in a large insurance firm.

Mrs. B's mother tongue is Ivrit, which is the couple's only common language in which they are both fluent. Although Mrs. B understands some of the Yiddish she heard in her parents' home, she knows no French or Flemish and has a very limited command of English, which she studied at her Beit Ya'akov high school. Although Mr. B would gladly speak Yiddish at home, as he studies in Yiddish at the Kollel, he acquiesces to Mrs. B's wishes to speak Ivrit, the language in which she is most comfortable. Similar choices are made in most families in the Gerrer community who use Ivrit in daily speech. There are, however, a small number of younger Gerrer Hassidim, particularly in the outlying Gerrer communities (Tel Aviv, Ashdod, Arad), who attempt to maintain their separatism by using Yiddish at home (El-Or 1994). Gender too is a factor: because their studies in higher yeshiva take place in Yiddish, the Gerrer men have a better command of Yiddish than the women. As we will see in the next chapter, children in the Gerrer schools I observed noted that while their fathers speak Yiddish fluently, their mothers know only the small amount of Yiddish that they have learned from their husbands or heard at home as children.

Despite his decision to use *Ivrit* at home, Mr. B finds himself using lexical transfers when speaking to his children, particularly from Yiddish (and at times from French), which enrich their language. His code switching often takes the form of Yiddish interjections in Ivrit sentences (*zoll zein mit glik,* "good luck"), or diminutive nouns (*keppele,* "head") when speaking to small children. While the B children cannot be considered fluent bilinguals, as Isaacs (1998a) points out regarding Haredi language patterns in general they are nevertheless being exposed to expressions from the common minority language of the Ashkenazi Haredi world.

The two older children in the B family are in school: the seven-year-old boy attends the Gerrer *Heder* (elementary school), and the five-year-old girl goes to a kindergarten connected with the Gur movement. The two younger children are in part-time daycare. Both of the older children study in Ivrit, and the boy is already being exposed to Loshon Kodesh with a small proportion of Aramaic in his religious studies. The parents of the B family keep tight control over the texts to which the children are exposed, including stories read to infants. These texts must be vetted by the Haredi community and bought in Haredi bookstores. As a result, the children do not know fairy tales; instead they hear Bible tales or stories with moral lessons. In her study of Haredi children's literature as a cultural phenomenon, Malhi (1993) notes that the language in these books is often stilted and archaic, although they are written in Ivrit.

The children's major exposure to non-Jewish languages takes place during visits with their paternal grandparents who speak to them in French or Yiddish. The children answer them in simple Ivrit. Among themselves, and with their parents, the children speak Ivrit with almost no colloquialisms or slang. While their Ivrit is almost indistinguishable from that of their non-Haredi Ivrit-speaking contemporaries, they substitute certain expressions of circumlocution (for example, in matters having to do with bodily functions) that are rarely heard from secular children. Throughout my observations I could note no difference in the language used by Mr. and Mrs. B toward their sons as opposed to their daughters, or in that used by boys as opposed to girls. This may be a function of age, as all the children are still young.

Although Mrs. B's Ivrit is colloquial and she is exposed to slang at work, she makes an effort not to use modern phrases or slang at home so that the children will be brought up hearing what she calls "proper language." Apart from what Mrs. B hears at work, the couple is exposed to few vehicles that would bring colloquial Ivrit into their home. The couple has no television set and rarely listens to the radio; the only daily newspaper to enter the house is *HaModia*. In addition, Mrs. B reads several family magazines such as *Marveh Latzame* and *Mishpacha*. Although in his youth he read secular literature, as a Kollel student Mr. B only reads the newspaper or religious writings. Mrs. B does not read secular literature other than the aforementioned family magazines.

According to Mr. and Mrs. B, their family's background, lifestyle, and linguistic patterns are typical of those of young Gerrer families in Jerusalem, Bnai Brak, and even those in outlying areas such as Ashdod and Arad. Gur is a sect that has attracted adherents from other Hassidic sects, particularly those from Poland and Galicia. This is seen in the case of the B family, where the husband, originally brought up in a Bobover Hassidic family, joined Gur. Noted for its adoption of Ivrit for daily speech, the Gerrer sect also has a minority of families that speak Yiddish at home. Most of these families are older or have European-born members, although there are also younger Israeli-born Gerrer Hassidic families who have chosen to speak Yiddish as a means of social and religious separatism (El-Or 1994). Yiddish becomes a part of Gerrer communal life primarily through higher yeshiva study, which takes place in Yiddish. As I show in the next chapter, spoken (but almost never written) Yiddish is introduced to boys in the Gerrer community usually at the high school level, as preparation for higher yeshiva study. As time goes by and fewer Gerrer families speak Yiddish, the active use of the language may disappear.

In an aside to me, Mr. B remarked that he is sorry that his children are not hearing enough Yiddish, which he referred to as "the language of his childhood," and that he hopes they will be exposed to more spoken Yiddish in the future. Although he now belongs to a sect that has adopted Ivrit as its main language of communication, he considers Yiddish to have both a nostalgic and a quasi-sanctified quality. In her study of Yiddish education in Israeli government-supported schools, Bogoch (1999) explains the historical, cultural, and associative basis for such an assertion. Yiddish's association with the Eastern European pre-Holocaust world grants it traditional status. The fact that Yiddish was the language of the martyrs of the Holocaust gives it religious sanctity. As Seidman (1997) states in her study of Hebrew and Yiddish, Yiddish has become the new Loshon Kodesh, the new "Holy Tongue," also known as lashon hakedoshim, the language of the Holy Martyrs. The identification of Yiddish with the Haredi world and lifestyle creates a cultural bond even between those Haredi groups who no longer use Yiddish for daily speech. These factors have combined to Yiddish a place of honor in the Haredi world and make it an identifying linguistic marker for the Ashkenazi Haredi world in the eyes of both its members and their fellow citizens.

Mitnagdim

The Mitnagdic family that I observed and interviewed (hereafter the C family) lives in the heart of Bnai Brak in an area populated by various Haredi groups. The family has four children aged 9 to 19. Both parents are in their early 40s.

The father, one of seven children in a veteran Mitnagdic clan, was born in South America to an illustrious rabbinical family whose patriarch had studied in a Mitnagdic yeshiva in Jerusalem. This is a common situation among middle-class and upper middle-class Mitnagdic families in the diaspora, who often send their children to study in Israel. Rabbi C's mother tongue is Spanish and he received his elementary schooling in that language; Jewish studies were taught in Loshon Kodesh with a high proportion of Aramaic. After moving to Israel as a young teenager to study in yeshiva, he became fluent in Ivrit. For many years after his marriage he was a full-time Kollel student, and he now teaches in a yeshiva in Bnai Brak.

The Israeli-born mother of the family, one of three children from a *Hardal* family, works as a secretary. This, too, is a common occurrence: as large numbers of children from *Hardal* families had tended toward a Haredi lifestyle from the 1970s onward, causing them to seek Haredi spouses and totally immerse themselves in the Haredi world. Before marrying the couple decided to speak Ivrit at home, as it is Mrs. C's mother tongue. Rabbi C speaks Spanish with his mother and siblings, and Mrs. C has made an effort to study the language and can now converse with her mother-in-law in simple Spanish. Apart from English, which she studied at her Beit Ya'akov school, Mrs. C is fluent in Yiddish, which she spoke with her grandparents. The children in the C family speak only Ivrit, and they communicate with their paternal grandmother in what they call *Ivrit kala* (easy Ivrit).

All four of the C family children study in strict Mitnagdic educational frameworks. The older son, in his early twenties, studied in a yeshiva *gevoha* (literally, "higher" yeshiva) for unmarried boys aged 18 and up; he is now married and studies in Kollel. The younger son studies in a yeshiva *ketana*, (literally, smaller yeshiva) for boys aged 14–18. In both the yeshiva and the Kollel all study takes place in Ivrit and Loshon Kodesh. Although both sons were supposed to have studied English in elementary school, in practice neither son has actually had formal studies in any foreign language, nor have they been exposed to Yiddish *shiurim*, something they might have encountered in the Mitnagdic world two decades ago. The younger daughter studies in an elementary school of the Haredi *Hinuch Atzmai* (Independent Haredi School Stream) system. The older daughter, who like her brother is married, studied at a Haredi girls' seminary (high school) in which most students are of a Mitnagdic background and is now completing her post–high school studies at the same seminary. Lessons are taught in Ivrit and Loshon Kodesh, and both girls study English in school. Like their parents, all four children speak colloquial Ivrit. Until recently there was little difference between the speech patterns used by the boys and the girls in the C family; however, the mother noted that lately the girls seem to express themselves more freely than the boys. Judging from my observations of Haredi society during this period, this is not a common phenomenon in the Haredi world in general or in the Mitnagdic world in particular. In this case, it may stem from a combination of personality and situation: the highly verbal interaction between mother and daughters in the C family, as opposed to her more limited verbal interaction with her sons, due to their absence from the home for study purposes.

The children use no derogatory expressions, but have instead substituted interesting equivalents that are frequently used at school. For example, when angry with his sisters, the younger son often calls one of them a "bulldozer," the expression that his age group in school uses as a parallel to the secular *ben zona*, figuratively "son-of-a-bitch." Since he began studying in higher yeshiva, the oldest son states, he has made efforts to refrain from using what he calls "street language." This includes expressions such as *haval al hazman* (don't waste your time, used in Israeli slang to either denote something terrific or something terrible), or *gadol* (great, equivalent to the American slang "awesome").

While the Ivrit that Rabbi and Mrs. C speak both inside and outside the home is interspersed with colloquialisms, they make an effort not to bring slang phrases into the house. They are aware that the children probably know slang that they do not use in front of their parents or other adults, but they try to minimize outside influences that can affect the children's speech. For the past few years the family has not kept a radio at home, nor do they read any newspapers. Mrs. C still listens to news and talk programs when she is at work and occasionally borrows Haredi magazines such as *Mishpacha* from her neighbors. The children read only Haredi children's literature which is usually written in a combination of Ivrit and Loshon Kodesh (Malhi 1993; Hovav 1994). Neither Rabbi nor Mrs. C uses Yiddish expressions in speech, although when agitated Rabbi C does occasionally use a Spanish phrase rather than express his anger in Ivrit. This follows a dictum kept by certain Haredim that no version of the Holy Tongue should ever be used in anger.

Rabbi and Mrs. C say that their family is typical of the more scrupulous Mitnagdic families found in both major Haredi centers like Bnai Brak and Jerusalem, and in outlying areas such as Beit Shemesh and Elad. Completely comfortable in Ivrit, unlike certain Hassidic groups, the younger Mitnagdim today rarely use Yiddish even for studying purposes. In spite of their command of colloquial Ivrit, such Mitnagdim expend great effort to ensure that unsuitable expressions make no inroads into their familial home. Unlike the girls, who study English at school as part of the educational preparation for their future task—supporting Torah scholars—the boys study no foreign languages at their school, which usually teaches a skeletal curriculum of secular studies, including Ivrit language classes (Friedman 1995; Bar-On 1999). When asked how they felt about this difference between the boys' and girls' schools, the boys in the C family expressed absolutely no desire to study English, claiming that they would not need it for their future as Torah scholars in Israel. As I will show in the next chapter, this follows the strict Mitnagdic norm of encouraging a certain amount of secular study for girls while almost forbidding it for boys. A different phenomenon is apparent among the more modern-style Mitnagdim, some of whom send their children to *Hardal*-type schools where both boys and girls study secular subjects. Boys from these families are solely prepared for a life of Talmud study but are also expected to have a profession or a trade.

The educational choices of the C family, whose mother is a graduate of one of the more modern Beit Ya'akov schools, are typical of the strict Mitnagdim. They appear to be part of the radicalization process evidencing itself among various groups of Mitnagdim, a group that used to be known for the high degree of interface its members had with the secular population in Israel. Particularly among the Mitnagdic elite one notes a more stringent interpretation of Haredi life in recent years, leading to the removal of any media elements from the home. For example, one of the conditions of admission at the seminary where the older C daughter studies is a signed statement that the family does not have a radio at home. Although she enjoyed listening to radio programs in the evening after dinner, Mrs. C agreed to remove the family radio from the house in order to ensure her daughter's continued education at an elite girls' seminary. This step, like the removal of the Mitnagdic newspaper *Yated Ne'eman* from the house, appears to be an additional removal of an object that could act as a vehicle for cultural and linguistic dynamic processes. As a tactic, it obviates the need for the parents to control the texts to which the children in the family are exposed. Except for stories read to small children—which being of the Haredi children's variety, are either didactic or realistic with heavy moral overtones (Malhi 1993; Hovav 1994)—the children themselves are heavily educated by their schools regarding the need for text censorship. As a result, they have developed a sense of self-censorship, purging the home of texts that, although accepted in general Haredi society, do not meet the ultrarigorous standards imbued in them by their schools.

In his study of the means by which Haredim confront the modern city, Friedman (1986) describes the process by which post–World War Two Haredim created voluntary cloistered communities stressing a heroic elite, centered on the Torah, and offering an alternative to modernity. Explaining how Haredi life acts an antidote to urban maladies, he shows how it fosters and preserves values and norms of modesty, spiritual riches, social togetherness, and respect for tradition. In the C family, the linguistic differences between the parents' and the children's generation highlight this ongoing process in the Mitnagdic world. While each parent is fluent in at least one language other than Ivrit and has a working knowledge of a third language, the children know either only Ivrit or, additionally, only a minimum of English. As for their knowledge of Ivrit, cultural constraints such as the removal of radio and newspapers attempt to narrow the scope of the language they use for everyday communication. Less than one generation ago a Mitnagdic family such as the C family would have been more moderate, perhaps sending its children to the schools where the professionally-minded A family children are being educated. Boys learn foreign languages and Hebrew grammar at such schools, and the more modern Beit Ya'akov schools offer matriculation exams rather than the internal diplomas of the radically separatist girls' seminaries. Today, the radicalization of Mitnagdic Haredi life makes this impossible for the C family. Each sex must be trained with a particular goal in mind: boys are to be Torah scholars and girls are to have the skills needed to support such scholars.

Discussion

A number of linguistic and cultural denominators are common to the families that I observed. All speak Ivrit at home, with the more colloquial form being spoken by the Habad and Mitnagdic families and the less colloquial by the Gerrer family. This seems to be directly related to the amount of cultural inter-face that each family has with their non-Haredi surroundings. Of the three families, all of the girls study, or will study, English at school, whereas only in the Habad family, which has chosen to give their children a more *Hardal* edu-cation for professional reasons, do both boys and girls study a foreign language. This gender difference is driven by an economic factor: girls who are expected to support their husbands study English, as they expect it to be of help in their professional future. While economics weighs heavily on the Habad family's de-cision regarding their children's schooling, their choices are equally influenced by the Habad focus on outreach: several of the children may ultimately serve as emissaries, which necessitates a knowledge of languages.

None of the children in any of the families speaks Yiddish, not even when one parent is fluent in that language. Only the boys in the Gerrer family will be exposed to Yiddish during their studies, although if the Habad family's sons study abroad, they, too, might be exposed to that language. The girls in the Gerrer family may also study Yiddish in school, but as a foreign language and not as the language of instruction. These groups consider Yiddish to be both a quasisacred language and a means of inter-Haredi suprageographical commu-nication. Although there are Habad, Gerrer, and even older Mitnagdic families that speak Yiddish at home, it does not appear at present that Yiddish will be-come the separatist linguistic characteristic of these sects, at least in Israel.

Literacy in the Haredi world is an important point of note. In the families I observed, all children over the age of five are literate in at least one language. Boys over the age of six acquire literacy in Loshon Kodesh and Aramaic, deter-mined by their age and level of study, and are also literate in Ivrit. Girls acquire literacy in Ivrit and Loshon Kodesh with a low proportion of Aramaic, and later in English, at least to a certain degree. With the exception of the boys in the A family, boys receive no instruction in English literacy and are taught lit-eracy in Ivrit literacy only to a limited degree. As I will show in the next chap-ter, in almost all Haredi schools lessons in Ivrit grammar are taught to boys in elementary school only, as the local vernacular is not considered a pivotal sub-ject of study or a necessary one for their future as Torah scholars. This is a practice found among Haredim throughout the world vis-à-vis boys formally studying the local vernacular (Fader 2001).

In her study of the sexual politics of Hebrew and Yiddish, Seidman (1997) explores the historical and literary roots of the cultural concept that Hebrew was a masculine language and Yiddish, a feminine tongue. Discussing the psy-chological backdrop of Hebrew-Yiddish bilingualism, linked with family roles and structures, she notes how in the pre-Holocaust world of religious Jews, Yiddish held an inferior status as the language of women while Loshon Kodesh and Hebrew were esteemed as masculine languages of worth. Even after the growth of Yiddishist ideology, it was Hebrew that held a position of institutional power in the Jewish world, despite the Yiddishist claim that such power did not in any way reflect objective cultural worth.

Here we note the opposite phenomenon. In two of the three Ashkenazi families, Yiddish is not the *mame loshen*—the "mother tongue"—but the father's tongue, forsaken in the family setting in favor of the mother's mother tongue, Ivrit. In fact, it is only upon reaching the totally male setting of the higher yeshiva that the boys will be initiated into the secrets of what was once considered a feminine language, Yiddish. In less than half a century, the cultural changes wrought by the physical decimation and demographic displacement of the Jewish world appear to have turned linguistic feminine into masculine, making Yiddish (a language to which certain groups of Haredi women have little access) a linguistic vehicle of male superiority. This process of linguistic role-switching is but an echo of a larger phenomenon of role-switching in the postwar Haredi world, best reflected in the cultural and economic spheres. While men, remaining in the world of Torah, will usually be conversant in Loshon Kodesh, Aramaic, and possibly Yiddish, women, having taken on the role of economic provider, are therefore exposed to Ivrit grammar lessons and even foreign language study in order to better support their family.

All of the children in the three families study in Ivrit and Loshon Kodesh. However, whereas the boys will learn Aramaic in depth for their Talmudic studies, the girls, who are not required to study Talmud, will only learn a few basic Aramaic terms as part of their studies in *Mishna* (Oral Law). None of the children has studied the languages in which their foreign-born parents communicate with their own parents, and they therefore speak to their grandparents in "easy" Ivrit. This phenomenon is common in much of Israel society, a society of immigrants.

A major difference between the various families is the extent of their interface with cultural vehicles of language and with non-Haredi culture, something that affects both the frequency of colloquialisms in their Ivrit and their attitude to foreign languages. In spite of the fact that in all three families the father is fluent in at least two languages, in two of them there is no attempt to teach the boys a language other than Ivrit. In two of the families the boys do not exhibit any desire to study an additional language, even when it would assist them in communicating with their grandparents. It is interesting to note that in each of the families examined the parents are fluent in a greater number of languages than are the children, and the grandparents speak (or spoke) a greater number of languages than do the parents. This linguistic pyramid appears, in part, to be a result of the geographical displacement that took place in the Jewish world during the twentieth century. It is also the result of the still growing cultural segregation that has characterized the Haredi world since the middle of that century. In the Habad family, where the goal of outreach nature predisposes members favorable toward foreign languages, the children of both sexes exhibit a desire to study the languages they assume will be necessary for their future activities in that sect.

In her study of language use in two Appalachian communities, Heath (1983) notes the significance of the gender and generational hierarchy evidencing itself in most of the families she observed: "the old know more than the young; men know more than women; and in case of a difference in views, the world of the old and the male holds." A similar hierarchy governs the patriarchal, authoritarian Haredi world. Heath notes that it is the woman, the mother, to whom fathers defer to in household practice, even if lip service is granted to the concept of male authoritarianism. Here, too, we see how in all three families the language chosen for daily speech within the family corresponds to the mother's mother tongue, how the fact that it was the local vernacular was not the sole determinant of that choice. In the B family the father would have preferred to speak Yiddish to his children; however, he acquiesced to his wife's desire to speak her mother tongue at home. This, again, may show how *de jure* patriarchal gender hierarchy, prevalent in the general cultural climate of a group, is often in abeyance within the family setting. Another explanation is the dichotomy between private and public space, the former being traditionally considered a female domain, and thus under the mother's authority, and the latter a male domain, and thus ruled by the father. As we will see in the next chapter, educational frameworks—a bridge between private sphere and public domain—are usually under male domination. This is true not only for boys' yeshivot, but also for those establishments that are solely dedicated to girls' education.

Public Domain: The Haredi Community

The linguistic landscape is an important marker of the relative power and status of linguistic communities inhabiting a particular territory. Billboards, street signs, commercial signs, and place names are all indicators of linguistic territory, delineating the geographical perimeters of a given language community. Government acceptance of these cultural/geographical distinctions is usually indicated by the use of a specific language on street signs, or its appearance on signs appearing on government buildings, conveying the expectation that one can be served in the in-group language within this establishment (Landry and Bourhis 1997). Commonly, the language (or even choice of words) appearing on commercial signs, posters, placards, and other unofficial forms of advertising is discordant with the language profile of official signs, communicating the multilingual ethnic identity of a particular neighborhood (Bourhis 1984b).

Language territories are rarely linguistically homogeneous (Bourhis 1992). As a result, it is possible to find neighborhoods where commercial signs or posters bearing different in-group languages or expressions appear side by side, in neighboring stores or on adjacent walls. In Israel, this is true in many, if not most Haredi communities whose linguistic landscape is a reflection of the various sects living in the area.

In order to examine the language used in the Haredi community, I explored the linguistic landscape of five Haredi neighborhoods throughout Israel. Three of the areas I chose have a high predominance of one sect (in Kfar Habad, Habad; in Arad, Gur; in Pardes Katz, Sefaradi Haredi). The other two neighborhoods— those in the center of Jerusalem and Bnai Brak—have a mixed Haredi population. Even in these two areas it is sometimes possible to identify a particular sign or poster as belonging to a specific Haredi sect. In addition, in three of the neighborhoods I observed the linguistic landscape accompanied by members of the families that are profiled in the previous section. Thus, I was able to note both audio as well as visual components of the Haredi community and had access to an insider's view of the linguistic dynamics evidencing itself in the Haredi public domain.

The first variable determining the linguistic landscape of a particular area was the language of its commercial signs or enterprises. In all of the areas which I explored it was difficult to determine which sect a store catered to by the language of its commercial signs. Most of the store names were written in Hebrew orthography, and the few that were not were written in English. Over a quarter of the stores in each area, and particularly the clothing emporiums, had names taken from non-Jewish languages ("Fancy" women's clothing store; "New Style" bedclothes; "Sensation" lingerie). Of these, a third were written solely in Hebrew orthography, another third had names written exclusively in English ("Designer Coat Experience"; "Kids-stop"), and the final third had names listed in Hebrew and English (*Bigdei Herayon Yokrati'im*—"Exclusive Maternity Wear"; *Sterling Senter*—"Sterling Center [Silver]"). This pattern largely prevailed among the five neighborhoods that provided my data on non-Hebrew store names, and even on the use of non-Hebrew orthography. This tends to support the claim that a global commercial culture exists in a similar form throughout Israel, affecting Haredim and non-Haredim alike. I also noted the same type of mistakes in transliterations from English (a Senior Citizens Home cares for patients suffering from *Halzheimers* instead of "Alzheimers" on its sign) and English orthography ("Motheres") that are commonly seen on signs throughout Israel.

One difference between these and non-Haredi stores was the absence of provocative names, logos, and women's pictures on store signs, including those for women's apparel. None of the stores that I observed had signs written in Yiddish, one of the primary means of identifying a Haredi store of almost any sect outside of Israel. In Israel, Yiddish language signs are found primarily in neighborhoods such as Mea Shearim in Jerusalem or the Belz and Vizhnitz Hassidic areas of Bnai Brak, where the commercial district caters to large numbers of primarily Yiddish-speaking Haredim.

Another way to chart this phenomenon in the Haredi world is to peruse the Haredi shopping guides that have become popular during the past few years, such as *Business Kehalacha* (Business According to Jewish Law) or the *Lainyan Haharedi* [Haredi Matters] *Shopping Catalogue*. A recent issue of *Business Kehalacha* (no. 17, 3 Nov. 2000) had advertisements for thirty four stores in the center of Jerusalem that cater to Haredim. Nine of the stores had non-Hebrew names ("Super Shopping," "Budget," "Pizza City," etc.), and in six of these advertisements the store name appeared in English orthography only with an explanation ("women's clothing emporium," "grocery store with discounts for Haredim") appearing underneath in Ivrit. Five stores advertised the name of the business in both English and *Ivrit*. A spring-summer 2001 issue of *Lainyan*

Haredi Shopping Catalogue, also from Jerusalem, ran advertisements for 144 stores and institutions catering to Haredim in Jerusalem and Bnai Brak. Twenty-one of the stores, educational institutions, or senior citizens' homes in the ads had non-Hebrew names ("American Hats," "First Class," "New York Delights," "My Chocolates"), and twenty-six of the stores or institutions advertised themselves using both Ivrit and English. One interesting advertisement appearing in Ivrit offered the services of a "Hassidish" Yiddish-speaking Haredi speech therapist who had worked in the U.S.A. with American children with speech problems, in other words, an advertisement in Ivrit for a Yiddish-speaking therapist with experience in an English-speaking country. Although it is doubtful that this ad was directed at either of the Hassidic communities upon which I focus, whose primary language in Israel is Ivrit, it is interesting to note its triglossic nature, characteristic of the Haredi world.

The evolution of the global informational mode of development, with its changing interaction between technology, semantics, and organizational structures, is known to have affected much of modern society. From worldwide systemic changes such as the restructuring of capitalism to the social transformations, resulting from better communications between continents, the global effect has touched many, if not most, facets of life in the Western world (Castells 1989). My findings regarding the names of Haredi stores and institutions support the supposition that a global consumer culture has made inroads into Haredi life, influencing marketing techniques that include choosing what appear to be attractive store names. Just as general Israeli society often appears to prefer stores with non-Israeli names, which impart a cosmopolitan flavor or the impression of the better quality that is expected from imported goods, Haredi society seems to have adopted the technique of deploying foreign names in its economic life.

A second variable determining the linguistic landscape consists of the signs posted on storefronts, placards, and wall posters. This is a central means of communication in the Haredi world that eschews television and often radio, and does not read a daily paper, even one of the Haredi variety. Unlike store names, which in the Ivrit-speaking Haredi world appear to follow an almost set pattern, placards and wall posters provide more insight into the language patterns prevalent within a particular sect. Recent posters appearing in Kfar Habad and on the outskirts of Bnai Brak (Habad wall posters rarely survive the Haredi infighting of central Bnai Brak and are usually torn down within a short time) announced a religious gathering, using a term (*Hitva'adut*) particular to Habad. Anyone familiar with Haredi terminology would be able to identify the sect towhich that particular poster belonged, even before noting the corner of the poster, which announced under whose auspices the gathering was being organized. Other posters found in Kfar Habad were of a general nature, announcing a dry goods sale in the local department store and various foods on sale at the local market. Such posters had no specific Habad nature and could have been found in any Haredi neighborhood in Israel.

Mitnagdic wall posters and store signs announcing lectures and gatherings taking place in the month of Elul also followed an identifiable formula, speaking of "raising" Torah knowledge, and for women, being more stringent in terms of modesty and refraining from gossip. Passing one of these signs with her family, the C mother stopped and talked to one of her contemporaries, making plans to attend a women's lecture to raise their level of *hakpada* (stringency). Here there was no talk of *lehit'hazek* (becoming stronger), a term that would rarely be used among Mitnagdim even to discuss changing one's orientation from lax to more stringent. The difference in terms is an indicator of the sociological composition and religious dynamics of each group. While the Sefaradi Haredi world is characterized by the religious returnee phenomenon, it is rare to see this trend among Mitnagdic society. Instead, Mitnagdim, who see themselves as the educational elite of the Haredi world, speak of improving their "learning," in other words, raising their level of Torah study.

As for the Gerrer linguistic landscape, with the exception of posters plastered on walls near the Gerrer *Beit Medrash* in Jerusalem inviting people to a Gerrer convocation, and two similar wall placards found near the Gerrer yeshiva in Arad announcing the same event, I saw no posters that were identifiably directed at the Gerrer sect. All of the posters in the neighborhood were of a general Haredi nature, offering services or announcing lectures and *shiurim* for the general public.

One of the common attributes of the many Haredi posters announcing lectures, speeches, and *shiurim* is a tendency exaggerate in descriptions of rabbis and speakers. Although each of the sects that I examined had its own favored terminology, the phenomenon is common to all four sects that I examined. Instead of a poster proclaiming "the esteemed Rabbi," a poster will instead speak of "the holy Rabbi, exalted in Torah, the light of the generation and the minister of Torah" when referring to Shas leader, R. Ovadia Yosef or of "the exalted leader of a generation, our Holy *Admor*," when announcing the Gerrer rebbe. This tendency toward hyperbole is not a general characteristic of religious sects throughout the world but one specific to Haredi life. Punctuating the Haredi world in general, it is expressed in everything from descriptions of household goods ("a bedroom set fit for a king and queen") to rabbinical figures (Munchick and Kantor 2000).

A final means of exploring the visual linguistic landscape is the examination of graffiti. In their study of linguistic landscape and ethnolinguistic vitality, Landry and Bourhis (1997) describe how graffiti can indicate the desire to replace a majority language with subordinated one. Graffiti are also used to express personal thought in a public setting or to unofficially place individual or group demands in the public eye. Here I have examined a narrow sample of graffiti, those appearing in areas of religious practice frequented by Haredim.

One type of Haredi graffiti was that located on the walls adjacent to graves of zaddikim, consists of requests for succor, assistance with children or matrimonial difficulties, and the like. One grave frequented by many different groups of Haredim is that of Rabbi Meir Ba'al Ha-nes, a second-century C.E. Palestinian scholar. His grave outside of Tiberias, which is now enclosed in an ornate building, has traditionally been a place of worship for many penitents and those seekers of physical, financial, or spiritual aid. In recent years it has become customary for groups of Haredi Jews—both men and women, Ashkenazi and Sefaradi, Hassidic and Mitnagdic—to frequent his grave during the month of Elul, and at various other occasions. Screened off into men's and women's areas of prayer, the walls of the graveside upon which one finds the invocation traditionally recited by Jews in need of urgent help—*Anenu Eloha D'Meir Aneuni* (Answer us, Lord of Meir, Answer us)—are covered with prayers and supplications written by those frequenting the site. I visited the grave in the late spring and early summer of 2001, noting "the writing on the wall." While the men's section was clean of graffiti, possibly due to the fact that the men visiting the grave usually spent their time immersed in prayer, the walls of the women's section were covered with notations. Furthermore, folded slips of paper containing requests protruded from almost every available crack, including the space behind the ancient-looking wall fan located high above the women's heads. While I considered it an invasion of privacy to unfold any of these papers, the graffiti was open to all to read.

Being aware of the codes of different Haredi groups and the ethnic origin of various names, it was possible to determine to which sect the petitioners belonged from the language used in some of the requests. From a random sampling of the requests on the wall it appears that most were written by Sefaradi Haredim (and Sefaradim in general) and were supplications for health and livelihood. *Briut Veparnasa avur Saba Sabbag, amen* (Health and livelihood for grandfather Sabbag, amen) was typical of the requests that included Sefaradi names. In the graffiti that bore Ashkenazi names, the two requests appearing most often were for assistance in studying (*yigdal baTorah*, "may he grow in Torah study") and in finding a life partner. In three cases of Ashkenazi Haredim looking for their future mate I identified names that are traditional in the Gerrer community—Simcha Bunim and Itche (Yitzhak) Meir—both names of former Gerrer rebbes. In general, the requests penned by those with Sefaradi names held a paucity of religious expressions, compared to those bearing Ashkenazi names.

In vivid contrast to the plethora of pleas written on the inner walls of the structure, no graffiti whatsoever were seen outside the enclosure. Two additional graves of *Zaddikim* in the area have no such graffiti, either inside or outside the structures in which the graves are housed, or on their outer walls. These are the graves of Maimonides and Rabbi Akiva, which are frequented by Haredim from all over the country, who make pilgrimages to the area. Since 1999 Maimonides' grave has been divided into men's and women's sections by a cloth that hangs over the top of the rounded grave, separating it into two halves. This is a cultural indication of the radicalization in Israeli Orthodox life, which was once a revolutionary Zionist movement dedicated to moderation, and now takes its cues from Haredi society.

It is difficult to base linguistic conclusions solely on such graffiti, primarily because it is impossible to conclusively identify the writers, even if their basic ethnic grouping can be determined. One must also keep in mind that in recent years these graves have been visited by growing numbers of modern religious and traditional Jews, in addition to the Haredi supplicants. Another difficulty is gauging the influence of the time factor; the only certain knowledge is that the older inscriptions are more likely to have come from Haredi women than from the barely traditional groups that have begun frequenting these sites only in the past year or two. Nevertheless, the language and topics of the requests are indicative of two broad differences between Sefaradi and Ashkenazi Haredim. The first difference is the paucity of religious language in the requests containing Eastern names. This corresponds to the returnee phenomenon among this group, which brings to the site large numbers of traditional and newly religious women, most of whom still uninitiated in the language of Haredi life. A second difference is the type of request that is made. Whereas the Sefaradi request aid in daily matters such as health and livelihood, the Ashkenazi requests are for strengthening Torah study and finding a mate. These wishes reflect the social, religious, and economic differences between the groups, where many, if not most of the men in the former are breadwinners, while a large number of men in the latter are full-time Torah scholars.

When I discussed this phenomenon with members of the families that I observed, the women of the C family stated that they had recently participated in such a pilgrimage themselves. When asked about the graffiti on the walls adjacent to the grave, Mrs. C replied that while both traditional and newly religious Sefaradi Haredi women would engage in such practices, it is much rarer to find a Mitnagdic woman today who would openly pen her requests on the wall next to the tomb. Neither Mrs. A nor Mrs. B has participated in such a pilgrimage, although Mrs. B is aware of women in the Gerrer community who have done so. In the Habad community supplicants fax their messages, which then are placed at the grave of the seventh rebbe in New York.

Spoken Language in the Public Domain

My final observations of the Haredi public domain were gleaned in public settings: on the street, at work, at study, or at prayer. As in my fieldwork among Haredi families, the period of observation spanned six months during the spring and summer of 2001. Observing Haredi men and women making their purchases in some of the aforementioned stores, or standing with a group of Haredi men discussing matters after prayer, it was difficult to determine from their speech what sect they belonged to. Almost all kept to the same formulaic responses (for example, using the phrase *kol tuv*, "all the best," instead of *shalom* for goodbye) (Helmreich 1982) and refrained from using immodest language. Instead it was their clothing that indicated their background. On the broadest level, it was easier to distinguish Ashkenazi Haredim from Sefaradi Haredim: however, that was more a matter of attire, coloring, and accent than of content of speech. Newly religious Haredim, both men and women, were more likely to continuously pepper their speech with the terms *baruch Hashem* (praise the Lord) and *be'ezrat Hashem* (with the Lord's help) than were veteran Haredim. Veteran Ashkenazi Haredim were more likely to insert Yiddish expressions into their speech then were newly religious Ashkenazi Haredim (like those in

Habad). Gerrer Hassidim were more likely to use Yiddish in study than any of the other groups I observed, while Sefaradi Haredim, even those who had studied in Mitnagdic yeshivot, rarely, if ever, used a Yiddish word of any kind. The Haredim I observed confirmed my findings regarding their ethnic and sectoral classification.

Members of all groups on the street or at work (where I observed the interactions experienced by both men and women from the families described herein) were heard using certain foreign words that have made their way into Ivrit, and certain slang phrases such as *balagan* (mess). On more than one occasion, two of the women (who later asked not to be identified), were heard using the slang expression *sheyelech kibinimat,* loosely translated as "he should go to hell."

The various places of worship and study are hotbeds of linguistic activity. Here too, formulaic expressions often take the place of flowing speech. In the study halls (Batei Medrash), as the material being covered is the same throughout most of the Haredi world, the vocabulary used is similar, merging Loshon Kodesh with a high proportion of Aramaic with the use of an additional basic language—either Ivrit or, in the case of Gur, Yiddish. The language used in Haredi educational institutions will be explored in greater depth in the next chapter. As for places of worship, all Haredi (and Orthodox) worship takes place in Loshon Kodesh with a certain proportion of Aramaic. However, the separate men's and women's shiurim—religious lessons—provide us with an additional vista in which to examine language praxis. Lectures on moral and religious topics are common social events in the Haredi world. Located in the twilight zone between public domain and educational frameworks, they provide a society devoid of frivolous entertainment with the opportunity to attend a social gathering with a religious-educational purpose, an act earning both a communal and a theological seal of approval.

All of the shiurim for men, which I attended, and women (from which I received recordings and observations consisted of lectures delivered in Bnai Brak, Kfar Habad, and Jerusalem during the spring and summer of 2001. All were delivered in Ivrit interspersed with Loshon Kodesh with a higher (for men) or lower (for women) proportion of Aramaic, similar to those lessons in yeshivot and kollelim of the four sects I have targeted. The shiurim delivered by lecturers speaking mostly to a newly religious public have the greatest number of colloquialisms. Thus, in deference to the fair number of *hozrim betshuva* in the audience, the Habad lectures were delivered in a very colloquial Ivrit, which included a number of slang expressions, such as *tshupar* (a prize) and even non-Ivrit words such as "champion." Meanwhile, in the Sefaradi Haredi shiurim both lexicon and phonology were often archaic, either consciously or unconsciously emulating the style used by R. Ovadia Yosef in his Saturday night sermons.

The Mitnagdic shiurim and those of Gur were delivered in less colloquial Ivrit, with more of an emphasis placed on Loshon Kodesh with a high proportion of Aramaic. The Ivrit spoken among themselves by all the men that I observed was virtually indistinguishable from that spoken in non-Haredi Israeli society. The only phrases missing were those of a questionable moral nature, as one of the major precepts of Haredi life of all sects is what is known as *lashon nekiya* (clean language).

In the Haredi world, women's shiurim are a major venue for social contact outside of the family. In all four sects that I have focused on, all women's shiurim were delivered in Ivrit, with only a select interspersing of Loshon Kodesh and only the occasional Aramaic word of the type that is part of daily Haredi speech. The women's shiurim of Habad, geared in part to the newly religious or those who are making their first steps toward religious life, were delivered in even more colloquial Ivrit than those of Gur and the Mitnagdim.

In general it appears that in comparison with the shiurim for men, those geared to women, even in the same sect, often utilize more simple language. This reflects the traditional Haredi attitude to women's study in the Haredi world, as documented by Friedman (1995, 1999) and Bar-On (1999): women are permitted to study on a "need-to-know" basis. One of the reasons for Haredi women's acceptance of this attitude, expressed (among other ways) in their limited access to sacred texts, is the belief that men's and women's roles and prestige are complementary to each other. While men garner prestige through religious study, women negotiate the public extensions of the domestic sphere and often support the family (Fader 2001). Consequently, their basic linguistic needs differ and are accomodated in frameworks designed for each of the sexes.

Both before and after these shiurim, the women spoke to each other in colloquial Ivrit. However, it is interesting to note that the modest tones documented by Uriah (1996) in her study of Haredi girls' speech, audible in close geographical and chronological proximity to the shiur, disappeared soon after. Lingering on the steps or walking homeward, one could observe the women speaking among themselves in louder tones, and occasionally even using a slang phrase that might have been unthinkable earlier, in the presence of the rabbi or *Rebbetzin* delivering the talk.

Studies of gender and language competency have shown that language choice practices are a site for reaffirming separate gendered realms of authority. The language used in men's and women's shiurim underscores the differences between men's and women's society in the Haredi world. Yet at the same time, the language that Haredi men and women in these sects use before and after the shiurim accentuates the fact that in adult daily life, there is little difference between the language used in men's society outside of Torah study, and that used in women's society. Any attempts to create a gendered language community with different language competency for the two sexes take place during the years of study, which for a large number of Haredi men may last through their third or even fourth decade. The educational frameworks that encourage the formation of these gendered linguistic communities are spotlighted in the next chapter.

Conclusions

The family is the primary framework for language socialization, socializing children through the use of language as well as socializing them to use language

(Schieffelin and Ochs 1986). The language community is a natural extention of the family whose dimensions enable growth in ethnolinguistic vitality, affording it control of language in private and even public institutions. This institutional control is the dimension of vitality *par excellence* available to ethnolinguistic groups wishing to maintain and assert their position as distinctive collective cultural entities within the intergroup structure (Sachdev and Bourhis 1991; Skutnabb-Kangas and Cummings 1988). In the case of subordinate ethnolinguistic groups in particular, family and community are expected to complement and support each other in the maintenance and furtherance of a linguistic, and thus cultural, agenda.

Friedman (1991) claims that Jewish religious society was the first to offer a family-type community in the modern world. Further developed by Haredim after the Second World War, this family-community model served as a framework in which children were resocialized, in terms of belief and praxis, in a more radical religious direction than their parents. As a result, although technologically more advanced than their parents, the younger generation of Haredim had, in many cases, more limited knowledge of and exposure to the secular culture that could have served as a linguistic vehicle. In spite of the suprageographical nature of the modern Haredi world, the demographic changes taking place since the Second World War have narrowed the natural scope of language knowledge, use, and literacy. In most cases the grandparents' generation (and in certain cases, as seen in the families I examined, even the parents' generation) were part of an immigrant culture and society, affording their members a broader natural exposure to a number of foreign languages. In contrast, Haredi children in Israel today have little or no natural exposure to foreign languages.

In addition, Ivrit's encroachment on the territory of daily speech in Ashkenazi Haredi society has relegated Yiddish—once a language of the Jewish masses—to an elite role as a language of higher Torah study (Ben-Rafael 1998). As a result of these factors, fewer languages are now heard in both the Haredi family and the Haredi community than were spoken, or at least understood, a generation ago. This parallels developments in much of post-immigration Israeli society. However, the unusually strong symbiosis between family and community in the Haredi world, ensuring a synchronization of goals between the two, limits the scope of outside linguistic influences to an unusual degree. The exceptions are certain English words that have entered Haredi life via Haredim immigrating to Israel from English-speaking backgrounds. As we will see in the next chapter, this symbiosis is supported by the seamless introduction of young Haredim into the successive educational frameworks, which is a pivotal factor in language management that both influences and supports the spread of Ivrit and the family-community symbiosis.

This interconnection of various elements in the Haredi world on the public level is mirrored on the private level as well, thus reinforcing cultural and linguistic norms. In the cases studied here, the continuous communal intertwining of Haredi society is exemplified by the social, neighborhood, educational, and even family connections between the families which I chose for observations, of which I had been almost completely unaware until commencing my research.

What sound like the usual convolutions of *shtetl* life become slightly more remarkable when one recalls that these families are from different sects, backgrounds, and even countries of origin. It is even more interesting to note that while the combined grandparents' generation in these families knew over a dozen languages and the parents know a total of nine languages, the children know only three languages with the future possibility of four languages for boys who will be exposed to Yiddish at yeshiva when they are older. Of these four, only three are spoken languages, and of these three, only one language is ultimately common to the men and women—Ivrit. In two of the families, only the women will study English, allowed as a tool in order to better facilitate the gendered equations of "woman equals breadwinner," providing short-term sustenance for the family in this world, and "man equals Torah scholar," providing long-term sustenance for the family in the world to come. While a number of scholars have expressed the opinion that Haredi women, being more exposed to secular language and culture, will ultimately act as the Haredi world's agents of socialization into modern society (El-Or 1994; Friedman 1995, 1991; Parush 2001), a different process appears to be developing. Although for the most part Haredi women have greater exposure in school to non-Jewish languages than do Haredi men, the extremist religious-cultural policies and educational constraints in force at many of the Haredi girls' educational establishments today have created a sharp line of demarcation between language and culture, permitting the first while forbidding the latter. This process will be examined in greater detail in the next chapter. Consequently, while Haredi women at work are at times exposed to Israeli culture, colloquial Ivrit, and slang expressions that they may often use at work themselves, in many cases these influences are left behind at the gates of the community or at the door of the home. Thus, not only are these Haredi women not agents of socialization for their families, but by accepting and internalizing the radical Haredi lifestyle of large families, and by removing cultural agents of modernization such as the radio and newspapers, they become the mainstay of Haredi society's continued cultural separatism (Golan 2000).

Within the family, on the street, and at work in the sects I have targeted, Haredi men, women, boys, and girls appear to coalesce into a single basic linguistic and cultural form. The differences between the sexes, and the sects, will become more apparent in the next chapter, where I examine the Haredi educational frameworks that are the basic institutional "greenhouses" fostering future generations of "men's society" and "women's society" in the Haredi world.

6

EDUCATIONAL FRAMEWORKS

In his study of Eastern European Jewish literature of the early modern era, Ya'akov Elboim (1990) explores the process by which a population, once open to outward influences, begins to close itself off to its surroundings. Until the seventeenth century, Eastern European Jews were familiar with local tongues and often even literate in non-Jewish languages (Maczak 1990). As part of a separation process that reached its height during the Jewish Enlightenment, observant Jews in Poland and Russia entrenched themselves in a world delimited by Loshon Kodesh and Yiddish, cutting themselves off from their surroundings in every sphere except the economic (Parush 1995). By the early twentieth century it was a rare observant Jew in Eastern Europe who had a full command—including literacy—of any non-Jewish language (Weinryb 1972).

My late father-in-law, who was a pupil in a Galician *Heder* before the First World War, liked to recall how the *melamed* (teacher) would chastise him for his passion for stamp collecting. Catching him at age ten running the *Heder's* "black market" in foreign stamps, the *melamed* tried to reason with him by pointed out that a good Jewish boy had no need for such activities as everything he would ever want could be found in the Torah. "One day I want to go and see these places," my father-in-law answered to the *melamed's* dismay, pointing to stamps from Argentina and the United States. "But how will you be able to talk to the Jews there?" answered the *melamed*, "I've heard that in America even in Heder boys learn in English and not in Yiddish like good Jews. Here we never study *goyish* [literally: the gentile language] and you'll learn whatever you need to know of it when it's time to go to work."

The attitude expressed by this teacher was the prevalent one among a large part of Eastern European Orthodox Jewry before the First World War (Corrsin 1990). Between the wars the acculturation process among Polish Jewry led certain young observant Jews to a knowledge of, and at times fluency in, the local vernacular (Weinryb 1972). While Torah learning for boys continued to be conducted in Yiddish and Loshon Kodesh, the newly founded Beis Ya'akov girls' school system initially began teaching in Polish, which had become the language spoken by large numbers of observant girls during the early 1920s (Weissman 1976; 1995). Only at a later stage was Yiddish reintroduced into the curriculum in an attempt to resocialize the young Jewish women into what the Haredi educators felt should have been their native tongue (Baumel and Schacter 1992).

The issue of educational institutions in their capacity as a framework for language socialization is implicit in a number of studies on education and language policy. In her study of two communities in the Carolinas, Heath (1983) shows how education is a framework for imparting information and skills to the younger generation as well as a central agent in their process of socialization. Using both written and oral discourse (known as "stories") in the primary grades, children learn a different taxonomy and new definitions of terms than they know from other contexts. The vocabulary and choice of language employed in the educational system socialize the young pupils to what is expected of them in broader society, in terms of verbal skills and literacy.

In his study of language policy in schools, Corson (1990) shows how education frameworks act as both mirrors of local linguistic tensions and agents of government or local language policy. In ethnic or religious communities the educational framework is often not an agent that links the familiar with the unfamiliar, but rather an extension of the community in question, a vehicle for strengthening ethnic heritage and religious beliefs by expanding the pupil's knowledge of these fields. As Corson (1999) shows in a later study, information taught or language used in these frameworks can also serve as a means of resocializing children from a society beset by outside influences into a community imbued with ethnic pride, religious beliefs, and native language. Apart from being the extension of a community, these educational frameworks are themselves forces that can strengthen and mold the community in turn, causing a subtle shift in one direction or another.

Haredi educational frameworks use various forms of overt and covert language management in order to shape the language ideology that I have already discussed into concrete language practice and thus, cultural expression. In order to explore this dynamic I examined the language taught and heard in various Haredi educational institutions at the primary and secondary level, and in post–high school frameworks. Of these, eighteen were male educational establishments and twenty were female educational frameworks, study in the Haredi world being sexually segregated. In speaking to administrators, teachers, and pupils I utilized the dual techniques of interviews and observation (Berdie 1974; Belson 1981; Briggs 1986; Foddy 1993; Arksey 1999; Holleman 2000), focusing first on a subject's background and social/linguistic norms and then on language policy as expressed in the relevant educational establishment.

My observations of language policy in Haredi educational frameworks were structured according to a four-tiered system corresponding to the four levels of language use in school-based settings noted by Heath (1983) and Corson (1990, 1999). The first is that of language management: the official language policy of the school in question. This includes the choice of the primary teaching language, teaching of grammar in the primary language, teaching of foreign languages, and official school attitude towards other languages spoken by pupils at home. The second level of use is an outgrowth of language management, although it also verges upon language practice: the language spoken by teachers to pupils within the school and the language in which students answer teachers. The third is more heavily grounded in language practice than it is in management: the language which the teachers in school speak among themselves. The fourth is most heavily based in the realm of practice: the language that the pupils in a school speak among themselves in the classroom, during recess, in the schoolyard, or when waiting for the school buses.

Although I questioned administrators and teachers to glean information about school language policy, my primary focus was the pupils in each establishment, whom I observed both in and out of the classroom, throughout their studies, and at play during recess. Sometimes the most enlightening information was collected outdoors, for example, by listening to a group of elementary school level yeshiva students outside their school in Arad, questioning a group of Arad Beit Ya'akov girls waiting for their bus pick-up, or in listening to a group of Kfar Habad children at play in their school courtyard. Here I learned much about the transition from official school language policy to that practiced in the Haredi community, and noted the effect that one framework has upon the other. In all, I was able to observe over 3,000 Haredi pupils of the four sects studied here, most of whom were enrolled in educational institutions ranging from kindergarten to high school.[1] As an aside one should note that the Israeli secular and modern religious school system is similar to the American one, encompassing K through grade 12 and corresponding to ages 5–18. The Israeli school system is compulsory until age 16 and is paid for by the government until age 18. The same holds true for Haredi schools receiving government aid. Tuition in these schools is usually not paid by the parents with the exception of the elite nationalist-Haredi (Hardal) schools such as Horev which will be mentioned further on.

As a first step to understanding the Haredi school system, let us examine their educational terminology. Haredi boys' elementary-level schooling in Israel takes place in a heder (literally: room), also pronounced *haider,* or in a Talmud Torah (Gillis 1987). While Talmud Torah nearly always spans the first to eighth grades, heder can last either from age three until age fourteen or from first to eighth grade. Boys aged 14–18 study in what is known as a yeshiva *ketana,* which among Sefaradim is called a *metivta.* Older unmarried boys study in a yeshiva *gedola* (lit: large) or *gevoha* (lit: higher), and after marriage they attend a kollel, a framework for married yeshiva students. First to eighth grade girls, on the other hand, study in elementary school. From ninth grade on they study in a *seminar* (seminary) a high school that often offers post-secondary courses leading to a teaching degree or vocational training. Another type of post–high school framework for girls, also known as a *seminar,* is not attached to a high school and only accepts girls who have completed twelfth grade. In addition, there are tertiary-level vocational frameworks for Haredi men, usually in their mid 30s who leave kollel for financial reasons and need training to make a living. A small number of Haredi men and women enroll in religious but non-Haredi educational institutions that offer a separate Haredi program for men or women and confer a B.A. or B.Ed. These include Lipschitz College and Touro College in Jerusalem, and Bar-Ilan University in Ramat Gan.

In undertaking my observations I faced two difficulties. The first was the issue of gender—specifically, the degree to which Haredi girls, used to a sexually segregated environment, were willing to talk to a strange man. When inside a girls'classroom, I was never introduced by the teacher but was permitted to observe silently from the side of the room. Under those circumstances, I was regarded by the girls either as part of the furniture—in other words, ignored— or as a sort of educational supervisor, with respectful glances. Outside the classroom, I would station myself near the school office, the playground, or outside the school gates. Some girls were happy to talk to me, usually when they were off their school turf, but others kept a marked distance from me and could be observed only from afar. Luckily, voices carry, and girls playing at a playground or waiting for a school bus, can be clearly heard shouting to each other, even from a distance of fifty feet.

A second problem was a more general one, that of the insider-outsider phenomenon discussed earlier. In all schools I introduced myself as someone doing research on Haredi language and culture. In almost all cases the teachers, administrators, and principals, both men and women, were happy to assist me. In one case the principal even asked me directly if I was writing a dissertation on the subject, showing no surprise or reluctance to assist when I answered in the affirmative. To all it was obvious that I was an outsider; however, because I appeared to be familiar with the Haredi world they had no difficulty in providing me with the information or introductions that I needed.

The children and students I observed had greater difficulty positioning me in their frame of reference than did the adults. To all schools I came dressed in what could be considered general Haredi attire: a white shirt, dark pants, and a black (knitted) skullcap. Meanwhile, although I have a mustache, I am not bearded, as males my age tend to be in the Haredi world. Consequently, youngsters I spoke to were often unable to determine what I was—insider, or outsider. On the one hand, I could speak their language, was familiar with their codes, could pick up a volume of the Talmud and learn with them in the *Beit Medrash* (study hall). I could join with them in prayer, knew many of the melodies of their songs, and recited with them the requisite blessings over foods that I was offered. On the other hand, I was definitely not one of them, being unbearded, with a knitted (albeit black) skullcap, and an American accented Ivrit. Although girls on school territory were often reluctant to talk to me (though many were very happy to do so outside the school gates), many of the boys were quite eager to talk to me both inside their school and outside the classrooms, over and above what was necessary for this study. A similar phenomenon regarding male Haredim is noted by Helmreich (1982) in his study of the yeshiva in the United States.

Haredi Education in Israel

Haredi education in Israel predates the establishment of the state. In the middle of the nineteenth century there were numerous Heders scattered throughout the Holy Land, not organized into any educational system. Arriving in Jerusalem in 1841, R. Shmuel Salant founded a large Talmud Torah for boys that ultimately metamorphosed into the Etz Haim school system (Sourasky 1967). Additional religious school frameworks for boys were later founded throughout the area, which was then a province of the Ottoman Empire. Only after the establishment of the Agudat Yisrael political movement in Poland in 1912 did Haredi education in the area begin to develop in the direction that it would maintain until today (Bentwich 1960).

Several educational frameworks were founded by the Agudat Yisrael movement in Palestine. The first were boys' schools—Talmud Torahs and yeshivot for younger students. In 1921 the groundwork was laid in Jerusalem for the first girls' Haredi educational establishment—a Beit Ya'akov school, based on the model established in Cracow by Sarah Schenierer at the end of the First World War (Weissman 1976, 1995), combining religious study with secular subjects. The first official Beit Ya'akov school in Palestine was founded by Rabbi Meir Scharansky in 1936, and today is considered one of the more modern schools of that educational system (Bar-On 1999). Agudat Yisrael was instrumental in establishing the Hinuch Atzmai system (Scharfstein 1965), an independent Haredi educational network subsidized by government allocations that taught in Ivrit (as opposed to the Old Yishuv that taught in Yiddish) and received state recognition after the reorganization of the Israeli school system in 1953 (Tzameret 1997; Bentwich 1960). This system was opposed by anti-Zionist sects such as Satmar and Neturei Karta, which did not desire government supervision and did not accept government allocations.

Consequently, three types of Haredi schools functioned side by side under different levels of government supervision or none at all functioned side by side. Recognized unofficial (*mukar she'aino rishmi*) schools such as the non-Zionist Hinuch Atzmai taught secular studies, received allocations, and were under government supervision. Exempt (*ptor*) schools, some non-Zionist and some passively anti-Zionist in their orientation, were not under state supervision and taught very little secular studies. Unsupported anti-Zionist Haredi schools taught religious studies; their only secular studies were basic reading, writing, and arithmetic for the lower grades. The latter two categories received no government allocations until 1975 when the government decided to overlook the fact that some of the exempt schools were passively anti-Zionist and granted them all allocations, primarily in response to political and demographic changes in Israel.[2]

Originally ranging from kindergarten to seminary and housing both boys' and girls' schools, during the 1950s and 1960s the boys' high school yeshivot that were part of the Hinuch Atzmai system ceased to function; only a few high schools remained open under the supervision of the Mercaz le-Hinuch Atzmai. Today the Hinuch Atzmai system supervises primarily elementary schools, including certain Heders, Talmud Torahs, and elementary schools of the Beit Ya'akov network for girls (Sourasky 1967). In addition, there are independent Haredi boys' and girls' schools, some of which, such as the Karlin, Vizhnitz, and Belz schools, are Hassidic-affiliated.

In certain subjects, such as mathematics, geography, and Jewish history, the Hinuch Atzmai system followed a curriculum similar to that of the National Religious schools. In other subjects, for many years there was no set curriculum or coordination of the policies of the various schools in the system, although it was accepted that these schools would teach secular subjects in order to continue to qualify for government allocations. The absence of a set curriculum enabled certain schools to avoid teaching a number of subjects or to limit their teaching, for instance in the case of teaching English to boys on the elementary school level, something that even today differs from school to school. In a discussion regarding this matter, Rabbi Binyamin Schreiber, the Inspector General of Haredi Education in Israel, was adamant in insisting that English is officially taught in all Haredi schools under ministry supervision. However, he stressed, the level of English taught may differ from school to school.[3] When asked about the use of a particular curriculum, Hava Schwimmer, the English language studies coordinator of the Hinuch Atzmai schools, stated that the Hinuch Atzmai schools developed their 1988 curriculum to parallel that of the Ministry of Education from the same year, aiming to maintain similar academic standards. Prior to that time, no organized Hinuch Atzmai English curriculum had existed anywhere in Israel, and every Haredi school that taught English, Hinuch Atzmai branches included, did so from a homemade curriculum uncoordinated with other schools.[4] This situation enabled various boys' schools to limit the teaching of English—considered a superfluous subject—on the elementary level and eliminate it entirely in high school.

Three curricular possibilities are open to Haredi schools in Israel. The path of least resistance is to adopt some form of the Ministry of Education curricula for particular subjects. The second possibility is to utilize a Hinuch Atzmai curriculum where it exists. The third option is to create a unique curriculum for a particular school. As Apple (1990) and Pinar (1995, 1998) show in their studies of the curriculum as political text, not only is each curricular choice an educational statement; it also carries with it ideological, theological, political, social, cultural, and even economic implications for those who formulate and apply the curriculum, let alone for those who are its recipients.

There are very few boys' Yeshivot *ketanot* (pl. of Yeshiva *ketana*) that are under government supervision, and most offer no secular studies at all. These schools are not under the supervision of any authority connected with the Ministry of Education. An exception to the rule is the elitist *Hardal* high school for boys, Yeshivat Harav Amiel in Tel Aviv, known as "Yishuv Hahadash," or "Yishuv" for short, and attended by the sons of certain modern Haredi families. This school is a hybrid, offering a full plan of Torah study for eight hours a day in addition to three daily hours of secular subjects. Haredi education for girls on the post-elementary level includes the Beit Ya'akov high school network and the Hassidic and Mitnagdic Haredi girls' high schools. The few Haredi trade schools, such as that in Kfar Habad, are another type of post-elementary education for Haredi boys. These schools often teach secular subjects as well as Torah learning and vocational training.

The differences between the various Haredi educational systems affect the type of pedagogical supervision under which they function. There is one General Inspector for all Ashkenazi Haredi education, employed by the Ministry of Education. There is an additional General Inspector for all Sefaradi Haredi education, also employed by the Ministry of Education. Unlike the municipal and state secular and religious schools, where each subject is supervised by a Chief Inspector as well as by various regional inspectors, the Hinuch Atzmai system employes no subject inspectors, nor does it have regional inspectors. Instead, various Haredi educational networks, such as the Beit Ya'akov system, have subject coordinators at the elementary and high school levels. The same holds true for the Habad girls' network and for the boys' high schools that are not yeshivot. Ma'ayan Hahinuch Hatorani uses its own subject inspectors in addition to the chief inspectors of the Ministry of Education. Other Haredi schools, particularly the yeshivot where no secular subjects are taught, have no inspection or supervision policy whatsoever.

Habad

Thousands of schoolchildren throughout Israel study at various Habad educational institutions, boys' and girls' schools, yeshivot, and women's seminaries. Despite variations in student body, curriculum, matriculation policy, and certification, all of these institutions follow the general Habad guidelines and most prepare their student body for a future position in the outreach movement. In an official Habad publication detailing the seventh rebbe's educational goals, Habad educators emphasize that the dual purpose of a Habad education is to provide students with facts and information while educating them morally to prepare them for a suitable leadership task upon reaching adulthood (Hartman 1984). These guidelines appeared to be a central factor in understanding Habad language policy in the education sphere, as expressed in most of the nine Habad schools (six boys' and three girls') that I visited, eight in Kfar Habad and one in Arad.

In eight of the nine Habad schools I visited, the primary teaching language is Ivrit. Hebrew grammar is taught as a subject of study in all of the elementary and high schools with the exception of the Heder and the Yeshiva, neither of which teaches secular studies. The grammar curriculum followed is that of the Israeli Ministry of Education, and the grammar textbooks are similar to those used in secular schools, although contents and illustrations are edited to ensure their suitability for Habad schools. In most cases, the rabbi of Kfar Habad is the final arbiter of what may or may not appear in a textbook used in a local Habad school.[5] In other communities with Habad schools (such as Arad), either the local Habad rabbi is consulted, or the Habad schools follow the directives issued for Kfar Habad.[6] Hebrew grammar studies include the topics commonly used in elementary schools—the study of speech forms (including pronunciation, stress and emphasis, spelling), writing forms (letter shape, using dictionaries, punctuation), word forms (inflections, compounds, metaphors), phrase and sentence structure, discourse structure (Corson 1999). All these are considered basic to the intellectual development that the Habad educational system cultivates in order to gain a fuller understanding of both Torah and the teachings of Habad. Religious studies are taught in a combination of Ivrit, Loshon Kodesh, and Aramaic.

In all of the schools that I observed, including the yeshiva devoted to high school and post–secondary courses (Tomchei Temimim), teachers spoke to each other in Ivrit, at times using slang expressions such as *ata brogez iti?* (are you mad at me?)[7] Pupils in both boys' and girls' schools speak to each other in Ivrit with the exception of the foreign pupils at the Tomchei Temimin yeshiva, who study in a mixture of English and Yiddish and speak to each other in their mother tongue (English, Russian, etc.). One difference between the boys' Ivrit and that spoken by the girls is the number of colloquialisms used by the two groups. While boys tend to speak to teach other in very colloquial Ivrit with a high proportion of slang the girls tend to use fewer slang terms.[8] This generally reinforces my observations in the family sphere, where boys tended to use more Ivrit slang than did their sisters. In Habad girls' schools, as was the case in the other three Haredi groups that I examined, I did not observe linguistic phenomena such as the use of "hedges" and "tag questions" that might characterize women's and girls' speech. At the same time, I noted a few cases where it was clear that a female teacher or pupil had adopted a male language strategy in terms of pitch, vocabulary, pronunciation, assertive style in group interaction, or prosodic features more typical of men's intonations (Coates 1993). This fits the gendered nature of the Haredi world, where separate spheres of influence and behavior codes typify Haredi life while not necessarily mirroring typical gendered behavior or spheres of influence in the secular world (Friedman 1999).

All teacher-pupil communication that I observed took place in Ivrit, including at the higher yeshiva that taught in Ivrit and Loshon Kodesh, but with the exception of the Kfar Habad Heder, where in the classroom, teachers spoke to pupils in Yiddish. Outside of the classroom, they used a mixture of Yiddish and Ivrit to communicate, and the exchanges that I overheard (*Ich hob a* ["I have a"—Yiddish] *michtav* [Heb.—letter]) were characterized by code switching.[9]

The Kfar Habad Heder (grades 1–8), where no secular studies are taught, differs from all of the other Habad schools I visited in that Yiddish is used as the primary language. In the lower Heder grades (1–6) pupils are taught in Loshon Kodesh with translation into Yiddish. Upper grades (7–8) study solely in Loshon Kodesh and Aramaic, complementing the level of their Talmud studies. Although teachers in the Heder speak to their pupils in Yiddish, they speak to each other in Ivrit. Similarly, the pupils speak to each other in Ivrit, and were even overheard using slang.[10]

Yiddish was initially the teaching language at the Kfar Habad Talmud Torah, established in the early 1950s, but in the early 1980s the school switched over to Ivrit.[11] Several of the veteran teachers mentioned to me that the policy of teaching in Yiddish had already been questioned in the late 1970s at the time that a number of Habad schools throughout the world made the switch from Yiddish to the vernacular.[12] According to the school secretary, the direct impetus for this change at the Kfar Habad Talmud Torah was an incident that took place while pupils were being tested in Bible knowledge. Asked to explain the Biblical verse regarding Abraham's planting a tree in Beersheva, the pupils translated the word *vayita* (to plant) into Yiddish as *gepflanzt*. When the examiner asked the boy what the Yiddish word meant, he answered, in Ivrit *"lirkod, kmo behatuna"* (to dance, like at a wedding), confusing the term with the similar-sounding Yiddish term *getantzt* (danced). When asked what the term *getantzt* meant, the pupil gave an erroneous answer, causing the examiner and other authorities to wonder whether the system of translating Loshon Kodesh into Yiddish was not detrimental to their educational goal of Torah study. They consulted with the seventh rebbe who replied that it was more important for the children to understand Torah than to know Yiddish, and were told to switch their teaching language to the one that the children understood—Ivrit.[13]

The use of Yiddish in Israeli Habad schools is often limited to the *maimar*, a talk given by the late rebbe, which Habad boys deliver at their Bar Mitzvah both in Israel and abroad. Today, with the exception of the Heder, both boys' and girls' schools in Kfar Habad use Ivrit as the language of instruction. Torah studies take place in Ivrit and Loshon Kodesh with a very low proportion of Aramaic, since the girls do not study Talmud. All girls studying at the Beit Rivka girls' junior high school are required to take one year of Yiddish (ninth grade), which is taught as a foreign language. As Habad considers the correct form of Yiddish to be the Russian-Lithuanian dialect of the last rebbe, that is the form of Yiddish taught in the school. Yet in spite of its Russian-Lithuanian orientation, Habad Yiddish has many borrowings from Ivrit in its vocabulary, making it easier for the girls to study than other dialects of Yiddish. The girls' elementary school is interested in setting up an extracurricular Yiddish club but has not yet been able to bring this plan to fruition.[14]

These details illustrate the unique role that Yiddish plays in Habad in general and in Habad education in particular. Although the use of Yiddish in Hassidism was originally a deliberate attempt to popularize the sacred, Habad's contemporary attitude towards Yiddish regards it as a quasi-sacred language. Although it was not declared an official sacred language, Yiddish was written in Hebrew characters and was therefore considered to be a holy tongue. In the days when it was the common language of Eastern European Jews, the rebbe would give various talks in Yiddish so that women and uneducated people would understand with ease. These talks were originally printed in Yiddish (*Likutei Sichot*), again in order to enable the masses of Jews to understand them.

Today, however, we note a reverse trend. By the 1960s and 1970s, when modern-day youth no longer spoke Yiddish, Habad schools throughout the world had begun teaching in the vernacular. This phenomenon was echoed at the Habad Talmud Torah in Kfar Habad during the early 1980s. In the mean-

timeYiddish—once a form of mass communication—began to be venerated because it was the language originally used by the rebbe. The fact that the rebbe
spoke in Yiddish ultimately underlays the growing educational belief in Habad
that girls should learn Yiddish in order to read the *Sichot* in the original language—which had been chosen in the first place so that the unlearned masses
could understand what was being said! Too, Yiddish was to be used for histor-
ical/theological reasons as it was the language that had unlocked the spiritual
power of the masses in the past (Glinert 1999a). These appear to be the origins of the desire to teach Yiddish to girls in Kfar Habad, although it should be
remembered that it is only taught as a foreign language and not used as a primary teaching language.

The study of English in Habad brings us to the dual issues of the Jerusalem
herem of the late nineteenth century that forbade the teaching of foreign languages (Spolsky 1993) and the general attitude toward the study of non-Jewish
languages in Habad. During the late nineteenth century, the poverty facing the
Jewish community of Jerusalem led several Ashkenazi schools under the anti-
Zionist Old Yishuv to request rabbinical permission to teach pupils Arabic in
order to enhance their prospects for employment. Fearing that knowledge of
foreign languages would weaken the barriers of ethnic Jewish separatism, a
number of Ashkenazi Rabbis sought to prevent the teaching of foreign languages, with a *herem* which was not accepted by rabbis in Egypt and Europe.
A more recent compromise allowed language study in very small groups of two
to three pupils. Here we see how economic pragmatism forced the hand of religious or ethnic separatism, as even the *herem* that was passed ultimately did
allow the teaching of foreign languages, albeit within a circumscribed framework. Over a century later, this *herem* is still considered by some to be in effect. For example, it was cited as the main reason for not teaching English at
the Talmud Torah of Kfar Habad.[15] It is also obeyed in some of the other schools
I investigated, including some where English is taught.[16]

In a discussion I had with the organizer of a Habad educators' conference
in Israel, one of the questions in point was the attitude toward teaching non-
Jewish languages, along with other secular subjects. Here it was explained that
whereas Ivrit and Yiddish are studied in primary shcools, there is a generally
negative attitude in Habad toward teaching non-Jewish languages and secular
subjects to young children under the age of nine. After that time, the attitude
towards languages is pragmatic. English is not taught at the Heder and Talmud
Torah English is not taught because of the *herem*. Other schools that I observed
circumvented the *herem* by teaching in small groups, thus eschewing the situation forbidden by rabbis in the late nineteenth century; however, these two
Habad institutions seek no loophole thorugh which to incorporate foreign language study into the curriculum. Apart from these schools, Habad elementary
and high schools in Israel teach English according to a curriculum that basically follows that of the Israeli Ministry of Education.[17] For example, at the
Habad Trade School (for boys, grades 9–12) English classes are very heterogeneous, and instead of using textbooks pupils receive individual worksheets
geared to their language level. The school, which caters primarily to under-

privileged boys, has developed its own English texts to suit its unique student body because none of the existing textbooks could bring pupils from the level of nonreaders to a three-unit matriculation in only four years.

Haredi schools choosing to teach English have several types of teaching materials at their disosal. They can use the same textbooks as secular and National religious schools, utilize these together with those produced by the Hinuch Atzmai or Beit Ya'akov network,[18] utilize only the Hinuch Atzmai/Beit Ya'akov textbooks, or use self-produced teaching aids in combination with others or exclusively, as is done at the Kfar Habad Trade School.

The same policy is followed at the Beit Rivka elementary school, which is guided by the English curriculum of the Ministry of Education but produces its own teaching materials, which deal in part with Habad subjects. Girls at the Beit Rivka high school use a combination of the books used by secular and National-religious schools, but for the most part receive photocopied pages for English study. Most of the worksheets deal with stories of Hassidic rebbes, or stories about the various Habad rebbes. Other handouts include reading comprehension material on various topics in print and script.[19] This choice is both ideological and sectoral, as Habad schools prefer their own material, stressing Habad topics, over the material produced by the Hinuch Atzmai, which has a more general Haredi nature. Habad has also been negotiating with the book company that publishes the English textbooks for secular and National-religious schools regarding the possibility of publishing "proper" (censored) versions of some of their textbooks that might be suitable for Habad, but as of yet nothing has developed in that direction.[20]

On the post–high school level, Habad takes a positive position regarding language study, particularly in view of its outreach ideology. For that purpose some Habad Hassidim study Russian "in order to bring Jews back to the fold," in the words of one of the educators I interviewed. Similarly, study of English and other foreign languages is encouraged explicitly in order to facilitate outreach work. These lessons, encouraged by Habad, take place in small groups outside the yeshiva, either under official Habad auspices or in private settings.[21]

Non-Jewish languages other than English are taught at only one of the Habad schools thatI visited—the trade school at Kfar Habad, which taught Arabic for several years when there was a demand among the student body. At that school, most of the teachers have a BA or a B.Ed., and at least one has a Ph.D. In other Habad schools teachers are usually graduates of the Habad educational system and have a Habad teaching degree.[22] Notably, of all the Haredi groups I observed, Habad—with its outreach ideology and more open attitude towards secular education—was the most likely to employ teachers with university degrees.

The language policy evidencing itself within the Habad educational frameworks appears to work in tandem with Habad ideology, as expressed in the various speeches and writings of the Habad rebbes. It thus acts as a form of language management, instilling this ideology into Habad youth through educational methods and personal example. Two fields where this is manifest are the use of daily speech and the Habad attitude toward Jewish vernaculars and non-Jewish languages.

While one hears Ivrit, even slang, spoken among both pupils and teaching staff in the Habad educational system, one will not hear improper speech, vulgar words, or expressions incompatable with the Habad/Haredi lifestyle and norms. Teachers set an example for their students in terms of behavior, dress, language, and lifestyle, and are hired accordingly. The vehicles used to promote the study of non-Jewish languages, such as English textbooks or handouts, are similarly scrutinized to remove improper influence and shaped to include educational messages about Habad, its leaders, and its beliefs.

Habad's positive attitude to Yiddish—a special Jewish vernacular—finds expression in the Habad educational framework, as does the fact that the language is afforded a quasi-sacred status by Habad. Even though most Habad schools teach in Ivrit, the local vernacular, Yiddish has a special status in the girls' schools and is taught to all pupils, both Ashkenazi and Sefaradi. (For many years, until the development of the Shas educational system, large numbers of Sefaradi girls studied at Habad schools.) The primary language of the boys' heder, where no secular studies are taught, is Yiddish, considered to be the traditional language of Habad as well as the traditional linguistic marker of Ashkenazi Haredim throughout the world. Yiddish had, in fact, been the original language of the Talmud Torah, until it moved toward Ivrit in the early 1980s. The desire for Habad children to know Yiddish, the acceptance of the fact that most do not, and the resulting changeover to Ivrit are indicators of the high level of linguistic pragmatism in Habad that stems from its ideological component of outreach.

The same pragmatic attitude applies to the study of non-Jewish languages. In principle, Habad prefers not to introduce non-Jewish language study at an early age, believing that those years should be devoted solely to Torah study, at least for boys. Yet those schools that follow the Israeli state curriculum (all girls' schools and some boys' schools) introduce the study of English in fourth or fifth grade. Habad high schools (not yeshivot) follow the same pattern, but all of them suit the teaching materials to the Habad ideology. Habad language study for adults is viewed in a positive light, as it is considered a major outreach tool and not only a means of obtaining employment, as it is for women in other Haredi groups.

In practice, the ideology of granting Yiddish special status is influenced by the pragmatism of accepting the use of the vernacular in everyday life. At schools in the Habad sector, I noted how the local vernacular was totally accepted as the primary language for study and daily speech, even by the pupils at a Yiddish-language school, the Heder. While teachers address pupils in Yiddish in the classroom, teachers speak among themselves in Ivrit outside the classroom, as do pupils. Outside the classroom Similarly, teachers will speak to pupils outside the classroom in Ivrit interposed with Yiddish terms. However, I observed one controversy in Yiddish outside the classroom.

It is impossible to fully understand an educational language policy without examining it in its a wider social context. In his study of the community context of language policy, Fitzpatrick (1987) mentions the importance of considering the material environment in which the community's families live. This includes the parents' formal education, reading material in the home, religious orientation of families, toys in the home, television viewing habits, parental attitude to school and education, the community language environment, language attitudes of parents, and language use in the home. In spite of the variations in social context that exist within Habad, a general line of language policy runs through Habad homes and communities. Here we see how the same policy—accepting the local vernacular as the mother tongue and primary teaching language, affording a quasi-sacred status to Yiddish, and taking a generally positive attitude to the study of non-Jewish languages—is reinforced in Habad educational frameworks. At the same time, these educational frameworks are often the first institutions to introduce children from newly religious families to the world of Habad. Thus, in addition to reinforcing Habad language policy among children from veteran Habad families, they also act as an agent of linguistic and cultural socialization for the children of secular families that have recently joined Habad.

Gur

When I began my research I was warned by Haredi friends that the Gerrer sect would be the most difficult of the four groups to "crack," and that it would be hard to make inroads into their educational institutions, particularly the ones for girls. Although the Gerrer sect adheres to the same religious, social, educational, cultural, and economic principles throughout the country, the advice of one Gerrer rebbi to whom I spoke was to initially visit Gerrer schools outside of Jerusalem, particularly in the Gerrer periphery.[23] Although they follow the same educational and language patterns as the Jerusalem schools, my informant explained, their administrators and teachers would be more open to observation by a non-Gerrer academic doing language research. In fact, he stated, the major differences between Gerrer communities in Jerusalem and elsewhere are that more foreign-born Gerrer live in Jerusalem and Bnai Brak, and that more Yiddish is spoken among younger Gerrer families in Jerusalem than among any Gerrer family living elsewhere.

I therefore focused my field study on Gerrer educational institutions in Arad—a city with approximately 200 Gerrer families—and Bnai Brak, one of the centers of Haredi life in Israel, where I observed pupils in three boys' and three girls' schools. Two boys' yeshivot and one girls' school served in the Gerrer community in Arad, a peripheral Gerrer community set up (along with Ashdod, Hatzor Haglilit, and Neve Sharret) during the late 1970s. Bnai Brak has one yeshiva and two girls' schools that have existed for several decades. I also visited a Bnai Brak institute for ongoing teacher education and training, that caters to Gerrer and Mitnagdic women.

A former Gerrer rebbe (the Beit Yisrael) was the guiding force behind the establishment of the Hinuch Atzmai system in Israel, just as his father (the Imre Emet) had been the original mainstay of the Beis Ya'akov girls' school system in Poland and later in Palestine. When referring to this girls' school network in the diapora I will refer to it by the Ashkenazic pronunciation used there and not by the Sefaradi-Israeli pronunciation, Beit Ya'akov, that I use when referring to the network in Israel. In Israel these schools all use Ivrit as their primary teaching language and have adopted a curriculum similar to that of the Ministry of Education, including the study of Hebrew grammar and the teaching of English.

It is interesting to note that in the past, English was often used as a term of reference regarding the level of pedagogical supervision among Haredi schools of the Hinuch Atzmai system. In November 1963 the inspector of recognized Israeli education requested that his counterpart in the Hinuch Atzmai system allow the professional pedagogical inspectors to supervise the general studies in Hinuch Atzmai along with the inspectors of English teaching in their system.[24] Apparently, English was considered an important enough secular subject at that time to warrant serious pedagogical treatment from the Hinuch Atzmai system. This is particularly true with regard to the girls' schools, where it was treated as one of the keys to obtaining the better employment they would need in the future to support their husbands as full-time Torah scholars (Friedman 1999).

As for secular studies, the present tiuation in the boys' schools in Hinuch Atzmai schools differs from that in the girls' schools. The polarization of Haredi life during the past decades has led many, if not most, of the boys' elementary schools under the supervision of the Hinuch Atzmai system to largely disregard the secular curriculum. In practice, they teach only the basic secular studies such as arithmetic and a certain amount of Hebrew grammar in the lower grades; no other languages are taught, not even English. Because supervision in these schools is entrusted only to Hinuch Atzmai inspectors, it is always possible to state that the boys are studying English, as they are required to do by the Ministry of Education curriculum, while actually they may know little more than the basic alphabet.

All of the Gerrer boys' schools that I visited were Talmud Torahs or yeshivot, as the Gur sect has no secondary boys' schools devoted to secular studies. In every case, the primary teaching language depended upon the age groups involved. At the Arad Talmud Torah, where both religious and secular subjects are taught, the primary teaching language is Ivrit. Teachers speak to each other and their pupils in Ivrit, and the children spoke to me and among themselves in what appears to be very colloquial Ivrit, albeit that of young children. The school, which enrolls children age five and over, does not teach English, but does teach Hebrew grammar and uses the standard Haredi textbooks on the subject, which differ from their secular counterparts primarily in the illustrations and the topics used for examples. Whereas the secular textbook shows pictures of a television set and uses stories about sports events to teach sentence structure, the Haredi version does not include illustrations that are inconsistent with the Haredi lifestyle and opts for stories about universal topics, for example, a trip to the grocery store.[25]

Yiddish is taught twice a week in the Talmud Torah in preparation for yeshiva study that takes place in Yiddish. In conversation with me, the children mentioned that while most of their fathers know how to speak Yiddish, their mothers only know what little Yiddish they have picked up from their husbands.[26]

Elementary school children begin their studies solely in Ivrit, but the schools' language policy begins to change during the years of study in the Gerrer Yeshiva *ketana,* in preparation for higher yeshiva. Although the boys study no secular subjects in the yeshiva *ketana,* the primary language of teaching is still Ivrit. Torah study is in Loshon Kodesh; *shiurim* given by the rabbis are in Ivrit. In the yeshiva *gedola,* however, they will be given in Yiddish. Teachers converse with pupils in Ivrit, and both groups speak among themselves in that language. A number of the pupils in the Arad yeshiva *ketana* told me that they speak Yiddish, another group mentioned that they speak Ivrit to each other but understand Yiddish, and a third group said that they know only Ivrit and understand no Yiddish as of yet. This last group was composed primarily of younger high school–age pupils; older boys are already being exposed to Yiddish at the yeshiva (in some *shiurim* and even, occasionally in speech with their rabbis) in preparation for the *shiurim* in Yiddish that they will hear in the higher yeshiva.[27]

Like the Arad yeshiva *ketana,* the Gerrer Yeshivat Imre Emet in Bnai Brak, a boarding school, also uses Ivrit as its primary language of study, while teaching only religious subjects. There, the school day begins early—at 5:30 A.M.—and the boys divide their time between *shiurim,* self review, and meal breaks continuing up to the enforced 9:30 bedtime. The school is trying to introduce Yiddish as a language of instruction for the older boys.[28] As opposed to the boys at the Arad yeshiva *ketana,* who were eager to speak to me both inside and outside the yeshiva, and whose Ivrit had a certain proportion of slang, the boys at the Bnai Brak yeshiva were more reticent—I was obviously religious, but obviously not one of them. Listening to their conversations in the *beit medrash,* I noted that their Ivrit appeared to have less slang than that of their counterparts in Arad.[29] It is possible, despite what might be considered the Arad Gerrer community's social insularity from its secular neighbors, that in this peripheral community the barriers separating the Gerrer youngsters from the surrounding society are actually more porous than those in Bnai Brak.

Despite their lack of formal secular education, at least one study of Haredi boys of high school age has shown cognitive superiority relative to their secular peers, in handling both abstract concepts and concrete problems (Dembo et al. 1997). The motivation of Haredi yeshiva students, the teacher-pupil relationship they experience, their method of thought, and the Haredi concept of study as a value unto itself may provide them with an advantage when facing new topics. In my discussions with Gerrer pupils in Arad, several of them laughed when I asked them how they would be able to make their way in the world without formal training in English or mathematics. "Don't worry about us," one of them said. "Just give us a few lessons when we are older and we will be able to cover all that the secular boys study in a year. After all, they 'study,' but we know how to 'learn.'"[30] The final word which was said in Yiddish (*lernen*), is the term commonly used for Torah study.

The purpose of introducing Yiddish to older students at the yeshiva *ketana* is to prepare them for studies at the Gerrer yeshiva *gedola,* where *shiurim* are taught in Yiddish and Loshon Kodesh with a high proportion of Aramaic. Nevertheless, even at the yeshiva *gedola*, students speak Ivrit to each other at most times. Outside of the *shiur* Rabbis speak to the students in Ivrit, and not in Ashkenazi Hebrew with a Yiddish inflection as is done by certain Hassidic or Ashkenazi Haredi groups in Israel. When students speak to one another, they do so in a mixture of Ivrit, Loshon Kodesh, and Yiddish.[31]

The existence of separate Gerrer community schools for girls as opposed to general Haredi girls' schools reflects the differences that comprise a social, ideological, and religious line of demarcation between this group and other Hassidic or Haredi groups in Israel. Although the Gerrer rebbe was instrumental in setting up the Beit Ya'akov girls' school system, which enrolls girls from various Haredi groups, today many girls from the Gur sect study in separate Beit Ya'akov elementary schools that were set up solely for girls from Gerrer homes. In addition, instead of continuing on to the regular Beit Ya'akov high school system, they attend Hassidic girls' high schools, some of which are in the framework of the Beit Ya'akov school system. This separation was enacted for sociocultural and religious-ideological reasons. Although both secular and religious studies in the Gerrer and general Beit Ya'akov schools have generally run along almost identical lines, in the upper grades girls from Gerrer families studying in the same classes with girls from Mitnagdic homes found themselves in a difficult social situation that was often exacerbated in view of the Gerrer attitudes toward relations between the sexes, even between husbands and wives. Upon reaching a marriageable age, Gerrer girls usually meet a prospective suitor only once or twice before marriage, not on dates in public but in a more domestic framework, with family members present. Some of their elegantly coifed and adorned Mitnagdic counterparts, who would regale them with tales of their introductions and outings with prospective grooms, looked down on the Gerrer girls owing to their stringent lifestyle in this sphere. Thus, their awareness of the differences between them and their schoolmates was an uncomfortable one. This was one of the initial factors in separating Gerrer girls' education from that of Mitnagdic girls in the Beit Ya'akov school system (El-Or 1994). A second factor was the growing schism between the Gerrer rebbe and the Mitnagdic leader R. Shakh in the late 1980s, which led up to the split within the Moetzet Gedolei Hatorah (Council of Torah Sages) that I described earlier in this study. As a result, girls from Gerrer families were made to feel ideologically uncomfortable in classes where the majority of pupils were from Mitnagdic backgrounds. The schism also had religious and economic repercussions: the two groups now use different kashrut supervisions (Badatz as opposed to She'erith Yisrael), raising another barrier between Mitnagdic and Gerrer Hassidic pupils. All these factors led to the establishment of a Gerrer elementary school system for girls, and the pactice of continuing in Hassidic Beit Ya'akov high schools.

I made observations at two girls' elementary schools one in Arad and one in Bnai Brak, which hold classes for girls in grades 1–8. Both schools operate under the auspices of the Hinuch Atzmai system. The primary teaching language in both schools is Ivrit, which is also the language that teachers and pupils speak among themselves and to each other. I noted no difference between Arad and Bnai Brak in the form of Ivrit used among girls of the Gerrer sect in Arad and Bnai Brak, which appeared to lack the colloquialisms that I heard among the boys of the same age.[32] This is similar to the findings by Uriah (1996) regarding Haredi girls in the Beit Ya'akov school system, who from their early youth are instilled with an understanding of the importance of modesty in dress and speech.

Both Gerrer elementary girls' schools that I visited follow the curriculum of the Hinuch Atzmai, including secular language study of Hebrew grammar and English. In addition, the girls in Bnai Brak (but not in Arad) in grades 1–6 study Yiddish one hour a week. The books used for Hebrew grammar are Haredi versions of those in the secular school system, with the differences in illustration and topics that I described earlier. English is taught using photocopied pages that deal with both grammar and literature, instead of the textbooks favored by both secular and modern religious schools.[33] Both the Arad and Bnai Brak elementary schools follow the English curriculum of Hinuch Atzmai.

The Hinuch Atzmai English curriculum differs from that of the Ministry of Education in several ways. One concerns matters of form: while the Ministry of Education English curriculum opens with a methodological introduction, that of the Hinuch Atzmai is solely topical and textual. A second difference is that of content. The Ministry of Education curriculum states the aims, objectives, and rationale behind teaching English according to its system, defining methodology and competence on various levels. The Hinuch Atzmai English curriculum simply lists the materials to be taught for each grade, so that the different types of Haredi schools can carry it out as they wish, fitting it to each school's own objectives. Thus, as opposed to the Minigstry of Education curriculum, the Hinuch Atzmai system offers no determination of levels and targets. In terms of practical level, the Hinuch Atzmai curriculum is slightly less comprehensive than that of the Ministry of Education: the ministry's lower school curriculum requires that English be taught from grade 5 until the end of grade 9, while the Hinuch Atzmai curriculum only goes up to the end of eighth grade (S. Baumel 1999).

Until the early 1980s girls from Gerrer homes usually continued on to the various Beit Ya'akov high schools, such as those of R. Wolff in Bnai Brak or R. Scharansky in Tel Aviv, or the Beit Ya'akov *hayashan* (old) in Jerusalem. In the wake of the schism between the Gerrer sect and the Mitnagdim, it became customary for Gerrer girls to continue their studies in Hassidic high schools such as the Beit Ya'akov of Vizhnitz. There they found a social and cultural milieu more akin to their home environment than that which had developed within many of the more modern, Mitnagdic-style Beit Ya'akov schools. Girls in most of these Hassidic high schools study in Ivrit, learn Torah studies in Loshon Kodesh with a low proportion of Aramaic, study Hebrew grammar from Haredi schoolbooks, and learn English from photocopied pages. Although there are Hassidic girls' high schools, such as those of the Satmar sect, that use Yiddish as their primary teaching language, Yiddish is rarely taught in the various Hassidic Beit Ya'akov schools, even as an elective foreign language.[34] This policy differs from school to school (Bogoch 1999).

At the end of their high school studies Gerrer girls in certain, more modern Beit Ya'akov schools take a matriculation equivalency exam called the Szold test, which must be passed to enroll in some of the post–high school Haredi seminaries and to receive a teacher's training certificate. Apart from the seminaries attached to the various high schools, several independent institutions, such as Beit Hamorah in Bnai Brak, a branch of the Beit Ya'akov teacher's training school in Tel Aviv, offer post-secondary courses for young Gerrer women. The language of instruction is Ivrit; English and Yiddish are being taught as fields of specialization along with computers, literature, mathematics, and gymnastics. The school also teaches preschool education, bookkeeping, art, hydrotherapy, and computer programming. The curricula used in all subjects, including language study, are composed by the Beit Ya'akov system, and graduates receive a B.Ed. at the end of their studies.[35]

Language policies at Gerrer girls' schools are very different from those in the boys' educational frameworks, reflecting the different gendered tasks allotted to the two sexes in the Haredi world. Boys are being prepared for a life of Torah but are also part of the worldwide Gerrer sect. Hence it is imperative that they study in Yiddish at some point, as it is to them a quasi-sacred language as well as an Ashkenazi Haredi linguistic marker throughout the world. Since they are not being prepared for the work force, it is less important for them to study Hebrew grammar or a non-Jewish language such as English. Boys in the Gerrer yeshivot therefore have no secular studies after eighth grade, nor do they spend time on subjects unconnected to the world of Torah.

While the boys are groomed for a life of scholarship and, if necessary, will take their place in the work force in trade or other sectors in which they do not need foreign languages, girls are being trained to support their future scholar-husbands. Furthermore, girls are not required (and in some Hassidic sects such as Satmar, not allowed) to study Torah and can therefore engage in secular studies, including languages, without having to worry about wasting time that should be devoted to religious studies. Thus they are not only encouraged to study secular subjects such as English that will enhance their position in the labor force, but are also provided with the opportunity to achieve advanced degrees. These include the teaching certificate issued upon passing the Szold test in high school, or in rare instances, a matriculation certificate from the Israeli Ministry of Education.

Gerrer language policy in the educational sphere differs from that of Habad in several aspects. Although in both groups the primary teaching language at the elementary and high school levels is usually Ivrit, the attitude to the study of Yiddish differs slightly. In Habad, whose world center is not in Israel but in Brooklyn, and whose primary language worldwide is not Ivrit but Yiddish, there are educational frameworks for boys that teach only in Yiddish from childhood on. Girls in Habad are also taught Yiddish from a young age, although girls' primary teaching language in Israel is never Yiddish, even in post–high school educational frameworks. In Gur, whose world center is in Jerusalem and many of whose members worldwide often speak Ivrit, there are no educational frameworks for younger boys (or girls) that stipulate Yiddish as the teaching language. Similarly, whereas in Habad most girls are exposed to Yiddish study at some point, there is no single policy regarding the study of Yiddish in girls' Gur schools. Some schools, like the Gerrer elementary school in Bnai Brak, teach Yiddish: others, like that in Arad, do not. Bur has no equivalent of the Habad desire to enable both boys and girls to read the rebbe's writings in the original Yiddish. Gerrer texts are all written in Loshon Kodesh and Aramaic.

While Habad higher yeshivot in Israel teach in Ivrit, Loshon Kodesh, and Aramaic, the Gerrer higher Yeshivot teach in Yiddish, Loshon Kodesh, and Aramaic. This teaches us something about the composition of the two sects, their ideology, and their attitude to Yiddish. The Gerrer sect is completely Ashkenazi, and the worldwide linguistic marker for Ashkenazi Haredim is Yiddish. Until the development of Shas, Habad had attracted large numbers of non-Ashkenazi followers for whom Yiddish was a foreign tongue. Although newly religious students do not study at Habad's Tomchei Temimim Yeshiva, the group's outreach ideology may still factor into the choice of primary teaching language, even in the higher yeshiva. Having no corresponding ideology, the Gur, like most Hassidic groups in Israel, teach higher yeshiva studies in Yiddish. Both groups treat Yiddish as a quasi-sacred language, venerating it in principle. But in practice, this treatment does not receive concrete expression in Habad higher yeshivot in Israel.

The study of English is another factor differentiating two groups. Girls study English in both Habad and Gur, but boys in Gur have only minimal language study during their elementary years. Unlike Gur, which teaches no English after elementary school, Habad boasts some boys' high schools—albeit usually those in the periphery or for underprivileged children—that teach English, even to a low matriculation level. On the post–high school level, Habad does not discourage men from studying foreign languages and even encourages it for outreach purposes; Gur, meanwhile, does not encourage its men to study anything except Torah. These distinctions are engendered by the ideology of each group, and its gendered view of Haredi society.

Mitnagdim

Although it may appear monolithic to the outsider, the Mitnagdic world today conceals a great amount of variation. At one end of the Mitnagdic scale we find professional, modern but modestly dressed, upper middle-class, clean-shaven men and women with smaller families, who wish to provide their children with both a top-notch religious and secular education. At the other end of the scale are the overly Haredi-looking, full-time homemakers and bearded Talmud students, living slightly above the poverty level in large families of seven or more children. Their main goal is for their children to follow in their footsteps by becoming full-time scholars or the wives of such men.

Because it is not a Hassidic sect with a single accepted leader, different trends have appeared in the Mitnagdic world based upon ethnic origin (Lithuanian versus German style), personal family background, and geography (Eastern

Europe, Western Europe, America, Israel) (Breuer 1992). While R. Shakh set the tone in the Mitnagdic world for many years, in daily praxis some Mitnagdim tended toward a more moderate or Zionist-oriented position, depending upon whom they considered to be not only their highest halachic authority but their ideological and political leader.

In order to examine a broad range of Mitnagdic education I visited fourteen schools and yeshivot in Tel Aviv, Bnai Brak, Ramat Gan, Givatayim, Petach Tikva, Rehovot, and Jerusalem. Eight were girls' schools and five were boys' schools. Five of the schools where I conducted my fieldwork were elementary schools (three boys', two girls'), of which two (one of either sex) were very modern while the other three were mainstream Mitnadgic, reflecting the tremendous variation within the Mitnagdic world. Of the eight high schools (two boys', six girls') I visited, two (one of either sex) may be considered very modern while the others ranged from mainstream to stringent Mitnagdic. In order to examine post–high school education I spent time at one higher yeshiva in Bnai Brak and at a girls' high school (featured in this study) that also maintains a post–high school seminary. All of the schools have been in existence for several decades, some for more than sixty years. A few schools have changed their orientation over the years, going from mixed Haredi to more Mitnagdic or from moderate to stringent in line with the general trend of separatism and radicalization characterizing the Haredi world (Friedman 1991). Because I had taught at one of the boys' high schools over a decade before, I had perhaps easier access there to the teachers and student body and could also chart curricular choices and changes that had taken place during that half-generation.

In all of the schools, yeshivot, and seminaries where I conducted my fieldwork, Ivrit was the primary teaching language and the mother tongue of almost all the Israeli-born pupils. In a very small minority of Mitnagdic higher yeshivot some *shiurim* are delivered in Yiddish, usually by older, European-born rabbis for whom Yiddish is both their mother tongue and language of choice. These rabbis also address many of the students—primarily those of the more stringent Mitnagdic type or those born in Europe or the United States—in Yiddish.

In all of the elementary and high schools, in the yeshiva *ketana*, and in the girls' seminaries, the teachers spoke to each other in Ivrit, pupils spoke to each other in Ivrit, and the teachers spoke to the pupils inside and outside the classroom in Ivrit. Unlike the Gerrer elementary school in Arad, where I heard teachers speaking to their young charges in Ivrit but often muttering to themselves in a combination of Ivrit and Yiddish, in the Mitnagdic schools all communication I observed up to the tertiary level for boys, and at any level for girls, took place in Ivrit. At one of the Mitnagdic boys' elementary schools a teacher spoke to me in Ivrit and continued talking to me in that language— even after our accents made it obvious that our common mother tongue was English, or that he could have spoken to me in Yiddish.[36]

It is difficult to define a Mitnagdic Talmud Torah. Mitnagdic boys will not be found studying at a blatantly Hassidic Talmud Torah such as that of Gur, Bobov, or Vizhnitz. However, they often attend what originally were Hassidic Talmud Torahs—such as the Ruzhin Talmud Torah in Bnai Brak—but have now come to attract the Mitnagdic elite. One explanation is that the polarization of the Haredi world had sent the upper-crust Mitnagdim, who themselves had both religious and secular studies in elementary school, in search of schools for their sons that teach a very limited amount of secular studies, if any at all. A second reason is related to sectarian separatism, but in a contradictory sense: during the past decades the desire for religious knowledge and elitism has often overridden Haredi sectoral separatism, binding members of various groups together in educational frameworks that strive for religious excellence. This also holds true for elite Sefaradi Haredim today, who often send their children to top-rated Ashkenazi Haredi Mitnagdic yeshivot and girls' seminaries, as will be seen in the D family observed in the next chapter and among other elite Sefaradi Haredim.

The official curricular policy of Mitnagdic Talmud Torahs, many of which receive government subsidies and are under the supervision of the Hinuch Atzmai school system, is to follow a curriculum that includes secular studies alongside religious ones. All religious studies are taught in Ivrit mixed with Loshon Kodesh with varying proportions of Aramaic, depending on the age of the pupils. Secular studies ostensibly include Hebrew grammar and composition, arithmetic, geography, history, and English. In practice, though, most Talmud Torahs teach religious studies for much of the day, leaving only the last hour and a half for secular studies. While these studies do include a certain amount of Hebrew grammar, taught from Haredi schoolbooks or worksheets, almost no composition is taught. Equally notably, the schools teach a minimum of arithmetic, no geography or history, no Yiddish, and very little, if any, English. At the Talmud Torah Hug Hatam Sofer in Bnai Brak, which has 180 pupils in kindergarten and first to eighth grades, English classes remain on a rudimentary level, concentrating on transliteration and very basic vocabulary.[37] When asked if the school teaches English, the principal stated that the school does not teach it at all, adding that he does not consider the minimal amount of English taught—with the aim of qualifying for a government subsidy—to be true study.[38] This situation is common among most Talmud Torahs with a large number of Mitnagdic pupils, such as that of Ruzhin.[39]

Yiddish is not taught in any of the Mitnagdic Talmud Torahs, although all of the Mitnagdic educators with whom I spoke expressed a desire for their pupils to know the language.[40] For example, the principal at the Talmud Torah Hug Hatam Sofer told me that he would have liked to teach Yiddish in the school, primarily as a means of keeping the boys separate from the general community. However, without continuous linguistic support and backup, meaning family use of the language, he understood that teaching Yiddish would be worthless. In the Mitnagdic families that he knows he noted, even when the father speaks Yiddish the mother generally does not. As much as he would have liked Yiddish to be taught in the school, he realized that ultimately the time and effort would be better spent on other things.[41]

Other arguments—some of them mirror images of the ones raised in the question of Yiddish teaching—were used to explain why English was not taught to any serious extent at Mitnagdic Talmud Torahs. One was that the schools' anti-assimilationist stance precluded teaching anything that might act as a conduit for secular culture. Another was that anything unessential that would take time away from Torah study should be limited. A third was that students have no use for English at their age and that there would be enough time to learn it in the future.[42] The arguments used against teaching English in particular, and against spending time on secular subjects in general, are a form of Mitnagdic language management on the educational level, as it relates to the religious, social, and cultural aspects of Haredi life and particularly the separatist tendency. Language management, as expressed in the decision not to teach Yiddish, also reinforces language use (or disuse) in the Mitnagdic community. Thus, the reluctance to teach Yiddish, which is influenced by the fact that Yiddish is not usually spoken in the younger Mitnagdic community, simultaneously reinforces that fact by insuring that the younger generation will have only a minimal—if any—understanding of that language. This situation differs from the conditions I observed only a decade ago, when *shiurim* in major Mitnagdic higher yeshivot, such as Ponivezh, were delivered in Yiddish; indeed, the over-40 generation of Mitnagdic men today are usually familiar with that language.

The situation changes diametrically when examining language policy as expressed in the extremely modern Horev elementary school system for boys, and the parallel one for girls, to which certain very modern Mitnagdim (along with *Hardal* families and some professional Habad families) send their children. This school (which teaches in Ivrit, spoken by pupils and teachers alike) follows the Ministry of Education/Hinuch Atzmai program and teaches both religious and secular studies to its pupils, including full Hebrew grammar and composition, English, and other subjects. Based on the German-Jewish Haredi philosophy of R. Samson Rafael Hirsch of "Torah and *Derekh Eretz*," the school sees secular studies as essential to the a modern Haredi man or women wishing to take his or her place in the world (Scharfstein 1960; Ben-Avner 1987; Breuer 1992). As a result, this school, which in the past had educated a generation of modern Mitnagdim, now tends to attract pupils from professional Mitnagdic families tending more toward a *Hardal* lifestyle.[43] Religious studies for both genders take place in Ivrit and Loshon Kodesh with a small proportion of Aramaic for girls and a larger proportion of Aramaic for boys, depending upon their age and level of study.[44]

The Horev school system, which also exists in Jerusalem, has become a hybrid system blending a more separatist Mitnagdic attitude with a more liberal *Hardal* educational attitude, depending on subject and grade. This is seen in the schools' choice of textbooks for language studies such as Hebrew grammar and English. While the school uses Hinuch Atzmai textbooks in the lower grades (3 to 5), it uses textbooks approved by the Ministry of Education, but not published by them, for grades 6 to 8.[45]

More mainstream Mitnagdic families usually send their daughters to Beit Ya'akov elementary schools, which like the Horev schools teach a full religious and secular curriculum, including language study. Unlike Horev, however, even the upper grades use Hinuch Atzmai textbooks for most subjects, including Hebrew grammar and English. One factor that forms the decision by various

Beit Ya'akov elementary schools to adopt a particular curriculum, a certain type of textbook, and so on, is location. In Jerusalem, Hinuch Atzmai elementary schools use the Hinuch Atzmai English curriculum but have freedom of choice in terms of schoolbooks, whereas outside of Jerusalem they are usually required by the Hinuch Atzmai Center to use only Hinuch Atzmai textbooks.[46] These are often similar to their secular and modern-religious counterparts, particularly on the elementary levels, but are tailored to the Haredi lifestyle. For instance, English textbooks of the Hinuch Atzmai/Beit Ya'akov system, passages on football, basketball, and other non-Haredi pastimes have been replaced by texts dealing with topics relevant to taken from the daily life of Haredi children, such as participation in religious activities or religious study. Along with the textual alterations came illustrative changes; while boys and girls continue to be depicted appear in the new textbooks, they are dressed appropriately for their new young readers.[47] The textbooks' educational level is approximately the same as their secular counterparts', just as the curricular expectations of the Ministry of Education and the Hinuch Atzmai system tend to converge in this matter.

Mitnagdic yeshivot and girls' high schools typically pattern with those of their Habad and Gerrer counterparts. Except for the extremely modern Yeshivat Harav Amiel ("Yishuv") in Tel Aviv, which attracts graduates of the Horev system whose parents wish them to receive a secular education, no Mitnagdic yeshiva teaches secular subjects. All Talmud study (and communication between and among teachers and pupils) takes place in a combination of Ivrit, Loshon Kodesh, and Aramaic. Two generations ago, when most Haredim in Israel were European-born, some of these yeshivot still taught in Yiddish and Loshon Kodesh. That phenomenon has all but disappeared, though several educators expressed regret that Yiddish has been forgotten by the younger generation.[48] In contrast, Hebrew grammar, composition, and English are not only taught at "Yishuv," but are taught using Ministry of Education textbooks as the school prepares its students for matriculation exams. This is the only boys' Mitnagdic yeshiva that prepares its students for matriculation, although the school only devotes three hours late in the day (5–8 P.M.) to secular studies.[49] A modernist Mitnagdic ideology guides the language policy makers at "Yishuv" and its corresponding girls' modernist Beit Ya'akov high school, similar to that of Horev. Unlike the Mitnagdic yeshivot and Beit Ya'akov schools, which only prepare their students to be Torah scholars or their wives, these schools consider good Hebrew grammar, knowledge of English, and a matriculation certificate to be the basic tools enabling their graduates to join the productive mainstream of life in contemporary Israel.

The elite, extremely modern Mitnagdic girls' schools that correspond to "Yishuv" are Beit Ya'akov Lustig in Ramat Gan and the Beit Ya'akov Hehadish (contemporary) in Jerusalem. Teaching in Ivrit, these schools offer the Ministry of Education language curriculum including Hebrew grammar, composition, and English. Lustig even offers a full matriculation program and teaches from Ministry of Education textbooks. The other Beit Ya'akov schools at which I carried out my fieldwork all use a modified Ministry of Education curriculum that includes Hebrew grammar, composition, and English, but no study of

Yiddish or any other foreign language. Teaching is in Ivrit, the only language I heard spoken in these schools, and religious studies take place in a combination of Ivrit and Loshon Kodesh with a low proportion of Aramaic. These less modern schools do not prepare their students for Ministry of Education matriculation examinations; however they do prepare students for the Szold examination, a type of modified matriculation. For example, the English Szold test is equivalent to the three-unit state matriculation exam in English.[50] Even before the reorganization of the Israeli educational system in 1953, certain Beit Ya'akov schools actively sought state recognition so that their pupils could take the matriculation examinations.[51] This policy has continued in only a very few Beit Ya'akov schools (such as Lustig in Ramat Gan), meanwhile undergoing a metamorphosis in others. These other schools prefer to use an examination that not only strengthens their separation from general Israeli society but prevents their graduates from having access to any higher education outside the Beit Ya'akov system.

In all of these schools—from the extremely modern Horev/Yishuv/Lustig to the more separatist Ruzhin/Darkei Moshe/Beit Ya'akov shel Harav Kahane—I overheard most pupils and teachers speaking in Ivrit that included a high proportion of slang, although it never verged on vulgar language. This phenomenon—which may denote a high degree of interface with or subliminal influence by the surrounding Israeli culture—was also reflected in the post–high school frameworks that I examined, the Ponivezh Yeshiva and the Beit Ya'akov seminary for grades 13 and 14 in Bnai Brak (Beit Ya'akov shel Harav Kahane). Despite the difference that no secular studies are taught in the higher yeshiva while the seminary prepares girls for a teaching degree in religious or secular studies, including English, the most striking difference contrast these two establishments was in the use of Yiddish.[52] In no elementary or high-school level Mitnagdic education establishment—for girls or for boys—did I hear Yiddish in the classroom. The only Yiddish that I heard was from a number of rabbis talking among themselves. Although *shiurim* at the Ponivezh Yeshiva used to be delivered in Yiddish and Loshon Kodesh with a high proportion of Aramaic during R. Shakh's tenure as head of the yeshiva, Yiddish has been replaced by Ivrit. This mirrors the generational linguistic changes that have taken place among Mitnagdic Jewry. When most Mitnagdic rabbis and teachers were European-born, Yiddish, their mother tongue, had been the preferred language of speech. Today, the vast majority of teachers, and even a great percentage of middle-aged rabbinical leaders in the Mitnagdic world, are native Israelis for whom Ivrit is the mother tongue. During their childhood some forty years ago, much of the Mitnagdic world in Israel had not yet been affected by the ultraseparatist cultural tendencies that now characterize much of the Haredi world. Yet even though Ivrit has taken over the Mitnagdic "street" and educational establishments, I did hear students in the Ponivezh *beit medrash* studying in Yiddish, and speaking to their rabbi in Yiddish. They were, however, in the minority as most of the conversation, lessons, and study that I heard and participated in during my observations at Ponivezh took place in Ivrit and Loshon Kodesh with a high proportion of Aramaic.[53]

Although my observations among Mitnagdic educational institutions were limited and included several extremely modern schools whose Mitnagdic status is questionable, they point to several trends in contemporary Mitnagdic language policy. Among the Mitnagdic mainstream, gender differences in language study are apparent, just as they are in the Gerrer schools and in some of the Habad schools, where boys are prepared for a life of Torah study. Girls are prepared to support these young men after marriage and thus are given a full secular education including English and may undergo a form of matriculation/ Szold test that allows them to be trained as teachers, including language teachers. A second trend has transformed the use and study of Yiddish. Unlike their peers in Habad and Gur, Mitnagdic boys learn no Yiddish until higher yeshiva and even then, as *shiurim* are usually no longer given in Yiddish, they have little exposure to the language. Mitnagdic girls are not exposed to Yiddish at all, unlike girls in Gur or in Habad who study it as a foreign language. Third, there are more modern frameworks for Mitnagdic boys and girls alike that offer a complete secular education than in any of the previously discussed groups. Such a course of study exists to a lesser extent for body in Habad and not at all for Gerrer boys. This prevalence of secular education opportunities may be a result of the broad spectrum of what may be considered contemporary Mitnagdic life, as mentioned at the opening of this section.

The extremely modern Mitnagdic schools such as Horev, or Yeshivat Harav Amiel and Beit Ya'akov Lustig have a socioeconomic impact as well as a political and religious-ideological one. For years, these three schools—the first initially established as part of the Poalei Agudat Yisrael movement—geared their educational policies to a particular Haredi socioeconomic group: families with a moderate Haredi lifestyle and a desire that their children receive an education combining the best of the secular world with the best of Haredi culture and values (Ben-Avner 1987). The more moderate Haredi stance of these families was also expressed in areas such as pupils' extracurricular activities. Up to the early 1980s, girls attending Beit Ya'akov Lustig were often active members of the moderate Haredi "Ezra" youth movement of Poalei Agudat Yisrael, a joint youth movement for boys and girls.[54] Even at that time, this type of behavior was frowned upon by many, if not most, Haredi rabbinical authorities; thus, from their inception onward, these schools were considered *treif* (unclean) by the more devout Mitnagdim, who would not consider sending their children to study there.

Despite the obvious polarization of Haredi society that has influenced even the more moderate Haredi sectors and particularly Mitnagdic youth (who, for example, no longer participate in the "Ezra" youth movement), the parents of these children and teens still maintain more moderate Mitnagdic Haredi educational demands. In many cases, it is the parents' desire for a combination of religious and secular education, more than their child's wish for a matriculation certificate, that determines whether the child is sent to a matriculation-oriented Haredi school. Torn between parents' ambition and children's more religious stance, educational institutions such as Yeshivat Harav Amiel and Beit Ya'akov Lustig still attempt to maintain secular educational standards similar to those of the general Ministry of Education. Their curriculum is that of the Ministry of Education; their textbook choice is that of the state and state-religious educational system; their matriculation policies parallel those of the state-religious high schools.[55]

Conclusions

In his study of the sociological perspectives of education, Reese McGee (1967) analyzes the role of education in social change. Under one set of circumstances, education may act as an agent of social change, at other times it serves as a condition of such change, and under a third set of circumstances it is primarily affected by the social change that has already taken place. All three possibilities come into play in observation and analysis of Haredi language policy and its cultural implications as evidenced in the educational frameworks of four Haredi groups in Israel. Initially, modern Haredi education in Israel, as opposed to that of the Old Yishuv, was meant to act as an agent of social change. During the early years of the state, Habad, Gur, and the Mitnagdim introduced boys' and girls' elementary schools at which a minimum of secular studies (including Hebrew grammar, composition, and English) was taught alongside religious studies. These were the critical years, as during the first years of the state only a minority of children continued schooling past age thirteen, the maximum age for compulsory (free) education at the time (Bentwich 1960). Even if Haredi boys studied only religious subjects after eighth grade, they at least had a basis for their future in the world. Language policy in the educational sphere aimed to enable graduates to eventually enter the workforce, harking back to the request of Haredim to study Arabic at the end of the nineteenth century to get better jobs (Spolsky 1993).

During the 1950s and 1960s, the desire of Haredi rabbis and educators to create what Friedman (1991) calls a "society of scholars" led to the erosion or elimination of secular (including language) studies at most of the boys' schools. Exceptions were the certain Habad and extremely modern Mitnagdic schools that continued to teach a secular studies program. Within another decade, an entire generation of Haredi men rarely had any choice other than to remain in this "society of scholars." Although groups like Gur and the Mitnagdim spoke Ivrit, their lack of formal language study, English language skills, and a matriculation certificate barred them from higher secular professional education. Having absorbed the ideology behind this "society of scholars," they demanded schools for their sons that would continue this trend. In these groups, as in Habad, Yiddish—once the usual linguistic marker for Ashkenazi Haredim— was slowly relegated to the sphere of higher yeshiva education, becoming an oral language in which fewer and fewer young men were actually literate. For men in these groups, Yiddish had become an almost vestigial structure symbolizing Haredi separatism rather than a tool in daily use to ensure continued separation. In Habad the outreach nature of the sect traditionally granted it more educational leeway, in language as in other fields. Nevertheless, even here a growing number of boys' educational frameworks began to minimize or abolish formal language study. Haredi boys' education, initially an agent of social change that later became a condition of social change, was ultimately affected by the social change it had encouraged.

An important issue in implementing language policy in educational frameworks is the question of teacher supply (Corson 1990). In Habad, a large percentage of whose members are formerly secular, teachers can be drawn from a population that has received secular education, or even earned graduate degrees in education. This phenomenon is uncommon in Gur and the Mitnagdic world, where the teaching pool is usually limited to men and women who have been educated in that group. The result is that would-be teachers receive an education based on the language policy of the sect in which they will teach, with their pre-service training reinforcing their in-service training, experience, and willingness to act as language managers, ensuring that the group's language ideology is carried out in practice. Under these circumstances, it is difficult to believe that any change in language policy will ever be initiated by actors in the educational sphere.

As Pinar (1995) states, a curriculum is a text that exhibits the dominant tone of the social or educational discourse of a particular society or population. At first glance, the Haredi discourse among each of the sects examined here appears to deliver a mixed message, teaching in the local vernacular and tacitly enabling cultural interface while preventing advancement in the secular world by not providing formal language skills. A deeper examination shows how this situation emerged alongside the sociocultural and religious-ideological developments in the Haredi world. To fully understand the discourse, it is necessary to remember the second half of the equation: how education (including language policy) initially acted as an agent of social change among Haredi girls and is now the result of social change in the Haredi world. In order to support the "society of scholars," the students of Haredi girls' schools (including Gerrer and Mitnagdic girls) were taught in Ivrit and provided with a full secular studies program, including formal language study, a matriculation (Szold) certificate, and ultimately, professional training. Girls in Habad, while not always trained to support their families, studied secular subjects and languages to further their future outreach work.

Fearing that knowledge of secular studies and language might lead to cultural interface with the secular world, Haredi educators inculcated these girls with a theological-ideological dictum: the belief that secular studies, among them language) were to be regarded as no more than economic tools (or in Habad, outreach tools), and that any cultural interface with secular language at work should be left outside the threshold of the home, or even at the edge of the neighborhood. Whereas in the past (Parush 2001) Haredi women had acted as agents of secular socialization owing to their study of languages, Haredi girls were now being educated about the dangers of this interface. This ensured that they remain what El-Or (1994) calls "educated and ignorant": literate (particularly in non-Jewish languages but not in a Jewish vernacular such as Yiddish), but inculcated not to use their literacy for anything beyond bare economic (or outreach) needs outside the Haredi world. Just as a surrounding community can be either an agent of tradition or a bad outside influence (Rosenack 1999), educational frameworks can either reinforce cultural and linguistic tradition or introduce dangerous foreign elements into the lives of the young pupils. In the Haredi world that I have examined here, educators appear to want to play both sides of the coin, particularly in girls' education, thus creating what may historically be seen as a fraudulent concept. On the one hand, they introduce foreign elements, like secular studies and non-Jewish languages into the curriculum. On the other hand they emphasize that these tools are to be used solely to reinforce what they want to project as traditional Haredi roles (women as bread-winners, supporting scholar-husbands), roles that, in fact, were never anchored in the broader or normative Jewish tradition.

Thus we have another example of a Haredi Gordian knot. Haredi language management in the educational frameworks of the groups examined is actually a reflection of Haredi language ideology, while also having been a factor that contributed to the formation of this (new) ideology in the first place. Both are ultimately reflected in Haredi language practice as expressed within these frameworks. In his study of language planning, Corson (1990) shows how the educational sector is frequently selected as the site for language planning. Here I have shown that it is also one of the sites, *par excellence,* of language management, particularly in view of the ideological nature of Haredi society and what is supposed to be the absolute obedience of a group's educational frameworks to its movement's ideology, at least in theory.

Until now I have concentrated primarily on the attitudes to language and culture among Ashkenazi Haredim. In the next chapter I will focus upon a different Haredi group whose cultural markers diverge, at times greatly, from those of the groups discussed heretofore: Sefaradi Haredim in Israel and abroad.

Notes

1. These schools include: Kfar Habad Talmud Torah; Kfar Habad Heder; Kfar Habad Trade School; Beit Rivka elementary school, Kfar Habad; Beit Rivka high school/seminary, Kfar Habad; Yeshivat Habucherim Kfar Habad; Yeshivat Tomchei Temimim, Kfar Habad; Kollel Habad Arad; Habad Heder, Arad; Yeshivat Lev Simcha, Arad; Beit Ya'akov Gur, Arad; Talmud Torah dehassidei Gur, Arad; Beit Ya'akov Gur, Bnai Brak; Yeshvat Imre Emet Bnai Brak; Seminar Beit Ya'akov shel harav Kahane, Bnai Brak; Beit Hamora, Bnai Brak; Yeshivat Harav Amiel, Tel Aviv; Beit Ya'akov Lustig, Ramat-Gan; Horev, Ramat-Gan; Horev, Givayatim; Beit Ya'akov, Petach Tikva; Beit Ya'akov Rehovot; Beit Ya'akov Hayashan, Jerusalem; Seminar Hassidi Beit Ya'akov, Bnai Brak; Ponivezh Yeshiva Bnai Brak; Mosdot Beit Meir, Bnai Brak; Talmud Torah Hug Hatam Sofer, Bnai Brak; Yeshivat Darkei Moshe, Bnai Brak; Talmud Torah Ruzhin, Bnai Brak; Mosdot Sha'arei Eliyahu, Bnai Brak; Yeshivat Birkat Efraim, Bnai Brak; Mosdot Bnai Zion, Kiriyat Sefer; Beit Ya'akov Vizhnitz, Bnai Brak; Mosdot Or Hahayim, Bnai Brak; Bnot Hayil Shas, Ramat Gan; Yeshiva Tichonit Ramat Gan; Ulpenat Ramat Gan; Lipschitz College, Jerusalem; Touro College, Jerusalem.
2. Author's telephone interview with Ya'akov Hellman, supervisor of Haredi education, 10 June 2002.
3. Author's telephone interview with Rabbi Binyamin Schreiber, 26 Aug. 1999.

4. Author's telephone interviews with Hava Schwimmer, 20 June 1999 and 17 July 1999 and interview, Jerusalem, 22 June 1999.
5. Author's interview with Zipora Vishatzky, principal, Beit Rivka high school for girls, 9 Sept. 2001.
6. Author's interview with Rabbi Yitzhak Meir of the Habad Kollel in Arad, 8 Feb. 2001.
7. Author's observations at the Beit Sefer LeMelaha (Habad Trade School), 6 Sept. 2001.
8. For example, at the boys' schools Kfar Habad Talmud Torah and Beit Sefer LeMelaha, as compared to girls at Beit Rivka elementary, high school, and seminary, September 2001.
9. Author's observations at the Kfar Habad Heder, 6 Sept. 2001.
10. Author's observations at the Kfar Habad Heder and interview with a teacher requesting anonymity, 6 Sept. 2001.
11. Author's telephone interview with Rabbi Naphtali Roth, organizer of the Habad educators conference, 18 July 2000.
12. Author's interviews with several teachers at the Habad Talmud Torah who requested anonymity, 6 Sept. 2001.
13. Author's interview with Rabbi Shimshon Ashkenazi, school secretary, Talmud Torah Kfar Habad, 6 Sept. 2001.
14. Author's interview with Luba Herzel, vice principal, Beit Rivka elementary school, 9 Sept. 2001.
15. Author's interview with Rabbi Shimshon Ashkenazi, school secretary, Talmud Torah Kfar Habad, 6 Sept. 2001.
16. Author's interview with Mrs. Pinter, school coordinator, Bnai Brak, 15 Feb. 1999.
17. Author's telephone interview with with Habad educator Rabbi Naphtali Roth, 18 July 2000.
18. Author's telephone interview with Miriam Karelenstein, 18 January 2000.
19. Author's telephone interview with English coordinator Lea Banker, of the Beit Rivka elementary school, 20 June 1999.
20. Author's interview with Etti Feldman, English coordinator at the Beit Rivka high school, 9 Sept. 2001.
21. Author's telephone interview with Rabbi Naphtali Roth, 18 July 2000.
22. Author's interview with Rabbi Fichman, secretary of the Kfar Habad trade school, 6 Sept. 2001.
23. Author's interview with Rabbi Dr. Yitzhak Alfasi, 14 Feb. 2001.
24. Letter M. Azaryahu to Mr. Wagshal, 22 November 1963, file 1331, Gal 1403, Division 71, Israel State Archives.
25. Author's observations at the Talmud Torah Dehassidei Gur, Arad, 8 Feb. 2001.
26. Author's conversations with children at the Talmud Torah Dehassidei Gur, Arad, 8 Feb. 2001.
27. Author's conversation with children at the Yeshivat Lev Simcha, Arad, 8 Feb. 2001.
28. Author's interview with Rabbi Mordechai Feldman, Yeshivat Imre Emet, Bnai Brak, 9 Sept. 2001.
29. Author's observations at Yeshivat Imre Emet, Bnai Brak, 9 Sept. 2001.
30. Author's conversation with teenagers at the Yeshivat Lev Simcha, Arad, 8 Feb. 2001.
31. Author's observations and conversations at Gur schools, Arad, 8 Feb. 2001.
32. Author's observation and conversations at Beit Ya'akov Dehassidei Gur, Arad, 8 Feb. 2001; Beit Ya'akov Gur, Bnai Brak, 9 Sept. 2001
33. Author's interview with Yehudit Lichtenstein, principal, Beit Ya'akov Gur, Bnai Brak, 9 Sept. 2001.
34. Author's interview with the assistant principal of Beit Ya'akov Vizhnitz, Bnai Brak, 21 Oct. 2001.
35. Author's interview with the school secretary at Beit Hamorah, Bnai Brak, 25 Sept. 2001.
36. Author's interview with Rabbi Donne, Yeshivat Darkei Moshe, Bnai Brak, 25 Oct. 2001.
37. Author's telephone interview with Shlomo, English teacher, Talmud Torah Hug Hatam Sofer, 20 June 1999.
38. Author's interview with R. Bodik, principal Talmud Torah Hug Hatam Sofer, Bnai Brak, 15 Oct. 2001.
39. Author's interview with Rebbetzin Z. Berman, Ramat Gan, 23 Sept. 2001.

40. I.e., the teachers and principals at the Talmud Torah Hug Hatam Sofer, the Darkei Moshe Yeshiva, the Talmud Torah, Ruzhin, etc.
41. Author's interview with Rabbi Bodik, Bnai Brak, 15 Oct. 2001.
42. Ibid..
43. Author's interview with Gita Kossovsky, Horev English coordinator, Ramat Gan, 8 Feb. 1999.
44. Author's interview with Dr. Leah Makovetsky, Ramat Gan, 10 June 1999.
45. Author's interview with Gita Kossovsky, Ramat Gan, 8 Feb. 1999.
46. Author's telephone interview with Miriam Karelenstein, 18 Jan. 2000.
47. Ibid.
48. For example, author's interview with Rabbi Donne, Yeshivat Darkei Moshe, Bnai Brak, 25 Oct. 2001.
49. Author's telephone interview with the school secretary of Yeshivat Harav Amiel, 4 March 1999.
50. Author's telephone interview with Zvia Kunzman, English teacher at Beit Ya'akov Hildesheimer, Petach Tikva, 15 Feb. 1999.
51. Letter, parents of eleventh graders in Beit Ya'akov Haifa to Rabbi K. Kahane, Deputy Minister of Education, 26 Nov. 1951, 17/11/4-34319 Gal 1109, Division 71, Israel State Archives, Jerusalem.
52. Author's interview with Mrs. Miriam Fisher, vice principal of Seminar shel Harav Kahane, Beit Ya'akov, 24 Sept. 2001.
53. Author's observations at the Ponivezh Yeshiva in Bnai Brak, September 2001.
54. Author's interview with Rebbetzin Z. Berman, Ramat Gan, 6 Jan. 2000.
55. Author's telephone interview with the school secretary of Yeshivat Harav Amiel, 4 March 1999.

7

LANGUAGE AND CULTURE
AMONG SEFARADI HAREDIM

Introduction

To members of a previous generation the use of the term "Sefaradi Haredim" might have appeared to be an oxymoron. As opposed to Ashkenazim, seen by some as having traditionally leaned toward religious extremism and sectoral strife, Sefaradim were known for their tolerance of variations within Judaic practice. Tending away from extremist or fundamentalist-style groupings, they even accepted what others might have considered deviant behavior, as long as it was nominally bordered by the framework of basic Jewish law. Even after immigrating to Israel, for many years Sefaradim were accepting of what was known as *mesorati* practice, which included a mixture of religious and secular behavior—such as profaning the Sabbath—that was unacceptable to their religious Ashkenazi brethren (Zohar 1998). Consequently, although the Ashkenazi Haredi community is clearly distinct from the rest of the Ashkenazi population, where secularism predominates, the same cannot be said for Sefaradi Haredim, who often move seamlessly within the general Sefaradi community and therefore do not constitute a community on their own.

For this reason I have devoted this chapter to discussing the language and culture of Sefaradi Haredim in the context of their political and religious frameworks, family settings, and educational institutions. In view of the strong connections maintained between Sefaradi Haredim in Israel and abroad, I have devoted the latter part of the chapter to the Sefaradi Haredim in France, the largest Sefaradi Jewish community today outside of Israel.

What are Sefaradi Haredim? The Political Background

Since the early 1980s an upsurge of religious revivalism has seethed among Oriental Jews in Israel, which combined with the Oriental ethnic action groups that had evidenced themselves almost a decade earlier, such as the Black Panthers. One result was the Shas movement, a social movement and a political party uniting an electorate ranging from the ultradevout, through the traditional to completely secular Oriental Jews who were searching for an expression of their ethnic pride. Shas is not the only group of Sefaradi Haredim in Israel, but it is the largest and the most prominent.

The internal dichotomy of Shas followers is depicted by the following story. In the 1990s, the popular Oriental singer Zehava Ben was chosen by the left-wing Meretz party to sing their pre-election jingle on prime-time Israeli television. Following the election, Ben—who at the time was enmeshed in a number of personal and family scandals—granted an interview to a women's weekly magazine. Asked about her connection to Meretz, she replied that she truly believed in much of the militantly secular party's platform. The interviewer then switched to family issues, asking Ben—who had grown up in a crime-ridden Beersheba slum—whether it was true that she had had to cut a performance short in order to post bail for her drug-dealing brother. When the singer replied in the affirmative, the topic shifted to Ben's own checkered past and her present activities involving money, men, and the hint of a connection to the criminal world. As a closing question, the interviewer asked Ben which party she had voted for in the recent elections. "What kind of question is that," replied Ben in surprise, "I voted for Shas, of course, because I'm religious."[1]

Depending upon whom you ask, the history of Shas is the story of a meteorically successful Israeli political party (Kopelowitz and Diamond 1998), the development of an ethnic revivalist movement (Willis 1993), the history of a social-welfare and educational action group (Peled 1998), or the revenge of a downtrodden minority in Israeli society that chose to identify with the ultra-Orthodox in an attempt to unbalance the equation that placed them closer on the demographic scale to the local Arab population than to the Ashkenazi Jewish one (Chetrit 2000). Shas was born in 1983 as a political list for the Jerusalem municipality elections. Earlier that year Sefaradi activists, claiming discrimination among the Ashkenazi non-Zionist Orthodox community and Agudat Yisrael, had decided to revive the idea of an ethnic list similar to those that had existed in the early years of the state. Ultimately garnering three out of thirty-one city council seats, the party began to develop into both a political force and an ethnic social welfare movement (Kopelowitz and Diamond 1998).

To understand how a municipal list could metamorphose into one of the strongest forces in the Israeli political world and create, almost *ex nihilo*, a Sefaradi-Haredi social and religious movement, we must examine three separate factors. The first is the growing privatization of Israeli society and the breakdown of the collectivist illusion. The second is the social cleavage affecting two groups of Israeli Sefaradim—the working-class *mesorati* and the elite who studied in Mitnagdic yeshivot—in the early 1980s. The third is the input of two rabbinical figures who were, in equal parts, politicians and theologians: the Mitnagdic R. Shakh, and the Sefaradi Rishon Letzion, R. Ovadia Yosef.

Since the late 1960s, Israel had found itself facing a breakdown of the collectivist ethic, leading to growing economic and cultural privatization. Although this was a natural response to the cohesion that had held an immigrant society together, the result was a sense of urgency concerning the growing ethnic cleavage that stemmed from the economic, educational, and social gaps between working-class Oriental Jews and mainstream Ashkenazi Israeli society. As early as the 1970s a Sefaradi "tent movement" had begun as a vehicle for social protest, but it soon folded because it lacked political support. In the 1981 elections there had been an attempt to woo traditional Sefaradi voters away from the right-wing Likud party in the hope that they would support the ethnic Tami list headed by former NRP (National Religious Party) activist Aharon Abuhatzera. But apart from its slogan "Stand tall!" Tami had little to offer, and Sefaradi voters remained loyal to religious or right-wing parties.

By 1984 the political constellation had changed. Embroiled in the Lebanese war, Likud was unable to put into practice much of its educational program, which was supposed to offer disadvantaged children additional opportunities, such as long school days and the like. Simultaneously, there was growing unrest among another group, the religious Oriental elite that had been studying for years in Mitnagdic yeshivot yet continued to be treated as second-class Haredim in terms of being offered educational and political positions, or marriage propositions. Into this recipe one must add an astute, recently unemployed Sefaradi rabbinical leader who was looking for a power base and framework in which to gather his ever-growing followers: the former Sefaradi Chief Rabbi, Ovadia Yosef (Zohar 1998). Born in Iraq in 1920, R. Yosef had moved to Jerusalem as a child, studying at the Sefaradi Porat Yosef Yeshiva and making his way up through the Sefaradi rabbinical courts. Having been a deputy chief rabbi in Egypt, he became the Chief Sefaradi Rabbi of Tel Aviv, and ultimately of Israel. A prolific author and witty speaker with a biting sense of humor, in 1983 he completed his ten-year term as chief rabbi and was told unequivocally that he could not stand for a second term. Finding himself without a political power base, R. Yosef was a guiding force behind the idea of a Haredi Sefaradi political party that would also become a social movement (Willis 1993).

Another factor in the Shas equation was R. Shakh's political manipulations. Embroiled in a polemic with Habad over its increasing interest in the Israeli political scene, R. Shakh sanctioned the creation of a Sefaradi-Haredi political party (Shas), partially in order to distance the Sefaradi electorate from what appeared to be their growing affinity with the Habad movement. Walking into the vacuum created by Tami, Shas gained four seats in the national elections by picking up disillusioned Likud voters and the support of the Mitnagdic Ashkenazi electorate. Thus, the framework for a national movement of Sefaradi Haredim was born.

Shas stressed Sefaradi unity. Promoting the slogan *Lehakhzir Atara Leyoshna* (to Return the Crown to its former glory) and developing a social/educational movement, Shas opened its own school network, Maayan Hachinuch Hatorani (The Torah Educational Spring), in 1988, offering inexpensive full-day education and free hot lunches (Kook 1998). In an attempt to popularize Shas, activists utilized folk methods and scare tactics such as blessings, curses, and amulets in order to charm voters and attract adherents to the movement. They also built the movement upon the lowest common denominator among Oriental voters—

ethnic pride and a long-simmering sense of social and economic discrimination. In trying to win over a traditional Sefaradi following, Shas fostered a *teshuva* (repentance) movement, circulating revivalist preachers, promising financial success (and Shas financial aid) to the newly religious, and threatening non-adherents with fire and brimstone. Shas soon became an anti-elitist movement, adopting the public discourse (an ethnic anti–Ashkenazi-Zionist rhetoric), promoting a direct cause and effect ("do good deeds and be rewarded"), and projecting an alternative mythical history. Although calling itself "Haredi," Shas became a general Sefaradi movement, with members as diverse as the rabbis of the Porat Yosef Yeshiva and the heads of the criminal Amidar Gang. In practice, its main supporters were working-class Sefaradim who saw the movement as an answer to the social and economic ingroup-outgroup dilemma they had long faced vis-à-vis the Israeli Ashkenazi middle class (Fisher 1999).

Although R. Yosef was overjoyed with his political success and enjoyed his manufactured charisma (his image appeared on posters, cassettes, amulets, and the like), R. Shakh was less ecstatic about the political developments. When Habad began to support Agudat Yisrael and joined the Gerrer Rebbe in the Moetzet Gedolai Hatorah, R. Shakh left that council to form his own Mitnagdic Haredi power base. Claiming that Sefaradim were as yet unable to manage affairs of state,[2] R. Shakh formed his own political party, Degel Hatorah (the Torah Flag), siphoning Mitnagdic voters from Shas and leaving the Sefaradi party completely dependent on an Oriental electorate. In response, Shas' leaders declared *de facto* independence from their Lithuanian patron. In 1992 Degel Hatorah joined forces with the Gerrer-led Agudat Yisrael movement to form a Haredi political coalition called Yahadut Hatorah (the United Torah Movement). This is an example of how all of the four groups that I have targeted—Habad, Gur, the Mitnagdim, and the Sefaradi Haredim—have become intertwined in the dynamic development of contemporary Israeli Haredi politics (Arian and Shamir 1995).

Shas is the strongest, of the groups that can be considered Sefaradi Haredi, but it is not the only one. In addition there is the divided Abuhatzera clan of Netivot (the "Baba Baruch"), Beersheba, and Ashdod, whose followers consider themselves Sefaradi Haredi although for many years they did not belong to the Shas movement. Other, smaller Sefaradi Haredi groups also exist in various development towns (which were established during the 1950s in order to absorb the large number of immigrants), and there is a hybrid group of Sefaradi nationalists led by another former Chief Rabbi, Mordechai Eliyahu, whose followers combine national religious beliefs with external Haredi trappings. Without negating the significance of these groups in the Haredi world, here I will concentrate primarily on R. Ovadia Yosef and Shas as the educational, social, and political expression of the large majority of Sefaradi Haredim.

Contemporary Sefaradim-Haredim

Shas is the largest group of Sefaradi Haredim in Israel. Combining a model of political mobilization with educational and social service institutions, the movement offers a new definition of Sefaradi ethnicity (Peled 1998). The choice of the word Sefaradi, as opposed to the politically and ethnically loaded term *Mizrahi* (Eastern), is indicative of the decision to keep this from becoming a radical social protest movement like the Black Panthers or the stillborn tent movement of the 1970s. Judging by electoral results, some claim that Shas has close to a million adherents. However, as the large majority of Shas voters do not maintain a Haredi lifestyle, the Haredi component is probably limited to fewer than 300,000 people. Although it is the last major Haredi sect to have formed in Israel, it is also the largest Haredi group in that country. Shas' stronghold is in Jerusalem but Sefaradi Haredi communities branch throughout Israel, particularly in development towns. Still other Sefaradi Haredim are found in France and Canada.

What makes a person a Sefaradi Haredi? Obviously, one prerequisite is being of the correct ethnic persuasion. In terms of philosophy of Judaism, it would be difficult for Sefaradi sages such as Maimonides, or more contemporary Sefaradi luminaries like R. Ben-Zion Uziel, to recognize accepted Sefaradi tradition among the antimodernist, amulet-carrying, folk-practicing Shas followers. Indeed, the recent proclamations of R. Yosef, which delegitimize Ashkenazi Judaism by claiming that the only "true" Jewish law or practices are those of the Sefaradim, have created a new Jewish philosophy of separatism. Shas's vacillations between a left-wing political orientation and a formerly right-wing territorial position are legitimized by R. Yosef's novel interpretation of the term *pikuach nefesh* (necessary for saving lives). His willingness to join coalition governments with all parties differentiates him from the leaders of Agudat Yisrael (such as those in Gur) and the right-wing Habad. Sefaradi Haredim emphasize practical Torah study over the *pilpul* method of endless arguments, customary in the Mitnagdic yeshivot. Similarly, instead of concentrating on the intellectual development of Judaism, Sefaradi Haredim are more concerned with mystical forces and the practical challenges of daily life (Willis 1993).

In appearance Sefaradi Haredim are similar to the Mitnagdim, although R.Yosef still wears the traditional garb of the Sefaradi *Hacham* (rabbi) and R. Baruch Abuhatzera, the Kabbalist R. Yitzhak Kadourie, and preacher Amnon Yitzhak dress in the long robes of Oriental Jewry. As opposed to Hassidim and Mitnagdim, Sefaradi Haredim usually do not wear their *tzitzit* out of their pants, and often do not grow beards or *peot*. Unlike other Sefaradi extreme groups, the followers of R. Mordechai Eliyahu wear the knitted skullcaps of the national religious movement, thus distancing themselves from the black skullcaps that have become the trademark of the Haredi world. Ever since R. Yosef forbade Sefaradi women to wear wigs, they cover their hair with hats or kerchiefs.

The lifestyle of Sefaradi Haredim is one of ethnic separatism and antimodernism. Many send their children to schools of the Maayan Hachinuch Hatorani, from daycare centers through yeshivot and girls' seminaries.[3] Catering to the working classes, the schools do not prepare students for white-collar professions outside of teaching or administrative work in the Shas school system. Although Sefaradi Haredim seek army exemptions and study in yeshivot and kollelim, many still serve in the army and go out to work, often as laborers, in services, trade, or clerical work. Large numbers of Sefaradi Haredi women work in childcare and housework, or in factories and services. Sefaradi Haredim usually do not continue on to secular higher education, although they have recently tried to academize their educational institutions, by requiring their teachers to pursue academic degrees from religious colleges. There have also been recent attempts to open a Shas technical college, comparable to the Ashkenazi Haredi efforts in that direction. These educational innovations will be covered in a future chapter.

Many Sefaradi Haredim venerate kabbalists such as R. David Batzri and R. Yitzhak Kadouri, but their highest rabbinical authority is R. Ovadia Yosef, referred to by his followers as Maran (our teacher). His separatist tendencies and attempts to delegitimize the Ashkenazi establishment led to the establishment of the Moetzet Hachmei Hatorah (Council of Sefaradi Torah Sages) under his leadership and created the Beit Yosef kashrut supervision. Long esteemed in both Ashkenazi and Sefaradi religious circles for his vast knowledge of Jewish law, R. Yosef is the chief authority not only in religious matters, but also in political decisions.

Communication forms among Sefaradi Haredim are a topic worthy of note. It seems often to express a linguistic dichotomy that pervades Sefaradi Haredi life. R. Yosef—whose Hebrew is not modern, and who knows a certain amount of Arabic—is a prolific author of halachic literature, having authored thousands of responsa and dozens of pamphlets and books dealing with the most minute issues of Jewish law affecting everyday life. This follows a traditional form of religious communication evolved to assist a religious leaders with their often heavy workload of matters of this kind. Side by side with this traditional form, R. Yosef and his followers have opened additional, less traditional channels of communication. For example, since the 1990s one of R. Yosef's main forms of communication with his followers has been mass-produced leaflets. In addition to distributing audio-cassettes containing lectures by R. Yosef and revivalist preachers, Shas also uses the cutting edge of technology to connect itself to several pirate radio stations throughout the country that cater to the *teshuva* movement (Anaki 1999). These stations carry live broadcasts from the Yazdim synagogue in Jerusalem of R. Yosef's weekly talks, one of the main forms of discourse between the leader of the Sefaradi Haredim and his followers. Other Sefaradi Haredi leaders, such as R. Baruch Abuhatzera, also utilize oral means to reach their followers. This choice of medium may be explained by the educational level of the Sefaradi Haredi masses, which respond best to oral communications.

Sefaradi Haredi Leadership and Publications

Since the early 1980s R. Ovadia Yosef has been the accepted leader of many Sefaradi Haredim in both spiritual and temporal issues. By focusing primarily upon R. Yosef, I am presenting only a partial picture of the leadership dynamics of the Sefaradi Haredi world; however, I have chosen to do so because of his central role in both cultural and language management of large numbers of Sefaradi Haredim.

As chief Sefaradi Haredi leader in both Israel and the world, R. Ovadia Yosef is a unique phenomenon, epitomizing the multifaceted nature of the contemporary Haredi world. Like Hassidic rebbes, he holds court for his followers. Instead of addressing the faithful at a *tish*, he delivers Saturday night *drashot* (sermons) at a Jerusalem Sefaradi synagogue. Like Habad, which would project the rebbe's *farbrengen* (gatherings) onto giant screens in Kfar Habad to enable mass, transatlantic participation, R. Yosef utilized the fruits of modern technology and agreed to have his talks broadcast live throughout Israel (Yosef 1998c). His written compositions include responsa (Yosef 1954, 1976, 1983, 1991), Talmudic commentaries (Yosef 1998b), recorded lessons (Yosef 1996), exhortations to followers (Yosef 1991, 1998a), transcribed eulogies, and printed speeches that he delivered during public gatherings (Sefer 2000).

R. Yosef speaks Hebrew and Arabic, but his sentence structure and vocabulary are archaic. Recently classified by journalist and author Adam Baruch as speaking Yehudit (Jewish) as opposed to Ivrit, R. Yosef's Ivrit differs from that of R. Shakh in that it includes the most up-to-date slang (Baruch 2000). His unique grammatical forms, such as the now-famous command to Israeli television reporter Nitzan Hen— *tetze bahutz* (go out), instead of the colloquial expression *tze hahutza*—and his convoluted sentence structures often make his spoken Ivrit incomprehensible to the average Israeli listener.

Similar to his spoken language, his Hebrew compositions are characterized by archaic, convoluted grammatical forms (Yosef 1998b). He appears to have no objection to foreign languages; one of his books even includes a long dedication in English mentioning the names of the donors who financed its publication (Yosef 1998b). This would have been unheard of among any of the Gerrer rebbes; the *Lev Simcha* once even condemned the English orthography embroidered as a dedication on the coat of a Torah scroll (Gerlitz 1995a).

All of R. Yosef's compositions are geared to a male audience, but he has been known to direct exhortations to women during his Saturday night *drashot*. There he simplifies his Loshon Kodesh to include almost no Aramaic, a form of gendered speech similar to the Lubavitcher rebbe's use of English in his *sichot* to women.

Several of his responsa deal with the issue of education, where he speaks of the superiority of a Torah education above all other forms. Advising a teenage boy who wishes to receive a Haredi Torah education, he informs him that he may oppose his parents' wishes if they want him to study in a yeshiva high school that combines secular and Torah studies. Unlike R. Shakh, he does not ascribe to an ideology that would cause him to issue a blanket condemnation against all forms of secular education, including the study of languages (Yosef 1983). In fact, in one of his Saturday night lectures he points to the story of Joseph in Egypt to emphasize the importance of knowing languages in the ancient Jewish tradition (Yosef 1998c, 213).

R. Yosef's efforts to include colloquial Hebrew expressions, and particularly slang, in his *drashot*, appear to be an attempt to play to his audience, a heterogeneous Sefaradi public. This appears to be a case where the speaker is linguistically influenced by his followers more than they are influenced by him. And if we bear in mind that his religious followers are also the electorate for his political party Shas, his seemingly populist linguistic overtures take on a political connotation as well as a social one.

Similar political connotations color the Shas weekly newspaper, *Yom Leyom* (Day to Day), published since 1992. Shas is the largest of the Haredi groups, but *Yom Leyom* has the smallest circulation of the Haredi papers; in mid 2001 it was published every Thursday in 16,000 copies, including several thousand subscriptions. This comparatively low circulation derives in part from the fact that unlike members of Habad, Gur, and the Mitnagdic communities, who are effectively captive audiences of their movement's journals, Shas members read the regular Israeli press. Meanwhile, like other Haredi papers, every edition of *Yom Leyom* is vetted by a board of spiritual censors. Each week's paper includes a Parashat Hashavua (Torah Portion of the week) section entitled Oneg Shabbat.

The first page of its main section is devoted to Israeli news. Over half of the subsequent pages deal with Shas issues: reports on Shas Knesset members and their activities, news from the religious world, coverage of former Shas leader Aryeh Deri's incarceration (for political financial fraud), and the doings of R. Ovadia Yosef. The main section also runs editorials, announcements, and advertisements. The supplement contains letters to the editor, op-ed pages, family pages, articles on such topics as economics, medicine, nature, computers and high-tech, classified advertisements, stories, and recipes.

The language of the Shas weekly *Yom Leyom* reflects the movement's desire for outreach. The paper's main section is written entirely in Ivrit, from its editorials through most of its advertisements and news columns, which rival any of the major dailies in snappy style and colorful format. The paper's Sefaradi Haredi nature is expressed almost solely in its editorials and coverage of Shas-related topics, where the language is often volatile. Taking its lead from the political-polemical style that R. Yosef employs in his *derashot*, many of the political columns feature biting plays on words, although they eschew the rabbi's archaic Hebrew grammar.

As in other Haredi papers, a noticeable amount of Loshon Kodesh appears in columns on religious topics or by rabbinical figures, which appear mostly in the weekly Torah Portion supplement *Oneg Shabbat*: summaries of R. Yosef's talks, his Torah lessons, excerpts from other rabbinical sources. These writings also include untranslated Aramaic quotations (*Yom Leyom*, 15 Feb. 2001). Yiddish is not found in *Yom Leyom*, since its mostly Sefaradi readers do not know it—although in the previous generation, a large number of Sefaradi Haredi yeshiva students were graduates of Ashkenazi yeshivot where Yiddish was the language of learning. English words that have made their way into Ivrit can be found in *Yom Leyom* (*hasiti*, the economic city-center; *retroaktivi*, retroactive, 7 June 2001) but English orthography appears only in advertisements.

Yom Leyom also has its expressions that are unique to it, as do each of the Haredi journals. The major term associated with Shas's outreach policy is *lehitch-azek* (to become stronger), which, used figuratively in an editorial (14 June

2001), op-ed article (1 Feb. 2001), or religious column (7 June 2001), describes the process of increased observance. The turn of phrase abounds in Shas radio programs, too. "Are you stronger?" "I have become stronger, but my wife isn't stronger yet." "My children are in the business of getting stronger, thank God, but they still have further to go before they are truly strong." (Brandeis 2001): thus went an exchange one uninitiated listener thought was a prelude to an ad for a gymnasium.

Unlike the other Haredi newspapers, *Yom Leyom* rarely uses abbreviations, although in line with the other Haredi journals, it does resort to them in the context of religious topics, particularly excerpts from religious books, or in summaries of R. Yosef's teachings.

It is difficult to categorize *Yom Leyom* when it is viewed alongside the rest of the Haredi press. On the one hand, its topical interests and specific linguistic practices define it as a Haredi paper. On the other hand, compared to other Haredi newspapers, it most resembles a secular newspaper in terms of language and format. This may reflect the cultural dichotomy prevailing among its readership, who belong to a Haredi Sefaradi political party that must consider the demands of its largely secular electorate. The paper must, hence, sit on a cultural fence without falling off—which is no mean feat, as much as it is also highly revealing about Shas's cultural ethos and direction.

The Realm of the Family

I have already discussed the nature of Ashkenazi Haredi families in which the crossing of racial boundaries is rare. This is often true of the Sefaradi Haredi rank and file, who tend to marry within the fold. Yet when a closer examination of the Sefaradi Haredi elite—in contrast to the rank and file which is often far from being Haredi in its lifestyle, but expresses itself primarily in its voting patterns—reveals a different phenomenon (Willis 1993). Not only is it not uncommon to find Sefaradi Haredi elite who have married religious-nationalist or *Hardal* Ashkenazim, but one also finds among them a considerable number of families whose wives were born abroad, particularly in the West (for example, in the family of former Shas Knesset member Rabbi Yitzhak Peretz). This is the case in the Sefaradi Haredi family that I observed and interviewed, where the husband was a typical member of the Sefaradi Haredi elite: educated in Mitnagdic schools, serving in a prominent public Sefaradi position, married to a woman born to an American *Hardal*-style family, and raising their ten children—culturally, educationally, and linguistically—as part of the Sefaradi Haredi elite.

This Sefaradi Haredi family (I will refer to them as the D family) lives in Jerusalem in a mixed Haredi neighborhood on the city outskirts. Eight of their ten children (aged 6 to 22) still live at home; the two oldest daughters are married. Both parents are in their mid 40s. The father, one of seven children, was born in Algeria and brought to Israel as an infant. After many years of study in yeshiva, he is now a *dayan* (rabbinical judge). Having been raised in a French-speaking home, he continues to speak his mother tongue with his parents, although he communicates with his siblings in Ivrit. In addition, he spoke Arabic with his grandparents and studied English at school. The mother was the only child of *Hardal*-style parents in a family of Holocaust survivors in the United States. Her mother tongue is English, and she also spoke German to her grandmother. She studied Hebrew at school and after moving to Israel in her late teens became fluent in Ivrit. Toward the end of her studies, a mutual friend introduced her to Rabbi D, who, like many elite Sefaradi Haredim of that time, was studying at a Mitnagdic yeshiva. Until the birth of her seventh child, Mrs. D worked in family mediation. Since then she has been a full-time homemaker.

Before their marriage Rabbi and Mrs. D decided to speak Ivrit at home. Rabbi D. communicats with his mother-in-law (who knows no Ivrit) in broken English, while Mrs. D speaks to her in-laws in what she calls "high school French." After the birth of their first child, Rabbi and Mrs. D. decided that they would speak to her in their mother tongues (French for him, English for her) and that their daughter would study Ivrit outside the home. When she began talking at age two, they were perturbed by her codeswitching ("*tni li* [Heb.] *la* [Fr.] plate"—"give me the plate") and decided to speak to the rest of their children in only two languages, Ivrit and English. By the time their fourth child was born, their older children were speaking among themselves in Ivrit, and both parents found themselves using Ivrit with their children, as they do to this day.

Although all the girls have studied English at school, only the three older daughters have a good command of spoken English. The boys, who have not been exposed to any formal foreign language study, know a few words of English that they have picked up listening to their mother. With the exception of the oldest daughter, the children do not understand any French, and they speak to their paternal grandparents in easy Ivrit. This is characteristic of a common language shift that has taken place among Sefaradi Haredim in Israel. Although French is the mother tongue or the strongest language of many middle-aged Sefaradi Haredi families with a North African background (such as the one in which Rabbi D was raised), it is rarer to find younger Sefaradi Haredi homes where French is spoken in contemporary Israel. Even the D family's oldest daughter, who is married to a man from an originally North African Sefaradi Haredi family that immigrated to Israel from France in the late 1980s, speaks Ivrit with her husband.

None of the children in the D family have studied in the El Hama'ayan educational system of Shas, which the parents consider inferior to that of Hinuch Atzmai. Rabbi D stated that this is the common belief among Sefaradi Haredi families whose boys study in Mitnagdic educational establishments. In this they differ from the mass supporters of Shas—many of whom are lower-class and themselves products of the state-sponsored religious educational system, and who now send their children to El Hama'ayan schools. All of the D family's children are enrolled or have studied in Haredi educational institutions that accept both Ashkenazi and Sefaradi pupils, although they have a primarily Mitnagdic student body. The education the children receive is similar to that of the Mitnagdic C family mentioned previously: the girls study English and Ivrit grammar at school and the boys have only a minimal amount of secular studies and no foreign language study at all. The boys in the D family are not exposed to *shiurim* in Yiddish. When asked how they feel about studying foreign languages, the older son (age 16) remarked that he understands English and was happy to show off his command of the language with the heavily accented phrase "I vant a kookee." The middle son (age 12) thought that he might want to study English some day and the youngest son (age 5) was still not sure that he even wanted to go to school! None of the children expressed a reluctance to study languages, and the older boys and girls both saw it as a pragmatic step that might help them later in life. This marks one contrast with the Mitnagdic family featured in an earlier chapter, whose boys showed no interest at all in studying any foreign language.

Both parents and children in the D family speak colloquial Ivrit. Nevertheless, the parents try not to use slang expressions at home, although Mrs. D often intersperses her speech with terms such as *walla* (wow), *yalla* (let's go), or at times parenthetic (pragmatic) particles from English ("like") inserted into an Ivrit sentence. The extent of Rabbi D's slang speech is the expression *Haval al hazman* (It's a waste of time) reserved for distress or excitement. The children also make an effort to refrain from speaking slang at home, although the boys, much more than the girls, do so with their friends. Mrs. D remarked that boys' Haredi society is more *shvitzer* (show-off) than girls' society, which is why the boys use more street language among themselves than do the girls. Although none of the children use "street curses"—Rabbi D's term for swearing, they feel free to call each other *metumtam* (stupid), *mefager* (retarded), *tipesh* (silly), or *meshuga* (crazy).

Both the adults and the children in the D family are exposed to various cultural vehicles that influence their vocabulary. The family reads *HaModia, Yated Ne'eman*, and occasionally *Yom Leyom* (depending, in Mrs. D's words, on what newspapers are left over at the *Beit Din* [religious court] each day). Rabbi D, who usually reads only religious books, remarked that his knowledge of colloquial Ivrit is often far beyond what he would like to know, as in his work he is exposed to the language used in all walks of Israeli society. He also remarked that he is commonly asked, by elderly Ashkenazi plaintiffs who have never before had direct contact with a Haredi, how it is possible for him to be a Haredi *dayan* and not speak Yiddish! He merely smiled. Mrs. D enjoys reading Haredi novels and biographies. Children's texts are not censored in the D family, but it is expected that they will not read anything unsuitable for Haredi children. There is a certain amount of self-censorship stemming from what the children hear from their peers about permitted and forbidden literature. This is common practice among young Sefaradi Haredi elite, as I learned during my observations among Sefaradi Haredi children studying in Mitnagdic schools. Among children studying in El Hama'ayan schools, I noted that this phenomenon had been taken a step further: children appeared to be more strict than their parents (who were generally less stringent, especially in religious matters than their offspring) when it comes to forbidden and permitted reading material. A likely source of the students' zeal is the influence of their teachers.

Both Rabbi and Mrs. D have modern religious and secular relatives who expose them to forms of speech not always used in the Haredi world. The children are less exposed to their secular family but do hear how their modern religious cousins talk with each other. The younger children read the Haredi newspapers' youth supplements (*HaModia Hatzair, Yated Shelanu*), and the girls also read secular classic novels, thrillers, and science fiction. All of the family listens to the radio, particularly news programs and talk shows.

According to Rabbi and Mrs. D, the family's lifestyle and language patterns are typical of a particular group of educated Sefaradi Haredim. Like Rabbi D, at least one parent in a great number of these families was born in a French and Arabic-speaking household. Despite the existence of a Sefaradi Haredi educational system, many such families prefer to repeat the educational choices of the previous generation by schooling their children in Mitnagdic yeshivot and girls' schools. The language education that the children receive—for boys, no foreign languages; for girls, study of English—is similar to the course of study I observed among the Mitnagdim.

In other respects the D family patterns with the general Sefaradi Haredi milieu in Israel rather than only the elite. Sefaradi Haredi families often have family ties to secular and modern religious Jews. As a result, they and their children are exposed—often on the daily level—to the language patterns prevalent among those groups. We have previously seen how this constant interface on the personal level with colloquial Ivrit or slang is not reflected in the Sefaradi Haredi press; certainly it differs from the Loshon Kodesh, Ivrit, and Aramaic that R. Yosef uses in his writings. But Sefaradi Haredi writings have little influence over the spoken word; rather, the colloquial nature of Sefaradi Haredi Ivrit appears to act as a constant influence on the language of R. Yosef's *drashot* or of the talks given by Sefaradi Haredi revivalists.

The Sefaradi Haredim espouse no separatist attitude that negates the study of foreign languages. Indeed, the Jerusalem *herem*, promulgated by Ashkenazi rabbis, was never accepted by the Sefaradi rabbinical leadership. So whereas Sefaradi Haredi boys may not study languages in their school framework, still they do not exhibit a negative attitude to the possibility of studying languages in the future. In order to understand the working of this linguistic policy let us turn to the nature of Sefaradi educational frameworks as they exist in Israel today.

Sefaradi Haredi Educational Frameworks

When the Shas Sefaradi Haredi school system known as Ma'ayan Hahinuch Hatorani was founded in the late 1980s by the El HaMa'ayan educational offshoot of Shas, it positioned itself as an additional form of Haredi education in Israel. Initially a response to the Sefaradi Haredi claim of educational discrimination in Ashkenazi yeshivot, the Shas educational network has grown to comprise over 350 institutions throughout the country. These include daycare centers, kindergartens, elementary schools, junior and senior high schools, yeshivot, and girls' seminaries.[4] Boys' and girls' kindergartens, elementary schools, and junior high schools are under the direct supervision of Ma'ayan Hahinuch Hatorani with a general supervisor in the Ministry of Education as the schools are considered recognized unofficial institutions. Boys' and girls' high schools are private, ideologically connected with Ma'ayan Hahinuch Hatorani but not under their direct supervision. A men's college providing teacher training—Mekor Ma'ayanot—is also affiliated with the Shas educational organization, as is a center for continuing study. Attempts have been made as recently as 2001 to establish a Shas-sponsored women's college not affiliated with Ma'ayan Hahinuch Hatorani.[5]

Thus, while Ma'ayan Hahinuch Hatorani claims to support over 350 institutions located around the country, from day-care centers to yeshivot and girls seminaries, in practice the network encompasses and supervises only preschool and elementary educational establishments and does not supervise high schools and yeshivot.[6] Meanwhile, there are Sefaradi Haredim who send their children to Habad and Mitnagdic schools and yeshivot—including the Beit Ya'akov system—higher yeshivot, and girls' seminaries.

During my observations of Sefaradi Haredi educational frameworks I surveyed ten schools, yeshivot, seminaries, and other higher education frameworks in which Sefaradi Haredim study. The schools are located in Bnai Brak, Kiriyat Sefer, and Jerusalem. Two elementary schools (one boys', one girls') belong to the Ma'ayan Hahinuch Hatorani framework, four (two girls' high schools and two yeshivot *ketanot*) were on the high school level, and four provide higher education (a yeshiva *gedola*, a girls' seminary, and one women's and two men's college programs). A majority of the institutions were geared almost fully to Sefaradi Haredim. One girls' high school, which operates in tandem with a post–high school seminary, is mixed Haredi, Sefaradi and Mitnagdic girls together. As do most Beit Ya'akov schools, this school maintains a tacit policy of ethnic quotas that is the cause of much heartache for elite Sefaradi Haredi parents who wish their daughters to receive what they consider to be a good Haredi high school education.[7]

At all of the Sefaradi Haredi schools where I carried out my observations, the primary teaching language was Ivrit. All pupils conversed among themselves in that language, and at all of the schools I heard them use Ivrit slang with each other. I heard more colloquial Ivrit among boys than among the girls, and the boys were often admonished by their teachers to "watch their language," an expression that I never heard during my observations at the girls' schools.[8] Teachers also conversed in Ivrit, although their speech was usually less colloquial than that of their pupils. The two frameworks in which the pupils' Ivrit was less colloquial than their teachers' were the colleges (Lipschitz and Touro programs for Shas teachers), where the teachers were usually nationalist-religious or *Hardal* and not necessarily Sefaradi. In those schools, teachers were heard to use slang expressions in conversation with students (such as *bechayecha*, used in the sense of "you must be kidding," or *katan alecha* "it's simple for your level"), while students usually refrained from using more colloquial phrases with their teachers and even with each other, at least when they were within earshot. This may stem from a respect for their teachers, but even when I over-heard them talking while thinking themselves unobserved, I noted the same phenomenon.[9]

Ma'ayan Hahinuch Hatorani elementary schools claim to follow the curriculum of the Ministry of Education by teaching a complete secular studies program that includes Hebrew grammar and English, along with a full religious studies program.[10] In practice, there are boys' schools that do not teach English at all, although they do teach Hebrew grammar, spelling, and composition. One example in this category is Mosdot Bnai Zion in Kiriyat Sefer, which follows a curriculum similar to that used in many Mitnagdic Talmud Torahs.[11] The books used in the elementary schools are those of the Hinuch Atzmai system, although Ma'ayan Hahinuch Hatorani has expressed a desire to develop its own textbooks for its school network. Girls' elementary schools of Ma'ayan Hahinuch Hatorani usually teach Hebrew grammar, spelling, composition, and English, although they teach no other foreign languages. Apart from the Hinuch Atzmai textbooks, these schools often use worksheets for English study as a means of implementing language management and strengthening political ideology, preferring homemade materials over those of the Hinuch Atzmai schools.[12] In general, there are those among the Sefaradi Haredim who believe that the level of many of the Ma'ayan Hahinuch Hatorani schools is lower than that of the Hinuch Atzmai, in both secular and religious studies. This attitude prompts upper-crust Sefaradi Haredi parents to send their children to Mitnagdic schools supervised by the Hinuch Atzmai system (Talmud Torahs and Beit Ya'akov), rather than to those of Shas.[13]

As high schools do not fall under Ma'ayan Hahinuch Hatorani jurisdiction, after eighth grade some Sefaradi Haredi children continue their studies at Sefaradi Haredi yeshivot and seminaries not necessarily affiliated with Shas. Three examples, all in Bnai Brak, are the two yeshivot *ketanot* that I observed—Mosdot Sha'arei Eliyahu, with 60 pupils, and Yeshivat Birkat Efraim, with 180—and the girls' seminary complex Mosdot Or Hahayim, where over a thousand pupils are enrolled in several study frameworks. Both of the yeshivot, although they cater to a mixed Sefaradi Haredi clientele (that is, from Shas and from other Sefaradi Haredi groups), claim to follow the study pattern of Mitnagdic yeshivot, where there are no secular studies and *shiurim* are delivered in Ivrit and Loshon Kodesh with a large proportion of Aramaic.[14] Pupils in both yeshivot spoke to each other in Ivrit with a moderate proportion of slang and teachers spoke to each other in Ivrit. Some of the teachers had studied in Mitnagdic yeshivot in their youth and had a minimal command of Yiddish, which they had never used in their teaching or their own later Talmud studies.[15]

Mosdot Or Hahayim, one of the first Sefaradi Haredi girls' high schools established in Israel (1953), was initially established under the guidance of a Mitnagdic luminary, the *Hazon Ish* (R. Avraham Yesha'ayahu Karlitz), as a Sefaradi parallel to R. Wolff's Beit Ya'akov, whose administration preferred it to remain a primarily Ashkenazi school (Sourasky 1967). Having largely failed in its attempt to become an elite Sefaradi Haredi school in the 1950s and 1960s, the school body metamorphosed; it is now an educational haven for Sefaradi

Haredi girls who, in the words of a member of the Sefaradi Haredi elite, are not considered "top educational material."[16] Like the Beit Ya'akov high school seminaries, Mosdot Or Hahayim teaches a complete secular program, including Hebrew grammar, composition, and English, alongside its religious studies program, which is taught in Ivrit and Loshon Kodesh with a small proportion of Aramaic. The school uses the textbooks of the Beit Ya'akov school system but worksheets replace these in English class, evidence of language management that mirrors the growing Sefaradi Haredi ideology of separating itself from the Mitnagdic establishment—the major force that founded and later funded the school.

All teaching and conversation that I heard at the school was in Ivrit, and I noted less Ivrit slang among the girls than I had at the boys' yeshivot. This follows what I had observed earlier among Sefaradi Haredi families, where the girls (who in practice may have more interface with secular culture) strive to use only proper language (Uriah 1996). As in most Beit Ya'akov schools, girls in Or Hahayim take the Szold test at the end of grade 12 in order to continue on to grades 13 and 14 at a teachers' training seminary that will give them a teaching certificate from the Ministry of Education. Among the subjects taught in the seminary are Hebrew language and grammar, and English.[17]

Not all Sefaradi Haredi children continue their studies in educational institutions that cater primarily or completely to Sefaradi Haredim. Since a large number of Sefaradi Haredi children come from families that were originally national-religious or even secular, some continue their high school studies in national-religious high schools such as yeshivot *tichoniyot* (national-religious yeshiva high schools) or national-religious girls' high schools.[18] Both schools of this type teach a full religious and a full secular curriculum, preparing graduates for state matriculation in exams in all subjects, including Hebrew grammar, composition, English, and at times an additional foreign language. This raises difficulties for boys who studied at certain Ma'ayan Hahinuch Hatorani elementary schools, some of which list secular studies in their curriculum but in practice put their main efforts into religious studies, leaving their graduates unprepared for the non-Haredi educational system. Graduates of schools that do not teach English, such as that in Kiriyat Sefer, have little chance of catching up to their non-Haredi peers, leaving them few options continuing their education. Similar policies apply in the vast majority of the Ashkenazi Haredi elementary schools and Talmud Torahs that I observed, and may be seen as a form of language management stemming from a separatist ideology. By producing graduates unable to mainstream into the national-religious educational system, Haredi educators hope to prevent their exposure to secular higher education and thus keep them within the fold.

On the other end of the spectrum are children from elite Sefaradi Haredi families who wish them to continue their studies at Mitnagdic yeshivot and elite Beit Ya'akov schools, just as their parents studied at these schools a generation earlier. The existence of a plethora of Sefaradi Haredi schools has encouraged the development of a stringent and discriminatory selection process at a number of the top-ranking Ashkenazi yeshivot *ketanot* and high-school seminaries, ostensibly to maintain high academic standards, but in practice causing much heartbreak to parents whose children are rejected only because of their ethnic origin. A well-known school in this category is the Beit Ya'akov Hayashan in Jerusalem, to which certain children of elite Sefaradi Haredi families apply (children of revered Rabbis, religious judges, educators, political figures) but are seldom accepted.[19] Sefaradi Haredi boys and girls accepted to Mitnagdic yeshivot follow the same curriculum as their Ashkenazi peers, as detailed in the previous section.

Sefaradi Haredim choose from a variety of post–high school educational frameworks, primarily higher yeshivot, kollels, and seminaries where they can continue their religious studies. One of the most famous Sefaradi Haredi higher yeshivot is Porat Yosef in Jerusalem, founded in 1922 under the spiritual auspices of Rabbi Yosef Haim of Baghdad, and with the financial support of the Nagid, Rabbi Yosef Abraham Shalom of Calcutta. The first modern Sefaradi yeshiva in Palestine to follow the learning tradition of Babylonian Jewry, Porat Yosef initially established classes from elementary school through higher yeshiva, including a small, elitist Kabbalistic yeshiva called Oz Vehadar operating within the framework of the larger institution. The primary teaching language in the yeshiva is Ivrit combined with Loshon Kodesh that has a very high proportion of Aramaic (Sourasky 1967).

Two additional educational frameworks for post–high school study are the academic training programs for Sefaradim Haredim that are being run at the national-religious Lipschitz College and Touro College, both in Jerusalem. The Lipschitz College program for Shas *ramim* (rabbi educators), whose several dozen annual graduates receive a B.Ed., is taught in Ivrit and includes courses in English, education, pedagogy, and other related topics. The teachers in the program speak among themselves in Ivrit, as do the students. However, the students typically use fewer colloquialisms and less Ivrit slang than do many of the teachers, who are usually from a national-religious background, and have a greater interface with contemporary popular Israeli culture than do their Haredi students.[20]

Touro College in Jerusalem runs a similar B.A. program for Sefaradi Haredim, taught in Ivrit and requiring study of English at a college level. Unlike the Lipschitz program, which is only for men, in addition to classes for Shas *ramim* Touro runs a parallel program for men teaching in the Ma'ayan Hahinuch Hatorani network and a third program solely for Sefaradi Haredi women.[21] Many of the men have studied little, if any, English until reaching this program, so the level of English taught to the men (as opposed to the women, who have usually had greater exposure to the language) is initially often closer to that of late elementary school or early high school. The same is true of the Lipschitz program. This lack of English language skills presents a pedagogical challenge for teachers, who have to bring their male students up to a college reading level within a year. At the same time, it creates a different kind of challenge for those students who view secular studies as a necessary evil one endures to gain the academization needed to continue teaching religious subjects in Shas schools. Some of these students even attempt to convince their teachers—themselves religious—of the futility of their spending time away from their Torah studies, in the hope of being able to complete their secular studies with as little investment of time and effort as possible.[22]

Like Habad and the Mitnagdim, Sefaradi Haredim offer young people a wide variety of educational possibilities tailored to their background, religious tendencies, and professional choices. The choice of school often takes them out of completely Sefaradi, or completely Haredi, frameworks, yet by definition of their ethnic background and home environment, not to mention their own daily lifestyle, they personally remain Sefaradi Haredi. This group does not include Sefaradi Haredim who have joined Habad, are educated at Habad institutions, and have adopted a Habad lifestyle. In contrast to this group, Sefaradi Haredim who study at Mitnagdic yeshivot and seminaries today usually remain Sefaradi Haredi in their religious practice, and can be considered as such.

The first common denominator of all the Sefaradi Haredi educational institutions I observed is that they teach in Ivrit, which is almost always the spoken language of choice among both pupils and teachers. Even those Sefaradi Haredi pupils and yeshiva/seminary students who were born in the French-speaking diaspora study Ivrit in school and speak it there and with their siblings, although they may continue to speak French at home with their parents.[23] This practice mirrors Sefaradi Haredi language ideology, where the local vernacular, as the language of daily speech and of study, is set apart from Loshon Kodesh, which is used for religious subjects.

There are no observable differences in vocabulary and syntax between the Loshon Kodesh of Sefaradi Haredim and that heard in Habad, Gerrer, and Mitnagdic yeshivot. The only difference I noticed was in pronunciation. In the yeshivot and girls' schools that I surveyed among Habad, Gur, or the Mitnagdim, certain words in Loshon Kodesh may be given an Eastern European (Ashkenazi, Yiddish-style) pronunciation, testimony to these groups' traditional and constant cultural interface with the Yiddish-speaking Haredi world. In contrast, the same words are given an Ivrit (Sefaradi) pronunciation in Sefaradi Haredi yeshivot and schools, in spite of the fact that many of the older Sefaradi Haredi rabbis and teachers are themselves graduates of Mitnagdic yeshivot. Thus, while Ashkenazim say *limaiseh* (actually), Sefaradi Haredim will say *lema'ase;* the Ashkenazic *aderabbeh* (even more so) becomes *adraba*, and so on. Modern-day Sefaradi Haredim who attend Mitnagdic yeshivot may adopt this pronunciation during their studies, but often they do not retain it after leaving the Ashkenazi educational world.[24] Yiddish and other Jewish languages are neither spoken nor taught at any Sefaradi Haredi educational institution. The absence of Yiddish is well understood, it not having been a traditional Sefaradi Jewish vernacular. However, the curricular absence of Arabic, French, or other foreign languages commonly spoken in Sefaradi homes is striking. One explanation may be the desire to teach only the minimum amount of secular study required by the Ministry of Education, thus leaving more time for study of religious subjects. From a second vantage point, this absence is a form of language management, reinforcing an ideology that divorces Sefaradi Haredi Jews from the non-Jewish cultures in which they lived in the diaspora, and emphasizes the importance of their life in the Holy Land.

A final point relates to the study of English among Sefaradi Haredim. Though they may emphasize ethnic separatism and stress how their movement is revitalizing the traditional Sefaradi religious culture, in practice Sefaradi Haredim seem to have taken their education cues from the Mitnagdic world, where many of them received their Torah education. As a result, girls begin learning English in elementary school, while most Sefaradi Haredi boys' schools have either a minimal English program or none at all. Sefaradi Haredi yeshivot on the high school level do not teach English; meanwhile, the girls' high schools and seminaries are adamant about teaching the subject and preparing students for matriculation-type (Szold) examinations, the common practice at Mitnagdic schools.

The desire to emulate the Mitnagdic Haredi educational framework may be seen in the following story. In the spring of 2001 the mother of a Sefaradi Haredi eighth grader who had great difficulty with English but was academically successful in other subjects asked to speak with the administration of the Or Hahayim high school. Explaining to the assistant principal that her daughter was planning to specialize in religious subjects, she asked whether her daughter could be excused from English studies, as she would not need that subject in the future. In response the assistant principal emphasized that English study was mandatory for all students in the school, and that whereas her daughter would be given remedial classes if necessary, being excused from English was not an option. "After all, we are just as good as Beit Ya'akov," she stated, "and no one is going to say that because we are Sefaradim our girls are less successful than those at *Rav* Wolff or Scharansky."[25]

Sefaradi Haredim Abroad: France

For many years Ashkenazi Haredim have been regarded as members of a transnational diaspora with international religious, linguistic, and cultural interconnections. Earlier chapters have highlighted various manifestations of this phenomenon in the family and educational frameworks. A different phenomenon characterizes Sefaradi Haredim, particularly in view of the fact that in many cases they are part of the general Sefaradi community. As a result, one finds constant connections maintained between Sefaradi communities throughout the world, Sefaradi Haredim being only one facet thereof. This sense of Sefaradi unity is exemplified by the case of France, the country with the highest concentration of Sefaradim outside of Israel today.

The Jewish community in France has changed considerably in terms of ethnic composition throughout the past sixty years. Before the Second World War the majority of Jews in France were of Eastern European origin. The destruction of a large proportion of Ashkenazi French Jewry under Nazi rule and the subsequent immigration of Jews from North Africa in the 1950s and 1960s, particularly from Egypt, Morocco, Algeria, and Tunisia, changed French Jewry's linguistic composition as Judeo-Arabic became the community's second language after French (Sachar 1985). The French Jewish Consistoire and the Fonds Social were prepared to support this change in rebuilding their communal lives.

Under their aegis, a major program of synagogue construction was launched throughout France. Care was taken to recreate the Sefaradi architectural pattern, to publish and distribute prayer books that followed the Sefaradi–North African rite, and to develop an Eshel Sefaradic seminary for training teachers, youth leaders, rabbis, and cantors (Bensimon-Donath 1973).

At the beginning of the twenty-first century France had a Jewish population of over 600,000 Jews—the second-largest Jewish population outside of Israel, after the United States. Over sixty percent of its population is Sefaradi; fifty percent of the total population are North African origin. The two largest Haredi groups in France are Habad and Sefaradi Haredim; populations of Gerrer and Mitnagdic communities are negligible.

Although over three fifths of the Jewish population of France is Sefaradi, only a small proportion of that group can be considered Sefaradi Haredi. In recent years there has been an upsurge of interest in Judaism among North African Jewry in France, a large number of whom always considered themselves traditional. This may be seen by the growth of consumers of kosher food, and kosher butchers continue to open new stores throughout the country (Ben Simon 2001).

Sefaradi Haredim speak French at home and in the street. The older North African–born generation is known to sometimes pepper speech with Judeo-Arabic (Sachar 1985). The Sefaradi Haredi communities in France use French for public notices, though an occasional store sign may contain Hebrew letters denoting ritual objects or kosher food (Ben Simon 2001). In terms of education, Sefaradi Haredim in France usually send their children either to Habad schools, or, more recently, to special Sefaradi schools that have opened during the past few decades.

There are 25,000 Jews registered in Habad communities in France, although larger numbers may be considered Habad supporters (Ben Simon 2001). Out of the 26,000 Jewish children who attend Jewish schools in France (Dossier 2001), 10,000 are enrolled in Habad schools. In spite of its being a Hassidic movement, Habad has made great inroads among Sefaradi Jews in France, and today the majority of the 10,000 children studying at all twenty-five of France's Habad schools are of North African origin. Habad representatives and rabbis run a network of Habad activities in twenty-five cities throughout France.[26]

Following the tradition of speaking the local vernacular, most Habad families in France speak French, and in Habad communities one can hear and see a combination of French and Ivrit. Landau (1993) notes that Yiddish is spoken among veteran Ashkenazi Habad families, and it is also understood by some of the Sefaradi Habad rabbis who studied at the Habad world center in Brooklyn.

The first Habad educational establishment in France, Beth Rivka, was opened in 1945 to educate young girls who were Holocaust survivors. There was no boys' Habad yeshiva in France until 1963, when Rabbi Sholom Mendel Kalmenson opened the Chné Or school for boys in Aubervilliers. A few years later a girls' school was established in the same city (Landau 1993). Additional Habad schools were opened throughout the next four decades. These included Sinaï (Paris, 1966), Beth Hanna (Paris, 1971), Beth Menahem (Villeurbanne, 1986),

Keren Menahem (Nice, 1988), Beth Hanna (Strasbourg, 1991), and Heikhal Menahem (Paris, 1996).

Today, the twenty-five Habad educational establishments in France teach both boys and girls. Religious studies are taught primarily in French and Loshon Kodesh with varying proportions of Aramaic, depending on the age and sex of the pupil, and secular studies take place in French. In most cases, the Habad school curriculum is fully recognized and pupils take state examinations (Landau 1993). The French-speaking, North African origin of much of French Jewry appears to explain the fact that Yiddish is not commonly used in Habad educational institutions in France.

Once larger numbers of North African Jews had immigrated to France, some families among them who wished their children to retain Jewish values began to promote the idea of sending them to Jewish schools (Dossier 2001)—in spite of these children's knowledge of French and ability to assimilate into the French educational system. With the growth of the Sefaradi World Federation—a worldwide organization that promotes Sefaradi tradition and education throughout the world—Sefaradi schools, some of which are Haredi oriented, have proliferated in France. Ozar Hatorah, an international Sefaradi movement, opened its first school, Torat Emet, in 1968. Today it runs seven schools, three of them in Paris and four in provincial towns (Dossier 2001). Other, smaller organizations are also active in Orthodox outreach among Sefaradim. In their return to Orthodoxy, it is possible to categorize some of these newly observant Jews as Sefaradi Haredi.

Some of France's Sefaradi Haredi elementary and high schools teach both religious and secular subjects. Religious subjects are taught in Ivrit and Loshon Kodesh with varying proportions of Aramaic, and secular subjects are taught in French. Secular studies include language study of Ivrit and even foreign languages such as German.[27] Bearing in mind the traditional orientation of French Sefaradi Jewry, including those who send their children to religious schools, it is often difficult to characterize these schools as Sefaradi Haredi. On the other hand, a number of the independent religious schools in France, have taken on more of a Sefaradi Haredi character in various spheres over the past decade. Examples of such independent schools are the Merkaz Hatorah complex at Raincy, which is under the tutelage of Rabbi Ya'akov Toledano, the École juive of Lyon under the direction of Rabbi Elie Maknouz, and the Chaaré Torah school under Rabbi Nabet (Dossier 2001). As opposed to the elementary and high schools, higher yeshivot teach only in Loshon Kodesh with a high proportion of Aramaic, using French as a second language of explanation. There is no organized Sefaradi Haredi school system in France with a political agenda, akin to that of Ma'ayan Hahinuch Hatorani in Israel.[28]

Conclusions

In this chapter we have seen how the unique nature of Sefaradi Haredim makes them a hybrid among the Haredi population. On the one hand, they have adopted

a lifestyle often characterized by attire unlike that of the local Sefaradi population, attend educational establishments outside the Sefaradi mainstream, and
have an active political orientation with social and religious manifestations.
On the other hand, however, they often do not form a separate community, as
Ashkenazi Haredim do, but rather remain part of the general Sefaradi community, albeit with a slightly different social and religious coloration. This can be
understood in view of the less modern, more traditional outlook of Sefaradi
Jewry, the acceptance of diversity within the community, and the strong communal ties that exist between family and community in much of the Sefaradi
world. This neighborly form of separatism holds true in both Israel and France,
the nation with the largest community of Sefaradim in the diaspora.

Is this attitude unique, or is it typical of Haredi life outside of Israel, and not
only that of Sefaradim? How does the attitude to language and culture among
Ashkenazi Haredim in Israel, as described previously, compare to the situation
among Haredim living abroad in a larger, non-Jewish society? I will address these
questions in the next chapter by examining Haredi language policy of Habad,
Gur, and the Mitnagdim in two countries outside of Israel with large Haredi
populations: Great Britain and the United States.

Notes

1. *Olam Haisha,* August 1996.
2, *Hamodia,* 14 June 1992.
3. *The Jerusalem Post,* 24 Dec. 1999.
4. *The Jerusalem Post,* 24 Dec. 1999.
5. Author's telephone interview with supervisor of the Mercaz Hishtalmuyot, 15 Oct. 2001.
6. *The Jerusalem Post,* 24 Dec. 1999.
7. Author's interview with Rebbetzin Gita Malka, Jerusalem, 3 Sept. 2001.
8. Author's observations at Mosdot Sha'arei Eliyahu, 15 Oct. 2001 and Yeshivat Birkat Efraim, 25
   Oct. 2001, as opposed to observations at Modsot Or Hahayim for girls, 17 Oct. 2001, all in
   Bnai Brak.
9. As a teacher in the Lipschitz program that provides academic training for Shas teachers, I have
   observed this phenomenon repeatedly among my colleagues and myself in comparison with
   my students. The same holds true in the Touro College academic training program for Shas
   teachers.
10. Author's telephone interview with curriculum coordinator at the Ma'ayan Hahinuch Hatorani
    center in Jerusalem, 15 Oct. 2001.
11. Author's interview with Yitzhak Yomtovian, Jerusalem, 15 April 2001.
12. Author's observations at Bnot Hayil Shas girls' school, Ramat Gan, 7 Nov. 2001.
13. Author's interview with Rebbetzin Gita Malka, Jerusalem, 3 Sept. 2001.
14. Author's interview with R. Sharabi, Mosdot Shaarei Eliyahu, Bnai Brak, 15 Oct. 2001, author's
    interview with secretary of Yeshivat Birkat Efraim, Bnai Brak, 25 Oct. 2001.
15. Author's interview with R. Sharabi, Bnai Brak, 15 Oct. 2001.
16. Author's interview with Rebbetzin Dina Ezri, Bnai Brak, 17 Oct. 2001.
17. Author's interview with the school secretary at Mosdot Or Hahayim, Bnai Brak, 17 Oct. 2001.
18. Author's observations at Yeshiva Tichonit Ramat Gan during the late 1990s and at the reli-
    gious girls high school in Ramat Gan during the same period.
19. Author's interview with Rebbetzin Gita Malka, Jerusalem, 3 Sept. 2001.
20. Author's observations and experiences in the Shas training program at Lipschitz College,
    1999–2001.

21. Author's telephone interview with Larissa, secretary of the Sefaradi Haredi program at Touro College, 7 Nov. 2001.

22. Observations of Prof. J. Baumel at Touro College, Jerusalem, 1995–1999 and of the author at Lipschitz College, 1999–2001.

23. Author's observations of the D family, studied in a previous section of this chapter.

24. Author's interview with Rabbi Moshe Edri Jerusalem, 5 Sept. 2001.

25. Author's interview with assistant principal of Or Hahayim girls' high school girls, Bnai Brak, 18 Oct. 2001.

26. List of Habad Shluchim in France, provided by Rabbi Aharonof (secretary for shluchim), Kfar Habad, Israel.

27. Author's interview with Prof. Jean-Paul Lellouche, Ramat Gan, 24 Sept. 2001.

28. Author's telephone interview with secretary of Ma'ayan Hahinuch Hatorani in Jerusalem, 16 Sept. 2001.

8

LANGUAGE AND CULTURE AMONG DIASPORA HAREDIM: A COMPARISON

The history, ideology, and daily practice of Orthodox and Haredi Jews have been the focus of numerous studies and several international conferences during the past few years. At one of the more recent conferences, held in Jerusalem in August 2001, a session was devoted to contemporary Orthodox and Haredi Jewry in the United States. Comparing Haredim in Israel with those in the United States, one of the speakers claimed that "although they look alike, they sound alike, and one could even think that they think alike," a major difference between Haredi Jews in Israel and in the U.S. is their sense of humor. To illustrate this point he brought the example of a store in a Haredi bungalow colony in upstate New York that sold baseball caps to Haredi men and boys on vacation. Two of the best-selling caps carried the slogans: "I keep *humrot* [strictures] which you haven't even heard of!" and "This was all I could afford after paying for my son-in-law's borsalino hat", referring to the Haredi tendency toward strict religious practice and their penchant for expensive headgear. While such vacation caps are acceptable among Haredim in The U.S., it would be difficult, if not impossible, to imagine most Israeli Haredim being able to laugh at their lifestyle—let alone wearing baseball caps on vacation.[1]

Is this the only difference between Haredim in Israel and those in the diaspora? Is it correct to say that "they sound alike," when speaking of Israeli Haredi sects which have adopted Ivrit as their language of daily speech? Haredi ideology, as expressed by the Da'at Torah of each sect regarding language use and study, is ostensibly considered suprageographical, with the leadership of each sect setting down policy for Haredim throughout the world. The ideology of the seventh Lubavitcher rebbe still guides Habad members in the United States, Israel, and even Katmandu; the Gerrer rebbe sets the tone for Gerrer Hassidim worldwide. Although the Mitnagdim had no central world authority, R. Shakh often attempted to influence Mitnagdic religious, cultural, and educational policies throughout the world. R. Yosef, leader of the Shas movement and one of the major leaders, if not the most important, in the Sefaradi Haredi world, has published halachic decisions on various subjects, including language study for Sefaradi Haredim outside of Israel. What, however, occurs when *de jure* decisions become *de facto* praxis? Does a single sect adhere to the same language practice both in Israel and throughout the diaspora? In this chapter I shall examine Haredi attitudes to language and culture in two countries with large Haredi populations, Great Britain and the United States, and compare them to Haredi language choices in Israel. While this is not intended as an in-depth examination of diaspora Haredim, I will nevertheless touch briefly on the three spheres of language and culture that serve here as a basis for compar-ison among Haredim: the domestic arena, the Haredi community, and Haredi educational institutions.

Unlike the previous chapters, for which I conducted extensive fieldwork, this chapter utilizes and synthesizes existing sources. These materials were sup-plemented and their findings corroborated by—or contrasted to—the results of numerous telephone interviews that I conducted with prominent leaders, rabbis, educators, and members of each community in the three countries surveyed.

The two coordinates of this chapter are geographical and sectoral. Even be-fore entering into the comparison with Israeli Haredim, I will present my broad-stroke research results geographically by analyzing the attitude to language and culture among the different sects in each of the three target countries. Only after this will I draw a comparison with the situation in Israel. I chose this method partly because the considerable overlap among Haredi groups within each country makes it difficult at times to differentiate one particular sect's com-munity or its educational institutions. I also wished to present a broader com-parative picture than the one that would ensue from lengthy and repetitive discussions by sector.

Great Britain

There are no precise data on the number of Haredim in Great Britain today. Es-timates range from 9,000–12,000 (Abraham-Glinert 1997) to 27,000 (Funke 1998). Of the estimated Jewish school population of 15,300, 36 percent study at strictly Orthodox schools, and most are Hassidim (Abraham-Glinert 1997). To cite the example of just one sect Rabinowicz (1997) writes that in the late 1990s over 1,500 children were enrolled in Habad schools in London alone, cared for by 80 teachers.

Several hundred Mitnagdic Haredim live in Britain, but a larger number of British Haredim belong to the various Hassidic sects. Habad communities, found throughout the British Isles, are centered in Stamford Hill, London, where over 250 Habad families reside, many newly religious (Rabinowicz 1997). In addi-tion, there are Habad communities in Cambridge, Brighton, Manchester, Leeds, and Oxford. While the Habad communities in Brighton, Manchester, and Leeds are veteran, stable communities, those in Cambridge and Oxford are primarily student communities with a changing population.[2]

Gerrer Hassidim have lived in Britain since the 1920s, and their yeshivot and *shteiblach* are concentrated in London. In 2001 there were approximately 170 Gerrer Hassidic families in Great Britain, mostly in London and Manchester, although the number of Gerrer sympathizers appears to be much greater.[3] There are no precise data on the number of Mitnagdim in Britain; estimates range from 500 to 1500 families.[4]

Although the original Jewish settlers of Britain were Sefaradim of Spanish and Portuguese descent, many descendents of these families have intermarried and virtually none have tended towards ultra-Orthodoxy. Although both they and the present-day Jews of Oriental origin are called Sefaradim, the two groups differ in origin, language, customs, and religious observance (Roth 1964). Today, the small number of Sefaradi Haredim in Britain are primarily Jews of Iranian and North African extraction who have little in common with the early Sefaradi Jews of Britain (Sachar 1985; Bermant 1972). In early 2001 there was an attempt to create a Shas movement in Britain, headed by an Irish convert to Judaism who has become Haredi. But despite the warm reception that Shas leader R. Yosef received in London, the movement has not yet taken off. Nor are there Shas educational institutions in Britain, although there are Sefaradi schools in London.[5]

The social and economic framework of British Haredim differs somewhat from that of their Israeli counterparts. Unlike their counterparts in Israel, where many Haredi men study into the fourth decade of their lives, Haredi men in Britain often leave the yeshiva and work after marriage, or, leave the kollel after their first or second child is born, at the latest. Haredi men are usually employed as religious functionaries, or in small businesses, manufacturing, education, the diamond industry, or the computer industry (Littlewood 1995; Dein 1992). Haredi women usually work in family businesses, as teachers, or as secretaries. Although in Israel it is rare to find Haredim studying in universities, Mitnagdic men in Britain occasionally attend institutions of higher education. Meanwhile, some Haredi women enroll in the British Open University, whose distance education system frees them from studying in classrooms together with men.

Habad

Although the basic language ideology of each of the four sects is suprageographical, certain variables can change according to location. For example, if a particular sect speaks in the local vernacular, that language will change from country to country. Thus, while most Habad Hassidim in Israel speak among themselves in Ivrit, in the majority of Habad homes in Britain the local vernacular—English—is spoken at home. This is particularly true among the newly religious, who make up a large number of the Habad sect in Britain (Littlewood 1995; Dein 1992). These are primarily Jews of Ashkenazic background, but some Sefaradim number among them as well. On the other hand, certain members of Habad, particularly those from newly religious backgrounds, have expressed a desire to study some Yiddish as a means of identifying with their new sect (Loewenthal 1990). Knowing Yiddish also makes it possible to study the seventh rebbe's teachings in the original (Isaacs 1999b).

Habad in Britain does not have its own local newspaper or periodical. Instead, Habad members may subscribe to the New York-based *Algemeyner Zhurnal,* a Yiddish-language weekly newspaper published by a Lubavitch-affiliated editor since 1972. Two hundred papers are delivered to subscribers in Britain every week (Mitchell 1999). Because of its unofficial Habad affiliation and its outreach mission, the paper appeals to various sectors of the Jewish community, not only the ultra-Orthodox. Yet it has not made inroads into much of British Haredi Jewry, partially because of its pro-Zionist position. Following Habad's political orientation, the *Algemeyner Zhurnal* takes a hard-line stand on Israeli territorial concessions, making it unacceptable reading matter in the more anti-Zionist Haredi circles. In general, British Haredim have a less Zionist attitude than their Israeli counterparts, something that I will explore further when dealing with Gerrer Hassidim in Britain.[6]

One of the missions that the *Algemeyner Zhurnal* has taken upon itself is the maintenance and promotion of Yiddish among Haredi Jews in general and Habad in particular. Presenting Yiddish as a language to treasure for future generations, in 1997, to commemorate the twenty-fifth anniversary of its founding, the paper sponsored a committee of rabbis and laymen who assumed a proactive role in this matter.[7] Explaining that promoting Yiddish was one way to prevent the assimilation of Jews into a wider gentile society, the paper's editor also alluded to the fact that by spreading knowledge of the language he was also giving Jews greater access to the Yiddish-speaking religious world.[8] Carrying announcements of international conferences and related events that promote Yiddish, the paper also serves the academic community, and with it the needs of the Lubavitcher rabbis at Habad houses and on university campuses throughout Britain and the United States (Mitchell 1999).

The attitude to Yiddish among Habad in Britain is a multifaceted one. By definition, the Haredi community—including all forms of Haredi public space—outside of Israel is distinguished by its use of signs in Hebrew orthography, with words in Loshon Kodesh or Yiddish. Although the large majority of Habad Hassidim in Britain speak English among themselves, a great number of their stores in Stamford Hill display signs that include Loshon Kodesh and Yiddish, the visible linguistic distinguishing marks of Ashkenazic Haredi culture in the diaspora. Yet apart from the occasional word found on a sign, or on the top of a poster announcing a religious event, a sale in a Haredi store, or an educational event, Yiddish among Habad in Britain today is used primarily as a vernacular for discussing sacred Jewish texts. Mitchell (1999) claims that speaking ability is limited mostly to men, many of whom have little proficiency in the written language. In contrast, Glinert (1999b) states that many Habad girls and women in Britain speak fluent Yiddish and are literate in the language, although they, too, are not always have proficient in written Yiddish. The discrepancy between these two claims might be attributable to Mitchell and Glinert's having examined different subgroups within Habad.

As in Israel, children in the British Habad movement study in separate boys' and girls' schools within the movement's own school system. Habad in London has a junior school and a senior school for girls, a boys' junior school, a mechina (preparatory yeshiva), a yeshiva, and a girls' seminary. Both the boys' and girls' Habad primary schools devote half the day to Jewish studies and the other half to secular studies. The language of teaching in all Habad schools is English. At the high-school level boys study for two years in the Habad Mechina, which devotes time to secular subjects, including English, after which they go on to the Lubavitch yeshiva in Golders Green.[9] In the girls' senior school secular subjects are taught; the girls are prepared for GCSE and A-level standards. English is taught as an A-level subject. Students at the boys' junior school and mechina, and in the girls' junior and senior schools, study their religious subjects in Loshon Kodesh. In addition, the boys' junior and girls' junior and senior schools teach Yiddish as a language, including the study of Yiddish texts. In the girls' senior school both Classical (Biblical) Hebrew and Ivrit are taught to the most senior classes (Glinert 1999b). At one time there was a government exam in them, but as of the 2000/01 school year it was no longer administered.[10]

Although Habad's attitude towards the vernacular is a positive one, Habad schools in Britain nevertheless put emphasis on studying Yiddish. Glinert (1999b) explains how until the late 1970s all Lubavitch schools in Britain operated entirely in English, with the exception of senior boys preparing to go to a yeshiva. When traditionalism intervened in the early 1980s, the schools were pressured to provide some Yiddish training. The boys' school responded by introducing a system whereby scripture was taught by oral translation from Hebrew into Yiddish, a language that few of the boys understood. In addition, there was one hour a day of Yiddish language instruction, using storybooks in the absence of a structured language course. Thus did Yiddish become part of the Jewish studies curriculum, although students gained proficiency not in grammar and writing but rather in oral use of the language. All Habad schools have adopted the Russian-Lithuanian pronunciation and spelling used by the rebbe, as opposed to the Polish or Hungarian dialects preferred by most Hassidic groups. Citing a recent controversy over this issue in the boys' junior school, where it was decided to stop the translation of scripture into Yiddish, the headmaster stated that he would prefer the school to be bilingual—Yiddish and English—since Yiddish is a language "for uniting Jews." In the senior boys' school the students study the rebbe's writings in the original Yiddish and Yiddish writing is taught, but the school does not promote Yiddish in place of English (Glinert 1999b). As in Israel, at their Bar Mitzvah, Habad boys also recite their *maimar*, a talk given by the late Rebbe, in Yiddish.

In contrast, the senior school for girls has a weekly period of direct Yiddish study that, in the words of the head teacher, "is to help them for the future and give them access to the Lubavitcher rebbe's writings" (Glinert 1999b). "The future" refers to their ongoing involvement in Habad activities, travel for outreach, and education in a Habad seminary in London, New York, or Manchester, which also has a Habad community. Unlike the boys, who are exposed to

Yiddish writing only in the latter part of their senior studies, the girls have structured Yiddish language study with textbooks and regular language lessons. This is partly a function of the greater status and extra time alloted to secular studies in the girls' curriculum. By age fourteen the girls are already reading the rebbe's Yiddish essays and listening to tapes of his talks; by sixteen they are writing in Yiddish. Glinert (1999b) cites educators who explain how some girls develop a passion for the language and seek out additional reading material; however, all the Yiddish they study in school revolves around Habad teachings and writings. One senior administrator of the Habad Girls Junior School in London remarked that in spite of this "passion" for Yiddish, the girls and the teachers all speak to each other in English, which remains the language of communication among Habad Hassidim in Britain.[11]

Habad's educational activities continue at the post-secondary level, both among students from Habad families who usually attend yeshiva and seminary and among Jewish students enrolled in other institutions of higher education in Britain. There is a Habad higher yeshiva and girls' seminary in London, and another in Manchester, both with international reputations.[12] While the yeshiva teaches in both English and Yiddish, the girls' seminary teaches primarily in English. Although few Habad students continue on to university, Habad rabbis are active among secular students on campuses via Habad Houses and social groups. These are organized by the Lubavitch Council for Universities and Colleges, which has organized weekend gatherings known as *shabbatonim* for Jewish students in Britain since 1966.[13] One of the better known rabbis of this sort in England was Rabbi Shmuel Boteach, an author of various books on religious family life, such as *Kosher Sex* and *The Jewish Guide to Adultery*, and the controversial founder and until recently, director, of the "Lechaim" society, the Habad center catering to Jewish students at Oxford. Speaking to groups in colloquial English, these Habad rabbis demonstrate the importance of a good command of the vernacular in an outreach movement.

Gur

In contrast to Habad, the Gerrer sect in Britain is very small, consisting of approximately 170 families. Most Gerrer Hassidim reside in London, which has three Gerrer *shteiblach,* one in Golders Green and two in Stamford Hill. The remainder live in Manchester, which has one Gerrer *shteibl.*[14] Until a generation ago Gerrer Hassidim in Britain, the majority of whom were refugees or Holocaust survivors, often spoke among themselves in Yiddish, their mother tongue. As the local Gerrer community grew and more Gerrer children were born in Britain, the language of daily use slowly switched from Yiddish to English, with parents speaking to their children in Yiddish and being answered in English, as in many immigrant communities. Today, a majority of British Gerrer Hassidim speak English among themselves.[15] Ivrit is also spoken in those Gerrer families where one parent was raised in Israel, a common occurrence among Gerrer couples. This observation was corroborated by the wife of the director of the London-based Gerrer Yeshiva of Europe, herself Israeli-born, who stated that international *shiduchim* (matrimonial matches) with Israelis are very common among Gerrer Hassidim, since the movement's center is in Israel.[16]

Although the Gerrer community in Britain, where comparatively more English is spoken, differs audibly from other British Hassidic communities, where one hears more Yiddish, its visible components are identical to those of the greater Hassidic surroundings.[17] This sameness appears to be a product of the relatively small number of Gerrer Hassidim in Britain and the high degree of overlap between them and their larger Hassidic surroundings. Hassidic-owned stores in Britain, particularly those dealing in ritual objects or foodstuffs under rabbinical supervision, may incorporate Hebrew orthography in their signs, or in smaller posters in their store windows, often using words in Yiddish or *Loshon Kodesh*, but Ivrit appear only rarely in these signs.[18]

Gerrer families in Britain sometimes subscribe to the English edition of *HaModia*, which is airmailed from Israel once a week. Several hundred copies of *HaModia*'s English edition go out to the UK and Western Europe every week, some to be sold at newsstands and others by subscription. A few families with one Israeli-born spouse also subscribe to the Friday edition of *HaModia* in Ivrit.[19]

The educational frameworks of the Gur sect again emphasize its overlap with other Hassidic sects in Britain. Gur does not have its own girls' junior and senior schools; instead, about half of the country's Gerrer girls study in two London Beis Ya'akov school—an elementary school for ages 4–11 and a secondary school for girls aged 11–17. Unlike the modern boys' Haredi schools in Britain, where secular instruction is in English but religious studies are in Yiddish (and sometimes in both Yiddish and Ivrit), the Beis Ya'akov schools teach all their subjects in English. Girls also study Ivrit after school, and Yiddish classes are held on Sunday mornings. Girls in the Beis Ya'akov schools take the GCSE and A-level examinations on a variety of subjects, including English, but are encouraged to postpone taking any university courses (if they so wish) until after marriage (Rabinowicz 1997).

The other half of the girls from Great Britain's Gur sect study at the Yesodei Hatorah school in London, which numbered over 1000 students in 2001. With separate boys' and girls' divisions, the school teaches—in the words of one of its headmasters, who happens also to be the son of the school's founder—"from cradle to seminary", meaning until the fifth form (grade 10, or about age 16).[20] The girls are given a choice of study group—English or Yiddish—and the majority choose Yiddish, although almost all of them speak English at home and among themselves. In addition to English and mathematics, which are taught according to the state curriculum in preparation for GCSE examinations, the girls learn what the headmaster calls "Biblical Hebrew," which is the equivalent of classical Hebrew, in which they also sit for a GCSE examination. Despite the great demand for Hebrew studies, this subject is not taught at Yesodei Hatorah in accordance with a decision made by the school's founder. Instead, it is taught off campus in the home of one of the teachers, and the girls are not tested in the subject. According to the headmaster, between a third and a half of the girls who graduate, including girls from the Gerrer sect, ultimately go to live in Israel and wish to have a good command of the local vernacular when they get there. In an aside he mentioned that his own daughters (his family counts itself among Gerrer sympathizers) had also taken this pragmatic path, as they knew that they would make *shiduchim* with boys from Israel and wanted to know the language in advance.[21]

The education that boys receive in the British Gerrer world involves more transitions than the girls'. Since Gerrer Hassidim in London do not have their own heder, some send their boys to the primary grades at Yesodei Hatorah, where they study religious subjects in Yiddish and Loshon Kodesh with a high proportion of Aramaic. Secular subjects are taught completely in English, and the school follows a state curriculum with emphasis on English and mathematics, in which GCSE examinations are given. Other Gerrer boys attend the Pardes House primary school, an all-male educational establishment with both Hassidic and Mitnagdic pupils. As in Yesodei Hatorah, the boys at Pardes House study secular subjects in English and religious subjects in Loshon Kodesh translated into Yiddish. Although only a few of the children already speak Yiddish when they start school at Pardes House, most of them pick it up quickly. As a state-aided school, Pardes House follows the national curriculum, offering standard exams in mathematics and English.[22]

Almost all Gerrer boys leave these two institutions between the ages of 10 and 13 to attend a more Hassidic-style school. The most popular schools for preadolescent Gerrer boys in Britain are the Vizhnitz school and the Gerrer Yeshiva of Europe, a London-based Gerrer institution for boys aged 13–17 from Britain and Western Europe that had approximately sixty pupils in 2001. Both institutions teach only religious subjects to their older pupils, in Yiddish and Loshon Kodesh, as do the London-area schools of other Hassidic sects such as Bobov, Belz, and Satmar (Abraham-Glinert 1997; Abraham 1999). These Haredi schools devote only a few hours a week to secular studies and teach all subjects in Yiddish. English is taught as a second language. Although they ostensibly conform to the national curriculum, in practice these schools do not teach more than six to ten hours a week of secular subjects and do not prepare their students to pass either GCSE or A-level examinations. Graduates of both sexes are actively discouraged from seeking admission to university, and girls are encouraged to continue in a teaching seminary of the particular sect.[23]

British Gerrer boys' command of Yiddish develops with age. Although they are supposed to have studied Yiddish as soon as they start school, in practice a large number of them are not yet fluent by the time of their Bar Mitzvah at age 13. Referring to this situation, one of my informants, well versed in the linguistic tendencies of the Haredi London community, pointed to examples from his own family to illustrate how, although most of these boys give their Bar Mitzvah *drush* (sermon) in Yiddish, they do not necessarily understand much of what they are saying.[24] This phenomenon occurs among ethnic groups preserving a linguistic heritage, whose children may have only a rudimentary command of that tongue (Mougeon and Nadasdi 1998).

Between the ages of 16 and 18, the Gerrer girls begin their studies in the seminary and the boys enter the higher yeshiva. Gerrer girls go to the Gateshead or Manchester seminaries; boys attend the Gateshead Yeshiva, the Gerrer Yeshiva in London, or a school in Israel (Rabinowicz 1997). Lessons at the Gateshead and Manchester seminaries all take place in English, and regardless of origin the girls usually speak to each other in English. In contrast, *shiurim* at Gateshead are delivered to the boys in Yiddish, even though many of the boys prefer to speak in English among themselves. Following the tradition that allows crossovers from almost all Hassidic sects and even from the Mitnagdim, boys from Gur sit side by side with Mitnagdim at Gateshead, and Gerrer girls at the Manchester seminary share a classroom with girls from Bobov and even Satmar. Yet in keeping with the same set of rules, which regard Lubavitch as outside the fold, no young man or young woman from Gur will study at a Habad yeshiva or seminary.[25]

Mitnagdim

There are no precise numbers regarding Mitnagdim in Britain, but estimates range between 500 and 1500 families. The largest numbers of Mitnagdim are found in London and Manchester, although small communities have taken root in several other cities, Oxford, Cambridge, and Bristol among them.[26] Most Mitnagdic families speak English at home. In view of the small numbers of Haredim in Britain, there is a great deal of overlap between the Hassidic and Mitnagdic communities. The audible Mitnagdic community is punctuated by less Yiddish than the Hassidic community, and the language usually heard is a combination of English and "Yeshivish," a term I will explain below.[27] As for the visual aspect, signs in stores catering to Mitnagdim may include the occasional word in Yiddish or Loshon Kodesh.[28]

Numerous Mitnagdim in Britain subscribe to *Yated Ne'eman* in English. Several thousand copies a week are sent from Israel to Haredi enclaves in Britain and Western Europe.[29] In addition, Mitnagdim occasionally also subscribe to the New York–based weekly the *Jewish Press,* a hybrid pro-Zionist/right-wing paper with a circulation of over 100,000 catering to English-speaking Hassidim, Mitnagdim, national-religious (Mizrachi), and Haredi nationalist groups throughout the world (Kranzler 1988). While a few such families can still be found reading the *Algemeyner Zhurnal,* it appeals mostly to the generation of Eastern European–born grandparents in their seventh and eighth decades, for whom Yiddish was their mother tongue.[30]

Educational frameworks in the Mitnagdic world of Great Britain are also characterized by overlap, both with Hassidic-affiliated institutions and with those that tend more toward the modern Orthodox world. Less than one generation ago Mitnagdim in London sent their children to Hasmonean Grammar School, an institution with modern Orthodox and Zionist tendencies.[31] In recent years, following the right-wing tendencies of the Haredi world, fewer Haredim are willing to send their children to a co-educational school. Most London Haredim now send their sons to Pardes House or Menorah Grammar School, which has separate classes for boys and girls in most subjects, and their daughters to Menorah, Yesodei Hatorah, or Beis Ya'akov.[32]

Most Mitnagdic children do not speak any Yiddish at home. The boys who study at Pardes House pick it up during the course of their religious subjects, which are taught in Loshon Kodesh and Yiddish. All secular subjects are taught in English. Because large numbers of Hassidic boys who study at Pardes House transfer to Hassidic schools in the upper grades of the junior classes (nearly half of the 260 boys in the junior school are Hassidic), the senior school, with 200 pupils, is primarily Mitnagdic. It strives for academic excellence in secular subjects, unlike many of the Hassidic schools, which teach little, if any, English, mathematics, or other secular subjects. Students at Pardes House take their English A-level examination a year ahead of their contemporaries in other schools. In addition, they take A-levels in Classical Hebrew and Ivrit. At the senior school students study French as well as Ivrit, and the occasional pupil elects to take German as well.[33] Menorah, equally devoted to academic excellence, teaches religious studies in Yiddish and Loshon Kodesh and secular studies in English. Like Pardes House, Menorah accepts the national curriculum in most subjects, having scrutinized it to rule out any clash with Jewish traditional teachings. Thus, as in many of the more modern Haredi schools in Britain, the boys study English, French, history, geography, mathematics, and physics in primary school, and later are prepared for the GCSE examinations of London University. The boys who attend these schools are highly motivated, and there is an examination pass rate of 80–90 percent. Many complete the GCSE in at least five subjects by the age of 15 (Rabinowicz 1997).

Ashkenazi Haredi language policy in Britain (or, for that matter, in the United States) cannot be described and analyzed without discussing a linguistic phenomenon that has become known as "Yeshivish" (Landau 1993). As Weiser (1995) states in *Frumspeak: The First Dictionary of Yeshivish,* this is neither a pidgin nor a technical jargon but rather a blend in which standard English is laced with words or expressions from Yiddish and Loshon Kodesh with varying proportions of Aramaic. The words in Loshon Kodesh always receive the Ashkenazic pronunciation, as opposed to the Sefaradi pronunciation commonly used in Ivrit. Although some may initially categorize Yeshivish as a mere dialect, it differs from English in three ways: sound or phonemic structure, lexical meaning, and syntax. Yeshivish is distinct from each of its component languages—English, Loshon Kodesh, and Yiddish—on each of these levels, leading to scholarly debate over whether it has become a separate language (Weiser 1995; Gold 1985). Almost solely an oral language, Yeshivish lacks grammar books laying out its rules, although a dictionary has recently been published (Weiser 1995). Yet as a modern offspring of traditional Jewish triglossia, Yeshivish has reached new heights of popularity among English-speaking Haredim, particularly Mitnagdim.

Yeshivish was born out of a number of factors. One was the desire expressed by Mitnagdic young men studying in yeshiva (who spoke English, as opposed to the Hassidim, who spoke Yiddish) to differentiate themselves linguistically from their parents, many of whom were already British- or American-born and well assimilated into the linguistic patterns of their country of origin. Yeshivish filled another gap by attempting to recreate an imagined linguistic pattern that had never really existed among nineteenth- and twentieth-century European Jews—not even among those who had immigrated to Britain and the U.S. in the waves of the great immigration (1881–1914), who either spoke Yiddish or mixed it with occasional English phrases. A third factor in the emergence of Yeshivish was the desire to create an internal type of language for yeshiva *bochurs* (students) to serve as an ingroup linguistic code among them. It is noteworthy that even the term *bochurs* is a choice influenced by Yeshivish. *Bochur*, a Biblical Hebrew word meaning "young man" that is used in both Yiddish and Hebrew, receives the English plural suffix "-s" instead of the Hebrew suffix "-im" or the Yiddish "-en."

Yeshivish has given birth to many interesting linguistic combinations besides the lexical transfers of Haredi Yiddish to English, but it also rests on a cultural component that defies explanation to anyone not part of a particular world (Isaacs 1999). One illustrative example is the Yeshivish translation of Antony's funeral oration for Caesar (Weiser 1995): "*Raboisai* [Heb.], Roman *oilam* [Yid.], *heimishe* [Yid.] *chevra* [Heb.], *herr zich ain* [Yid.]"—"Friends, Romans, countrymen, lend me your ears." Another is the Gettysburg Address in Yeshivish, which appeared several years ago in the English section of the *Algemeyner Zhurnal* and was reprinted in Weiser's dictionary (1995), beginning with the sentence: "*Be'erech* [Heb.] a *yoivel* [Heb.] and a half ago, the *meyasdim* [Heb.] *shtelled avek* [Yid.with Eng. suffix] on this *makom* [Heb.] a *naiya* [Yid.] *malchus* [Heb.] with the *kavana* [Heb.] that no one should have *bailus* [Heb.] over their *chaver* [Heb.], and on this *yesoid* [Heb.] that everyone has the *zelba* [Yid.] *zchusim* [Heb. with Yid. suffix].[34] To an older English speaker who knows Yiddish and Loshon Kodesh, this Yeshivish version of "Fourscore and seven years ago our forefathers brought forth on this continent a new nation, conceived in liberty, and dedicated to the proposition that all men are created equal" appears laughable. But to large numbers of Mitnagdic young men it is a completely understandable form of speech (Helmreich 1982).

Sefaradi Haredim

The first Jewish families to settle in Britain when Cromwell decreed that Jews may return to England were of Spanish and Portuguese origin, and only a small number of their descendents are still Jewish today. Like their counterparts who found refuge in the New World in the seventeenth and eighteenth centuries, large numbers of British Sefaradim abandoned the faith of their forefathers, marrying into the local population and even into the British aristocracy (Roth 1964). Most of the Sefaradim in Britain today are not descendents of these original settlers; rather, they are of Oriental descent, immigrants from Islamic lands, particularly Iran, and North African countries. A small number are former Israelis who have made their home in Britain. Of this group, only a minute number can be considered Haredi, and almost all of these live in the Stamford Hill section of London, the site of several Sefaradi and Sefaradi Haredi synagoguges.[35] It is difficult to speak of a Sefaradi Haredi community with its own characteristics because of the small numbers of people involved.

Sefaradi Haredim born outside of Britain usually speak to each other in their mother tongue—Farsi, Ivrit, or French—just as many immigrants prefer to speak the language in which they are most comfortable, or try to maintain proficiency in their native language.[36] In the same fashion, Sefaradi Haredi children born or raised in Britain usually speak English to each other and answer their parents in English, even when they are addressed in their parents' preferred language.

There are Sefaradi school systems operating in London, of which the best known is the Od Yoseph Chai system of schools ranging from a newly opened kindergarten to higher yeshiva. Teaching in English and Loshon Kodesh with varying proportions of Aramaic, these schools cater to the Sefaradi population but cannot be considered Sefaradi Haredi–oriented like the Ma'ayan Hahinuch Hatorani schools in Israel. Most Sefaradi Haredi children in London study at Ashkenazi schools such as Hasmonean or Yesodei Hatorah. In the latter institution, the boys are first exposed to Yiddish, like the Sefaradi Haredi boys in Israel who only one generation ago studied Yiddish in Mitnagdic Yeshivot. Sefaradi Haredi girls attend either Yesodei Hatorah, where they usually choose to study in English, or Beis Ya'akov.[37] Although R. Yosef was afforded a warm welcome when he came to speak, as was the Israeli Sefaradi Haredi revivalist Amnon Yitzhak during his September tour of that year, the movement does not appear to be taking off in Britain. There has as yet been no attempt to open a Sefaradi Haredi school system similar to Ma'ayan Hahinuch Hatorani, nor any attempt to create a political framework similar to that of Sefaradi Haredim in Israel.[38]

Discussion

In comparing the language and culture of British and Israeli Haredim belonging to the Habad, Gur, Mitnagdic, and Sefaradi sects, several similarities and differences come to light. Before breaking down my conclusions to the sectoral level, I should note that on the geographical level it appears that overall, British and Israeli Haredim use similar language frameworks—although not necessarily the same languages themselves—in the domestic sphere. All four sects among both Israeli- and British-born Haredim prefer to use the local vernacular at home—Ivrit for the first group, English for the second. Immigrant Haredim of these groups in Britain appear to use less local vernacular with their children than do their Haredi immigrant counterparts in Israel—perhaps because to the Haredi sects in question, Ivrit, the local vernacular in Israel, enjoys a tacit, quasi-sacred status owed to its linguistic connection with Loshon Kodesh.

As for Haredi communities and neighborhoods, within the Ashkenazi Haredi groups one hears and sees more Yiddish in Britain than in Israel. This does not seem to be connected to the age of the Haredim found within these communities, as both in Britain and in Israel one finds that these Haredi groups comprise all ages. The linguistic difference between the British and Israeli Haredi communities may derive from fact that in the diaspora, Yiddish is usually considered the ingroup language, the linguistic marker of all Ashkenazi Haredi life, regardless of sect. Even if a particular sect's members do not tend to speak Yiddish among themselves in Israel, their vocabularies are richer in Yiddish expressions in the diaspora. This appears to be the fruit of the crossover between the various Haredi groups in the diaspora and the greater mixing of these groups in educational institutions there.

The contrasts and similarities are most abundant in a comparative examination of the four Haredi sects' educational systems in Britain and in Israel. On the whole, Haredi girls' schools in both countries appear to be more open than boys' schools to the outside world. While the girls' schools in both countries often administer state or state-equivalency language exams in the upper grades, the boys' schools rarely do, with the exception of the more modern Mitnagdic-style schools. Few Hassidic boys in either country study any secular subjects after reaching high school. Older Gerrer and Mitnagdic boys study in Loshon Kodesh with a large proportion of Aramaic and Yiddish, as do Sefaradi Haredi boys who are educated in Ashkenazi frameworks. Elite Sefaradi Haredi girls in both countries often study in Ashkenazi frameworks, and all girls' seminaries of the four sects conduct their lessons in the local vernacular. Both in Israel and in Britain, girls study foreign languages to prepare themselves for their economic future. In Britain, many Haredi girls study Ivrit, even off campus, to prepare themselves for marriages that will take them to Israel. For them, knowledge of that language has both social and economic significance for their future. Similarly, Haredi girls in Israel study English to prepare themselves for the work force. At times, knowledge of English may also help an Israeli Haredi girl make and sustain an international matrimonial match, as in the case of the Gerrer Rebbetzin in London, who was a Haifa-born English teacher in Israel before her marriage.

A number of differences mark British and Israeli Haredi language and culture in the four targeted sects. In general, it appears that in these sects, and particularly among the Mitnagdim and Sefaradi Haredim, more boys in Britain than in Israel attend schools that teach language studies, meaning the study of English as well as foreign languages such as French or German. More Mitnagdic and Sefaradi Haredim in Britain are open to the idea of higher education for men—often within the framework of the British Open University, but also at times in regular university study—because in Britain large numbers of Haredi men expect to join the work force. Therefore certain Haredi boys' schools tend to emphasize subjects necessary for making a living, including English language study.

In the Israeli Haredi world, there are almost no boys' high schools, besides the yeshivot *ketanot,* which rarely offer any real form of language study and which discourage their pupils from seeking higher education. Boys are expected to study in higher yeshiva and then in kollel for a major part of their first married decades. Consequently, there is no need for them to study the secular subjects that would assist them in progressing economically.

British and Israeli Haredi language policy also differ in the field of girls' studies. More Yiddish is taught at British Haredi girls' schools of the three targeted Ashkenazi sects than at their Israeli counterparts, where all study takes place in Ivrit. More girls in Britain choose Yiddish as the language of instruction for secular subjects as well, to an extent that has no parallel in Israeli Habad, Gur, or Mitnagdic girls' schools in Israel. Girls learning English and foreign languages in the British schools use state textbooks, often edited to expunge unsuitable pictures or texts, whereas with only a few exceptions, most Haredi girls' schools in Israel use their own home-produced material.

A final striking difference is the absence in Britain of Shas-sponsored Sefaradi Haredi schools, along the lines of the Ma'ayan Hahinuch Hatorani system in Israel.

In general, Habad language policy in Britain is similar to that in Israel—an openness to language stemming from the movement's ideology of outreach. Although Gur was traditionally considered a more Zionist-oriented Hassidic sect than other Haredi groups, the Gerrer Hassidim in Britain are less Zionist-oriented than their Israeli counterparts. Yet one still finds Gerrer families in Britain who speak Ivrit at home when it is one of the parents' mother tongue. The Mitnagdim in Britain are usually more open to the wider society than are those in Israel, particularly in their attitudes toward higher education and employment. As a result, they have a more liberal attitude to language study for men than do many Israeli Mitnagdim. Sefaradi Haredim in Britain are reminiscent of those in Israel a generation earlier, who sent most of their children to Haredi Ashkenazi schools, including schools that taught Yiddish.

The United States

The situation in the United States differs somewhat from the one I have described in Great Britain in view of the demographic differences between the two countries, particularly the proliferation of American Haredim during the latter half of the twentieth century. As in Britain, it is difficult to determine the exact number of Haredi Jews living in the United States; estimates range from 60,000 to over 110,000 (see, for example, Glinert 1999a as opposed to Mintz 1992 and Kranzler 1995a). The main centers of Haredi life are in and around New York City, with the majority of Haredim concentrated in Brooklyn (Williamsburg, Borough Park, and Crown Heights) or in Haredi communities such as the Satmar enclave of Kiriyas Yoel in Monroe, New York (Ben-David 1999). In addition, in recent years one can find Haredim scattered throughout all of the fifty states. American Ashkenazi Haredim include both those of Mitnagdic background and of Hassidic affiliation, with a number of Hassidic rebbes having built their postwar courts in America after escaping from Europe. Among them were the leaders of the Bobover Hassidim, the Habad Hassidim (which according to some accounts are the largest Haredi group in the U.S.), the Skverer Hassidim (Dar 2001), and even one American Hassidic institution that has spread to Israel: the Bostoner Hassidim. The Gerrer community in the U.S. is located in Brooklyn, which has eight Gerrer *shteiblach* (Landau 1993). Growing numbers of Sefaradi Haredim of Oriental and Middle Eastern background live in the U.S., mainly in New York, New Jersey, Los Angeles, or Miami. More

Haredi educational institutions on all levels are found in the United States than in any other country of the diaspora.

As in Great Britain, Haredi men in the United States usually join the work force after marriage or after beginning their family (Bomzer 1985). But in view of the polarization of Haredi life in the United States, the kollel movement for married men, which urges study for two to five years after marriage, has grown considerably. Helmreich (1982) states that in 1950 there were no more than fifty to a hundred young men studying in kollels in the United States. By 1980 there were over 1,000 such students, and today kollels exist throughout the United States, from New York City, South Fallsburg, New York, and Stamford, Connecticut, to Los Angeles.

It is more common for Mitnagdim to study in kollelim after marriage than it is for Hassidim, who traditionally go out to work shortly after marriage. For example, only in 1965 did the Satmar Hassidim open a kollel for married students, as the rebbe had long held that married men should work to support their families (Kranzler 1995a; Rubin 1997). While Hassidic men are usually employed in trade, printing, the diamond industry, education, and computers or as religious functionaries (Redekop 1987; Shaffir 1974), it is possible to find small numbers of Hassidic men and larger numbers of Mitnagdic men who have attended college. The New York–based religious educational establishment, Touro College, founded in 1970 by Dr. Bernard Lander, offers separate classes for men and women, but Haredi men sometimes go to secular colleges leaving yeshiva (Helmreich 1982). In addition, various Mitnagdic yeshivot offer a full Torah study program but permit older students to take college courses in the evenings. These include Torah Voda'at Yeshiva in New York City and Ner Israel Yeshiva in Baltimore (Gurock 1988). Mitnagdic men work in the same trades as Hassidic men, as well as accountancy, law, advertising, and even medicine. Haredi women usually work in teaching, clerical work, and computer programming, or in trade. Among adherents of Habad, which is the largest Jewish outreach group in the United States (Shas is not particularly active in America), one finds both male and female college graduates.

Habad

There are no precise numbers of Habad Hassidim in the United States, although counting Habad sympathizers, they claim to be the largest Haredi group in America.[39] As in the British Lubavitch movement, American Habad members usually speak English among themselves, particularly in view of the fact that large numbers of the sect are newly religious. There are some Habad families in America who speak Yiddish at home, but they are the minority.[40] In general, the Habad communities throughout America are English-language communities, but one must differentiate between the Habad communities outside of New York and the one found around the Habad world center in Brooklyn. During the High Holiday month of Tishrei, when Habad members the world over customarily travel to New York and congregate near the rebbe's residence, the streets are filled with Hassidim speaking various languages, especially Ivrit and

French. Many of the French speakers are of Sefaradi ethnic origin and have become members of Habad in countries such as France, Britain, Israel, and the United States.[41]

Today the Crown Heights Habad community, the seat of the Habad world center, is a mixed one, with many members from Israel and outside the United States. The language on the street is similarly mixed, with English predominating although among Habad Hassidim Yiddish is also heard, primarily the Lithuanian-Belorussian dialect (Jochnowitz 1968). Among American Habad members English is the primary language of communication, although Yiddish is afforded "great respect," in the words of a Habad family living in Crown Heights.[42] Commercial signs are usually in English, while signs of a religious nature are often in English and/or Ivrit. Because large number of Israeli Habad members live in the area for some period, many classified-type notices (help wanted, apartments for rent) are in Ivrit.[43]

Following what Landau (1993) calls their bibliophilical tradition, Habad Hassidim are known as voracious readers. Apart from the daily American press, which many Habad Hassidim read, many Yiddish-speaking American Habad members read the weekly *Algemeyner Zhurnal,* whose editor has a Lubavitch orientation. Some Habad members read the English-language weekly, the *Jewish Press* mentioned earlier, which caters to a broad religious and Haredi public within the Zionist spectrum. Shaffir (1974) notes that there are Habad families who read *Di Yiddishe Heim.* Unlike the *Algemeyner Zhurnal,* where articles and advertisements can relate to non-Haredi, general Yiddish activities in the Jewish world, these two latter papers are geared to a religious/Haredi public, particularly *Di Yiddishe Heim,* which is a Lubavitch publication. This is one example of how the Habad community in the United States, immersed in outreach and in constant touch with the outside world, attempts to resist secular culture by providing members with a separate Haredi alternative (Davidman 1990). Other Hassidic groups in the U.S. also have their own newspapers or magazines, such as the Satmar Hassidim's *Der Yid,* a communal organ claiming a circulation of 30,000, that was founded in 1953 as an offshoot of the now defunct Yiddish daily *Morgen Zhurnal* (Kranzler 1988, 1993). These Yiddish papers include a large number of English words, which have blended into the text and into daily Yiddish speech (Poll 1965). As a result, readers in Israel who are unfamiliar with English expressions such as *gewaschen de vinde* (washed the window) often find it difficult to fully understand the American Haredi Yiddish press.

From kindergartens to higher yeshivot, Habad educational institutions are found in communities throughout the United States. Most Habad schools outside of New York teach secular studies in English and religious studies either in Loshon Kodesh or in a combination of English and Loshon Kodesh, as they often cater to a newly observant clientele (Fishkoff 2001). Habad schools usually follow a state curriculum in secular studies, including the study of English and foreign languages.[44]

The center of Habad education is in Brooklyn, home to the largest number of Habad schools in any one geographical location. In Crown Heights, boys' and girls' schools educate children from nursery schools through higher ye-shiva (known as *Beis Medrash*, (study hall) and girls' seminary. There are two main Habad boys' elementary schools in Brooklyn, Oholei Torah and Achei Temimim (Sharot 1991). The first teaches exclusively in Yiddish with no secu-lar program and no language study (Mintz 1992); the second teaches religious subjects in Loshon Kodesh, Yiddish, and English and offers a secular studies program taught in English. Studies at the Habad *Beis Medrash* are in Loshon Kodesh and Yiddish. There is also a yeshiva for boys of college age with no re-ligious background, where studies take place primarily in English with some *Loshon Kodesh*.[45] While it is common to hear Yeshivish among Habad boys and men, it is less common to hear it among girls and women, who do not study Talmudic texts (Benor 1999, 2001).

Habad in New York has one main elementary school for girls, Beis Rivka, and two smaller Habad girls' schools in the area. The main school generally teaches all of its secular classes in English. Religious studies are in English and Loshon Kodesh, although there is generally one class per grade (out of approx-imately six parallel classes) where the language of instruction is Yiddish. One of the new girls' schools teaches all its subjects in Yiddish and Loshon Kodesh; at the other, religious studies are in English and Loshon Kodesh, and secular studies are in English. The main girls' elementary school runs a high school, also belonging to the Beis Rivka network, that teaches religious studies in En-glish and Loshon Kodesh and secular studies in English. In the autumn of 2001, the Yiddish elementary school opened a girls' high school where religious stud-ies are taught in Yiddish and Loshon Kodesh and secular studies, in Yiddish. All of the girls' schools—including the Yiddish-language ones—teach English as a subject of study. Beis Rivka also runs a girls' seminary where the languages of instruction are English and Loshon Kodesh.

In contrast, discussing Habad in Canada, Shaffir (1974) notes that Habad boys' schools in Montreal, are divided into two streams, one studying only in Loshon Kodesh and Yiddish, and the other working in Loshon Kodesh in the morning and in English in the afternoon, when secular subjects are taught. As in the United States, Yiddish is the most commonly heard language among Hassidim in Canada, although Shaffir notes that Habad Hassidim are more likely than any other sect to know English. Bearing in mind that these obser-vations are more than three decades old, and that the outreach component of Habad has grown since that time, Habad in Canada today can be expected to have seen a proliferation of English (or French), as the first language learned and the favorite language for speech, similar to that experienced by American Habad members.

Gur

The small Gerrer community in the United States is congregated primarily in Brooklyn. Speaking English, Yiddish, and, in the case of families with one or more members from Israel, Ivrit at home, the Gerrer community uses these three languages in its public space as well, with more Yiddish than is customarily heard in Gerrer neighborhoods in Israel. This is probably a result of the crossover between various Hassidic groups in the diaspora, and may also reflect the fact that Yiddish is considered the Haredi linguistic marker, regardless of whether a particular sect uses Yiddish as its most commonly spoken language. Visually, the Gerrer neighborhoods, like American Hassidic neighborhoods in general, have signs and posters in a combination of English, Ivrit, and Yiddish, depending on the nature of the notice.[46]

Some Gerrer Hassidim in the United States subscribe to the English-language edition of *HaModia,* which is flown in from Israel once a week.[47] There are a small number of Gerrer Hassidim who read the *Jewish Press,* a paper whose growing hard-line Zionist orientation in recent years has alienated it from large groups of American Hassidim (such as the Bobover Hassidim) who used to read the paper in the 1960s and 1970s.[48] Other Gerrer Hassidim subscribe to the Yiddish monthly *Dos Yiddishe Vort,* a Yiddish-language magazine founded in 1954 by Agudat Yisrael in America and edited by Joseph Friedenson, an elderly Holocaust survivor from Warsaw with family connections to the Gerrer sect (Poll 1965). Some Gerrer families subscribe to *The Jewish Observer,* the English-language monthly sponsored by Agudat Yisrael in America.[49]

Gerrer Hassidim have lived in the United States since the end of the Second World War and have a long established educational system. In New York they have their own yeshiva system ranging from elementary to higher yeshiva. Secular subjects are taught only in the elementary schools, in English and in the afternoon, and religious studies are conducted in Yiddish and Loshon Kodesh with a low proportion of Aramaic. From high school age onward all studies are religious and are taught in Yiddish and Loshon Kodesh with a high proportion of Aramaic.[50] Girls from the Gerrer sect study in the Beis Ya'akov school system, founded in the United States in the early 1940s. Teaching religious studies in English and Loshon Kodesh and secular studies in English, these schools follow the state curriculum and prepare their pupils for state examinations, although they discourage them from pursuing higher education (Rosengarten 1992; Weissman 1976, 1995).

In contrast to the Beis Ya'akov schools, a number of Hassidic-oriented schools for boys and girls teach primarily in Yiddish. An extreme example is that of the Satmar Hassidim. While some Haredim speak English to their children from birth in the United States, the Satmar, like certain other Hassidic sects, deliberately shield their children from English before the age of eight, speaking only Yiddish to them. Although at times they speak English among themselves, girls from these sects study in Yiddish only, whereas boys are taught in two languages—Yiddish and Loshon Kodesh with varying proportions of Aramaic depending upon their age. When these children begin studying English, it is taught as a foreign language (Eisenberg 1995) and usually not given much respect. English teachers, who are often not even considered "teachers" by their pupils, are treated more like babysitters than educators (Fader 2001; Albarelli 2001). This separatist attitude is expressed again in the general attitude these Haredim hold toward secular studies, of which English is considered a part. As a result, it is less acceptable to teach English and secular subjects to boys among the Satmar Hassidim (Rubin 1997) than it is among more modern Hassidic sects such as Habad and Bobov (Kamen 1985; Shaffir 1974).

Mitnagdim

The Mitnagdic community in the United States is larger than its British counterpart, with an estimated 10,000 to 30,000 members.[51] Based primarily in New York City, Mitnagdim have spread to communities in major Jewish centers: Boston, Philadelphia, Miami, Los Angeles, Chicago, Cleveland, and recently, additional areas in the continental United States.[52] A wide variety of observances and lifestyles flourish in what is called the Mitnagdic community, from heavily separatist members to those whose lifestyle is almost indistinguishable from what is known as "centrist," or even what was once called modern Orthodox (Heilman 1982).

One aspect of this variation emerges in the sphere of domestic language. Although older, European-born Mitnagdim may still speak Yiddish at home, since the 1960s most American-born Mitnagdim have usually chosen to speak English among themselves, a sign of the community's Americanization.[53] As the Mitnagdic community shifted rightward in terms of religious observance and separatism, some in the younger generation (usually more men than women) began to speak Yeshivish. Men were the first to use Yeshivish—the name itself refers to the all-male world of the yeshiva, where the phenomenon developed. But Mitnagdic women, some of whom possess extensive Jewish learning and have even studied Mishnaic (and occasionally Talmudic) texts, also began using a moderate form of Yeshivish by incorporating large amounts of Yiddish and even Loshon Kodesh into what was once their everyday English speech. They have also changed their syntax and altered the meanings of various words that still retain the form of their original language.[54] Certain families even went over to speaking a form of Yiddish at home, although their members had never received formal instruction in the language; the men had usually picked up what they knew during yeshiva studies.[55]

The Mitnagdic communities today are primarily English-speaking. Certain store signs, primarily those advertising kosher food and religious objects, contain Hebrew words. Dry-goods or even furniture stores may also have signs with Yeshivish expressions such as *sforim shank,* meaning large bookcases for religious books.[56] The same combinations of linguistic expressions appear in the American Haredi press (Kantor 1997).

Certain Mitnagdim throughout the United States read the *Jewish Press,* although in the greater New York area there are a handful of subscribers to the English-language edition of *Yated Ne'eman.*[57] In recent years, the language in many columns of the *Jewish Press* has become quite Yeshivish, particularly in the family and household sections, and in the *Machberes* (notebook) section, which details the comings and goings of rabbinical figures in the Haredi world, both Hassidic and Mitnagdic.[58] Mitnagdim also read the *Jewish Observer,* and the Yiddish-speaking contingent also often reads *Dos Yiddishe Vort.*[59]

Mitnagdic educational frameworks in the United States are well developed, particularly in the major cities with large Jewish populations. The Mitnagdic school system has separate boys' and girls' schools. It is best exemplified in New York, where Mitnagdic boys and girls have a large number of schools to choose from at both the primary and secondary levels. From the German-Jewish–style R. Samson Rafael Hirsch ("Breuer's") girls' school to the more traditional Beis Ya'akov schools (Rosengarten, 1992) for girls, and from the more modern Chofetz Chaim boys' elementary and high school yeshiva to the more traditional Torah Voda'at high school and higher yeshiva, all of these schools have several common denominators. The first is the language of education. All Mitnagdic elementary and high schools teach secular studies in English and religious subjects in either Loshon Kodesh with various proportions of Aramaic and English, or Loshon Kodesh with various proportions of Aramaic, English, and Ivrit. A second common denominator is the study of other languages. Almost all of the girls' schools, and a large number of the boys' schools, teach Ivrit as a subject. Many of the schools also teach foreign languages such as French.[60]

Another common denominator is the general curriculum. Unlike many of the Hassidic schools, which do not teach secular subjects past junior high school age, all of these elementary and high schools follow a state curriculum. Even the most traditional teach a minimum number of secular subjects in high school, preparing students for state examinations such as the New York Board of Regents' Examinations, or even college preparatory exams like the SAT (Scholastic Aptitude Test). For their secular studies, almost all of these schools use the state program's textbooks. A final common denominator is preparation for further study. A number of these schools ready children for higher education, even if they are encouraged to continue at a yeshiva or seminary instead of a university.[61]

Considerable variation marks the Mitnagdic yeshiva world's attitude to college-level study. No higher yeshiva will agree to the primacy of secular study over religious study, but some are more pragmatic than others in permitting college study on a limited basis (Helmreich 1982). Then again, there are yeshivot, such as the Mirrer Yeshiva, that unequivocally forbid college study to their students currently attending the yeshiva, and discourage graduates from involvement in secular study afterwards. Other Mitnagdic higher Yeshivot, for instance Ner Israel in Baltimore or Torah Voda'at in Brooklyn, allow their students to pursue a college degree while continuing their yeshiva studies and even have agreements with nearby colleges, such as Johns Hopkins in Baltimore, on transferring credits for yeshiva study. The arrangement is a purely practical one, as the yeshiva considers college to be no more than vocational training. Students may study subjects that will be of professional use, but do not receive permission to study subjects like history, philosophy, or literature, which might be at odds with their yeshiva studies (Landau 1993). Languages are permitted topics of study, if they are for future professional use. Yet even in cases of yeshivot such as Lakewood and Telshe, which forbid college attendance for students boarding at the school, a substantial number of alumni attended college either before they enrolled or after they left the yeshiva (Helmreich 1982). This would not be possible without the training in secular subjects, including language, that these alumni received at their Mitnagdic yeshiva high schools.

Aware of the difficulty of stemming the tide of students who wish to arm themselves with a secular degree before entering the work force, Mitnagdic yeshiva leaders (and even the rare Hassidic rebbe) in the United States also recognize that the yeshiva world stands to gain a great deal from the fact that some of their students attend college. In his study of the American yeshiva world, Helmreich (1982) shows how such secular education, by providing prestige, financial advantage, and general stature in the Orthodox community at large, ensures that people sympathetic to the interests of the yeshivot will ultimately serve in key positions throughout the community. Such individuals form a cadre of core supporters whose influence will affect the political and economic support that yeshivot receive on various levels.

Mitnagdic higher yeshivot exist throughout the United States but are concentrated primarily in cities with large Jewish populations, chiefly New York (Chaim Berlin, Torah Voda'at, Central Yeshiva Beth Joseph Rabbinical Seminary, Mirrer Yeshiva, Beth ha-Talmud Rabbinical College, Kamenitzer Yeshiva of Boro Park, R. Samson Rafael Hirsch Yeshiva), but also in Lakewood, New Jersey (Beth Medrash Govoha of America), Philadelphia (Talmudical Academy of Philadelphia), Baltimore (Ner Israel Rabbinical College), and Cleveland (Rabbinical College of Telshe) (Helmreich 1982). Many of these Mitnagdic yeshivot, like their Hassidic counterparts, have European antecedents in that the original faculty members were European or the entire school had been transferred to the U.S. from Europe. Although the original language of teaching in these yeshivot was a combination of Yiddish and Loshon Kodesh with a high proportion of Aramaic, in recent years English has seeped into the *shiurim*, which in certain yeshivot are delivered in a form of Yeshivish. In spite of what appears to be the cultural insularity of the Mitnagdim, mentioned previously, there do exist yeshivot that allow their students to take college courses at night, in addition to their religious studies. This appears to be a pragmatic arrangement, acknowledging that not all students are suited for life as religious functionaries or in Jewish education, and that a professional education will enable them to progress financially instead of remaining in trade and small manufacturing.

Mitnagdic girls often continue their post–high school studies at teachers' seminaries such as those run by the Beis Ya'akov system, where studies are in a combination of Loshon Kodesh with a small proportion of Aramaic, and English. A minority of young women continue on to college in the expectation that they will have to help support their families, particularly in the first years after marriage, if their husband is still studying. It is tacitly agreed among the more modern Mitnagdic groups that such study for girls, while not the optimal choice, is often a pragmatic decision made for economic reasons.[62]

Sefaradi Haredim

Although Sefaradim of Spanish and Portuguese descent were the original Jewish settlers in North America, and though Sefaradi communities have existed in the New World since the late seventeenth century, the massive influx of Central and later Eastern European Jews turned their descendents into a small minority of American Jewry. To those American Sefaradim whose descendents remained Jewish, one must add the small Sefaradi migration from the Middle East (primarily Syria) that reached North America at the beginning of the twentieth century. These groups were augmented by Jews from Iran and North Africa, as well as Sefaradim from Israel, who began coming to the United States in the 1960s (Sachar 1985).

As in Great Britain, the relatively small numbers of Sefaradi Haredim in the United States today are almost all of Oriental Sefaradi background. American Sefaradi Haredi communities—in New York, New Jersey, Miami, Los Angeles, and a number of other locations—are populated primarily by relatively recent Oriental and Israeli immigrants. In other cases, Sefaradi Haredim end up joining existing Sefaradi Orthodox communities, such as those in Queens and Long Island, thus giving these communities a more Haredi orientation. It is possible to find Sefaradim who became Haredim by joining or being sponsored by Hassidic groups such as Habad (Iranian Jews) and Satmar (Yemenite Jews), and whose Haredi linguistic expressions, study framework, and religious practice have come to resemble those of their adopted group. By virtue of birth, these people are Sefaradim; by virtue of affiliation they are Haredi. Yet by no means can they be considered Sefaradi Haredim in the sense this term has conveyed up to now in this study.[63]

Being immigrants, some older Sefaradi Haredim often speak to each other in their mother tongue—Farsi, Ivrit, or French—while their Americanized children speak to them in English and use that language among themselves. A few Sefaradi educational establishments, from kindergarten to higher yeshiva, may be found in various parts of the United States, for instance the Sefaradi kollel in Deal, New Jersey (Helmreich 1982). Following a religious and secular curriculum similar to those in Mitnagdic schools, these Sefaradi schools teach secular studies in English and religious studies in Ivrit, Loshon Kodesh with a high proportion of Aramaic, and sometimes English, the common language used for explanations. Some Sefaradi Haredi institutions in the United States engage in Sefaradi outreach, among them the Midrash Ben Ish Hai Institute in Great Neck, New York, where extremely modern Orthodox activities such as the "Date N 8" meetings go on alongside Sefaradi Haredi religious activities. The institute also sponsors a Sefaradi boys' yeshiva high school, Midrash, which offers religious and general studies, the former in Loshon Kodesh with a varying proportion of Aramaic and English, and the latter only in English. As in Mitnagdic yeshiva high schools, at Midrash Ivrit is taught as a subject.[64] This phenomenon is typical of Sefaradi and Sefaradi Haredi education in the United States. Although there are individual Sefaradi yeshivot, the U.S. has no organized Sefaradi Haredi educational network similar to that of Ma'ayan Hahinuch Hatorani in Israel.[65]

Discussion

Despite the suprageographical nature of Haredi life, American Haredim appear to live in a world slightly different from that of their Haredi brethren elsewhere, even in Great Britain, another country whose vernacular is English. Subtle differences are apparent in all sectors, from the domestic through the public domain, and up to educational frameworks. As in the case of Britain, Habad and Gerrer families speak more Yiddish in the U.S. than they do in Israel.[66] But being the Habad world center, the Habad community in Crown Heights, Brooklyn, is even more multilingual than Habad communities elsewhere. American Gerrer Hassidim speak less Ivrit than Gerrer in Britain or, of course, Israel. American Mitnagdim tend to speak less Yiddish and more English than their British counterparts. The Sefaradi Haredi domestic sphere and public domain in the U.S. are different from those in Israel where most Sefaradi Haredim come from families that have been in Israel for at least one generation, if not longer.[67] Linguistically paralleling their British counterparts, American Sefaradi Haredim live primarily in an immigrant society that is often less than one generation removed from the immigration experience and the mother tongue.

Differences between the groups—and between members of each sect in different countries—express themselves most vividly in the educational frameworks. British and American Habad appear to be similar in terms of the religious praxis, outreach programs, and Zionist orientation that underlie their positive attitude toward the local vernacular. Yet only in New York does there exist a complete Habad educational system that teaches solely in Yiddish, without any English language study. This may be the veteran Habad groups' response to the threat of over-Americanization that can result from the nature of the sect and its members' close contact with American culture. It may also be a way for newly religious Habad members to immerse themselves fully in Haredi culture, facilitating what they might see as a seamless transition into the diaspora Haredi (Yiddish-speaking) world.

At first glance, the Gerrer sect in Britain and in the United States appear to be cut from the same linguistic cloth. But closer observation confirms that much more Ivrit can be heard among Gerrer Hassidim in Britain than in the U.S. American Gerrer Haredim are characterized by their use of Yiddish, possibly because it is considered the linguistic marker of the Haredi world. In general, both American and British Gerrer Hassidim speak more Yiddish than do their Israeli counterparts.[68]

The greatest differentiation among the groups becomes apparent when American Mitnagdim are compared to those found in Britain and Israel. All three groups tend to speak in the local vernacular, with those in English-speaking countries, particularly the younger generation, often inclining towards Yeshivish. While Mitnagdim in both Britain and the United States receive much more secular education than their Israeli counterparts, only in the U.S. is it commonplace to find yeshivot that permit their students to simultaneously pursue a college degree, something that would be incomprehensible in Israel. This variation is grounded in social and economic logic, stemming from awareness of the difficulty of forbidding something so ingrained in American Jewish society as higher education, and from Mitnagdic leaders' respect for the economic (and at times political) benefits of large numbers of alumni being college graduates and professionals. In practical terms, secular study, including language study, is seen as an investment that will be recouped by the community, as future Haredi professionals can cover the costs of running educational establishments and underwriting tuition for poorer students.

Sefaradi Haredim in the United States are a small group who have for the most part been absorbed into the existing Sefaradi congregations. Their language use in America is similar to that in Britain, and in both of locales it is influenced by their membership in a society of recent immigrants, unlike in Israel. Some Sefaradi Haredim in the U.S. are actually part of the Ashkenazi Haredi community, having been absorbed by Habad.[69] The Yemenite Jews, who came directly from Yemen to the U.S. in the 1990s, have been sponsored by other Hassidic communities, primarily Satmar, and their children are being absorbed into the cultural separatism and Yiddish-language milieu of that community.

Satmar is one of a few Hassidic groups that attempt to maintain total linguistic separatism in their educational establishments, teaching no English at all (Rubin 1997). In view of the growing cultural separatism that has evinced itself among American Haredim over the past three decades, a broader question comes to mind: If the addition of secular subjects—including English—in the strict Haredi curriculum is usually considered a negative influence, then why are they taught at all? The main reason is financial: a full secular curriculum entitles the school to receive government funding. This is true of schools where the secular program is tacitly accepted, and of those where students are discouraged from too much, or any, participation in secular studies.

The American Haredi attitude to the teaching of secular subjects in general, and English in particular, seems to relate to gender as well as to a finance. In almost all of even the strictest Haredi girls' schools that provided data for this study, there appears to be a greater willingness to teach English and other secular subjects than there is in boys' schools. This attitude applies to all parties involved: the Haredi educational authorities, the parents, and even the students. The school authorities' opinions are evident, even at the classroom level, and influence children's willingness to study. For example, at one Satmar boys' school, the same pupils who were enraptured by Jewish studies disrupted the secular classes. The opposite situation was observed at the parallel girls' school, where the secular studies held the pupils enthralled and there was less interest in Jewish studies (Rubin 1997).

The girls' relative lack of interest in religious studies and desire to study secular subjects may seem surprising, but scrutiny of the motives of those who set Haredi language policy renders the picture less complex. Apart from the generally lax attitude to teaching secular studies to girls, who are not required to devote themselves to Torah, the emphasis on English and secular studies for girls reflects the Haredi interpretation of the Talmudic prohibition on teaching Torah and other religious studies to girls. In certain strict Haredi educational institutions in the United States, religious studies for girls are actively discouraged. As a result, apart from selected material from rabbinical sayings, all that is left for them to study are the secular subjects (Landau 1993). The result is a Haredi separatist girls' school that provides its students with what is primarily a secular education.

Conclusions

In his study of reproduction in society, education, and culture, Pierre Bourdieu (1970, this ed. 1990) examines the factors in societies and their cultures that contribute to maintaining and reproducing various characteristics, both desirable and undesirable. Building on this study, Corson (1990) shows how language is a key factor in reproducing and maintaining the features of cultures and societies, enabling individuals and groups to shape societies to serve their own ends. Heath (1983) shows how the home and the community are central institutions in the linguistic process of cultural reproduction. To this, Corson claims (1990, 1999), one must add the educational system, in which language, knowledge, and studying are triangulated to enable pupils to achieve linguistic, communicative, and analytical competence. In pluralistic societies, modern schools often face various language problems rooted in the diverse social and cultural makeup of their student body. At schools that are run exclusively by ethnic or religious minorities but exist within a pluralistic society, language problems often arise from a clash between the language policies of the specific minority and surrounding society (Corson 1990). This situation is typical of a number of the Haredi schools examined in the countries targeted in this chapter.

Three issues come to the fore when attempting to compare the attitudes of Israeli and diaspora Haredim to language and culture. The first is the influence of sociological factors, particularly with regard to the use of Yiddish. The second is the issue of gender-related language practice and the third is the study and use of Ivrit and its connection to contemporary Israel and/or Zionism.

Although each of the four sects targeted in this study has initially adopted the local vernacular—Ivrit, English, or French—as their domestic language, they differ in their attitude to, and use of, what is often considered the traditional Ashkenazic Haredi vernacular, Yiddish. Compared to Israel, we find that in the case of the three Ashkenazi Haredi groups targeted—Habad, Gur, and the Mitnagdim—the amount of Yiddish characterizing the language patterns of the domestic sphere and community grows considerably in Britain and the United States, and somewhat less in France. This appears to be a result of a supra-Haredi influence, and of the fact that in the diaspora, more than in Israel, Yiddish is considered the ultimate Ashkenazi Haredi linguistic marker.

A similar pattern appears to carry over to the educational frameworks. In Israel, very little Yiddish is taught in the three Ashkenazi sects in comparison with the situation in Britain and the U.S. In Israel, only a small amount of Yiddish is taught to many boys (except in the Yiddish-speaking Talmud Torahs) or to girls in Habad. None is taught to the Mitnagdim in Israel, where today, Yiddish is only used in a few of the higher yeshivot. Girls in Gur learn very little Yiddish, and it is not a language of instruction but only a studied language. As for boys, the Gerrer sect in Israel introduces Yiddish to boys at high-school age, and its higher yeshivot teach in a combination of Yiddish and Loshon Kodesh with a high proportion of Aramaic. In contrast, in Britain and the U.S. Yiddish is introduced to children in Gur and Habad as early as the elementary school level. In the more polarized schools in Britain, particularly those with a mixed Mitnagdic-Hassidic school body, boys and girls study Yiddish in primary school. In the case of the boys, this prepares them for Yiddish *shiurim* in higher yeshivot; for the girls, Yiddish is thought to supply them with the linguistic key to Haredi life in the diaspora. In the U.S. Mitnagdic girls do not study Yiddish at all, and Mitnagdic boys usually are not exposed to Yiddish in school until they reach the level of higher yeshivot, similar to the pattern in Israel. However, in both countries the boys, and some of the girls, are exposed to Yeshivish, which includes many expressions in Yiddish.

Two conclusions stand out from this overview. First, among all Hassidic groups in the diaspora—including those that utilize the local vernacular as their home language, such as Habad—Yiddish appears to play a more central role in their community and as an educational language than it does in Israel. In Britain and the U.S., countries with growing Ashkenazi Haredi populations, Yiddish is considered the insider language, the linguistic marker for all Ashkenazi Haredim. Thus, even those Haredi groups—and particularly the Hassidim among them—that choose the local vernacular as their home and neighborhood language offer studies in Yiddish, to enable their followers to seamlessly blend into the general Haredi society.

Second, the greater cultural or economic interface that Mitnagdim in both Israel and the diaspora tend to have with their secular or non-Jewish surroundings, as opposed to Hassidic groups, results in a minimal, if any, study of Yiddish as a language, or study in Yiddish, at the primary and secondary level for both boys and girls. Among Mitnagdim in Britain and the U.S., Yiddish seems to have been replaced by Yeshivish at both the educational level and that of the Haredi community. This allows them a certain amount of linguistic interface with all Haredi society—characterized by Yiddish—while Yiddish is not actually taught as a subject or utilized it as a complete language in everyday life. This conclusion is reinforced by the observations that in Britain, the only Mitnagdic children who study Yiddish do so in schools catering to a mixed Hassidic-Mitnagdic student body, and that in both Israel and the United States, the frequency of Yiddish *shiurim* in higher Mitnagdic yeshivot is slowly diminishing with the demise of the older generation of European-born rabbis.

A second issue in this comparison of Israeli and diaspora attitudes is that of gender-related language patterns, particularly within the educational frameworks. Language study for boys appears to follow no single pattern for each sect worldwide with regard to the study of the local vernacular, foreign languages, and preparation for matriculation examinations. In Israel, boys in the Gerrer and Mitnagdic schools study only a minimum of the local vernacular (Ivrit) and a foreign language (English), taking no state examinations in either. This is similar to certain Hassidic sects in Britain and the U.S. that teach only the minimum amount of English necessary for state requirements and no foreign languages. Mitnagdic boys in Britain and the U.S. who attend Mitnagdic-geared schools study in the vernacular, study foreign languages, and take state language examinations. Sefaradi Haredi boys in Israel, Britain, and the U.S. pattern similarly in all countries, studying in the local vernacular and often seeking instruction in foreign languages as well.

On the other hand, girls in Habad, Gur, Mitnagdic, and Sefaradi Haredi schools worldwide usually study in the local vernacular and take state examinations in that subject. In Israel they all study English as a foreign language, usually in line with the state curriculum, using photocopied English handouts or Haredi-oriented textbooks based on the state curriculum, and some schools prepare young women for matriculation examinations. In Britain and the U.S. girls in these sects often study foreign languages in addition to Classical Hebrew or Ivrit.

The explanation for the gender differences in language study appears to be twofold. Their first source is the general permissiveness among Haredim regarding teaching secular subjects to girls. The second cause of gender differences is women's status as future breadwinners for their family, which necessitates education in secular subjects, including languages, that may assist them in obtaining employment. Another, tacit reason for this phenomenon may relate to the dissonance between girls being, considered on the Haredi declarative level, more in need of protection from the local environment, while in practice they often have greater contact with this environment than do their male peers. As for method and curriculum, in all four sects, some version of the local or state curriculum is often employed, even if it is modified so as not to offend religious sensibilities.

Economics can also help explain the willingness of boys' schools in all countries—at least on the declarative level, in places with lax government supervision—to teach a certain amount of both the local vernacular and foreign languages. All Haredi schools in the countries examined receive government financial assistance if they comply with government policies. Haredi schools wishing to receive government aid therefore must implement a partial or full language program. In Israel, where Israeli government supervision of the Hinuch Atzmai educational system was sporadic in the first decades of the state's existence, Haredi boys' schools got away with teaching a minimum of language study (Tzameret 1997). In Britain and the U.S., where there was heavier government supervision, there was more language teaching in most Haredi boys' schools than in Israel, at least on the elementary levels.

The third issue is the study of Ivrit and its connection to contemporary Israel and/or Zionism. As the language of modern Israel, it is intrinsically connected either with the Zionist ideal, or with the concept of a practical language needed by anyone wishing to settle in Israel, with or without an ideological connection to Zionism. In Israel, all four groups teach certain subjects in Ivrit, as it is the local vernacular that they regularly speak at home. This does not have any impact on their attitude to Zionism, as neither Gur nor the Mitnagdim can be considered Haredi groups with Zionist affiliations. In Britain, older Habad girls study Ivrit as a foreign language, although they do not do so in the U.S.. This difference appears to stem from practical demand and not Zionist orientation, as in the case of the Gerrer and Mitnagdic girls who, attending the various British schools that do not teach Ivrit on campus, arrange for private lessons in their homes as training for future international *shiduchim* or study at an Israeli seminary. In other British Haredi schools Mitnagdic boys and girls study Ivrit as part of their foreign language studies, not because of Zionist leanings but because it will be of use in future study or life in Israel. In the U.S. only Mitnagdic boys and girls study Ivrit, their Hassidic counterparts do not. This is because it is Yiddish, not Ivrit, that they see as the Haredi linguistic marker, necessary for them to become one with the suprageographical Haredi society. Sefaradi Haredim in Britain and the U.S. teach Ivrit, possibly because growing numbers of Sefaradi Haredim are of Israeli origin, or—unlike their Ashkenazi Haredi counterparts—are more Zionist-oriented.

In view of the previous analysis, can we speak of a supraterritorial Haredi language policy? Is Ben-Rafael (1998) correct in commenting that the Israeli Haredi is Hebracized more than his American contemporary is Anglicized or his Belgian contemporary is Flemicized? To begin with, there appears to be no single Haredi language policy, but rather a dialectical relation opposing moderate Haredi policies to the more separatist ones of Satmar and other extreme-separatist Hassidic groups. Both the moderate and the separatist policies evident in Israel are paralleled in Great Britain and the United States. It is therefore difficult to make any blanket statements concerning Haredi language policy worldwide, particularly in view of the differences between the various groups in each country. In addition, gender differences relating to secular studies in general and language teaching in particular appear among Haredi groups in all of the countries surveyed. In all countries there appear to have been clashes with government authorities over the stricter Haredi schools' policies of teaching few secular subjects, including English. In some cases, such as the Satmar Hassidic communities of Kiriyas Yoel, the Haredi separatist attitude has won out. In others, there has been a slow but steady encroachment of English into the lives of their young people as ethnic separatist groups find themselves unable to hold out against the majority culture. In reaction, these groups' schools have doubled their efforts to teach in Yiddish and keep English to a minimum. This is true both in Israel, where Haredi schools that formerly taught English have removed it from the curriculum (such as the Talmud Torah Zichron Meir in Bnai Brak), and abroad, where Satmar Hassidim have redoubled their battle with local authorities to form their own school district apart from the Monroe County district in which they reside (Ben-David 1999). Adaptability may be a well known component of Haredi life, but moderation and compromise are not.

Notes

1. Prof. Gershon Bacon mentioned this matter during the conference on "The Study of Jewish Orthodoxy: New Perspectives," held at the Hebrew University, Jerusalem, 9 August 2001.
2. This information was received from the office of R. Aharonov, Mercaz Zeirei Habad, Kfar Habad, and from the Habad website of Northeast England.
3. Author's telephone interview with R. Avraham Pinter, principal, Yesodei Hatorah school, London, 6 Sept. 2001.
4. Author's telephone interview with Menny Klausner, former president of the Mizrachi in Great Britain, 5 Sept. 2001.
5. Author's telephone interview with Menny Klausner, 5 Sept. 2001.

6. Author's telephone interview with R. Avraham Pinter, 6 Sept. 2001.
7. *Algemeyner Zhurnal,* 18 July 1997, p. 3.
8. *Algemeyner Zhurnal,* 27 August 1997, p. 1.
9. Author's telephone interview with secretary of the Lubavitch Junior Boys School, London, 6 Sept. 2001.
10. Author's telephone interview with Mrs. Spivak, Lubavitch Junior Girls School, London, 6 Sept. 2001.
11. Author's telephone interview with Mrs. Spivak, 6 Sept. 2001.
12. Author's telephone interview with secretary of the Lubavitch Junior Boys School, London, 6 Sept. 2001.
13. *The Jewish Chronicle,* 18 February 1966, p. 1.
14. Author's telephone interview with R. Avraham Pinter, 6 Sept. 2001.
15. Author's telephone interview with Menny Klausner, 5 Sept. 2001.
16. Author's telephone interview with Rebbetzin Rosenbaum, wife of the director of the Gerrer Yeshiva of Europe in London, 6 Sept. 2001.
17. Author's telephone interview with Rebbetzin Rosenbaum in London, 6 Sept. 2001.
18. Author's telephone interview with Marcus Komarsky, 6 Sept. 2001.
19. Author's telephone interview with subscription department of *HaModia,* 27 July 2001.
20. Author's telephone interview with R. Avraham Pinter, 6 Sept. 2001.
21. Ibid.
22. Author's telephone interview with Mrs. Kusmiesky, secretary, Pardes House Primary School, 6 Sept. 2001.
23. Author's telephone interview with R. Avraham Pinter, 6 Sept. 2001.
24. Author's telephone interview with Menny Klausner, 5 Sept. 2001.
25. Author's telephone interview with R. Avraham Pinter, 6 Sept. 2001, 10 Sept. 2001; author's telephone interview with the secretary of the Gateshead Yeshiva, 10 Sept. 2001; author's telephone interview with the secretary of the Gateshead Seminary, 10 Sept. 2001.
26. Author's telephone interview with the secretary of the Gateshead Seminary, 10 Sept. 2001.
27. Author's telephone interview with Menny Klausner, 5 Sept. 2001; author's telephone interview with A. Weisskopf, 6 Sept. 2001.
28. Author's telephone interview with Michael Kronenfeld, 6 Sept. 2001.
29. Author's telephone interview with the representative of the English edition of *Yated Ne'eman,* 23 July 2001.
30. Author's telephone interview with Michael Kronenfeld, 6 Sept. 2001.
31. Author's telephone interview with Menny Klausner, 5 Sept. 2001; author's personal communication with Prof. Lewis Glinert, 5 Sept. 2001.
32. Author's telephone interview with Menny Klausner, 5 Sept. 2001.
33. Author's telephone interview with Mrs. Kusmiesky, 6 Sept. 2001.
34. I would like to thank Prof. Gershon Bacon of the Department of Jewish History at Bar-Ilan University for providing me with the "Yeshivish" translation of the Gettysburg Address.
35. Author's telephone interview with Menny Klausner, 5 Sept. 2001; personal communication with Israel Meiri, 7 Sept. 2001.
36. Personal communication with Prof. Lewis Glinert, 5 Sept. 2001.
37. Author's telephone interview with R. Avraham Pinter, 6 Sept. 2001.
38. Author's telephone interview with Menny Klausner, 5 Sept. 2001.
39. Author's personal communication with the office of Habad shlichut, Kfar Habad, 10 Sept. 2001.
40. Author's personal communication with Dr. David Kranzler, Brooklyn, N.Y., 10 Sept. 2001.
41. Author's personal communication with Baila Eisenberg, Brooklyn, N.Y.. 6 Sept. 2001.
42. Author's personal communication with Chanie Eisenberg, New York City, 10 Sept. 2001.
43. Author's personal communication with Baila Eisenberg, Brooklyn N.Y., 6 Sept. 2001.
44. Author's interview with Steven Eisenberg, Ramat Gan, 8 Oct. 2001.
45. Author's personal communication with Chanie Eisenberg, New York City, 10 Sept. 2001.
46. As per presentation by Prof. Samuel Heilman, "The Call from the Walls: Using Posters and Handbills to Understand the American Orthodox World," at the conference on "The Study of Jewish Orthodoxy: New Perspectives," held at the Hebrew University, Jerusalem, 9 Aug. 2001.

47. Author's telephone interview with the subscription department of *HaModia,* 27 July 2001.
48. Author's personal communication with Bobover Hassid Elias Bergman, 5 Sept. 2001.
49. Author's interview with Joseph Friedenson, New York City, 22 July 1989.
50. Author's personal correspondence with Dr. David Kranzler, 6 Sept. 2001.
51. In 1977 there were over 5,500 young men attending Lithuanian yeshivot in the U.S. (Helmreich 1982).
52. Author's telephone interview with R. Hershel Schacter, 23 August 2001.
53. Author's personal communication with Shimon Margoliot, 9 Sept. 2001.
54. Author's interview with Dr. Deborah Dienstag, Jerusalem, 4 Oct. 2001.
55. Author's interview with Sadie Pitkowsky, Jerusalem, 24 Sept. 2001.
56. Author's interview with Leah Schiffer, Jerusalem, 13 Sept. 2001.
57. Author's telephone interview with *Yated Ne'eman* representative, English edition, 23 July 2001.
58. *The Jewish Press,* 6 Sept. 2001.
59. Author's interview with Joseph Friedenson, New York City, 22 July 1989.
60. Author's personal communication with Daniel Eisenberg, New York, 7 Sept. 2001.
61. Author's telephone interview with R. Hershel Schacter, 23 August 2001.
62. Author's interview with Dr. Deborah Dienstag, Jerusalem, 4 Oct. 2001.
63. Various websites set up by Sefaradi communities throughout the United States make clear that they include groups that may be considered Sefaradi Haredi while catering to a larger Sefaradi population. See, for example, the Midrash Ben Ish Hai website, and those of the World Sefaradi Federation.
64. Source: Midrash Ben Ish Hai website, an extremely comprehensive site with an interactive component, a monthly newsletter, educational explanations, curricula (including language study) of the school system, and communal activities.
65. Author's telephone interview with secretary of Ma'ayan Hahinuch Hatorani in Jerusalem, 16 Sept. 2001.
66. Author's personal communication with Baila Eisenberg regarding the Habad communities in New York and Israel, 6 Sept. 2001; author's personal communication with Michael Leitner regarding the Gerrer communities in New York and Israel, 24 Sept. 2001.
67. Author's personal communication with Jeffrey Behar, New York City, 21 Sept. 2001.
68. Author's personal communication with Dr. David Kranzler, Brooklyn, NY, 6 Sept. 2001.
69. Author's personal communication with Baila Eisenberg, Brooklyn, N.Y., 6 Sept. 2001.

9

CONCLUSIONS

In the eyes of the uninitiated, research often appears to be a never-ending project. But all researchers come to a moment in the life of every researcher when they are forced to stop and take stock while undertaking a litmus test of the issues being examined. Mine occurred as I was concluding my observations at one of the many Haredi schools that I visited during my fieldwork. Accompanying me out of the school building, the assistant principal stopped at the bottom of the stairs and turned to me with a half-smile. "Tell me," he said, "why are you interested in any of this? Who cares what we speak or in what language we teach? What good is it to the world if it can't help someone?"[1]

I don't remember how I answered him then, apart from probably biting back the instinctive, jocular retort that first and foremost it will help this budding researcher obtain a higher academic degree. However, these innocent, pointed questions from a Haredi educator who did not understand the purpose of my research, yet had been willing to offer me great help as a fellow Jew, have propelled my thoughts in that direction over and over again since that time.

It is well known that one of the allures of academic research in certain disciplines is the validation of viewing it as an end unto itself, a worthy intellectual exercise that at most will serve as the starting point for additional worthy intellectual exercises that may never have practical application. It was the fear of being enticed into such a never-ending loop that drove me always to keep in mind the broader significance of my research and its possible applications in practice, whether by educators, language planners, anthropologists, or even Israeli politicians dealing with the Haredi community. In order to formulate this, however, it was first necessary to pinpoint where I locate the Haredim in general, and the Haredim that I examined in particular, within the general framework of ethnic and linguistic minorities.

Haredim as a Linguistic Minority Group

My foray into the homes, streets, synagogues, educational institutions, religious writings, and cultural frameworks of Haredim impressed on me the extent to which they cross boundaries. By virtue of shared ethnic background, and maintenance of ethnic dress and customs, various groups of Haredim are obviously ethnic minorities (Fishman 1991). Though their members may be second- and third-generation Israeli, American, English, etc., some still consider these groups an ethnic immigrant minority.[2] Finally, the common religious ties and theological framework that guide their everyday life categorize them as a religious minority, although they lack the rural background often shared by groups in that category (Sharot 1991).

Additional factors to take into account are their declarative separatist nature, evolved to shield the impressionable from the surrounding culture, and the fundamentalist character that is often ascribed to their religious and cultural behavior (Heilman and Friedman 1991). In short, it appears that the broadest, most comprehensive typology for Haredim would describe them as an ethno-religious, third-generation immigrant, urban fundamentalist-separatist minority—in other words, a bit of almost everything.

Although a scholar searching for minute categorical precision may imagine this hybrid, boundary-crossing typology as complicating matters, its all-encompassing nature can also serve to simplify things. By exhibiting a large number of typological variations, this categorization of Haredim does not remain within a circumscribed perimeter but can lead us instead to a unique, broad-scale understanding of the cultural complexities of this group.

Contemporary Haredi Culture and Language

In majority and minority groups alike, language is both an indicator of cultural values and a factor in molding these values. Culture, however, is a catchall term that includes social, political, economic, and religious variables. Sociologists, linguists, and anthropologists have shown the impact of language on all their fields. Fishman (1989, 1991) discusses language as an expression of ethnicity, nationalism, and ethnocultural identity, and explores how the social pressures of society craft the attitudes towards languages among various ethnic minorities. Grin (1990, 1993), Coulmas (1992), and Chiswick and Miller (1992, 1995) have examined language as an indicator of economic development and show how economic pressures affect ethnic minorities' attitudes to the use of majority and minority languages. Hostetler, (1968), Redekop (1989), and Kraybill (1989) have analyzed the role of theological constructs that influence minority groups' language policies. Ruiz (1990) and Ager (1996) focus on the dichotomy of language as a "right," a "resource," and a "problem" and discuss how political pressures and counterpressures can bring about maintenance or loss of an ethnic minority's language. All of these variables receive expression in the language and culture of Israeli Haredim.

In his study of reversing language shift, Fishman (1991) emphasizes that on the socioethnic level language is an important determinant of identity, and asks whether it is possible to truly be considered a member of a particular group without having knowledge of the group's language. In response, he claims that language is not the sole variable or guarantor of a cultural pattern, yet when language is lost, it is more likely that other socioethnic props of a group will be lost as well. According to Fishman, the reversal of language shift begins with reconstructing the language and its study among adults, cultural interaction involving the community-based older generation, and intergenerational use of the language in the home, family, and neighborhood. From this stage, the social level expands to include internal-group and official schools for literacy in and acquisition of the language, and use of the language is normalized in the local work sphere, then in local mass media and government services, and finally in education, work, mass media, and governmental operations at a higher and nationwide level.

In the case of the four Israeli Haredi groups that I have examined, Ivrit is used as the vernacular, but at least two of the groups express the desire to use a minority in-group language—Yiddish—for higher religious study. Furthermore, among certain groups (men more than women, younger more than older), the vernacular actually includes a local, Israeli version of what is termed Yeshivish abroad, in itself a variation of what may be considered a minority language.

Are the language and cultural patterns of Israeli Haredim similar to other religious minorities'? In his analysis of Amish society, Hostetler (1968) shows how at the optimum, Pennsylvania Dutch is the in-group vernacular, English is used on forced occasions with out-group members, and Amish High German is reserved for preaching and formal ceremonial religious occasions. Despite the fact that schooling in the Amish community takes place in English, members of the group recognize and accept the use of an ethnic language (which is not used only by them but also by other, ethnically connected groups) and a religious language that is used under ritual circumstances. The encroachment of English into daily speech, particularly among the youth, does not detract from the group's separatist religious nature, which is reinforced by the use of a special language for religious activities, even if the knowledge of that language is more passive than active among most members. As long as the group, reinforced by the teachings of their elders, maintains this linguistic tradition, they can retain their religious separatist nature. Redekop (1989) notes a similar pattern among Mennonite society as a whole.

This is similar, but not identical, to the situation among many Haredim. Loshon Kodesh is used as a religious language, based on ongoing religious tradition and the support of the religious communal leadership. This is also true for Orthodox Jews worldwide, not only for Haredim. The use of Yiddish as an ethnic language (vernacular) among Haredi groups facilitates the maintenance of separation, but as I have shown in this study, it is not an essential linguistic component of Haredi separatism. It does, however, reinforce the religious separatist nature among certain Haredi groups that use Ivrit as their vernacular, yet utilize Yiddish as a language for higher Talmud study. As long as Loshon Kodesh is used for religious purposes (with knowledge of Aramaic often being passive, like to the knowledge of High German among the Amish or the Mennonites), even among Haredi groups using Ivrit as their vernacular, the group can sustain its religious separatist nature. The use of an Israeli form of Yeshivish, particularly among Sefaradi Haredim, who have no ethnic language as their own, also emphasizes their sense of separatism from the Israeli secular and modern Orthodox public.

Economics is a crucial factor actively affecting Haredi language choices and, tacitly, Haredi acculturation. In his study of the Amish, Kraybill (1989) points to the inherent connection between religion and economics. Reiterating the Amish claim that religious values lie at the bottom of their objections to consolidated, modern education, he shows how the spiritual explanations were often bolstered by economic ones. The demands that children have an eight-month school year and leave school after eighth grade were not only meant to ensure their religious separatism, but also to free up child labor that was essential to the maintenance of the traditional Amish labor-intensive farm economy. Indeed, as Lawrence (1989) shows in his study of the fundamentalist revolt against the modern age, the fundamentalist-versus-modernist struggle has often been tacitly impelled by economics, especially modernization's economic impetus and great economic implications for the minority/fundamentalist groups.

To this we must add the absolute economic value of language. As Coulmas (1992) has shown, although language is considered an asset to the speaker, multiplicity of languages is inversely conducive to social wealth. The economic utility of a language grows not because of its cultural value but because the number of its speakers increases. English, a major player in the world economy, is still considered the best-adapted and most widespread language in the world.

All of these factors come into play in an analysis of the language and culture of Israeli Haredim. Using either a separate ethnic language (such as Yiddish) or a hybrid derivative of the majority language (such as Yeshivish) for in-group communication, even the most separatist Haredi groups are aware of the economic utility and efficiency of majority language use in out-group communicative settings. One possibility preferred by many Haredi groups is to minimize the amount of out-group communication, and even economic activity, in order to mitigate the linguistic influences that a market economy will have on the group. These groups base their individual economic survival on a gendered society in which women support their families; meanwhile, the group's economic viability relies on political allocations. Another majority-language strategy is to teach languages like English to women—the breadwinners—all the while attempting to nevertheless maintain their cultural separatism so as to better empower them economically.

The gendered component of Israeli Haredi language and culture appears to differ from that of other religious minorities and fundamentalist groups. In traditional Mennonite society the women, as the subgroup least exposed to outside influence, are therefore the group that best maintains the ethnic language (*The Economist* 2000). Although Haredi women prefer to be employed in a

Haredi environment that is conducive to maintaining their culture, it is they who are most exposed, through employment, to modern Israeli language and culture, even among those Haredi groups that use Yiddish as their vernacular. So whereas in Mennonite society women are the mainstays for minority language maintenance, in certain Haredi groups women are the main agents introducing the majority language into minority society (Fader 2001). Nevertheless, scholars are divided over whether Haredi women are agents of socialization. Although they are often exposed to secular Israeli culture at the workplace, they can consciously refrain from bringing this culture home. However, awareness that their daughters, who are being trained to support their future families, will also be exposed to this culture, creates a sense of parallel, gendered lives in the Haredi community. Men learn Torah, and live in a Haredi culture. Women work, spend up to half of their waking hours exposed to secular Israeli culture, and then return home to a Haredi culture. It is difficult to say how long this dichotomy can continue before the cultural interface becomes porous.

Politics also plays a role in forming Haredi language policy and its cultural constructs. Ager (1996) states that a language problem is often a symbol of problems in other areas, and is particularly likely to be a surrogate for economic or social policy. This can be seen among Israeli Haredim, where political policy vis-à-vis Haredim and Haredi language has economic implications, but also mirrors an ongoing social and ideological process in the country. One example is the 2002 decision of the Israeli Ministry of Education to follow through with supervision of secular studies, including teaching of Hebrew and English, in all Haredi schools receiving government allocations. "If they are going to receive our money, they had better learn our language," said one government clerk interviewed on Israeli prime-time television.

A final factor in forming the attitudes of Israeli Haredim to language and culture is leadership. Although many religious minorities often have a traditional or hereditary leadership that maintains a static language or cultural policy, a change in leadership via death or schism can bring about a revolution in this area. Among Haredim this may occur at the time of succession or when a sect splits.

Nationalization and Transnationality among Haredim

One of the phenomena that I have noted among Haredim both in Israel and abroad is the adoption of the dominant languages of the different countries as community languages. Can this trend be considered a weakening of the transnationality that has traditionally characterized Haredi life?

It is impossible to conceive of the Western world today without bearing in mind the impact of globalization. Globalization of technical communication as expressed by the availability of the Internet and even hand-held satellite communicators; the ubiquity of the English language, even in countries like France that struggle to maintain linguistic purity; and, of course, economic and political globalization of all kinds.

Against this backdrop, then, we turn to the true nature of contemporary Haredi society. Noting that they appear at times to function as separate entities, we have already explored the extent to which the Haredim, both in Israel and abroad, are surrounded by permeable linguistic and cultural barriers, making them at times an integral part of their surroundings. The adoption of national languages for community use by Haredim in various countries can therefore be seen as a natural process stemming from economic and practical factors and not necessarily an indicator of nationalization. Haredim still remain conversant in Loshon Kodesh and can use it in communication with foreign Haredim when necessary. Loshon Kodesh, Ivrit, and at times, either Yiddish or English for Ashkenazi Haredim of various sects, or French in the case of Sefaradi Haredim, can also be used by rabbinical leaders to communicate with their followers. They are also the languages used by Haredi family and visitors to communicate with Haredim abroad, either orally or in writing. In general, however—through with a few notable exceptions—when crossing boundaries between various Haredi groups today, with a few exceptions, the lingua franca of rabbis and other leaders is Ivrit mixed with Loshon Kodesh.

Furthermore, the spread of knowledge regarding the "biblical" and modern forms of Ivrit, as we have seen in the case of Haredi girls studying the language in Britain, and the continuation within this community of supranational marital ties, in which the lingua franca of the couple is usually English or Ivrit—and much less often, Yiddish— negate the idea of a complete cultural nationalization of Haredim in various countries. Rather, the process is a slow and complex one of boundary blurring, whose ultimate outcome is obscured.

The Israeli case, particularly regarding the slow loss of Yiddish among Ashkenazi Haredim, is striking. In a certain cultural sense, the adoption of Ivrit and loss of Yiddish, at least at the level of community and family life, signals the "Israelization" of Haredim in that country and an erosion of their separatism from the rest of Israel's Jewish society. But again, as we have seen, that barrier is permeable only in one direction. The Haredim have become much more cognizant of processes in contemporary Israeli society, while the surrounding secular society still considers the Haredi world and cultural norms—let alone their linguistic patterns—to be primarily closed to them. A case that exemplifies this process is the gendered concept, discussed in previous chapters, of educated women serving as agents of change. To some observers outside the Haredi community, the fact that Haredi women are receiving increasingly modern and vocational education, including knowledge of English and other non-Jewish languages, signifies that they are not only changing their own image in the community but also are becoming agents of change in that community. However, as I have shown previously, Haredi educators have already grappled with this challenge, inculcating in women the belief that such education should be left at the doorstep of the family home and community in order to maintain existing ways of life and forestall potential change. This is the true challenge of Haredi women today, as projected by educators and rabbinical leaders: to use their education solely for breadwinning purposes, eschewing any practical application in home or communal settings, in order to reinforce the existing gendered, social, cultural, and religious norms.

Conclusions

Throughout this study I have emphasized how language is at one and the same time a form of communication, a tool for expressing and reinforcing identity, and a means of making a statement about one's relationship with the surrounding world. In Haredi circles "you are what you speak,"[3] and the choice of language, or even the form of the local vernacular chosen for everyday communication, reflects the speaker's thoughts, values, and *weltanschauung*. The Orthodox Jewish world, and even more so the Haredi world, has always sought to impose controls on words and language. Even in the primary grades, children's education is imbued with traditional phrases such as *Mila Bisela, Shtika Bitrei* (A word is worth one coin, silence is worth two, *Kohelet Raba* 5:3), teaching the importance of absence, or *Ki derekh nikiyei hada'at lidaber bilshon nikiya* (Those with clean minds speak clean language), impressing upon them how the existence of even a single untoward word can allude to a deeper phenomenon. "To pronounce useless words is to commit murder," stated the Hassidic master R. Menahem-Mendl of Riminov (Wiesel 1972). In Haredi society, the warning "Watch your language!" is much more than a parental admonition to an impudent child. It is a statement denoting the boundaries of identity, culture, and existence.

The Haredi preoccupation with language, its existence or absence, perpetuates many stories revolving around these concepts. It is told that the first time R. Mendel, the son of the zaddik of Vorki, met R. Eleazar, the grandson of the Maggid (preacher) of Koznitz, the two retired to a room and sat in silence for a whole hour to prepare themselves for their followers. In one of his magical tales, the Ba'al Shem Tov was saved from robbers by his scribe's reciting the letters of the Hebrew alphabet. Unlike some of their later counterparts, who lived in a world bordered by Yiddish, the early Hassidic masters were familiar with the vernacular; R. Yisrael of Koznitz was known to speak to God in Polish (Buber 1948).

The Haredi world is a dynamic one, and even in the field of language many things have changed. In the late eighteenth century R. Zusya of Hanipol would speak of his pious mother, who did not pray from a book because she could not read. Today, not only are Haredi women literate in Loshon Kodesh and the vernacular, but—usually more than their male counterparts—they also study foreign languages. In contrast, although the first Gerrer rebbe often stated that he devoted himself to the study of Hebrew grammar because he realized that the secrets of the Torah depend upon it (Buber 1948), few of his male disciples in Israel today have had more than a modicum of grammar study, and much less than is mandated by the Ministry of Education.

Visiting Heders in Bnai Brak, Jerusalem, Arad, or Kfar Habad I could imagine the changes that have taken place in the Haredi world during the course of a century. Unlike my late father-in-law who learned by gaslight in his small Galician town at the beginning of the twentieth century, the little boys here sat under electric lights with rotating ceiling fans to keep them cool. In place of the bare walls that had surrounded him and his young classmates, these little boys gazed upon large glossy poster-prints depicting rabbis and rebbes at events that had taken place throughout the world. And while he and his friends had taken their fledgling steps in the world of Torah in Yiddish, in a large number of Haredi heders that I visited, the boys were speaking to their rebbes in Hebrew, or more precisely, in colloquial Ivrit, which even the most erudite early twentieth-century *melamed* would have found almost impossible to follow. Had that same *melamed* glanced over the children's shoulders, he would have seen the illustrated primers and coloring books used by Haredi boys today, which bear such titles as *Ligdol Batorah* (To Grow in Torah), or *Der Heder Yingel* (The Heder Boy). Leafing through the booklets, he might have sighed happily upon seeing a familiar picture of Abraham, Isaac, and Jacob in *streimel* and *kapoteh* or upon reading exhortations to modesty, respect for parents, and the importance of learning Torah that are identical to those that he had taught his small charges almost a century ago. In the Haredi world, language, words, and expressions can undergo many changes, but certain values remain eternal.

Notes

1. Author's interview with the assistant principal of Yeshivat Imre Emet, Bnai Brak, 9 Sept. 2001.
2. Discussions of ethnicity among Hassidim and questions of whether Haredim are an ethnic minority are a central discussion point in the film *The Hassidim of Boro Park*.
3. Author's interview with Rabbi D, 7 Oct. 2001.

GLOSSARY

admor—Hassidic rabbinical leader
Aliya—Immigration to Israel
badatz—High Court of the Eda Haredit
bagrut—matriculation
beit medrash (beis medrash)—a hall of study where boys and men review and
    study Talmud on their own or hear lectures from rabbis and rebbes
Beit Ya'acov (Beis Ya'akov)—a Haredi girls' school network
bekiut—in-depth knowledge
bochur—unmarried young man
da'at Torah—religious beliefs as formulated or interpreted by a religious
    leader
daven—pray
dayan—religious judge
Degel Hatorah—The Torah Flag (a political movement)
derasha—speech (pl. *derashot*)
devekut—cleaving to God through prayer
drush—sermon
fabrengen—hassidic gathering
gartel—Hassidic prayer belt
Gedolim—great sages (lit: great)
gemilut hasadim—kindness and charity
ger—convert to Judaism
goy—gentile (pl. *goyim*)
hacham—Sefaradi rabbi (literally: wise)
halacha—Jewish law (adj.—halachic)
Hardal—Nationalist Haredi Jew
Harifut—sharpness
Haskala—Jewish enlightenment
Hayashan—the old

heder—religious elementary school
herem—ban
hesed—charitable deeds
Hinuch Atzmai—independent Haredi school system
hitva'adut—religious gathering (in Habad)
hozrim betshuva—newly religious
humash—Bible
humrot—strictures
kapoteh—Hassidic-style coat
kavannah—proper intention in carrying out one's good deeds
kipah—skullcap
klalei nikayon—rules of cleanliness
kollel—study framework for married men
Leumi—national (Israeli)
lehit'hazek—to become stronger
limud—study of Torah
Loshon Kodesh—the holy tongue
Loshon nekiya—clean speach
ma'amarim—speeches
Ma'ayan Hachinuch Hatorani—The Torah Educational Spring (of Shas)
mamash—actually (used for emphasis in Habad)
mame loshen—mother tongue
mamlachti dati—modern religious state
Maran—our teacher
Marbitzim—to teach (lit: to hit)
maskilim—Enlightened Jews
mechina—religious elementary school for boys (lit: preparatory)
melamed—religious teacher
mesorati—traditional
metivta—yeshiva for high school–age boys
mezuzah—small box put on doorpost containing four bible segments
mizrahi—eastern (Oriental)
Moetzet Gedolei Hatorah—Council of Torah Sages
mussar—ethics
netilat yadayim—ritual washing of hands
nusach Eretz Yisrael—liturgical form used in Eretz Yisrael in the sixteenth
     century
nusach Ha'Ari—liturgical form used by the Ari, Rabbi Shlomo Luria
     (sixteenth cent.)
nusach Sefarad—liturgical form derived from nusach Ha'Ari and used by
     Hassidim
peot—sidelocks
pidyon—a sum of money given to a Hassidic rebbe in exchange for the
     rebbe's intercession in prayer
pikuach nefesh—necessary for saving lives
pilpul—endless Talmudic arguments

ptor—exemption
Ram—male religious teacher (pl. ramim)
Rebbe—Hassidic rabbi
Rebbetzin—rabbi's wife
Redyn—talks
rishon Letzion—Sefaradic chief rabbi
rosh yeshiva—yeshiva director (pl. *roshei yeshivot*)
seminar—seminary
shiduchim—matrimonial matches
Shisha Sidrei Mishna—the six books of the Mishna
shiurim—religious lessons
shlita—May he be blessed with a long life
shmussen—informal talks
shtadlan—interceder
shteiblach—small Hassidic synagogues (s. *shteibl*)
shtetl—small town
shuhkelin—swaying in prayer
sichot—chats
simcha—joy
slichot—penitential prayers
spodik—Hassidic high fur hat
streiml—Hassidic broad fur hat
succot—tabernacles (also a holiday by the same name)
tefilin—phylacteries
teshuva—repentance
tish—table
Tisha Be'av—the fast of the ninth of Av
treif—ritually unclean or impure
tzitzit—fringes
tzniut—modesty
Yahadut Hatorah—The United Torah Movement (political party)
yehudit—Jewish
yeshiva gedola—higher yeshiva (post–high school age)
yeshiva gevoha—higher yeshiva (post–high school age)
yeshiva ketana—smaller yeshiva (high-school age)
yeshiva tichonit—modern religious yeshiva high school
Yishuv—pre-state Israel
zaddik—holy man
zman—time, school study term in a yeshiva

BIBLIOGRAPHY

Archival Sources

Israel State Archives, Division 71 (Ministry of Education Archives), Jerusalem, Israel.
Mercaziya Pedagogit, Mercaz Hinuch Atzmai, Archives (English studies syllabi), Jerusalem, Israel.
List of Habad Shluchim in Britain, provided by Rabbi Aharonov, Mercaz Zeirei Habad, Kfar Habad Archives, Israel.
List of Habad Shluchim in France, provided by Rabbi Aharonov, Mercaz Zeirei Habad, Kfar Habad Archives, Israel.
Statistical Abstract of Israel, 1949, 1958–1998, Jerusalem

Interviews

On Site

Interview with Dr. Muhammad Amara, language specialist, Ramat-Gan, 20 Jan. 2000.
Interview with Rabbi Shimshon Ashkenazi, school secretary, Kfar Habad, 6 Sept. 2001.
Interview with the assistant principal of Yeshivat Imre Emet, Bnai Brak, 9 Sept. 2001.
Interview with the assistant principal, Or Hahayim, Bnai Brak, 18 Oct. 2001
Interview with Rebbetzin Z. Berman, Haredi mother, Ramat Gan, 6 Jan. 2000, 23 Sept. 2001.
Interview with Rabbi Bodik, principal of Talmud Torah Hug Hatam Sofer, Bnai Brak, 15 Oct. 2001.
Interview with Dr. Deborah Dienstag, Hardal mother, Jerusalem, 4 Oct. 2001.
Interview with Rabbi Donne, Haredi educator, Yeshiva Darkei Moshe, Bnai Brak, 25 Oct. 2001.
Interview with Rabbi Moshe Edri, Haredi educator, Jerusalem, 5 Sept. 2001.
Interview with Steven Eisenberg, Hardal student, Ramat Gan, 8 Oct. 2001.
Interview with Rebbetzin Dina Ezri, Haredi educator, Bnai Brak, 17 Oct. 2001.
Interview with Etti Feldman, English Coordinator, Beit Rivka High School, Kfar Habad, 9 Sept. 2001.
Interview with Rabbi Mordechai Feldman, Gerrer educator, Bnai Brak, 9 Sept. 2001.

Interview with Rabbi Fichman, secretary, Kfar Habad Trade School, Kfar Habad, 6 Sept. 2001.

Interview with Mrs. Miriam Fisher, Haredi educator, Bnai Brak, 24 Sept. 2001.

Interview with Joseph Friedenson, Haredi activist, New York City, 22 July 1989.

Interview with Luba Herzel, vice principal, Beit Rivka Elementary school, Kfar Habad, 9 Sept. 2001.

Interview with Gita Kossovsky, Horev English coordinator, Ramat Gan, 8 Feb. 1999.

Interview with Prof. Jean-Paul Lellouche, Professor from France, Ramat Gan, 24 Sept. 2001.

Interview with Yehudit Lichtenstein, principal, Beit Ya'akov Gur, Bnai Brak, 9 Sept. 2001.

Interview with Dr. Leah Makovetsky, Haredi educator and mother, Ramat Gan, 10 June 1999.

Interview with Rebbetzin Gita Malka, Haredi mother, Tel Aviv, 8 Aug. 2001.

Interview with Rabbi Yitzhak Meir, Haredi educator, Arad, 8 Feb. 2001.

Interview with Bernard Merzel, Belgian Haredi Holocaust Survivor who lived in France, Jerusalem, 13 Sept. 2001.

Interview with Mrs. Pinter, Haredi educator, Bnai Brak, 15 Feb. 1999.

Interview with Sadie Pitkowsky, American Jewish activist, Jerusalem, 24 Sept. 2001.

Interview with Leah Schiffer, American Jewish activist, Jerusalem, 13 Sept. 2001.

Interview with school secretary, Beit Hamorah, Bnai Brak, 25 Sept. 2001.

Interview with school secretary, Mosdot Or Hahayim, Bnai Brak, 17 Oct. 2001.

Interview with secretary, Yeshivat Birkat Efraim, Bnai Brak, 25 Oct. 2001.

Interview with R. Sharabi, Haredi educator, Mosdot Sharei Eliyahu, Bnai Brak, 15 Oct. 2001

Interview with teacher, Habad Heder, Kfar Habad, 6 Sept. 2001.

Interview with Yechezkel Tydor, Polish Holocaust survivor, Ramat Gan, 20 June 1988.

Interview with Zipora Vishatzky, principal, Beit Rivka High School, Kfar Habad, 9 Sept. 2001.

Interview with Yitzhak Yomtovian, Haredi educator, Jerusalem, 15 April 2001.

By *Telephone*

Telephone interviews with Rabbi Dr. Yitzhak Alfasi, Hardal historian,14 Feb. 2001; 30 Aug. 2001.

Telephone interview with assistant principal, Beit Ya'akov Vizhnitz, 21 Oct. 2001.

Telephone interview with Lea Banker, English coordinator Beit Rivka, 20 June 1999.

Telephone interview with E. Dar, Haredi reporter for *Mishpacha*, 26 July 2001.

Telephone interview with Dvora, advertising section of *Olam Hahasidut*, 25 July 2001.

Telephone interview with Ya'akov Hellman, supervisor of Haredi education, 10 June 2002.

Telephone interview with secretary, Gateshead Yeshiva, 10 Sept. 2001.

Telephone interview with secretary, Gateshead Seminary, 10 Sept. 2001.

Telephone interview with Haya, *Yom Leyom* subscription department, 23 July 2001.

Telephone interview with Miriam Karelenstein, Haredi educator and author of English textbooks, 18 Jan. 2000.

Telephone interview with Menny Klausner, former president of the Mizrachi in Great Britain, 5 Sept. 2001.

Telephone interview with Marcus Komarsky, activist of the Mizrachi in Great Britain, 6 Sept. 2001.

Telephone interview with Michael Kronenfeld, American Jewish educator and activist, 6 Sept. 2001.

Telephone interview with Zvia Kunzman, English teacher at Beit Ya'akov Hildesheimer Petach Tikva, 5 Feb. 1999.

Telephone interview with Mrs. Kusmiesky, secretary, Pardes House primary school, 6 Sept. 2001.

Telephone interview with Larissa, secretary of the Sefaradi Haredi program at Touro College, 7 Nov. 2001.

Telephone interview with secretary, Lubavitch Junior Boys School, 6 Sept. 2001.

Telephone interview with secretary, Ma'ayan Hahinuch Hatorani, 16 Sept. 2001.

Telephone interview with secretary, *Ma'ayan Hashavua*, 13 Sept. 2001.

Telephone interview with secretary, *Marveh Latzame*, 23 July 2001.

Telephone interview with N. M., *Yated Ne'eman* editorial staff, 23 July 2001.

Telephone interview with Malka, Haredi secretary, 26 July 2001.

Telephone interview with Ya'akov Pali, assistant general manager of *Mishpacha*, 26 July 2001.

Telephone interview with Rabbi Avraham Pinter, principal of Yesodei Hatorah, London, 6 Sept. 2001; 10 Sept. 2001.

Telephone interview with Pnina, *Yated Ne'eman* staff, 23 July 2001.

Telephone interview with Rachel, secretary of *Olam Hahasidut*, 25 July 2001.

Telephone interview with Esti Rider-Reichmann, editor of *Mishpacha Tova,* 26 July 2001.

Telephone interview with Rebbetzin Rosenbaum, wife of the director of the Gerrer Yeshiva of Europe in London, 6 Sept. 2001.

Telephone interview with H. R., *Hamodia* subscription department, 23 July 2001.

Telephone interview with Z. R., *Yated Ne'eman* subscription department, 23 July 2001.

Telephone interview with representative, *Yated Ne'eman,* 23 July 2001.

Telephone interview with representative, English *Yated Ne'eman,* 23 July 2001.

Telephone interview with Rabbi Naphtali Roth, Israeli Haredi educator, 18 July 2000.

Telephone interview with Rabbi Hershel Schacter, American Jewish activist, 23 Aug. 2001.

Telephone interview with B. S., Haredi educator, 25 July 2001.

Telephone interview with school secretary, Yeshivat Harav Amiel, 4 March 1999.

Telephone interview with Rabbi Benjamin Schreiber, Israeli Haredi educational supervisor, 26 Aug. 1999.

Telephone interview with Hava Schwimmer, Israeli Haredi educator, 20 June 1999, 17 July 1999; interview, Jerusalem, 22 June 1999.

Telephone interview with Dr. Ephraim Shakh, son of R. Elazar Menachem Shakh, 14 Feb. 2001.

Telephone interview with Shlomo, English teacher at Talmud Torah Hug Hatam Sofer, Bnai Brak, 20 June 1999.

Telephone interview with Mrs. Spivak, Lubavitch junior girls school, London, 6 Sept. 2001.

Telephone interview with S. Steinmetz, Kfar Habad administrator, 16 July 2001.

Telephone interview with subscription department, *HaModia*, 27 July 2001.

Telephone interview with supervisor, Mercaz Hishtalmuyot, 15 Oct. 2001.

Telephone interview with A. Weisskopf, Haredi educator, 6 Sept. 2001.

Correspondence and Personal Communications

Personal communication with Jeffrey Behar, 21 Sept. 2001.

Personal communication with Elias Bergman, 5 Sept. 2001.

Personal communication with Baila Eisenberg, 6 Sept. 2001.
Personal communication with Chanie Eisenberg, 10 Sept. 2001.
Personal communication with Daniel Eisenberg, 7 Sept. 2001.
Personal communication with Prof. Lewis Glinert, 5 Sept. 2001.
Personal communication with François Grin, 20 Oct. 2001.
Personal communication with office of Habad shlichut, Kfar Habad, 10 Sept. 2001.
Personal communication with Dr. David Kranzler, 10 Sept. 2001.
Personal communication with Michael Leitner, 24 Sept. 2001.
Personal communication with Shimon Margoliot, 9 Sept. 2001.
Personal communication with Israel Meiri, 7 Sept. 2001.

Printed Sources

Haredi Press

Algemeyner Zhurnal (Yiddish, New York)
Der Yid (Yiddish, New York)
Der Yiddishe Heim (Yiddish, New York)
Dos Yiddishe Vort (Yiddish, New York)
HaModia (Hebrew, Jerusalem)
HaModia (English, Jerusalem)
The Jewish Observer (English, New York)
Kfar Habad (Hebrew, Kfar Habad)
Marveh Latzameh (Hebrew, Bnai Brak)
Mishpacha (Hebrew, Bnai Brak)
Mishpacha Tovah (Hebrew, Bnai Brak)
Olam Hahasidut (Hebrew, Jerusalem)
Olam Haisha (Hebrew, Bnai Brak)
Yated Ne'eman (Hebrew, Bnai Brak)
Yated Ne'eman (English, Bnai Brak)
Yom Leyom (Hebrew, Jerusalem)

Newspapers

The Jewish Chronicle (London)
The Jewish Press (New York)
The Jerusalem Post (Jerusalem)
Yediot Acharonot (Hebrew, Tel Aviv)
Ha'aretz (Hebrew, Tel Aviv)
Ha'aretz (English, Tel Aviv)

Haredi Community Publications

Business Kehalacha
Lainyan Haharedi Shopping Catalogue

Writings, Collected Speeches, and Responsa of Haredi Leaders

Alter, Abraham Mordechai. 1925. *Hatorah Vehadat Meeretz Yisrael: Michtavim* (Torah and
    Religion from Eretz Yisrael: Letters) (Heb.). Warsaw: n. pub.

Alter, Abraham Mordechai. 1937. *Osef Michtavim Vedivarim* (Collected Letters) (Heb.). Warsaw: n. pub.

Alter, Pinchas Menachem. 1990. *Sefer Toratcha Shaashuai* (Torah is My Joy) (Heb.). Bnai Brak: Rosenthal.

Alter, Pinchas Menachem. 1995. *Likutei Ya'akov Ze'ev: Libaei Hatzar Gur (Shmussen LeHag Hashavuot 5755)* (Compilations of Ya'akov Ze'ev: For Those Coming to the Gur Court: Talks for the Shavuot Holiday 5755) (Heb.). Jerusalem: n. pub.

Alter, Pinchas Menachem. 1997. *Pnai Menachem: Amirot Vehidushei Tora* (Pnai Menachem: Sayings and Torah Vignettes) (Heb.). Jerusalem: Hotzaat Pnai Menachem.

Alter, Pinchas Menachem. 1998. *Shmussen Al Shabbat Shuva Veasseret Yimei Teshuva* (Shmussen for Shabbat Shuva and the Ten Days of Repentence) (Heb.). Jerusalem: n. pub.

Alter, Simcha Bunim. 1992. *Lev Simcha: Amirot Vehidushei Tora* (Lev Simcha: Sayings and Torah Vignettes) (Heb.) Jerusalem: Hotzaat Lev Simcha.

Alter, Simcha Bunim 1993. *Uviyemei Ratzon Vesimcha* (And During the Days of Joy) (Heb.). Jerusalem: Hotzaat Lev Simcha.

Alter, Simcha Bunim. 1994. *Hem Zichronam* (Their Words are their Memorial) (Heb.). Jerusalem: Hotzaat Lev Simcha.

Alter, Simcha Bunim. 1994. *Ma'amarei Kodesh* (Holy Sayings)(Heb.). Jerusalem: Hotzaat Lev Simcha.

Alter, Yisrael. 1978. *Beit Yisrael: Sefer Ozer Yisrael* (The House of Israel: The Book Ozer Yisrael) (Heb.). Compiler. Zvi Marks. Jerusalem: Hotzaat Beit Yisrael.

Amirot 1994. *Amirot Vehidushei Torah meet Raboteinu Zichram Yagen Aleinu Amen: Haimrei Emet Migur Vsiftei Zadik Mipilts.* Jerusalem: n. pub.

Maamorei, Admur Hoemtzoee. 1991. *Kuntresim.* Brooklyn: Kehot.

Schneerson, Dov Baer. 1991. *Maamorei Admur Hoemtzoee: Kuntresim.* Brooklyn: Kehot.

Schneerson, Menachem Mendel. 1964. *Likutei Sichot* vol. 4. Brooklyn: Zeirei Agudat Habad.

Schneerson, Menachem Mendel. 1965. *Likutei Sichot* vol. 2. Brooklyn: Zeirei Agudat Habad.

Schneerson, Menachem Mendel. 1977. *Sefer Halikutim Dach Tzemach Tzedek, ot shin.* Brooklyn: Otzar Hahasidim Kehot.

Schneerson, Menachem Mendel 1992. *I Await his Coming Every Day,* Brooklyn: Kehot.

Schneerson, Menachem Mendel.1994a. *A Partner in the dynamic of creation: Womanhood in the teachings of the Lubavitcher Rebbe, Rabbi Menachem M. Schneerson.* Edited by Uri Kaploun. Brooklyn: Sichos in English.

Schneerson, Menachem Mendel. 1994b. *In the Garden of the Torah.* Brooklyn: Sichos in English.

Schneerson, Menachem Mendel. 1994c. *In the Paths of our Fathers: Insights into Pirkei Avot.* Brooklyn: Kehot.

Schneerson, Menachem Mendel. 1973. *Likutei Sichot* (Talks) (Heb.). Brooklyn: Kehot

Sefer. 2000. *Sefer Hazicaron Knesset Ezra* (Knesset Ezra memorial book in memory of Rabi Ezra Atiya) (Heb.). vol. 2. Jerusalem: Havaad lehotzaat kitvei maran.

Shakh, El'azar Man. 1948–1993. *Sefer Avi Ezri: Beurim Beinyanim Shonim Lefi Seder Harambam* (The Avi Ezri Book: Commentaries on Different Issues According to the Order of Maimonides) (Heb.). vols. 1–13. Bnai Brak: n. pub.

Shakh, El'azar Man. 1970. *Divarim Sheneemru Biyishivat Ponevezh al Yidei Ehad Hashomim [Nachman Galinski]* (Things Which Were Said at the Ponevezh Yeshiva, written by one who heard them [Nachman Galinski]) (Heb.). vol. 1. Bnai Brak: Ponevezh Yeshiva.

Shakh, El'azar Man. 1971. *Divarim Sheneemru Biyishivat Ponevezh al Yidei Ehad Hashomim [Nachman Galinski]* (Things Which Were Said at the Ponevezh Yeshiva, written by one who heard them [Nachman Galinski]) (Heb.). vol. 2. Bnai Brak: Ponevezh Yeshiva.

Shakh, El'azar Man. 1978. *Da'at Torah Al Hamatzav Bieretz Yisrael* (Da'at Torah about the Situation in Israel) (Heb.). Bnai Brak: n. pub.

Shakh, El'azar Man. 1983. *Hapitaron Atzat Tora* (The Solution is the Advice of the Torah) (Heb.). Bnai Brak: n. pub.

Shakh, El'azar Man. 1986. *Haamitiyim* (The Real Ones) (Heb.). Bnai Brak: n. pub.

Shakh, El'azar Man. 1988. *Michtavim Uma'amarim* (Letters and Articles) (Heb.). Bnai Brak: n. pub.

Shakh, El'azar Man. 1992. *Ubikanes Torah* (And When The Torah Was Brought In) (Heb.). Bnai Brak: Ponevezh Yeshiva.

Shakh, El'azar Man. 1993. *Kovetz Hadracha Liven Hayeshiva* (A Guide for the Yeshiva Student) (Heb.). Bnai Brak: n. pub.

Shakh, El'azar Man. 1995. *Kriya LeIsur Hachzakat Utzfiya Batelevizia* (A Call to Forbid Having and Watching Television) (Heb.). Bnai Brak, n. pub.

Shakh, El'azar Man. 1998a. *Bezot Ani Boteach* (I Trust in This) (Heb.). Bnai Brak: n. pub.

Shakh, El'azar Man. 1998b. *Sichot* (Talks) (Heb.). Bnai Brak: n. pub.

Shakh, El'azar Man. 1998c. *Shiurim Yomiyim Bimasechet Nedarim* (Daily Lessons in the Nedarim Tractate) (Heb.). Bnai Brak: n. pub.

Shakh, El'azar Man. 1999. *Rav Schach Speaks*. Bnai Brak: A. Bergman.

Shneur Zalman of Liadi. 1982. *Maamori Admur Hazoken Bereishis-shmos* (The Sayings of the Elder Admor on the Books of Genesis-Exodus). Brooklyn: Kehot.

Shneur Zalman of Liadi. 1987. *Lessons on Tanya*. Elucidated by R. Yosef Wineberg. Edited by Uri Kaploun). Brooklyn: Kehot.

Yosef, Ovadia. 1954. *Sheelot Uteshuvot Yabia Omer* (Responsa Yabia Omer) (Heb.). Jerusalem: n. pub.

Yosef, Ovadia. 1976. *Sheelot Uteshuvot Yabia Omer* (Responsa Yabia Omer) (Heb.). Jerusalem: n. pub.

Yosef, Ovadia. 1983. *Sheelot Uteshuvot Yechaveh Da'at* (Responsa Yechave Da'at) (Heb.). Jerusalem: n. pub.

Yosef, Ovadia. 1991. *Sheelot Uteshuvot Hazon Ovadia* (Responsa Hazon Ovadia) (Heb.). Jerusalem: n. pub.

Yosef Ovadia. 1996. *Mishiurei Harishon Leziyon Ovadia Yosef* (From the Lessons of the Chief Rabbi Ovadia Yosef) (Heb.). Jerusalem: n. pub.

Yosef, Ovadia. 1998a. *Dinei Hinuch Katan Uvar Mitzvah* (The Laws of Educating the Minor and the Bar Mitzvah) (Heb.). Jerusalem: n. pub.

Yosef, Ovadia. 1998b. *Halichot Olam* (The Laws of the World) (Heb.). Jerusalem: Maor Yisrael.

Yosef, Ovadia. 1998c. *Mishiurei Maran Harishon Lezion Rabeinu Ovadia Yosef Shlita* (The Lessons of Maran the Rishon Lezion Rabbi Ovadia Yosef Shlita) (Heb.). Jerusalem: n. pub.

Studies

Abraham-Glinert, Joan. 1997. "How Much English Has the British Education Act Required? The Secretary of State for Education vs. A Hasidic Yiddish-speaking School." *Journal of Multilingual and Multicultural Development* 18 no. 6: 443–450.

Abraham, Joan E. 1999. "Perceptions of English learning in a Hasidic Jewish sect." *International Journal of the Sociology of Language* 138: 53–80.

Ager, Dennis. 1996. *Language Policy in Britain and France*, London and New York: Cassell.

Albarelli, Gerry. 2001. *Teache! Stories From A Yeshiva*, Vermont: Glad Day Books.

Alfasi, Yitzhak. 1993. *Tiferet Shebatiferet: Beit Gur Letoldoteha* (Wonder of Wonders: The House of Gur) (Heb.) (3rd ed.). Tel Aviv: Sinai

Anaki, Ofer. 1999. *Mi Vami Baolam Haharedi* (Who is who in the ultra-religious world). (Tel-Aviv?): Or-am.

Apple, Michael. 1990. *Ideology and Curriculum*. New York: Routledge and Kegan Paul.

Arian, Asher, and Michal Shamir. 1995. *The Elections in Israel*. Albany: SUNY Press.

Arksey, Hilary. 1999. *Interviewing for Social Scientists: An Introductory Research With Explanations*. London: Sage.

Bacon, Gershon. 1986. "Da'at Torah Vihevlei Mashiach: Leshe'elat Haidiologia shel 'Agudat Yisrael' Bepolin." (Daat Torah and Pangs of the Messiah: Towards the Question of the Ideology of "Agudath Israel" in Poland) (Heb.). *Tarbitz* 52: 497–508.

Ball, P., H. Giles, and M. Hewstone. 1984. "Second Language Acquisition: The intergroup theory with catastrophic dimensions." in H. Hajfel, C. Fraser and J. Jaspars, eds., *The Social Dimension: European Developments in Social Psychology*, vol. 2. Cambridge: Cambridge University Press.

Bar-On, Herzliah. 1999. "Haisha Haharedit Hamaskelet" (The Educated Haredi Woman) (Heb.). *Hemdaat: Shnaton Michlelet Hemdat Hadarom*, Netivot B: 174–183.

Baruch, Adam. 2000. *Seder Yom: Hayey Yom Yom Beriee Hahalacha* (Daily Routine: Daily Life as Mirrored by Jewish Law) (Heb.). Jerusalem: Keter.

Baumel, Judith Tydor, and Jacob J. Schacter. 1992. "The Ninety-three Bais Yaacov Girls of Cracow: History or Typology." J. J. Schacter, ed., *Reverence, Righteousness, and Rahamanut: Essays in Memory of Rabbi Dr. Leo Jung*. New York: Jason Aronson. Pp. 93–130.

Baumel, Simeon D. 1999. *English Language Policy in Israeli Charedi Schools*. Seminar paper, Ramat Gan.

——— 2000. *The Pit and the Pendulum, or Is Yiddish swinging back as a vernacular among the children of Haredim in Israel?*. Seminar paper, Ramat Gan.

Becker, Gary S. 1976. *The Economic Approach to Human Behavior*. Chicago: University of Chicago Press.

Belcove-Shalin, Janet Sera. 1989. *A Quest for Wholeness: The Hasidim of Boro Park*. Ph.D. Dissertation, Cornell University.

Belson, William A. 1981. *The Design and Understanding of Survey Questions*. Aldershot, Hantshire: Gower

Ben-Avner, Yehuda. 1987. *Vom orthodoxen Judentum in Deutschland zwischen Zwei Weltkriegen*. Hildesheim: Olms.

Ben-David, Calev. 1999. "Class Conflict." *The Jerusalem Post Magazine* 10 December, pp. 10–13.

Benor, Sarah Bunin. 1999. ms. "The gendered use of Hebrew and Yiddish loan words and the creation of an Orthodox Jewish identity." Presented at: New Ways of Analyzing Variation (in English) 28, Toronto.

——— 2001. "Sounding Learned: The Gendered Use of /t/ in Orthodox Jewish English." In *Penn Working Papers in Linguistics: Selected papers from NWAV 2000*. Philadelphia: University of Pennsylvania.

Ben-Rafael, Eliezer. 1998. "Nitzhona Shel Hasafa Hanechuta" (The Victory of the Inferior Language) (Heb.). *Panim* 7: 38–44.

Ben Simon, Daniel. 2001. "Shareholders in the Business of Israel." *Ha'aretz English Weekend Edition* (22 June).

Bensimon-Donath, Doris. 1973. *L'integration des Juifs nord-africaines en France*. Paris.

Bentwich, Joseph. 1960. *Hinukh Bemidinat Yisrael* (Education in The State of Israel) (Heb.). Tel Aviv: Y. Chichik.

Berdie, Douglas R. 1974. *Questionnaires: Design and Use,* Metuchen, N.J.: Scarecrow.

Berger-Sofer, Rhonda. 1978. *Pious Women: A Study of the Women's Roles in a Hasidic and Pious Community.* Ph.D. dissertation. Providence, R.I.: Brown University Press.

Bermant, Chaim. 1972. *The Cousinhood.* New York: Macmillan.

Bernstein, B. 1975. *Class, Codes and Control, volume 3: Towards a Theory of Educational Transmission.* 2nd Ed. London: Routledge and Kegan Paul.

Bogoch, Bryna. 1999. "Gender, Literacy and Religiosity: Dimensions of Yiddish Education in Israeli Government-supported Schools." *International Journal of the Sociology of Language* 138: 123–160.

Bomzer, Herbert W. 1985. *The Kollel in America.* New York: Shengold.

Bourdieu, Pierre (with J. C. Passeron). 1990. *Reproduction in Education, Society and Culture.* Los Angeles: Sage.

Bourhis, Richard Y. 1984a. "Cross-cultural Communication in Montreal: Two field studies since Bill 101." *International Journal of the Sociology of Language.* 46: 33–47.

——— 1984b. "Introduction: Language Policies in Multilingual settings." In R. Bourhis, ed., *Conflict and Language Planning in Quebec.* Concord: Multilingual Matters.

——— 1992. "Language policies and language attitudes: le monde de la francophonie." In E. Bouchard Ryan and H. Giles eds., *Attitudes towards Language Variation: Social and Applied Contexts.* London: Edward Arnold.

Bourhis, Richard Y. and Itesh Sachdev. 1989. "Two decades of language planning in Quebec: Issues and controversies." *The London Journal of Canadian Studies* 6: 36–46.

Brandeis, Yochi. 2001. "Hava Venitchazek" (Let's Get Stronger) (Heb.). *Yediot Acharonot* (13 July).

Breuer, Mordechai. 1992. *Modernity Within Tradition: The Social History of Orthodox Jewry in Imperial Germany.* New York: Columbia University Press.

Briggs, Charles L. 1986. *Learning to Ask: A Sociolinguistic Appraisal of the Role of the Interview in Social Science Research.* Cambridge: Cambridge University Press.

Brown, R. 1973. *A First Language: The Early States.* London: George Allen and Unwin.

Buber, Martin. 1948. *Tales of the Hasidim.* New York: Schocken with Farrar Straus and Young, Inc.

Castells, Manuel. 1989. *The Informational City: Information Technology, Economic Restructuring, and the Urban-Regional Process.* Oxford (Eng.) and Cambridge, Mass.: Blackwell.

Cebollero, Pedro Angel. 1945. *A School Language Policy for Puerto Rico.* San Juan de Puerto Rico: Impr. Baldrich.

Challenge: An encounter with Lubavitch—Chabad in Israel 1973. London: Lubavitch Foundation.

Chetrit, Sami Shalom. 2000. "Mizrahi politics in Israel between integration and alternative." *Journal of Palestine Studies* 24, no. 4: 51–65.

Chiswick, Barry R. and Paul W. Miller. 1992. "Language in the Immigrant Labor Market." In Barry R. Chiswick, ed., *Immigration, Language and Ethnicity: Canada and the United States.* Washington: American Enterprise Institute. Pp. 471–476.

——— 1995. "The Endogeneity Between Language and Earnings: International Analyses." *Journal of Labor Economics* 13: 246–288.

Clark, H.H. and M.F. Schober. 1992. "Asking questions and influencing answers, what is to be done?" In J.M. Tanur, ed., *Questions about Questions; Inquiries into the Cognitive Bases of Surveys.* New York City: Russell Sage Foundation. Pp. 15–48.

Coates, Jennifer. 1993. *Women, Men and Language.* London: Longman.

Cohen, Asher and Bernard Susser. 2000. *Israel and the Politics of Jewish Identity: The Secular-Religious Impasse.* Baltimore and London: Johns Hopkins University Press.

Corrsin, Stephen D. 1990. "Language use in cultural and political change in pre-1914 Warsaw: Poles, Jews, and Russification." *Slavonic and Eastern European Review* 68, no. 1: 69–90.

Corson, David. 1990. *Language Policy Across the Curriculum*. Clevedon: Multilingual Matters.

———— 1999. *Language Policy in Schools*. Mahwah, N.J. and London: Lawrence Erlbaum Associates.

Coulmas, Florian. 1992. *Language and Economy*. Oxford: Blackwell.

Dalfin, Chaim. 1998. *The Seven Chabad-Lubavitch Rebbes*. Northvale, N.J. and Jerusalem: Jason Aronson.

Dan, Joseph. 1989. "Rikudo Shel Rabi Elimelech" (Rabbi Elimelech's Dance) (Heb.). *Politika* 24 (Jan.): 10–13.

———— 1998. "Haharediyut Hamishtakeret: Totzar Shel Yisrael Hachilonit" (The Intoxicated Haredism: The Result of Secular Israel) (Heb.). *Alpayim* 15: 234–253.

Dar, Sarah Leibovich. 2001. "Sha'agat New Square" (The Call of New Square). *Ha'aretz Weekend Magazine* (9 March), 56–62.

Davidman, Lynn. 1990. "Accommodation and resistance to modernity: A comparison of two contemporary Orthodox Jewish Groups." *Sociological Analysis: A Journal in the Sociology of Religion* 51 no.1: 35–51.

Dein, Simon. 1992. "Letters to the Rebbe: Millennium, messianism and medicine among the Lubavitch of Stamford Hill, London." *International Journal of Social Psychiatry* 38: 262–272.

Dembo, Yoram et al. 1997. "Haredim Vehilonim: Pitaron Baayot Bikerev Talmidim Bishnei Migzarei Hinuch" (Haredim and Secular: Solutions for Schoolchildren's Problems in Two Educational Sectors) (Heb.). *Megamot* 38 vol. 4: 469–503.

Dossier. 2001. "Dossier. École juive." *L'Arche* 520 (June); 30–48.

Dresner, Samuel H. 1960. *The Zaddik*. New York: Schocken.

The Economist. 2000. "Im Hagav Lemoderniyut, Im Hapanim Liyeshu" (With their backs towards modernity, with their faces towards Jesus) (Heb.). *Ha'aretz* (17 Jan.), section B, p. 5 (translated from *The Economist*).

Eisenberg, Robert. 1995. *Boychiks in the Hood: Travels in the Hasidic Underground*. San Francisco: Harper San Francisco.

Elboim, Ya'akov. 1990. *Ptihut Vehistagrut: Hayetzira Haruhanit Hasifrutit Bepolin Uveartzot Ashkenaz Beshilhay Hamea Hashesh Esreh* (Openness and Seclusion: Religious Literary Compositions in Poland and Ashkenaz at the End of the 16th Century) (Heb.). Jerusalem: Magnes.

Elior, Rachel. 1998. "The Lubavitch Messianic Resurgence: the historical and mystical background 1939–1996." In Peter Schafer and Mark Cohen, eds., *Toward the Millennium: Messianic Expectations from the Bible to Waco*. Leiden: Brill. Pp. 383–408.

El-Or, Tamar. 1994. *Educated and Ignorant: Ultraorthodox Jewish Women and Their World*. Boulder and London: Lynne Rienner Publishers.

Epstein, Shifra. 1999. "Going Far Away in Order to Better Understand the Familiar: Odyssey of a Jewish Folklorist into the Bobover Hasidic Community." *Journal of American Folklore* 112 no. 144: 200–212.

Erickson, F. 1984. "School Literacy, Reasoning, and Civility: An anthropologist's perspective." *Review of Educational Research* 54: 525–546.

Etkes, Immanuel. 1989. "The Gaon of Vilna and the Haskalah Movement: Image and Reality." *Binah* 2: 147–175.

———— 1996. "The Study of Hasidism: Past Trends and New Directions." In Ada Rapoport-Albert, ed., *Hasidism Reappraised*. London: Vallentine Mitchell. Pp. 447–464.

Fader, Ayala. 2001. "Literacy, Bilingualism, and Gender in a Hasidic Community." *Linguistics and Education* 12 no. 3: 261–283.

Faierstein, Morris M. 1991. "Hasidism: The Last Decade in Research." *Modern Judaism* 11 no. 1: 111–124.

Feldman, Anat. 2001. *Gormim Betzmichat Miflaga Hadasha: Hitachdut Hasfaradim Shomrei Tora (Tenuat Shas)* (Causes for the Development of a New Political Party: The Sefaradi Torah Guardians [Shas Movement]) (Heb.). Ph.D. dissertation, Bar Ilan University.

Ferdman, Bernardo M. 1991. "Literacy and Cultural Identity." In Masahiko Minami and Bruce B.Kennedy, eds., *Language Issues in Literacy and Bilingual/Multilingual Education,* Cambridge: Harvard University Press. Pp. 347–371.

Fisher, Shlomo. 1999. "Tenuat Shas" (The Shas Movement) (Heb.). In Adi Ofir, ed., *Hamishim Learbaim Ushmoneh.* Jerusalem: Van Leer; Tel Aviv: HaKibbutz Hameuchad. Pp. 329–337.

Fishkoff, Sue. 2001. "The Moose in the Mikve." *The Jerusalem Post Magazine* (2 March), pp. 16–20.

Fishman, Joshua A. 1969. "National Languages and Languages of Wider Communication in the Developing Nations." *Anthropological Linguistics* 11 no. 1: 111–135.

———— 1989. *Language and Ethnicity in Minority Sociolinguistic Perspective.* Clevedon: Multilingual Matters.

———— 1991. *Reversing Language Shift: Theoretical and Empirical Foundations of Assistance to Threatened Languages.* Clevedon, Philadelphia, Adelaide: Multilingual Matters Ltd.

Fitzpatrick, F. 1987. *The Open Door.* Clevedon: Multilingual Matters.

Foddy, William. 1993. *Constructing Questions for Interviews and Questionaires: The Organization and Practice in Social Research.* Cambridge: Cambridge University Press.

Friedman, A. Eliyahu ha-Kohen. 1997. *Days of Awe, Days of Joy: Chasidic insights into the festivals of the month of Tishrei, compiled and adapted from the talks and writings of the Rebbes of Chabad-Lubavitch.* Brooklyn: Kehot.

Friedman, Menachem. 1975. "Religious zealotry in Israeli society." In Solomon Poll and Ernest Krausz, eds., *On Ethnic and Religious Diversity in Israel.* Ramat Gan: Bar-Ilan University Press.

———— 1986. "Haredim Confront the Modern City." In Peter Y. Medding, ed., *Studies in Contemporary Jewry II,* Bloomington: University of Indiana. Pp. 74–96.

———— 1991. *HaChevra HaCharedit-Mekorot, Megamot Vetahalichim* (Charedi Society-Sources, Trends and Processes) (Heb.). Jerusalem: Machon Yerushalayim Liheker Yisrael.

———— 1992. "The Lost 'Kiddush' Cup: Changes in Ashkenazic Haredi Culture—a Tradition in Crisis." In Jack Wertheimer, ed., *The Uses of Tradition: Jewish Continuity in the Modern Era.* New York: Jewish Theological Seminary. Pp. 175–186.

———— 1995. "Haisha Haharedit" (The Haredi Woman) (Heb.). In Yael Atzmon, ed., *Eshnav Lihayeihen shel Nashim Bahevrut Yehudiyot: Kovetz Mechkarim Bein-Techumi.* Jerusalem: Mercaz Shazar. Pp. 273–290.

———— 1999. "Kol Kvoda Bat Melech Hutza: Haisha Haharedit 'Baruch She'asani Isha'" (All Honor of a King's Daughter Outward: The Haredi Woman "Blessed Art Thou for making me a Woman") (Heb.). In D.Y. Ariel, M. Libovitz, Y. Mzor, eds., *Haisha Beyahadut—Mehatanach Vead Yameinu.* Tel Aviv: Yediot Aharonot, Sifrei Hemed. Pp. 189–205.

Funke, Phyllis Ellen. 1998. "The Jewish Traveler: London." *Hadassah Magazine* 80 no. 4: 28–32.

Garlick, Harry. 1999. *The Final Curtain: State Funerals and the Theatre of Power.* Amsterdam-Atlanta, Ga.: Rodopi.

Gerlitz, Mordechai. 1995a. *Libam Shel Yisrael*. Jerusalem: Machon Amudei Haor.

——— 1995b. *Rabbi Simcha Bunim Alter Haadmor Migur* (Rabbi Simcha Bunim Alter, the Gerrer Rebbe) (Heb.). n. pub.

Gillis, Miriam. 1987. *Min ha"Heder" el Hamachshev: Mea Shnot Horaat Kriat Ivrit Beyisrael* (From the "Heder" to the Computer: One Hundred Years of Teaching Hebrew Reading in Israel) (Heb.). Ramat Gan: Bar-Ilan University Press.

Glinert, Lewis. 1999a. "Foreword." *International Journal of the Sociology of Language* 138: 1–4.

——— 1999b. "We Never Changed our Language: Attitudes to Yiddish Acquisition Among Hasidic Educators in Britain." *International Journal of the Sociology of Language* 138: 31–52.

Glinert, Lewis, and Yosseph Shilhav. 1991. "Holy Land, Holy Language: A Study of an Ultraorthodox Jewish Ideology", *Language in Society* 20: 59–86.

Golan, Avirama. 2000. "Achot Lo Rechoka" (Not Distant Sister) (Heb.). *Meimad* 20 (Sept.): 13–15.

Gold, David. 1985. "Jewish English." In Joshua Fishman, ed., *Readings in the Sociology of Jewish Languages*. Leiden: E.J. Brill. Pp. 280–298.

Greenberg, Gershon. 1992. "Assimilation as Churban According to Wartime American Orthodoxy (Chabad Chassidism)." In Menachem Mor, ed., *Jewish Assimilation, Acculturation and Accommodation: Past Traditions, Current Issues and Future Prospects, Proceedings of the 2nd Annual Symposium of the Klutznick Chair*. Lanham, Md.: University Press of America. Pp.161–177.

Gries, Zeev. 1987. "Hasidism, The Present State of Research and Some Desirable Priorities." *Numen: International Review for the History of Religions* 34 no.1: 97–108; 34 no. 2: 179–213.

Grin, François. 1990. "The Economic Approach to Minority Languages." *Journal of Multilingual and Multicultural Development* 11: 153–161.

——— 1993. "European Economic Integration and the Fate of Lesser Used Languages." *Language Problems and Language Planning* 17: 101–116.

Gurock, Jeffrey S. 1988. *The Men and Women of Yeshiva*. New York: Cambridge University Press.

Hakuta, H., B. M. Ferdman, and R.M. Diaz. 1987. "Bilinguilism and Cognitive Development: Three perspectives." In S. Rosenberg, ed., *Advances in Applied Psycholinguistics vol. 2: Reading, writing and language learning*. New York: Cambridge University Press. Pp. 284–319.

Halliday, Michael A. K. 1978. *Language as a Social Semiotic*. London: Edward Arnold.

Hartman, Joseph. 1984. *Hahinuch Bemishnat Habad* (Education in the Teachings of Habad) (Heb.). Kfar Habad: Oholei Yosef Yitzhak Lubavitsch Network.

Hasdai, Yaacov. 1988. "The Origins of the Conflict Between Hasidim and Mitnagdim." In Bezalel Safran, ed., *Hasidism: Continuity or Innovation?* Cambridge, Mass. and London: Harvard University Press. Pp. 27–45.

Heath, Shirley Brice. 1983. *Ways with Words: Language, Life and Work in Communities and Classrooms*. Cambridge: Cambridge University Press.

Heilman, Samuel C. 1982. "The Many Faces of Orthodoxy." *Modern Judaism* 2 no.1: 23–51.

——— 1992. *Defenders of the Faith: Inside Ultra-Orthodox Jewry*. New York: Schocken.

Heilman, Samuel C., and Menachem Friedman. 1991. "Religious Fundamentalism and Religious Jews: The Case of the Haredim." In Martin E. Marty and R. Scott Appleby, eds., *Fundamentalisms Observed*, Chicago and London: University of Chicago Press. Pp. 197–264.

Helman, R. 1994. *Habeit Yisrael: Me'at Al Rabbi Yisrael Alter Haadmor Migur* (The Beit Yisrael: A Bit About Rabbi Yisrael Alter, the Gerrer Rebbe) (Heb.). n. pub.

———— 1997. *Hapnei Menachem: Me'at Al Rabbi Pinchas Menachem Haadmor Migur* (The Pnai Menachem: A Bit About Rabbi Pinchas Menachem, the Gerrer Rebbe) (Heb.). n. pub.

Helmreich, William B. 1982. *The World of the Yeshiva: An Intimate Portrait of Orthodox Jewry.* New York: Free Press.

Holleman, Bregje. 2000. *The Forbid/Allow Asymmetry: On the Cognitive Mechanisms Underlying Wording Effects in Surveys.* Amsterdam and Atlanta, Ga.: Rodopi.

Hostetler, John A. 1968. *Amish Society.* Baltimore: Johns Hopkins University Press.

Hovav, Lea. 1994. "Sifrut Yiladim Haredit—Realistit oh Didaktit?" (Haredi Children's Literature—Realistic or Didactic?) (Heb.). *Sifrut Yiladim Venoar* 20 no. 3–4: 20–35.

Hundert, Gershon David. 1997. *Jews in Early Modern Poland.* London: Litmann.

Hurvitz, Avi. 1996. "Ivrit Vearamit Bitkufat Hamikra—Sugiyat be'Aramismim' Bimechkar Haivrit Hamikrait" ("Hebrew and Aramaic in the Biblical Period—The Problem of 'Aramaisms' in the Linguistic Researach of the Hebrew Bible") (Heb.). In Moshe Bar-Asher, ed., *Studies in Hebrew and Jewish Languages: Presented to Shelomo Morag.* Jerusalem: The Hebrew University and the Bialik Institute. Pp. 79–94.

Hymes, Dell. 1967. "Models of the interaction of language and social setting." *Journal of Social Issues* 23 no. 2: 8–38.

———— 1974. *Foundations in Sociolinguistics: An Ethnographic Approach.* Philadelphia: University of Pennsylvania Press.

Isaacs, Miriam. 1998a. "Yiddish in Orthodox Communities of Israel." In Dov Ber Kerler, ed., *Politics of Yiddish.* Walnut Creek, Calif.: Altamira Press. Pp. 85–96.

———— 1998b. "Yiddish "then and now": Creativity in contemporary Hasidic Yiddish." In Leonard Jay Greenspoon, ed., *Yiddish Language and Culture Then and Now.* Omaha: Creighton University Press. Pp. 165–188.

———— 1999. "Haredi, Haymish and Frim: Yiddish Vitality and Language Choice in a Transnational Multilingual Community." *International Journal of the Sociology of Language* 138: 9–30.

Jochnowitz, George. 1968. "Bilinguilism and Dialect Mixture Among Lubavitcher Hasidic Children." *American Speech* 43 no.3: 182–200.

Kaddari, Menachem Z. 1990. "Davka Bilshonam Haivrit Shel Amoraei Bavel Uvilshon Haaramit shel Hatalmud Habavli" (Davka in the Hebrew of the Amoraim of Babylon and in the Aramaic of the Babylonian Talmud) (Heb.). *Moreshet Ya'akov* 4: 126–144.

———— 1993. "Confronting the Hebrew of Responsa: Intensifiers in the syntax of Rabbi Meir of Rothenburg." In Lewis Glinert, ed., *Hebrew in Ashkenaz: A Language in Exile.* New York: Oxford University Press. Pp. 88–98.

Kahane, Henry. 1986. "A Typology of the Prestige Language." *Language* 62 no. 3: 495–508.

Kamen, Robert Mark. 1985. *Growing Up Hasidic: Education and Socialization in the Bobover Hasidic Community.* New York: AMS Press.

Kantor, Hadassah. 1989. "Al Tofa'at Hahilun Bilshon Yameinu Vehashlachoteh al Hora'at Haivrit" ("Regarding the secularization phenomenon in contemporary language and its repercussions on teaching Hebrew") (Heb.). In A. Ulstein, D. Zissenwein, and E. Shohami, eds., *Haivrit Kekoach Meahed Behinuch Hayehudi Batfutzot.* Tel-Aviv: University Publishers. Pp. 157–170.

———— 1992. "Ekologia Leshonit: She'elot Gluyot Usmuyot min Ha'anglit Bilshon Haitonut" (Language Ecology: Overt and Covert Questions from English in the Language of Newspapers) (Heb.). *Balshanut Ivrit* 33–35: 235–242.

———— 1997. "Triglossia Baitonut Haharedit Beartzot Habrit" (Triglossia in the American Haredi Press) (Heb.). *Balshanut Ivrit* 41–42: 131–139.

Kaplan, Robert B., and Richard B. Baldauf Jr. 1997. *Language Planning: From Practice to Theory.* Clevedon: Multilingual Matters.

Katz, Maidi. 1998. "Secular Studies at the Volozhin Yeshiva." In Micah D. Halpern and Chana Safrai, eds., *Jewish Legal Writings by Women.* Jerusalem: Urim.

Katzover, Yisrael. 1999. "Masa El Eretz Hahatzerot" (Journey to the Land of the Hassidic Courts) (Heb.). *Panim* 9: 24–31.

Kook, Rebecca. 1998. "In the name of G-d and our rabbi: The politics of the Ultra-Orthodox in Israel." *Israel Affairs* 5 no. 1: 1–18.

Kopelowitz, Ezra, and Matthew Diamond. 1998. "Religion that Strengthens Democracy: an Analysis of Religious Political Strategies in Israel." *Theory and Society* 23 no. 5: 671–708.

Koskoff, Ellen. 1995. "The Language of the Heart: Music in Lubavitcher Life". In Janet S. Belcove-Shalin, ed., *New World Hasidim: Ethnographic Studies of Hasidic Jews in America.* Albany: SUNY Press. Pp. 87–106.

Kranzler, George Gershon. 1988. "The Voice of Williamsburg: Mass Media in a Hasidic Community." *Tradition* 23 no. 3: 53–59.

———— 1993. "The Women of Williamsburg: a contemporary American Hasidic community." *Tradition: A Journal Of Orthodox Jewish Thought* 28 no. 1: 82–93.

———— 1995a. "The Economic Revitalization of the Hasidic Community of Williamsburg." In Janet S. Belcove-Shalin, ed., *New World Hasidim: Ethnographic Studies of Hasidic Jews in America,* Albany: SUNY Press, pp. 181–204.

———— 1995b. *Hasidic Williamsburg.* Northvale: Jason Aronson.

Krauss, Michael. 1992. "The World's Languages in Crisis." *Language* 68 no. 1: 4–11.

Kraybill, Donald B. 1989. *The Riddle of Amish Culture.* Baltimore: Johns Hopkins University Press.

Kutscher, Eduard Y. 1982. *A History of the Hebrew Language.* Jerusalem and Leiden: Magnes and Brill.

Labov, William. 1973. "The Linguistic Consequences of Being a Lame." *Language in Society* 2: 81–115.

Landau, David. 1993. *Piety and Power: The World of Jewish Fundamentalism.* London: Secker and Warburg.

Landry, Rodrigue, and Richard Y. Bourhis. 1997. "Linguistic Landscape and Ethnolinguistic Vitality: An Empirical Study." *Journal of Language and Social Psychology* 16 no. 1: 23–49.

Laskier, Michael Menachem. 1991. "Egypt and Beyond: The Jews of the Arab Countries in Modern Times." *AJS Review* 16 nos. 1–2: 199–210.

Lawrence, Bruce B. 1989. *Defenders of God: The Fundamentalist Revolt Against the Modern Age.* San Francisco: Harper and Row.

Levin, Yehuda Leib. 1977. *Admorei Gur: Mitoldot Chayeihem upoalam* (The Rebbes of Gur: Tales of their lives and deeds) (Heb.). Jerusalem: Hamodia, Mossad Harim Levin.

Levy, Amnon. 1989. *Haharedim* (The Haredim) (Heb.). Tel Aviv: Am Oved.

Littlewood, Roland. 1995. "The Effectiveness of Words: Religion and Healing among the Lubavitch of Stamford Hill." *Culture, Medicine and Psychiatry* 19 no. 3: 339–383.

Lobenstein, Yosef. 1998. *Days of Destiny: The Jewish Year Under a Chassidic Microscope: Adapted and translated from the works of the Lubavitcher Rebbe.* Brooklyn: Sichos in English.

Loeb, Laurence D. 1995. "HaBaD & Habban: 770's Impact on a Yemenite Jewish Community in Israel." In Janet S. Belcove-Shalin, ed., *New World Hasidim: Ethnographic Studies of Hasidic Jews in America.* Albany: SUNY Press. Pp. 69–86.

Loewenthal, Naftali. 1990. *Communicating the Infinite: The Emergence of the Habad School.* Chicago: University Press Books.

——— 1993. "Hebrew and the Habad Communication Ethos." In Lewis Glinert, ed., *Hebrew in Ashkenaz: A Language in Exile.* New York: Oxford University Press. Pp. 167–192.

——— 1994a. "Hasidism, Mysticism and Reality." *The Jewish Quarterly* 153 (spring): 52–53.

——— 1994b. "The Paradox of Habad." *Jewish Studies* 34: 65–73.

——— 2000. "'Daughter/Wife of Hasid'-or: 'Hasidic Woman'?" *Jewish Studies* 40: 21–28.

Maczak, Antoni. 1990. "The Jews in Poland and Western Europe in the 16th–18th Centuries, Problems in Comparative Research." *World Congress of Jewish Studies* 10 B2. Pp. 281–288.

Malhi, Esther. 1993. "Sifrut Hayiladim Haharedit Ketofa'a Tarbutit Yisraelit" (Haredi Children's Literature as an Israeli Cultural Phenomenon) (Heb.). *Beemet?! Maasef LeIyun Horaa Umechkar Bisifrut Yiladim* 6–7: 27–47.

McGee, Reese. 1967. "Education and Social Change." In Hansen and Gerst, eds., *On Education—Sociological Perspectives.* New York: J. Wiley. Pp. 67–104.

Meyer, Michael. 1986. *Response to Modernity.* New York: Oxford University Press.

Michelson, Menachem. 1990. "Itonut Haredit Beyisrael" (Haredi Newspapers in Israel) (Heb.). *Kesher* 8: 11–22.

Mindel, Nissan. 1969. *Rabbi Shneur Zalman of Liadi.* New York: Kehot.

Mintz, Jerome R. 1992. *Hasidic People: A Place in the New World.* Cambridge, Mass.: Harvard University Press.

Mitchell, Bruce, J. 1999. "London's "haredi" periodicals in Yiddish: Language, literature and ultra-Orthodox ideology." *European Judaism* 32 no. 2: 51–66.

Morgenstern, Aryeh. 1998. "Rabbi Elijah, The Gaon of Vilna and his Historical Influence." In Rachel Schnold, ed., *The Gaon of Vilna.* Tel Aviv: Beit Hatfutzot. Pp. 68–86.

Mougeon, Raymond and Terry Nadasdi. 1998. "Sociolinguistic Discontinuity in Minority Language Communities." *Language,* 74 no. 1: 40–55.

Munchick, Malka and Hadassah Kantor. 2000. "Al Tearim Yehudiyim Lenashim Ulegvarim Bamodaot Haharedim" (Special Expressions Given to Women and Men in Haredi Advertisements) (Heb.). *Balshanut Ivrit* 45: 53–60.

Netzer, Nissan. 1999. "Lidmuto shel Happoal Gazur Hashem Bamikra—Al Basis Hapealim Gezurei Hashemot Lieven Bilam (On Denominative Verbs in the Bible) (Heb.). In Shimon Sharvit, ed., *Studies in Ancient and Modern Hebrew in Honour of M.Z. Kaddari.* Ramat Gan: Bar-Ilan University Press. Pp. 61–82.

Nir, Raphael. 1978. *Semantika Shel Haivrit Hahadasha* (Semantics of Modern Hebrew) (Heb.). Tel Aviv: Amichai.

Parush, Iris. 1995. "The Politics of Literacy: Women and Foreign Languages in Jewish Society of 19th Century Eastern Europe." *Modern Judaism* 15 no. 2: 183–206.

——— 2001. *Nashim Korot: Yitrona Shel Shuliyut* (Reading Women: The Benefit of Marginality in Nineteenth Century Eastern European Jewish Society) (Heb.). Tel Aviv: Am Oved.

Paulston, Christina Bratt, and G. Richard Tucker, eds. 1997. *The Early Days of Sociolinguistics: Memories and Reflections, Publications in Sociolinguistics.* Dallas, Tex.: The Summer Institute of Linguistics.

Peled, Yoav. 1998. "Towards a Redefinition of Jewish Nationalism in Israel? The enigma of 'Shas'." *Ethnic and Racial Studies* 21 no. 4: 703–727.

Piekarz, Mendel. 1986. "'Hanekuda Hapnimit' Etzel Admorei Gur VeAlexander Kebavua Likosher Histaglutam Litmurot Haitim" ('The Internal Point' Among the Admorim of Gur and Alexander as a Reflection of their Adaptational Capabilities to Changes Taking Place) (Heb.). In J. Dan and J. Haker, eds., *Mechkarim Bekabala, Befilosofia Yehudit, Ubesifrut Hamussar Vehehagut.* Jerusalem: Magnes. Pp. 617–660.

Pinar, William. 1995. *Understanding Curriculum: An introduction to the study of historical and contemporary curriculum discourse.* New York: Peter Lang.

——— 1998. "Time, Place and Voice." In *Contemporary Curriculum Discourses.* Scottsdale: Gorsuch Scarisbrick. Pp. 264–278.

Poll, Solomon. 1962. *The Hasidic Community of Williamsburg.* New York: The Free Press of Glencoe.

——— 1965. "The Role of Yiddish in American Ultra-orthodox and Hassidic Communities." *YIVO Annual of Jewish Social Science* 13: 125–152.

——— 1995. "The Charismatic Leader of the Hasidic community: the Zaddiq, the Rebbe." In Janet S. Belcove-Shalin, ed., *New World Hasidim, Ethnographic Studies of Hasidic Jews in America.* Albany, SUNY Press. Pp. 257–275.

Poplin, Dennis E. 1979. *Communities: A Survey of Theories and Methods of Research.* New York and London: Macmillan.

Rabi, Ya'akov. 1974. "Hala'az Beitonei Yisrael: Hiyuv Ushlila" (Foreign Words in Israeli Newspapers: Positive and Negative) (Heb.). *Sefer Hashana Shel Haitonaim.* Pp. 304–312.

Rabin, Chaim. 2000. *The Development of the Syntax of Post-Biblical Hebrew.* Leiden: Brill.

Rabinowicz, Harry. 1982. *Hasidism and the State of Israel.* Rutherford: Fairleigh Dickenson University Press.

——— 1997. *A World Apart.* London: Vallentine Mitchell.

Redekop, Calvin. 1987. "Communal organization and secular education: Hutterite and Hassidic comparisons." In Yosef Gorni, Ya'akov Oved, and Idit Paz, eds., *Communal Life: An International Perspective.* Efal: Yad Tabenkin; New Brunswick, N.J.: Transaction Books. Pp. 342–357.

——— 1989. *Mennonite Society.* Baltimore and London: Johns Hopkins University Press.

Redman, Barbara J. 1992. "Strange Bedfellows: Lubavitcher Hasidim and Conservative Christians." *Journal of Church and State* 34 no. 3: 521–548.

Robinson, Ira. 1995. "The Zaddik as Hero in Hasidic Hagiography." In Menachem Mor, ed., *Crisis and Reaction: The Hero in Jewish History.* Omaha: Creighton University Press. Pp. 94–103.

Rosenack, Michael. 1999. "Mokdim shel Haktzana Datit: Hebetim Hinuchiyim" (Centers of Religious Fanaticism: Educational Aspects) (Heb.). *Hagut BeHinuch Hayehudi* A, pp. 155–172.

Rosengarten, Sudy. 1992. *Worlds Apart: The Birth of Bais Yaakov in America: A Personal Recollection.* New York: Targum and Feldheim.

Roth, Cecil. 1964. *A History of the Jews in England.* Oxford: Oxford University Press.

Rubin, Israel. 1997. *Satmar: Two Generations of an Urban Island.* New York: Lang.

Ruiz, R. 1990. "Official Languages and Language Planning." In K. L. Adams and D. T. Brinks, eds., *Perspectives on Official English: The Campaign for English as the Official Language of the USA.* Berlin: Mouton de Gruyter. Pp. 11–24.

Sachar, Howard M. 1985. *Diaspora: An Inquiry into the contemporary Jewish World.* New York: Harper and Row.

Sachdev, Itest, and Richard Y. Bourhis. 1991. "Power and Status Differentials in Minority and Majority Group Relations." *European Journal of Social Psychology* 21: 1–24.

Salinger, Peter Shmuel. 1991. "Publishing developments of Habad teaching, 1794–1989." In Diana Rowland Smith and Peter Shmuel Salinger, eds., *Hebrew Studies Colloquium,*

Papers presented at a colloquium on resources for Hebraica in Europe, London, September 1989. London: British Library. Pp. 105–110.

Schacter, Jacob J. 1990. "Haskalah, Secular Studies and the close of the Yeshiva in Volozhin in 1882." *Torah U-Madda Journal* 2: 76–133.

Scharfstein, Zvi. 1960. *Toldot Ha-chinuch Be-Yisrael Badorot Ha-Achronim* (The History of Education in Israel during the Last Decades), vol. 2 (Heb.). Jerusalem: Reuven Maas.

———— 1965. *Toldot Ha-chinuch Ha-Ivri Be-Eretz Yisrael* (The History of Hebrew Education in the Land of Israel) vol. 4 (Heb.). Jerusalem: Reuven Maas.

Schieffelin, Bambi B. and Elinor Ochs. 1986. "Language Socialization." *Annual Review of Anthropology* 15: 163–191.

Schiffman, Harold E. 1996. *Linguistic Culture and Language Policy.* London and New York: Routledge.

Schwarzfuchs, Simon. 1992. "The Alliance Israelite Universelle and French Jewish Leadership vis à vis North African Jewry 1860–1914", in: Selwyn Ilan Troen and Benjamin Pinkus, eds., *Organizing Rescue: National Jewish Solidarity in the Modern Period.* London: Frank Cass. Pp. 77–90.

Schwarzwald, Ora R. 2001. *Modern Hebrew.* Munich: Lincom Europa.

Seidman, Naomi. 1997. *A Marriage Made in Heaven: The Sexual Politics of Hebrew and Yiddish.* Berkeley: University of California Press.

Shaffir, William. 1974. *Life in a Religious Community: The Lubavitcher Chassidim in Montreal.* Toronto: Holt, Rinehard and Winston of Canada.

———— 1993, "Haredi Jewry: Safeguarding a Distinctive Way of Life." *Qualitative Sociology* 16 no. 4; 455–462.

Sharot, Stephen. 1991. "Hasidism in Modern Society." In Gershon David Hundert, ed., *Essential Papers on Hasidism: Origins to Present.* New York and London: New York University Press. Pp. 511–531.

Sharvit, Shimon. 1996. "Pe'alim Tlat Atariyim Hamichilim Mashlim Shem Poal Bilshon Hatanaim" (Three-Place Verbs in Tannaitic Hebrew) (Heb.). In Moshe Bar-Asher, ed., *Studies in Hebrew and Jewish Languages: Presented to Shelomo Morag.* Jerusalem: The Hebrew University and the Bialik Institute. Pp. 223–236.

Shilhav, Yosseph. 1993. "The Emergency of Ultra-Orthodox Neighborhoods in Israeli Urban Centers." In Efraim Ben-Zadok, ed., *Local Communities and the Israeli Polity: Conflict of Values and Interests.* Albany: SUNY Press. Pp. 157–187.

Shnall, Yitzhak. 1989. "Hahibadlut Hamerhavit shel haHaredim Beyisrael" (The Spatial Separatism of Haredim in Israel) (Heb.). *Beeri* 1: 151–171.

Silber, Michael K. 1992. "The emergency of Ultra-Orthodoxy: The invention of a tradition." In Jack Wertheimer, ed., *The Uses of Tradition: Jewish Continuity in the Modern Era.* New York: Jewish Theological Seminary. Pp. 23–84.

Skutnabb-Kangas, Tove and Jim Cummings. 1988. *Minority Education.* Clevedon: Multilingual Matters.

Sourasky, Aharon. 1967. *Toledot Ha-chinuch Ha-torati* (History of Torah Education) (Heb.). Bnai Brak: Or Hachayim.

Spolsky, Bernard. 1993. "Language Conflict in Jerusalem—1880 and 1980." In E. H. Jahr, ed., *Language Conflict and Language Planning.* Berlin: Mouton de Gruyter. Pp. 179–192.

———— 1998. *Sociolinguistics.* Oxford: Oxford University Press.

Spolsky, Bernard and Shohamy, Elana. 2000. "Language practice, Language Ideology and Language Policy." In Richard D. Lambert and Elana Shohamy, eds., *Language Policy and Pedagogy, Essays in Honor of A. Ronald Walton.* Amsterdam and Philadelphia: John Benjamins Publishing Company. Pp. 1–42.

Stampfer, Shaul. 1988. "Hasidic Yeshivot in Inter-War Poland." *POLIN* 11: 3–24.

———— 1995. *Hayeshiva Belita Behithavuta* (The Lithuanian Yeshiva in its Development) (Heb.). Jerusalem: Mercaz Zalman Shazar Litoldot Yisrael.

Steinberg, Milton. 1939. *As a Driven Leaf.* New York: Behrman House.

Stillman, Norman A. 2000. "Frenchmen, Jews, or Arabs: The Jews of the Arab World Between European Colonialism, Zionism and Arab Nationalism." In Benjamin H. Hary, John L. Hays, and Fred Astren, eds., *Judaism and Islam: Boundaries, Communication and Interaction: Essays in Honor of William M. Brinner.* Leiden: Brill. Pp. 123–138.

Suttles, Gerald D. 1972. *The Social Construction of Communities.* Chicago and London: University of Chicago Press.

Tourgeman, Refael. 1999. "Tofaot Morfologiyot Bilshon Hatefilot Shebasidurim Hakedumim" (Morphological Features in the Language of Early Siddurim) (Heb.). In Shimon Sharvit, ed., *Studies in Ancient and Modern Hebrew In Honour of M.Z. Kaddari.* Ramat Gan: Bar Ilan University Press. Pp. 133–145.

Tzameret, Zvi. 1997. *Alei Gesher Tzar: Itzuv Ma'arechet Hachinuch Biymei Ha'aliyah Hagedola* (On a Narrow Bridge: Shaping the Education System during the Great Immigration Wave) (Heb.). Sde Boqer: Mercaz Moreshet Ben-Gurion.

Uriah, Shlomit. 1996. "'Shalom Tznua—Nefesh Tznua': Dfusei Tikshoret Miluliyim Bikerev Banot Venashim Harediot" (Modest Greeting—Modest Soul': Verbal Communication Forms among Haredi Girls and Women) (Heb.). *Balshanut Ivrit* 41–42: 7–19.

Webster's. 1958. *Webster's New World Dictionary of the American Language.* Cleveland and New York: The World Publishing Company.

Weinreich, Max. 1973. *The History of The Yiddish Language.* Trans. Shlomo Noble and Joshua Fishman. Chicago: University of Chicago Press.

Weinryb, Bernard D. 1972. *The Jews of Poland: A Social and Economic History of the Jewish Community in Poland From 1100 to 1800.* Philadelphia: Jewish Publication Society.

Weiser, Chaim M. 1995. *Frumspeak: The First Dictionary of Yeshivish.* Northvale: Aronson.

Weissman, Deborah. 1976, "Beis Yaakov: A historical model for Jewish feminists." In E. Koltun, ed., *The Jewish Woman.* New York: Schocken. Pp. 139–149.

———— 1995. "Bais Ya'akov as an innovation in Jewish women's education: A contribution to the study of education and social challenge." *Studies in Jewish Education* 7, pp. 278–299.

Wiesel, Elie. 1972. *Souls On Fire: Portraits and Legends of Hasidic Masters.* New York: Vintage.

Wilensky, Mordecai L. 1991. "Hasidic-Mitnaggedic Polemics in the Jewish Communities of Eastern Europe: The Hostile Phase." In Gershon David Hundert, ed., *Essential papers on Hasidism: Origins to present.* New York: New York University Press. Pp. 244–271.

Wilson, Fiona, and Bodil Folke Frederiksen. 1995. *Ethnicity, Gender and the Subversion of Nationalism.* London: Frank Cass.

Willis, Aaron P. 1993. "Sephardic Torah Guardians: Ritual and the Politics of Piety" Ph.D. dissertation, Princeton University.

Ya'akovson, Yoram. 1986. "Emet Veemuna Behasidut Gur" (Truth and Belief in Gur Hassidism) (Heb.). In J. Dan and J. Haker, eds., *Mechkarim Bekabala, Befilosofia Yehudit, Ubesifrut Hamussar Vehehagut.* Jerusalem: Magnes. Pp. 653–616.

Zilberschlag, Dudi. 1998. "A Gesunter Ra'ayon" (A Healthy Idea) (Heb.). *Panim* 7: 76–77.

Zohar, Zvi. 1998. "Hachmei Hatorah Vehamoderna: Al Ortodoksia, Hachmei Hamizrach Vetnuat Shas" (The Torah Sages and Modernization: About Orthodoxy, the Sages of the East and the Shas Movement) (Heb.). In Meir Rot ed., *Hatzionut Hadatit Beriiya Mehudeshet.* Ein Tzurim: Neemanei Tora Veavoda. Pp. 161–178.

Haredi English Textbooks

Adler, Miriam, Hanna Goldhirsh, and Yocheved Halevy. [n.d.]. *Using English*. Bnai Brak: [n. pub.].

Alter, Mindy. [n.d.]. *Selected Readings*. [n. pub.].

Averbuch, Leah. [n.d.]. *High to High*. [n. pub.].

Goldhirsh, Hanna. [n.d.]. *English From A to Z*. Bnei Brak, [n. pub.].

Karelenstein, Miriam. [n.d.]. *English for US*. (series includes textbooks, workbooks, readers, and summer books), [n. pub.].

Karelenstein, Miriam. [n.d.]. *Spell and Speak*. [n. pub.].

Segev, Shifra. [n.d.]. *Let's Study the A,B,C*. (a study workbook), [n. pub.].

Shtub, Elisheva. [n.d.]. *Short Ones*. [n. pub.].

INDEX